A HISTORY OF THE IRISH SHORT STORY

HEATHER INGMAN

CAMBRIDGE
UNIVERSITY PRESS

CAMBRIDGE UNIVERSITY PRESS
Cambridge, New York, Melbourne, Madrid, Cape Town,
Singapore, São Paulo, Delhi, Tokyo, Mexico City

Cambridge University Press
The Edinburgh Building, Cambridge CB2 8RU, UK

Published in the United States of America by Cambridge University Press, New York

www.cambridge.org
Information on this title: www.cambridge.org/9780521349574

First published 2009
First paperback edition 2011

A catalogue record for this publication is available from the British Library

Library of Congress Cataloguing in Publication data
Ingman, Heather, 1953–
A history of the Irish short story / Heather Ingman.
p.   cm.
Includes bibliographical references.
ISBN 978-0-521-86724-5 (hardback)
1. Short stories, English–History and criticism.   2. English fiction–Irish
authors–History and criticism.   3. Ireland–In literature.   1. Title.
PR8804.I64 2009
823′.01′099415–dc22
2009006850

ISBN 978-0-521-86724-5 Hardback
ISBN 978-0-521-34957-4 Paperback

However depressing the facts may be, the story will always be excellent.

(Frank O'Connor, *The Bell*, May 1942)

Contents

Acknowledgments

A study as wide-ranging as this is indebted to many works that have gone before. The ones that have been most useful are acknowledged in the bibliography and footnotes, but I read many more and their traces have also gone to make up this work. Many of the books cited were written by my colleagues in the School of English at Trinity College, Dublin and I am fortunate to work in a department where the study of Irish literature is flourishing. I am indebted, too, to students of my Irish Women's Writing course for their enthusiasm and challenging queries down the years. I would also like to thank the staff of Trinity College library, particularly the Early Printed Books section, for their unfailing courtesy and helpfulness.

My thanks must go to Ray Ryan of Cambridge University Press, who suggested this project to me and whose wise guidance helped to keep me on course. I would also like to express heartfelt thanks to CUP's anonymous readers for their always perceptive comments and challenging questions.

I would like also to thank Jerusha McCormack for her advice, particularly for pointing me in the direction of Sarah Orne Jewett's Irish stories.

Finally, this book could not have been completed without my husband's unfailing encouragement and my sons' patient forbearance with a mother seemingly tied to the computer.

CHAPTER ONE

Introduction

The Irish short story has been read, debated and lectured about to generations of students. A study by Deborah Averill, *The Irish Short Story from George Moore to Frank O'Connor*, came out in 1982, while two important collections of essays have been devoted to the subject: *The Irish Short Story*, edited by Patrick Rafroidi and Terence Brown, published in 1979, and *The Irish Short Story*, edited by James Kilroy, published in 1984. In recent years there have been as well many studies of the short stories of individual authors like James Joyce, Mary Lavin, John McGahern, William Trevor, Bryan MacMahon and others. Irish practitioners of the art, notably Seán O'Faoláin and Frank O'Connor, have written influential studies of the form, and there have been volumes devoted to the Irish short story in particular contexts, such as Michael Storey's *Representing the Troubles in Irish Short Fiction* (2004). We think we know very well what the modern Irish short story is, to the extent that another overview may well seem redundant.

Yet for a form often regarded, particularly in relation to the novel, as the pre-eminent Irish prose form, this handful of studies is numerically small. Even in Ireland, short fiction has been relegated to the margins of critical discourse, the short stories of major short story writers like Elizabeth Bowen treated as minor or apprentice pieces in comparison with their novels. The relative lack of attention to the genre is reflected in the fact that, for example, the *Field Day Anthology of Irish Writing* has no separate section for the short story. Recent studies, such as *The Irish Novel in the Nineteenth Century*, edited by Jacqueline Belanger, and John Wilson Foster's *Irish Novels 1890–1940: New Bearings in Culture and Fiction*, have gone some way towards up-dating our view of the Irish novel, but there have been no comparable volumes devoted to the Irish short story. Moreover, earlier studies were naturally unable to take account of Irish writers' increased interest in the form during the last two decades of the twentieth century, an interest which shows no sign of abating in the first decade of the twenty-first. The huge number of excellent short stories by a variety of contemporary Irish authors, including, for the first time, women writing in large numbers, urges a fresh consideration of the form.

In general terms, the short story, perhaps more than any other form, has been associated with modernity, both in terms of experimentation and theme. In her brief but insightful comments on the short story, Nadine Gordimer argues that the art of the short story, seeing 'by the light of the flash', makes it an art always of the present moment and that its 'fragmented and restless form' renders it ideally suited to the modern age.[1] The association of the short story with modernity would come as no surprise to Elizabeth Bowen, who judged the short story to be the most modern of forms, 'the child of this century', she wrote in 1937, and connected it with that other modern art form, film.[2] In the specific context of the Irish short story, however, these comments pose a challenge to the long-perceived relationship between the literary short story and the tradition of oral storytelling in Ireland, a relationship that has often been adduced to account for the centrality of the genre in the Irish canon. To compare Bowen's preface to *The Faber Book of Modern Short Stories* (1937) with Vivian Mercier's introduction to *Great Irish Short Stories* (1964) is to become aware of two entirely different ways of looking at the genre. Whilst Bowen stresses the form's newness and lack of tradition, Mercier's specific focus on the Irish short story leads him to emphasize its strong roots in the oral folk tradition.

Like Mercier, many writers and scholars have argued that the vibrancy of oral storytelling in Ireland is one of the reasons why the short story established itself as a characteristically Irish form, never suffering from the inferiority complex that plagued the Irish novel.[3] Other scholars have drawn a clear distinction between the copious and dramatic art of the storyteller and the tautness of the modern short story, operating through irony, suggestion and precision; between the oral tale's emphasis on chance and the unexpected, and the short story's demand for a logical and psychologically plausible sequence of events.[4] In his 'Observations on the Works of Nikolai Leskov', Walter Benjamin outlines the essential differences between oral storytelling and the literary short story. Whereas oral storytellers used tone, gesture and facial expression and relied on a shared sense of values with their community to help them tell their story, the modern short story writer, Benjamin argues, cannot rely on such shared experience and has only language as a tool. Benjamin goes on to point out that the subject matter is different: oral storytellers aimed to convey something useful to their community, either a moral, some practical advice or a maxim. Though personality intruded heavily on the narration, storytellers rarely told stories about themselves and character development was unusual, character generally being presented in a single stroke.[5]

In his study of the contrasts between oral and literate cultures, Walter Ong goes further and argues that to write down oral material is irrevocably to alter it since the aims of oral and written narratives are entirely different.[6] In oral cultures, theme was dictated by the need to organize and conserve knowledge (of the history of the tribe or the tribal king). Style was governed by mnemonic needs, as in the use of formulas, patterns, repetitions, antithesis, alliteration, assonance, maxims and other techniques of the oral storyteller. The change to writing resulted in profound alterations, both in our thought processes and in narrative modes. Writing became analytical, inward-looking, sparsely linear, experimental; it eschewed the heroic and moved into the everyday. All these are characteristics of the modern short story.

The distinction between the oral tale and the modern short story seems clear, yet in Ireland the distinction breaks down. If the short story has generally been regarded as the characteristic Irish prose form, this implies a sense of community that challenges Benjamin's denial of shared values. Irish authors of short fiction often use the form to convey a message to their community, from Sheridan Le Fanu's submerged warnings to the Anglo-Irish, to Yeats' vision of a new order in *The Secret Rose*, to feminists' exposure of the hidden realities of Irish women's lives in the 1970s, 1980s and 1990s, sometimes drawing on motifs from Irish folklore. This suggests consciousness of an audience, however distanced it might seem in comparison with the storyteller's circle of listeners. Moreover, the advent of radio allowed writers to prolong the oral tradition through their readings. Notwithstanding his emphasis in *The Lonely Voice* (1962) on the solitary, critical reader, Frank O'Connor, when reading his stories for the radio, would alter or excise passages in the written story that interfered with his ability as a storyteller to engage directly with his audience. His work in the form reveals a preoccupation with retaining a warm human speaking voice that would reach out to the reader or listener; indeed, one of his criticisms of Joyce was that he had abandoned that voice.

The oral culture may be, literally, another world but it is one that in Ireland shadows even the English language short story. Elements of the storytelling tradition are visible in the work of William Carleton, George Moore, Seumas O'Kelly, Daniel Corkery, James Stephens, Frank

O'Connor, Bryan MacMahon and Benedict Kiely, to name only a few of the writers who have endeavoured to incorporate into their short fiction the speaking voice of oral tradition. If themes as well as techniques are considered, the list of Irish writers interested in the myths and legends, fairy and folk tales of oral tradition lengthens considerably to include writers as diverse as Sheridan Le Fanu, Oscar Wilde, W. B. Yeats, Éilís Ní Dhuibhne and Angela Bourke. Folk themes may have largely fallen into disfavour in the period following the Irish Revival, but more recent research into the oral tradition has prompted a fresh awareness of the complexities and subtleties of oral tale-telling so that to be an Irish short story writer even today is to be aware at some level of this other tradition.

Nonetheless, it is also true that one of the greatest Irish short story writers, namely Joyce, produced in *Dubliners* a collection that stylistically, at least, bears no connection with the oral tradition, and while William Carleton's *Traits and Stories* may have begun with storytelling around Ned M'Keown's fireside, the urgency of his desire to comment on Irish circumstances was such that he quickly found the storytelling tradition too constraining for his purposes and moved towards an omniscient narrator and standard English. Yeats may have joined Lady Gregory and other Revivalists in collecting Irish folk tales but his interest in folklore rapidly became subordinate to his personal literary and occult enthusiasms. Daniel Corkery was a strong exponent of the Gaelic storytelling tradition but it came to him second-hand, and the realist mode he adopted for his stories could not help but record its passing. Even a writer like Liam O'Flaherty, who was born into an Irish storytelling family, attested to the influence of foreign authors such as Maupassant and Gorky in his stories. In 'The Search for the Lost Husband' (*The Inland Ice and Other Stories*, 1997), Éilís Ní Dhuibhne draws on folklore but rewrites the traditional ending to render it more attuned to contemporary women's lives. Time after time, we will find that where Irish authors draw on the oral tradition they do not seek so much to reproduce oral techniques as to combine them with modern literary forms and themes.

There were other factors besides the link between the Irish short story and the Irish tradition of storytelling that account for the centrality of the form within the Irish canon. The material conditions in which Irish writers lived and worked influenced the development of the form. Financial necessity, for instance, impelled writers like Wilde and Yeats to make forays into short fiction at the end of the nineteenth century when the demise of the three-volume novel in England and the rise of small literary magazines encouraged writers' work in the genre. In the twentieth century, the lucrative nature of the American magazine market stimulated development of short fiction generally and a large Irish American readership encouraged Irish writers towards the form. Magazines like the *New Yorker* did much to publicize the Irish short story at mid-century, and chapter six of this study examines the way in which their relationship with the *New Yorker* shaped Irish writers' handling of the form.

Sometimes, however, it was simply the case that the short form suited a writer's particular skills. This was notably true for Frank O'Connor, Seán O'Faoláin and Mary Lavin, though again, the material circumstances in which they were writing should not be underestimated: O'Faoláin despaired of encapsulating Ireland's contradictions in the novel form and Lavin admitted that her domestic responsibilities militated against producing novels. The pre-eminence of the form in the middle years of the twentieth century in Ireland may be partly accounted for by the international prominence of critical writing on the short story by Irish practitioners such as O'Connor and O'Faoláin. Both O'Connor's *The Lonely Voice* and O'Faoláin's *The Short Story* (1948) were important Irish contributions to establishing the short story as a serious art form with its own distinctive aesthetics. Their thesis that while the novel form suits a stable, structured society like nineteenth-century England, the short story prospers at times of social upheaval, was hugely influential on subsequent writers and critics. The lingering effects of this may be seen in John McGahern's explanation for the flourishing of the short story in Ireland – 'the short story is often stronger in less structured societies where locality and individualism are rampant'[7] – as well as in scholarly works presenting Ireland as a society uncongenial to the novel form.[8]

Ireland, however, was not unique in the inability of its culture to cohere into the novel form. As Graham Good points out, in nineteenth-century Germany, where delay in developing industry, national unity and a solid middle class hindered the introduction of the social novel, the novella became the favoured fictional genre, adapted as it was to the atypical and the regional.[9] In the United States, also, preconditions for the social novel were not fully present till the late nineteenth century and the tale became a popular form. In her preface to *The Faber Book of Modern Short Stories*, Bowen associates the American short story with the Irish short story, characterizing both as products of an uncertain society. The centrality of the short story to the American canon arguably played its part in the eagerness with which the work of O'Connor, O'Faoláin, Lavin and others, was promoted by American reviewers and publishers mid-century; in other words, the importance of the short story in the

American canon may have influenced the enthusiasm of American readers and publishers to associate Irish writing also with the form. Irish writers, in turn, acknowledged the skill of American short story writers in handling the genre, witness O'Connor's admiration for Sherwood Anderson and J. D. Salinger in *The Lonely Voice* and O'Faoláin's for Hemingway in *The Short Story*.

Since Ireland is not unique in regarding the genre as central to its national canon, the moment of emergence of the modern Irish short story needs to be set in its international context, something O'Connor himself did in *The Lonely Voice*, where he did not limit himself to study of the Irish short story but dealt with a range of international writers. If writers like O'Connor and O'Faoláin later came to admire the American short story, it was French and Russian authors who first caught their attention, and it was their influence that enabled the Irish short story to shed some of the limitations of the oral tradition and develop as a modern literary form. Chapter four considers the influence of Russian writers, particularly Turgenev and Chekhov, and of French writers like Flaubert and Maupassant on the development of the modern short story in Ireland. Foreign authors continued to influence Irish writers after that date, of course; witness Mary Lavin's admiration for Chekhov, Turgenev, Katherine Mansfield and Eudora Welty, or John McGahern's repeated allusions to Chekhov and Proust.

Definitions of the short story are notoriously tricky to pin down but any history of the genre needs to consider, at least briefly, the distinction between the short story and other forms of fiction to which it is adjacent. For Valerie Shaw in *The Short Story* (1983), hybridity is the essential characteristic of the short story, embracing as it does fable, fairy story, ghost story, anecdote, sketch, tale and novella: 'the short story is an independent yet hybrid genre, which connects with other art forms at various points and keeps eluding definition except as an interplay of tensions and antitheses'.[10] Suzanne Ferguson has likewise argued that the short story as a genre possesses no distinct characteristics; she regards it simply as part of the general emergence of the impressionist movement.[11]

Despite these warnings about the fluidity of the genre, there have been attempts at more precise definitions. One of the earliest came in 1842, in Edgar Allan Poe's review of Nathaniel Hawthorne's *Twice-Told Tales*, in which he defined the short prose tale as distinguished from and superior to the long narrative by its unity of focus and singleness of effect. For Poe, it was the short form's intensity and compression that distinguished it from the novel, or even the novella, and it was its artistic patterning that differentiated it from the anecdote. Events, he insisted, should only be included where they contributed to the overall theme: 'the unity of effect or impression is a point of the greatest importance'.[12] In the hands of a writer like Poe, the nineteenth-century tale approaches the modern short story in its intensity but remains distinguished from it on account of the characters' lack of inner consciousness; in a tale by Poe or, in the Irish context, James Stephens, characters generally represent a state of mind or a psychological trait.

Following on from Poe, practitioners like Chekhov and theorists like Susan Lohafer have argued that it is the focus on the ending that distinguishes the short story as a form.[13] Whereas the novel may contain incidental events, everything in the short story has to be selected and controlled in preparation for the conclusion. The novel may illustrate by means of accumulating detail; the short story achieves its effects through compression, relying on suggestion and implication rather than multiplicity. The first drafts of a writer like Mary Lavin may have extended to over a hundred pages and contained seven or eight characters, but in the revised versions they were cut down till everything irrelevant to the overall effect and purpose had been ruthlessly stripped away and only two or three characters remained. This editing process was not simply to suit the publication requirements of the literary magazines in which Lavin's stories were initially published but was an essential part of her methods as an artist, geared to achieving maximum focus and clarity.[14] The novel provides us with a world we can sink into, whereas in the short story artistic considerations are paramount. This is perhaps what Frank O'Connor was getting at when he wrote: 'What Turgenev and Chekhov give us is not so much the brevity of the short story compared with the expansiveness of the novel as the purity of an art form that is motivated by its own necessities rather than by our convenience.'[15]

Poe characterized the short story not only by the unity of its effects, but also by its element of suggestion, requiring from the reader an attentiveness to what is going on beneath the surface equal to that of the writer. This attentiveness he termed 'a kindred art'.[16] In her study of the form, Clare Hanson, too, stresses the liminality of the short story, hovering on the border between known and unknown worlds and, like Poe, points to the concomitant effort required by readers to exert their imagination to fill in the gaps in an often elliptical text.[17] In a modern short story we accept elision and mystery, hence its appropriateness for exploring themes related to hauntings and terror: Elizabeth Bowen wrote many ghost stories, but only one, not particularly successful, novel of a haunting. Charles May, editor of the influential study, *The New Short Story Theories*, sees the form as maintaining an affinity with the transcendent and the mythic: 'the tradition of the short story as descended from myth, folk tale, fable and romance forms, drives it towards focusing on eternal values rather than temporal ones and sacred or unconscious reality rather than profane or everyday reality'.[18] A historical survey allows us to see that while in Ireland this definition may hold true for writers of the Irish Literary Revival and for some contemporary writers such as Éilís Ní Dhuibhne and Angela Bourke, it does not suit the mimetic fictional worlds of mid twentieth-century Irish writers like Frank O'Connor, Seán O'Faoláin and Michael McLaverty. May's further characterization of the short story as an intuitive form dealing with the subconscious, operating through dreams and metaphor, foregrounding style and rejecting chronology in favour of artistic patterning, suggests an alliance with modernism that in Ireland finds its flowering in Joyce's *Dubliners* and is later picked up by writers like John McGahern and William Trevor.

In relation to other forms, as early as 1901, Brander Matthews distinguished the short story from the sketch by positing that 'while a Sketch may be still-life, in a Short story something always happens'.[19] This is a distinction that will be valuable when we come to Liam O'Flaherty's work, where his nature sketches take on aspects of the short story through movement. The novella is another form adjacent to the short story and adopted by several of our writers, notably Mary Lavin, Maeve Brennan, William Trevor, and Colum McCann. Graham Good judges the novella to be mid-way between the novel and the short story, permitting a more complex line of action to be developed, yet never moving too far from the single focus of the short story. A novella may redevelop a situation, allowing for more lengthy character revelation and a more extended time frame than a short story, while retaining greater thematic intensity than a novel.[20] Yeats' 'John Sherman' is one example, discussed in the interchapter to chapter three.

Frank O'Connor dated the appearance of the first literary short story to 1840 with the publication of Nikolai Gogol's 'The Overcoat'.[21] Later critics have tended to concur, sometimes adding in the names of Nathaniel Hawthorne and Edgar Allan Poe, both of whom were writing tales in the 1830s and 1840s that marked the transition from older forms of romance and folk tale to the tightly woven structure and psychological plausibility of the modern story form.[22] There are disputes, however, as to when the modern Irish short story began. Frank O'Connor and Deborah Averill locate its origins some sixty years after Gogol's 'The Overcoat' with the appearance of George Moore's collection, *The Untilled Field*, in 1903. O'Connor's influential anthology, *Classic Irish Short Stories*, originally published as *Modern Irish Short Stories* in 1957, begins with George Moore and ranges in a typical trajectory through the stories of, among others, Edith Somerville and Martin Ross, Daniel Corkery, James Joyce, James Stephens, Liam O'Flaherty, Seán O'Faoláin, O'Connor himself, Michael McLaverty, Mary Lavin, James Plunkett and Elizabeth Bowen. For some scholars, such as Patrick Rafroidi, the publication of Somerville and Ross' *Some Experiences of an Irish R.M.* in 1899 marks the beginning of the Irish short story.[23] Others, like Seamus Deane, go back to the stories of William Carleton.[24] Vivian Mercier's anthology, *Great Irish Short Stories* (1964), emphasizes the link between the oral tradition and the modern literary short story by including translations and adaptations from folk tales by John Millington Synge, Augusta Gregory, Douglas Hyde and Gerald Griffin, before commencing his selection of literary short narratives with Carleton. Benedict Kiely demonstrates his commitment to the oral tradition in his *Penguin Book of Irish Short Stories* (1981) by printing two early Irish tales, one translated by Augusta Gregory, the other by himself, before beginning with Carleton. William Trevor's anthology, *The Oxford Book of Irish Short Stories* (1989), is wider-ranging than any of these, finding room for Seumas MacManus' retelling of a Donegal fairy story, as well as for Anglo-Irish writers like Maria Edgeworth, Oliver Goldsmith and Sheridan Le Fanu, and a handful of contemporary women writers.

To some extent, the starting-point for any study of the short story is always going to be arbitrary since stories, in one form or another, have been around as long as human life. An examination of the Irish language short story might have a completely different time scale going back, as the anthologies of Mercier and Kiely indicate, to the tales of the Ulster cycle or the twelfth-century story-ballads of the Fianna. Since the object of this book is not to discuss storytelling in general, nor folk lore, nor the Irish language tradition, all of which would require separate studies, twentieth-century pioneers of the short story in the Irish language, such as Patrick Pearse, Pádraic Ó Conaire, Máirtín Ó Cadhain, Seán Mac Mathúna, Biddy Jenkinson, have had to be excluded. Nevertheless, rather than beginning simply with Moore, this volume adopts the practice of recent anthologists in going back into the nineteenth century to take a look at precursors of the modern short story in Ireland. This longer historical perspective will allow us to bring forward hitherto neglected writers. In studies of the Irish short story dating from the 1970s and early 1980s, the contribution of writers such as Frank O'Connor, Seán O'Faoláin and Liam O'Flaherty was naturally seen as central; with a longer historical vantage point, new writers come into focus. The rise in the number of Irish women published during the 1980s and 1990s, for example, encourages us to look back and uncover a strong, though neglected, tradition of Irish women's attention to the short story form. The historical context will give us not only the well-known examples of Somerville and Ross, Elizabeth Bowen and Mary Lavin, but lesser-known early writers such as Rosa Mulholland and Emily Lawless, both of whom wrote noteworthy short fiction, as well as neglected early and mid twentieth-century writers like Norah Hoult and Maeve Brennan. In the contemporary period, the extraordinary flowering of short stories by women writers has as yet received little critical attention.

A fresh examination of the way in which Irish women have used the short story raises the question as to whether their treatment of the form modifies our view of the Irish short story. O'Connor's association of the short story with voices excluded from the ruling narrative of the nation seems peculiarly appropriate for Irish women, an often submerged population group within the public life of the nation. At the same time, the stories of Somerville and Ross, Mary Lavin and Éilís Ní Dhuibhne, for example, resist his theory of 'the lonely voice' by writing out of and to a community. Indeed O'Connor had difficulty fitting Mary Lavin into his framework for the Irish short story: 'The point of view is perhaps too exclusively feminine,' he confessed.[25] It is a statement that would seem to reveal a pressing need for the canon of the Irish short story to be looked at again in a way that would allow for the admission of short stories by Irish women. Attention to representative stories by male and female writers of each period in the interchapters will, it is hoped, go some way to redressing the gender balance and to determining whether giving equal weight to women writers alters our view of the Irish short story itself.

Clearly there is a tension between the Irish short story as a transmitter of tradition and its current position as the form that perhaps best expresses Irish modernity. It cannot be a coincidence that the renewed Irish interest in the short story form in the last two decades of the twentieth century happened at a time when the country was undergoing an unprecedented period of change and growth. The short story's ability to encapsulate fleeting insights allowed it to reflect more easily than the novel, which requires a more comprehensive vision, the rapid succession of changes that Ireland underwent in the 1990s. The short story's presentation of brief moments of existence, 'something glimpsed from the corner of the eye, in passing' in V.S. Pritchett's words,[26] permitted snapshots of the effects of the Celtic Tiger, immigration, the decline of the Catholic church, changes in the family unit, and other still current Irish issues. Although the 'mini-world' of the short story, to use Joe Cleary's term, may never be able to set out a detailed vision of Ireland's new place in the global world order, what it can provide are initial soundings.[27] The definitive novel of the Celtic Tiger years has yet to be written; in the meantime, as we shall see in chapter eight, a variety of excellent short stories provides an insight into the liberations, dislocations and alienations consequent on the seismic changes the country underwent during those years.

The development of critical thinking in relation to the Irish nation in the areas of postcolonialism, new historicism, feminist theory and gender studies plays a crucial part in this interrogation. In recent years, both the essentialism and exclusivity of Irish nationalism's meta-narrative and the binary focus of arguments between nationalist historians and revisionists have been challenged. Cultural critics like Luke Gibbons have argued for a rethinking of the national tradition in terms which would recognize its variety and dynamism and locate, within Ireland's past, strands of pro-gressive thinking. Other writers have emphasized Ireland's hybrid iden-tity, residing between two worlds, the Gaelic and the Anglo-Irish, and they have linked this to a postmodern sense of the fragility of identity. In *Inventing Ireland*, Declan Kiberd invokes Karl Marx's description of Ireland as a crucible of modernity, whilst in *Transitions*, Richard Kearney describes Ireland as a place of identities in transition and defines the Irish imagination as essentially migratory. In his study of John Banville, Derek Hand glosses this to indicate that Irish experience is fundamentally modern because it is always in a state of transition.[28] Feminist scholars, among them Patricia Coughlan, Anne Fogarty and Ann Owens Weekes, have pointed to the way in which Irish women's writing challenges the notion of a homogeneous Irish nation and critiques a masculinist nationalism that until recently set up women as idealized symbols of the Irish nation whilst offering them little in the way of a public voice. Likewise, recent work on sexuality and gender in Irish writing by scholars such as Éibhear Walshe has explored the challenge to a homogeneous state posed by gay and lesbian voices. Talk of the Irish nation has given way to discourse on Irelands, a multi-layered text the strength of which lies not in uniformity but in plurality.

Given the lengthy association of the short story form with the Irish nation, these types of argument will have repercussions for the way we view the short story form. If our view of Irishness has changed and expanded in recent years, this poses challenges to our received under-standing of a form regarded as the national genre to the extent that it was often used in the past, by Yeats and others, to propagate the notion of an essential Irish identity. If Ireland has always been a place where identity is made and unmade, arguably the Irish short story will reflect this. 'The hour of change, of metamorphosis / of shape-shifting instabilities' is the hour claimed by Eavan Boland for her art.[29] This in-between place of shifting identities, of change and transformation, is the realm in which the Irish short story also operates. Seen in this context, the Irish short story may become a form less wedded to the portrayal of quotidian reality than to tracking fragmentation and dissolution, as works by writers as diverse as Sheridan Le Fanu, Elizabeth Bowen, John McGahern and Éilís Ní Dhuibhne illustrate.

With its sidelong glance and its marginal status in comparison with the novel, the short story, by its very nature, is, it has been argued, ideally suited to playfulness and subversion. Yet in Ireland, where the short story has been seen not as marginal but as the characteristic Irish genre, this subversive quality has often been downplayed and the form has become associated with early to mid twentieth-century attempts to portray the life of the Irish nation, employing a drab rural or urban realism to do so. The association of the short story form with experimentation and modernity poses a challenge to the traditional affiliation of the Irish short story with the mimetic fiction of writers like Frank O'Connor and Seán O'Faoláin. The mid twentieth-century hegemony of O'Connor's view of the Irish short story as an epiphany in the realist mode may well have obscured other important trends in the Irish short story and clouded our judgment, particularly when we look back to the short fiction of the nineteenth century and forward to stories of the 1990s. A longer historical overview allows us to assess the extent to which the form's alliance with realism may be limited to a certain historical moment and reminds us that while realism in the short story might seem the norm, it is not the only mode in which the Irish short story operates.

In his conclusion to *Inventing Ireland*, Declan Kiberd argues that it is literature and popular culture that will provide us with the insight into individual responses to Ireland's ever-changing situation over the past century and a half.[30] The short story, focusing on the stories of indi-viduals but also tied, through its links with oral storytelling, to popular culture, is admirably suited to chart the inner experience of those from different historical periods caught up in the process of change. In the nineteenth century, the Anglo-Irish tale often revealed the buried fears and anxieties of a class that anticipated its imminent demise. Too brief to provide the 'slice of life' realism that characterized the English novel in this period, short fiction in the hands of practitioners like Sheridan Le Fanu expressed, through dreams, fantasy and the supernatural, what could not be said out loud. His narratives are pervaded by the theme of dissolution associated with Irish short fiction in some of its guises: dissolution of place, political structures, language and even personal identity. In the closing decades of the twentieth century, the narrator-autobiographer of Aidan Higgins' 'Sodden Fields' picks up this theme of dissolution and fragmentation: 'Who am I? Am I or am I not the same person I have always taken myself to be?'[31] In 'Frère Jacques, Bruder Jacques', Higgins' narrator highlights this fragmented self as a peculiarly Irish characteristic: 'For my father, the hardest thing to believe in, to credit, was his own existence, a very Irish trait.'[32] Paul Muldoon says something similar in *To Ireland, I*, where he argues that successive invasions have resulted in 'a sense for many so-called native Irish people of their own invisibility'.[33]

Following the example of Higgins and Muldoon, one might argue that the contemporary short story's awareness of the fragility of identity is not only peculiarly modern, or even postmodern, but also particularly Irish, the consequence of prolonged imposition of an alien identity. As the example of Le Fanu attests, this anxiety about identity is confined neither to the contemporary Irish short story nor to 'native Irish people'. Dissolution of identity is a particularly Anglo-Irish anxiety, and indeed is a dominant theme in Elizabeth Bowen's writing. After independence, the short stories of even a supposedly realist writer like Seán O'Faoláin dwell on the suppressed desires, buried fears and haunting memories of their protagonists. In the modern period, John McGahern and William Trevor use the short story to present social change, while Éilís Ní Dhuibhne links the theme to the shape-shifting of Irish folk tale. It will be one of the aims of this study to probe these themes of fragmentation and dissolution in the Irish short story as it responds, in different historical periods, to the changing pressures of living in a society struggling to establish a sense of national identity and then to modify, expand and deconstruct that identity.

The main focus of this study is not Irish storytelling per se but to track the development of the modern Irish short story as an art form, going back to its roots in the short narratives of the nineteenth century and tracing its evolution down to the present day. Setting the form in its historical and cultural context will allow us to investigate the way in which the Irish short story mirrored or even, given its affinity with the modern, anticipated and sought to influence changes in Irish society. Consideration of the material culture will allow us to determine the extent to which publishing outlets – newspapers, magazines, journals, anthologies – influenced the development of the genre. Given the broad historical sweep of this study, it is expected that discussion will uncover not one but several, perhaps even conflicting, strands in Irish short story writing. In any case, the focus will always be on the individual stories themselves. As the anonymous reviewer of an edition of *Irish Short Stories* by George Birmingham (Reverend James Hannay) reminded readers of *The Bell*, yoking the form to a particular view of Irish history in order to tease out the characteristics of a typical Irish short story is at best con-straining and at worst leads to inaccurate generalizations.[34] This was sage advice, particularly given Birmingham's theory of the Irish short story as characterized by an absence of introspection, a judgment that was not particularly valid when it was promulgated in the 1940s and has become even less so in the light of subsequent developments in Irish short story writing in the hands of writers like Edna O'Brien and John McGahern. I have aimed to follow the advice of *The Bell*'s anonymous reviewer in this respect and, while looking at the historical context and endeavouring to tease out certain recurring themes, I have tried to keep faith with the protean nature of the stories themselves.

CHAPTER TWO

The nineteenth century: nation and short story in the making

If the modern Irish short story has frequently been concerned with identities in transition, it is interesting to observe that short narratives dealing with Irish themes began to emerge in the nineteenth century in large numbers at a time when the country was going through one of its most traumatic periods. The attempt by Irish Protestants to define themselves as a nation ended with the failure of Grattan's Parliament, and a series of events during the course of the nineteenth century, beginning with the Act of Union in 1800 and including Catholic emancipation (1829), the tithe wars, the famines and the 1848 rebellion, weakened the moral and political claim of the Ascendancy to rule Ireland. The tales of a writer like Sheridan Le Fanu reveal the anxiety induced by this loss of prestige. At the same time, the efforts of Catholics to establish a nation-state were beginning: in the 1820s Daniel O'Connell, aided by the Catholic Association, was orchestrating a mass movement to demand rights for the Catholic population. In order to make progress with this, O'Connell believed that Ireland needed to abandon the Irish language and learn the language of the country's administrators. Short fiction dealing with Irish themes started to proliferate at the moment when the Irish language and the oral tradition were being jettisoned in favour of English and the printed word. Research has highlighted the enormous implications of this shift from oral culture to print, not only for social structures, but also for patterns of thought.[1] Conscious that access to the past lay in the language and habits of the Irish-speaking peasantry and that Gaelic culture was dying around them, scholars and writers began collecting Irish folklore. Often this also involved its adaptation and manufacture, for the impetus behind the retrieval of Ireland's past was not simply historical but part of a political and cultural engagement in shaping Ireland's future identity at a time of transition. The emergence of Irish short fiction in the nineteenth century was entangled in the rise of national consciousness.

Across Europe the romantic quest for the past prompted historical research into ancient cultures, of which Ireland was an obvious and accessible example. In Ireland this quest gained added impetus after the Act of Union stimulated English interest in that part of the empire. During the first decades of the nineteenth century, depictions of Irish life and customs and collections of folklore and travelogues, often wrapped up in a quasi-fictional form, became immensely popular. Much of this early nineteenth-century writing, though about Ireland and arguably establishing the beginnings of a national literature, was published in England and addressed to an English readership.[2] In 1844, an article titled 'Twaddling Tourists in Ireland' in the *Dublin University Magazine*, complained bitterly of the number of 'rash, ignorant and ill-informed tourists' who were writing books on Ireland: 'There probably never was a country so completely overrun by the book-making generation as this land of ours.'[3]

Nineteenth-century literary periodicals reveal that though short fiction by Irish writers was frequently published, just as the Irish state had yet to come into being, so the Irish short story had yet to stabilize as a genre. There is an enormous difference between the modern short story with its lyrical intensity, tight structure and focused viewpoint, and the nine-teenth-century form where 'a tale' could mean anything from a brief sketch, anecdote or fable to a novella or even a three-volume novel. The appearance of William Carleton's autobiographical and anti-clerical tale, 'The Lough Derg Pilgrim', in the anti-Catholic periodical, *The Christian Examiner and Church of Ireland Magazine* in 1828, placed his fiction alongside anti-Papal polemics, biblical exegesis, church history, religious poetry and reviews of sermons. The material context of his tale's publi-cation inevitably drew attention to its didactic elements rather than to its literary qualities. Indeed, one of the main differences between the nineteenth-century story or tale and its modern form is that nineteenth-century writers used their short fiction for purposes other than telling a story. The nineteenth-century tale evolved out of a hybrid mix of trav-elogue, memoirs, sketches, tales and legends. Whether written by Anglo-Irish Protestants or middle-class Catholics, much of it was inspired by extra-literary considerations and propelled by anxiety: to record the beliefs and habits of Irish peasant life before they got lost for ever, to defend and explain the Irish to the English, to rectify the many and obvious faults in the Irish character. The nineteenth-century Irish short narrative, in its various different shapes, was involved as much in intervention in Irish life as in representation. Under pressure from the turbulent times, the realistic framework of the fiction frequently collapsed – into Gothic or melodrama, sentimentality or didactics.

The Act of Union led to a dawning realization on the part of the Anglo-Irish that they were in fact as much Irish as English, and with this realization came a concomitant desire to explain, defend and justify their country to the English. In the early years of the nineteenth century, the didactic element came to the fore in the Anglo-Irish short narrative. The turn of the century saw an upsurge in morally uplifting tales for children, among them those of Maria Edgeworth, who published a series of children's tales exemplifying the educational ideals set out by her father and herself in *Practical Education* (1798). It was through writing the simple stories for young children featured in *The Parent's Assistant* (1796) that Edgeworth began to detach herself from her father's influence and find her distinctive fictional voice. This volume was followed by *Moral Tales for Young People* (1801) and *Early Lessons* (1801–2). As the titles suggest, Edgeworth's aim was primarily didactic, not only to instruct parents in the right way of educating their children, but also English readers into an understanding of the Irish way of life, essential if the Anglo-Irish were to rule Ireland effectively.[4] Her tales already possessed a hybrid quality which was to become more pronounced in Irish short fiction as the century wore on: 'The White Pigeon' in *The Parent's Assistant* is addressed both to Irish readers in its justification of an Irish informer and to English readers in its plea for more resident landlords like Mr Somerville.

Edgeworth's *Popular Tales*, published in London in 1804, aimed at an artisan readership. 'The Limerick Gloves', from this collection, was written between the 1798 rebellion and the Act of Union, at a time when relations between Ireland and England were at their most strained. The entire tenor of the tale was to promote favourable feelings towards Ireland and allay English anxieties, parodied in Mr Hill's exaggerated prejudice against his daughter's would-be suitor, Brian O'Neill. The tale, though witty and engaging, is not without condescension towards the Irish: O'Neill may be a good man, generous and brave, but he is also impulsive and careless with money. Edgeworth's use of the vernacular adds to the attraction of 'The Limerick Gloves' but, as Brian Hollingworth has pointed out, use of the vernacular in her writing does not necessarily imply sympathy with it.[5] In 'Rosanna', the other story in *Popular Tales* with an Irish setting, Edgeworth's suspicion of the vernacular is evidenced by its association with the slothful Simon O'Dougherty; O'Dougherty's neighbours, the hard-working and thrifty Gray family, use standard

English. In 'The Limerick Gloves', after various opportunities for mis-understandings between the Irish and the English, Mr Hill comes to recognize that he has misjudged O'Neill and the tale concludes with their reconciliation and a barely disguised plea for friendship between England and Ireland to their mutual trading benefit. Maria Edgeworth's tales represented modernity to the extent that they were an active intervention in the debate about Ireland's future and indicated a desire to reform the management of Irish estates. Her novel, *Castle Rackrent* (1800), pioneered regional writing in English, and her tales deserve to be seen as part of this: the *Dublin University Magazine* described them as 'the first truly Irish sketches'.[6] Unlike the tales of emerging nationalist writers, however, Edgeworth's tales were intent on preserving the status quo and were thus implicated, as a recent critic has argued, 'in national stability and imperial expansion'.[7]

If the impulse behind Edgeworth's short fiction was primarily didactic, she did have the virtue of letting her lively and readable tales tell them-selves; in Anna Hall's writing, the fictional framework all but collapses under the weight of her message. Like Edgeworth, Anna Hall, born in Ireland of Huguenot descent but residing for much of her life in England, strove to explain Ireland to the English, with the aim of benefiting both countries.[8] Her *Sketches of Irish Character*, published in London in 1829, centred on the parish of Bannow in County Wexford where Hall's early life was spent and were enormously popular: by 1854 they were into the fifth edition. They included the type of subject matter her English readers would have expected: portraits of dirty and idle Irish peasants, tales of violence in the Irish countryside and local stories of fairy and folklore. Many of the characters were drawn, Hall claimed, from life, making these sketches more akin to travel documentary or sociological observation than to the modern short story, but guaranteeing them authenticity in the eyes of her contemporaries.

Whilst the examples of Edgeworth and Hall reveal the story in the early nineteenth century to be an unstable form veering between travelogue and morality tale, other writers from the Protestant tradition exploited Ireland for the entertainment and instruction of English readers by publishing collections of folklore. The best-known of these writers was Thomas Crofton Croker, credited with achieving the breakthrough of Irish popular narratives into respectable literature to be read by English and Anglo-Irish readers who would have disdained to come into contact with the living oral tradition of the Irish peasantry.[9] The first volume of his *Fairy Tales and Legends of the South of Ireland*, published anonymously in London in 1825, was widely praised by such figures as Sir Walter Scott and the Brothers Grimm. As the son of an army major Croker was, as W.B. Yeats pointed out in his introduction to *Representative Irish Tales*, an outsider to the culture he was presenting. In his hands, fairies became not, as Yeats thought they should be, a subject for nobility and splendour, but an occasion for humour. 'The Confessions of Tom Bourke', for example, is told from the point of view of someone from outside the peasant community, an omniscient narrator who speaks educated English, is sceptical of the peasants' beliefs and feels obliged to explain aspects of Irish life to the reader. Croker relied on stereotypes about the Irish character and, like Hall, was unable to refrain from interrupting his story with comments and explanations. Despite this, his tale flows smoothly, with touches of humour and tension and incorporating some passages of natural-sounding dialogue, bearing out Yeats' comment that Croker 'could tell a story better than most men'.[10] Nevertheless, the main purpose of Croker's stories was to exploit the comic potential of the peasants' beliefs for the entertainment of English readers. In the end, Croker was neither pure folklorist nor pure storyteller. In the preface to the second edition of *Fairy Tales*, he admits that he was not aiming for originality and that his stories were representative of those in circulation among the peasantry in the south of Ireland. He often embellished the stories he heard, or received them second-hand from a correspondent.[11] Croker's significance lies not as a fiction writer but in being the first to present Irish folklore to a European audience.

When the Catholic writers, John and Michael Banim, came to write about their country, they had the advantage over Edgeworth, Hall and Croker in being closer to the people they were writing about. Wishing to counter the portrayal of the Irish peasant as buffoon, the Banims aimed for a serious portrait of contemporary rural hardship and thereby came a step nearer to bringing an Irish national literature into being. The first series of *The Tales of the O'Hara Family* was published in London in 1825, 'at once acquiring popularity', according to *The Illustrated Dublin Journal*.[12] As far as the short story form was concerned, however, less progress was made, *The Tales of the O'Hara Family* containing historical tales sufficiently large-scale to qualify as novels.

In the demoralized years following on the Act of Union there was virtually no indigenous Irish publishing. In 1833, the first volume of the *Dublin University Magazine* was gloomy about that magazine's chances of survival, musing on 'the disadvantages that attend a literary periodical in Dublin' and pointing out that 'numberless Irish periodicals have already failed'. In comparison with England and Scotland, it lamented, 'there rests upon our metropolis the stigma of never having supported a good general Magazine'.[13] The extent to which the Irish publishing scene was still dominated by London and Edinburgh is apparent in the life and work of William Maginn. Born in Cork in 1794 and a graduate of Trinity College, Dublin, he left Ireland for London in 1824 in order to pursue a literary career. His stories, published variously in *Blackwood's Edinburgh Magazine*, *Bentley's 'Miscellany'* and *The Literary Souvenir*, illustrate the range of the nineteenth-century short narrative, from the Gothic horror of 'The Man in the Bell' (*Blackwood's Magazine*, 1821) and 'A Night of Terror' (*Bentley's 'Miscellany'*, 1836), to tales of comic misunderstanding ('The Two Butlers of Kilkenny', *Bentley's 'Miscellany'*, 1836) and humorous tales of military life ('Bob Burke's Duel with Ensign Brady of the 48th', *Blackwood's Magazine*, 1834). Maginn also participated in the Gaelic renaissance with tales of fairy folk such as 'The Legend of Bottle Hill' and 'The Legend of Knockgrafton', included in Thomas Crofton Croker's *Fairy Legends*. Maginn featured posthumously in the 'Portrait Gallery' of the *Dublin University Magazine*, which presented him as a ruined genius, on account of time spent in a debtors' prison where he contracted the tuberculosis that caused his premature death. Maginn thus became an early example of an Irish writer failing to flourish abroad, and the magazine remarked on publishers' reluctance to republish his work. The portrait concentrated on Maginn's poetry and passed over his tales in silence, an indication of the relative unimportance of the prose tale in the hierarchy of literary genres at this period. Maginn's skills as an oral storyteller in London drawing rooms were highlighted, however, foreshadowing the reputation of Oscar Wilde later in the century.[14]

Gerald Griffin was another Irish writer obliged to move to England in the 1820s in order to further his literary ambitions. Born into the Catholic merchant class that had come into existence partly as a consequence of the Penal Code, whereby Catholics were excluded from most areas of public life, Griffin began writing his first collection of short tales in London in 1826. He found that gaining entry to the London literary world was not easy for an unknown Irishman:

You have no idea what a heart-breaking life that of a young scribbler, beating about, and endeavouring to make his way in London, is: going into a bookseller's shop, as I have often done, and being obliged to praise up my own manuscript to induce him to look at it at all; for there is so much competition, that a person without a name will not even get a trial.[15]

The primary urge behind Griffin's *'Holland-Tide'; or, Munster Popular Tales*, published in London in 1827, was not to shape a short story collection but to map out and explain Irish customs and life for English readers, doing for his country what Sir Walter Scott's tales had done for Scotland. The remarkable cross-fertilization of influence between Scotland and Ireland in this period is illustrated by the fact that it was Maria Edgeworth's tales of Ireland that prompted Scott to write about Scotland, and he in turn inspired both Griffin, a Catholic, and in the following decade, the Irish Protestant, Samuel Ferguson, to write about their own country. Griffin's biographer quotes a letter from Griffin asking his family to supply him with regional stories: 'My anecdotes are all short stories, illustrative of manners and scenery precisely as they stand in the south of Ireland.'[16] There is, however, little uniformity in *'Holland-Tide'*. A story like 'The Brown Man' is a brief, effective folk tale, not easily distinguishable from Croker's *Fairy Legends*. Like Croker, Griffin prefaced his folk tale with an explanation by an educated narrator. However, when a contemporary reviewer drew a comparison with Croker, Griffin was enraged, indicating that his aim in *'Holland-Tide'*, even if not always successfully executed, was to distance himself from Croker's exploitation of Irish stereotypes for the amusement of English readers.[17] In contrast with 'The Brown Man' 'The Aylmers of Bally-Aylmer', a rambling tale of revenge between smugglers, runs to almost 200 pages and shows Irish short fiction continuing to be marred by loose structure, digressions and authorial comment. Irish short narratives also continued to be hampered by the fact of being written for an English audience. 'The Aylmers of Bally-Aylmer' is full of asides and explanatory footnotes for Griffin's English readers: '(it is turf we speak of, gentle London reader)', 'the haggard (Irish-English for hay-yard)'.[18] Griffin's use of an educated narrator not only interrupts the flow of his stories but also creates an impression of the writer's willed distance from the experiences he is describing. The form suffers as a result of being caught between Griffin's desire to present Irish peasant life but also to impress his English readers by establishing his superiority to it.

Griffin's *Tales of the Munster Festivals*, also published in 1827, marked a step forward both in his handling of prose narrative and his portrayal of his compatriots. It was favourably received: 'The critics now began to load him with praise, and the publishers to vie, with one another, for his favours.'[19] Rather than referring to tales heard or recounted, Griffin is conscious in this collection of inheriting an Irish tradition of the *written* story. He pays homage to Maria Edgeworth's depiction of Ireland and to

the Banims' *Tales of the O'Hara Family* whilst nailing his colours firmly
to the mast as a regional writer who feels uncomfortable writing about
Dublin, territory of Edgeworth and the Banims, but regards Munster as
'unsifted soil'.[20] In Griffin, therefore, we find a writer who was aware
that, as far as Irish short fiction was concerned, an indigenous literary
tradition was beginning to take shape.

The collection, containing just three lengthy stories, 'Card Drawing',
'The Half-Sir' and 'Suil Dhuiv, the Coiner', still displays Griffin's
fondness for melodrama and improbable coincidences, but also reveals
Griffin coming into his own as a regional writer whose tales, often chaotic
in form, aptly reflect the chaos of his country in the years before the Great
Famine. 'Card Drawing', for instance, though melodramatic and
unstructured, portrays a society struggling to come to terms with an alien
code of justice and learning to express itself in an alien language. However, it is in 'The Half-Sir' that Griffin displays his gifts in vivid depiction
of the Irish rural scene and a psychological intensity that moves Irish
narrative away from folk tale and anecdote towards the modern short
story. 'The Half-Sir' gains in vividness and authenticity from its setting in
the recent past: opening in 1822, a time of epidemic and famine, it
communicates a real feeling of Griffin writing as events in Ireland were
unfolding. The tale's psychological intensity is focused on the 'half-sir',
Eugene Hamond, and draws its force from autobiographical elements:
Eugene, educated by a wealthy second cousin of his father beyond the
peasant class but refused enough money to be independent, reflects
Griffin's own uncomfortable position as a middle-class Irish Catholic,
caught between the peasant class and the Anglo-Irish gentry. The
description of Eugene's emotions as he quits Ireland has an autobiographical ring but also captures the situation of the emergent Catholic
middle class of the period: 'Hamond . . . was leaving a land, which was,
and was not, his home – and where he had filled a nameless place in
society, without stamp and station – preserving claims to various conditions, and properly belonging to none.'[21] Fiction yields to propaganda
as, in an ending that suppresses both the implications of the horror of the
famine scenes and Eugene's rebellious nature, Eugene is reconciled with
the woman he loves and both prosper as good landlords who look after
the needs of their tenants. In the wake of the political disempowerment of
the Ascendancy class and in the years before Catholic emancipation,
Griffin was advertising his faith in a respectable Irish Catholic bourgeoisie
ready to take over the country. It is not the ending that creates the force
and originality of this tale, however, so much as the vivid depiction of the

devastation of the Irish countryside during a period of famine and the acuteness of Griffin's psychological observation of Irish identity in a moment of evolution.

Griffin's gifts for psychological observation are evident in one of his finest tales, 'The Knight of the Sheep', published in later editions of *'Holland-Tide'*. 'The Knight of the Sheep' is a *King Lear*-type tale of a prosperous Catholic farmer, Bryan Taafe, who divides his property between his two eldest sons but, out of hastiness and ill temper, rejects his youngest son. Though the tale is divided into two chapters, it runs to a mere fourteen pages, is tightly structured and, apart from the opening paragraph where the title 'Knight of the Sheep' is explained for the benefit of the English reader, largely avoids intervention by an omniscient narrator. The rural Irish are treated with seriousness, as in the Banims, and Griffin abstains from a happy ending: vanity and misjudgment have caused Bryan Taafe to trust his two unworthy eldest sons at the expense of his third, and though he himself learns from his mistake there is no reconciliation. The psychological tragedy of a father–son relationship gone awry is somewhat undermined by the folk tale ending of Taafe's tricky revenge on his eldest sons for their greed and self-interested love. Nevertheless, tales like 'The Knight of the Sheep' and 'The Half-Sir' show Griffin shifting the Irish short narrative away from one-dimensional characters who simply react to events or are illustrative of some moral point.

Griffin is often judged, and found wanting, because of his distance from the lives of the peasants he portrayed, but his tales are a vital record of the emergent Catholic identity in the years between the Act of Union and the Great Famine. A contemporary reviewer placed him alongside Carleton, Edgeworth and the Banims as 'an able delineator of our national feelings'.[22] The wording of this suggests that, in the minds of Griffin's contemporaries, national themes continued to take precedence over matters of style when assessing short fiction. In 1861, *The Illustrated Dublin Journal* featured Griffin in the first of its series of 'National Tintings', proclaiming that 'no national writer has excelled him in his delineation of Irish character'. It was this journal's opinion that 'Gerald Griffin fell just short of being the Irish Walter Scott', a judgment that has often been endorsed by subsequent critics.[23] If Griffin's stories were often chaotic in form, this is understandable, given the chaotic nature of the times and his own lack of formal education. Ireland's turbulence could not easily be contained within the conventions of European literary realism and that in itself is perhaps another reason for looking at nineteenth-century Irish short fiction in different terms, as a form concerned not so much with reproducing the conventions of European realism as developing a way to express the dissolution of an old culture and the emergence of a new nation and language. The efforts of Griffin and, later Carleton, to defend and explain their nation are quite different from the mimetic impulse behind the realism of the mid twentieth-century Irish short story. It is on account of Griffin's ability to portray the chaos of his times and the plight of his people that his biographer, John Cronin, regards him as a forerunner of writers like Moore and Joyce.

In the 1820s Griffin and Maginn had to go abroad to pursue their literary careers. In the following decade there would be more opportunities for Irish writers to publish at home. Until the Catholic Emancipation Act of 1829 the only Irish magazines that had flourished since the Union had been involved, along tribal lines, in political and religious propaganda, like the anti-Catholic periodical, *The Christian Examiner and Church of Ireland Magazine*, published by the Protestant proselytizer, Caesar Otway, in which the first stories by William Carleton appeared.[24] After 1829, the stirrings of national consciousness prompted the setting up of new Irish literary periodicals (though still often published in London). *The Belfast Magazine and Literary Journal*, started in 1825, was an early journal that expressed its desire to promote literature over religious and political polemic. Like many non-sectarian journals in a sectarian age, it survived less than a year. A cultural journal aspiring to promote a more inclusive nationalism was the *Dublin Literary Gazette*, which started in January 1830 and in July emphasized its aspirations to form an Irish national consciousness by changing its name to *The National Magazine*. It ran until April 1831. Though still Protestant managed, *The National Magazine* was both more intellectually substantial and less partisan than *The Christian Examiner*. It published fiction by Anna Hall, William Carleton and Samuel Lover. Its Catholic counterpart, the *Irish Monthly Magazine of Politics and Literature*, with which Samuel Lover and James Mangan were associated, also hoped to avoid religious bigotry. It lasted for two years (1832–4) and it too published short fiction.

Despite the pessimism of its opening editorial, the *Dublin University Magazine* became highly influential, running from 1833 until 1877. By the 100th volume, it was congratulating itself that: 'Previous to or since the Union, no Irish Magazine or Review ever attained the circulation, or existed for the same length of time we have now reached.'[25] The *Dublin University Magazine* was founded by a group of Conservative and Protestant young men affiliated to Trinity College, including such names as Caesar Otway, Isaac Butt and Samuel Ferguson. In the wake of the

Reform Bill of 1832, it opposed agitation for social change, any concessions to democracy and the politics of Daniel O'Connell. Despite its politics and its mainly Protestant readership, it aimed to project a sense of the cultural unity of the Irish nation, proclaiming its wish to create 'a literature which should be NATIONAL without degenerating into mere PROVINCIALISM'. By 1841 it was priding itself both on its service to the literary life of the nation – 'Much of the literary talent of Ireland we have been the means of retaining at home, that, were it not for us, had sought some other market' – and on its nurturing of new talent: 'we have educed and brought forth, who had else probably never written a line'.[26] In practice, the fiction the magazine published tended to fall in, with varying degrees of subtlety, with support for the Ascendancy, though the tales of a writer like Sheridan Le Fanu pointed to the anxieties and uncertainties underlying its conservative, counter-revolutionary ethos. Contributors included Anna Hall, James Mangan, William Carleton, Samuel Lover, Charles Lever, who became editor in 1842, and Sheridan Le Fanu, who later owned and edited it. Its Catholic counterpart was the London-based *Dublin Review*, which lasted from 1836 until 1969, and became the leading Roman Catholic periodical in Britain.

In addition to these expensive magazines for the intelligentsia were the popular penny magazines which began to appear in 1830s and where Anna Hall, for one, found a market for her work: the *Dublin Penny Journal* (1832–6), the *Irish Penny Magazine* (1833–4), edited by Samuel Lover, and the *Irish Penny Journal* (1840–1), to which both Hall and Carleton contributed. In the North, *The New Belfast Magazine* (Belfast 1833–4) included short fiction, as did the later *Ulster Magazine* (Belfast 1860). The rise of indigenous literary periodicals encouraged both the emerging national consciousness and, because of their format, the popularity of short narratives. The rapid development of Irish publishing may be measured in the distance between the first series of William Carleton's *Traits and Stories*, the slim, anonymous volumes of 1830, to the lavishly illustrated edition of 1842, complete with etchings and woodcuts by contemporary artists, which went into eleven impressions before 1870. The instant success of the first series of *Traits and Stories*, published by William Curry of Dublin, followed by an equally successful second series in 1833, encouraged other writers to publish in Ireland, and Carleton took justifiable pride in his contribution to developing an Irish publishing industry: 'it was now clearly established that an Irish writer could be successful at home without the necessity of appearing under the name and sanction of the great London or Edinburgh booksellers'.[27]

Though the 1830s may have brought more indigenous publishing opportunities, Irish writers' approach to the short narrative continued to vary widely. Samuel Lover, like Croker a member of the Protestant Ascendancy, stood outside the life of the community from which he collected folk tales but endeavoured to impersonate the voice of the Irish storyteller. The first edition of his *Legends and Stories of Ireland* appeared in 1832, a second series in 1834 and a third, *Further Stories of Ireland*, posthumously. In his introduction to the first series, Lover explained that the collection evolved from stories he told to his friends around his fireside 'recited in the manner of those from whom I heard them'.[28] Subsequently he published two of them in the *Dublin Literary Gazette* and their favourable reception led to the appearance of his first volume, an example of the stimulus given by the newly established literary magazines to the development of the genre.

The oral quality of his tales explained, Lover argued, why they suffered on being transferred to the printed page, notably from digressions: 'the Irish are so imaginative that they never tell a story straightforward, but constantly indulge in episode'.[29] Certainly his collections illustrate how the Irish story had yet to stabilize as a genre. 'Paddy the Piper' from the first series is little more than an amusing anecdote moved along by its dialogue, which a prefatory paragraph asks the reader to imagine being delivered 'by a frolicking Irish peasant, in the richest brogue and most dramatic manner'.[30] In the second series, 'New Potatoes' is simply a dialogue between two street hawkers, whereas 'Barny O'Reirdon, the Navigator', originally serialized and highly praised in the first issue of the *Dublin University Magazine* in January 1833 and later selected by Yeats as one of his thirty best Irish books, runs to more than thirty pages and is divided into two chapters.[31] Lover's narratives are generally framed by opening and closing paragraphs in the voice of an educated and highly condescending narrator. The tales are readable and amusing – unlike Anna Hall, Lover lets a story tell itself – but ultimately his aim was not, as Yeats' would be, to create a national literature but, like Croker's, to exploit peasant material for the amusement of his readers by combining it with the caricature of the stage-Irish found in seventeenth- and eighteenth-century playwrights. In 'Paddy the Piper', set at a time of martial law, the darker aspects of the tale of a corpse hung by rebels are thrust into the background in order to provide the English reader, haunted by the spectre of starvation and rebellion in the Irish countryside, with a welcome distraction in the form of a frolicking entertainment as the corpse's boots are stolen by the eponymous Paddy.

For another writer from the Protestant tradition, Samuel Ferguson, short fiction had a higher purpose. In a review of Lover's work in the *Dublin University Magazine*, he dismissed *Legends and Stories of Ireland* as 'the grinning heartlessness of mere brogue and blunder'.[32] Born in Belfast, Ferguson belonged not so much with Big House Protestantism as with the world of Victorian urban middle-class intellectuals and professionals.[33] The first two stories of Ferguson's early work, *Hibernian Nights' Entertainments*, appeared in *Blackwood's Edinburgh Magazine* in December 1833 and February 1834, and the following five were serialized in the *Dublin University Magazine* from December 1834 to May 1836, but the collection was not published in book form until 1887. *Hibernian Nights' Entertainments* was the first collection from the Protestant tradition in which there is a clear association between the short narrative form and modernity, as Ferguson tried to shape an Irish identity in transition. *Hibernian Nights* is a series of national tales inspired by Walter Scott but drawing also on *Tales of the Arabian Nights* for its loose fictional framework of tales told in 1592 by Turlogh O'Hagan, hereditary bard of the O'Neills, to entertain Hugh O'Donnell and his fellow captives during their imprisonment in Dublin Castle. Ferguson's aim, however, was not primarily recuperative but to set out his particular perspective on Irish history at the moment of Ireland's transition from an aristocratic society to a merchant class. The words of Brother Virgil in 'Corby MacGillmore' proclaim the essence of Ferguson's ideal for civic life based on a prosperous and settled middle class and an urban market economy: 'I see these wild woods, now the refuge of the wolf, yielding to the fair green fields of a civilized and prosperous people . . . The hum of cheerful labour sounds from the populous city like the message of the summer beehive.'[34] 'The Rebellion of Silken Thomas' uses the episode of Thomas Fitzgerald's rebellion against the crown to depict the decline of the feudal system and the rise of an urban merchant class. Ferguson's tales endeavoured to impose a coherent perspective on a variety of historical periods from pre-Christian and medieval Ireland through to the Elizabethan period. It was an ambitious project and the collection remained unfinished, with only fourteen out of a projected twenty-one tales. Nevertheless, Ferguson's attempt to use the short narrative form to shape a vision for Ireland, together with his interweaving of history and myth, anticipates Yeats' *The Secret Rose*.[35]

As the 1830s wore on and the situation in the Irish countryside continued to be marked by outbursts of agrarian violence, the entertainments of Lover and Croker began to be regarded, even by the *Dublin University*

Magazine, with different eyes: 'The time is, indeed, now past, when the unnatural absurdities of Teagues or O'Blunders can pass for genuine pictures of Irishmen and we now seldom find an Irish character introduced in a tale merely to amuse by his extravagance and discharge the humble task of the buffoon in an old play.'[36] For the benefit of the magazine's middle-class readership, Samuel Ferguson depicted the scene outside his study window: 'the wanderers of Connaught, ragged, diminutive, and of abortive feature, the mis-creations of hardship and neglect, crowding to the quays, upon their weary way to the English harvest'.[37] The political situation had its effect on Irish writers: in 1834, defeated by the realities of the people's suffering and her distance from them, Maria Edgeworth ended her career as a fiction writer.[38] In *Lights and Shadows of Irish Life*, published in London in 1838, Anna Hall was still using the word 'sketch' to describe her tales inspired by scenes and people she had met in Ireland during the autumn of 1834, but the picture of Ireland had darkened. In 'Beggars', she remarks that it is impossible for English readers to understand the depth of Irish suffering. At the same time as she portrays Irish beggars' misery, however, she blames them for not having the habit of saving. Hall's sketches are lively and entertaining but marred by her tendency to ascribe the increasingly dire political and economic situation to moral failings on the part of landlords and peasants, constantly intervening as an omniscient (and right-thinking) narrator to explain Irish life to the English reader and inserting lengthy didactic passages on how to improve Irish conditions. Having been reared in Ireland, Hall felt that she knew that country better than most English commentators (in the 'Groves of Blarney' she is sharply critical of ignorant English outsiders who write uninformed books about Ireland); at the same time, her writing reveals that she had imbibed many of the colonial and class prejudices of her English readers, with the result that her narrative voice veers uncertainly between defending and explaining the Irish to the English reader and speaking as an Englishwoman who believes that English virtues can transform Irish life. Reviews of Hall's work varied from the glowing (*Dublin University Magazine*, August 1838) to the misogynist, Samuel Ferguson suggesting, perhaps with good reason, that she steer clear of 'masculine' subjects like politics and stick to 'the social and domestic'.[39]

For the Banim brothers, as for Hall, fiction was not a reliable enough witness to the increasing poverty and wretchedness of Irish life. In 'The Stolen Sheep', subtitled 'An Irish Sketch', appearing in *The Bit O'Writing*, a collection of tales published in London in 1838 under the pseudonym

'The O'Hara Family', the authenticity of the Banims' tale has to be bolstered by the claim that it is drawn from life, in this case not from personal observation but from a newspaper account. 'The Stolen Sheep' opens with a cautious statement of the narrators' aims:

The faults of the lower orders of the Irish are sufficiently well-known; perhaps their virtues have not been proportionately observed or recorded for observation. At all events, it is but justice to them, and it cannot conflict with any established policy or do any one harm to exhibit them in a favourable light to their British fellow-subjects, as often as strict truth will permit.[40]

Unlike Lover, the Banims were not reluctant to portray the horrors suffered by the peasants during a time of famine and fever, emphasizing that 'in almost every third cabin there was a corpse daily'. Yet they were careful to keep an eye on their English readership: 'then came England's munificent donation – God prosper her for it!'[41] 'The Stolen Sheep' breaks off to describe examples of Irish virtue under these appalling circumstances personally witnessed by the authors. This fracturing of the narrative under pressure from the times is an illustration of the strain under which nineteenth-century Catholic writers on Ireland were working. Caught between a desire to portray the full horror of their countrymen's suffering and their need to conciliate the English reader, it was the Banims' art that suffered. Ireland's turbulent times resisted being constrained within the bounds of fiction with the result that Irish short fiction continued to be a mixture of special pleading and moral fable.

After this explanatory introduction, 'The Stolen Sheep' focuses on a case study of an individual peasant, Michaul Carroll. The situation of Michaul's father being compelled to testify against his son, a submission to colonial authority that would have been approved of by Edgeworth and Hall, and in Lover made the excuse for farcical complications, is here treated as a tragedy between two noble and dignified characters. Dialect is used in the story, not to ridicule the peasants, but to illustrate their natural way of speaking: shorn of the extravagance and outlandishness of Lover's peasants' language, the speech of Michaul and his father comes across as restrained, affectionate and pious. Michaul's action in stealing the sheep is not presented, as it would have been in Hall, as the result of flaws in his character, but of the impossible economic situation in which he finds himself. Apart from the opening two paragraphs, 'The Stolen Sheep' refrains from direct intervention by the narrator and is tightly structured, without digressions, maintaining the tension until the end. Yet the primary impulse behind the narrative is didactic: to display the

Irish peasant in such a noble light that even English readers would be moved. Because of this, the writing cannot avoid sentimentality, melo-drama and, despite the generally realistic tone, an unrealistically happy ending ensuring that the conscience of the English reader would be soothed rather than pricked.

As the successive famines began to take hold, Anna Hall's dual national allegiance became troubling to her, and her earlier certainties about how Irish society should develop gave way to doubts and a darker portrait of Irish life in *Stories of the Irish Peasantry* (1840). Each of the sixteen tract-like tales in this later collection deals with a particular Irish failing such as alcoholism, idleness, violence and improvidence but, despite the stri-dently didactic tone, Hall cannot quite push out of sight that this is a dying country. Her portrayal of the despair of a character like Sandy in 'Too Early Wed!' and her observations of the growing desolation and emptiness of Dublin's streets provide ample evidence of a country in crisis. Although Hall's stories, like Edgeworth's, can hardly be associated with modernity, nevertheless her sense of a culture in crisis put pressure not only on her sense of identity but also on her use of the short narrative form, as her writing came increasingly to reflect what a recent study has called 'her basic uncertainty in...[her] vision of herself'.[42] Hall's strengths as a writer lay in travelogue, in her evocative descriptions of the Irish countryside and her early lively sketches of Irish peasants. Her handling of the form is much less certain in *Stories of the Irish Peasantry*, where she can never quite trust the story to tell itself. As Hall's hybrid national identity proved increasingly fraught, its complexity and con-tradictions became difficult to contain within the format of her tales.

Sheridan Le Fanu was another writer from the Protestant tradition whose work in the 1830s expressed both personal and political anxieties. Le Fanu's short fiction is filled with themes of dissolution, not only the dissolution of political boundaries consequent on the rise of the Fenians who, he feared, would dispossess the Protestant gentry as the latter had dispossessed the Catholic gentry after 1690, but also the dissolution of barriers between the human world and the world of spirits. Le Fanu had heard such stories from the local storytellers in Abington in his youth, but in his hands the folk tale became transformed into highly crafted stories for a literate, sceptical audience, allowing for both supernatural and psychological explanations and, anticipating Yeats, mingling Swedenborg with Irish folklore.

'The Fortunes of Sir Robert Ardagh', first published in March 1838 in the *Dublin University Magazine*, aptly illustrates the difference between popular folklore for a sympathetic audience and literary tales of the supernatural addressed to a sceptical readership; indeed, the composition of this tale may well have been influenced by Le Fanu's knowledge of the expectations of the *Dublin University Magazine*'s readers.[43] The tale opens by recounting the traditional story of Sir Robert Ardagh, a man so morose and solitary that he appears to have sold his soul to the devil in the shape of a foreign companion. This devil/foreigner later returns and drags him over the edge of a precipice. Le Fanu's narrator is the Reverend Francis Purcell, an eighteenth-century Catholic priest, antiquarian, collector of folklore and Swedenborgian. Purcell proceeds to distance himself from this simple and melodramatic tale by recounting a very different story he claims to have heard from a female eyewitness. Unlike the folk tale preceding it, Purcell's tale is precisely dated: Sir Robert Ardagh inherits an impoverished estate on the borders of County Limerick and spends the years 1742 to 1760 abroad. Purcell's narrative transposes Le Fanu's anxieties about the declining fortunes of his family and class into a Gothic tale of Jacobite times, a period fascinating to Le Fanu because it seemed to prefigure his own family's decline. In his later rewriting of this Faustian bargain tale, 'Sir Dominic's Bargain', published in 1872 in the London magazine, *All the Year Round*, edited by Charles Dickens, the Jacobite connection is made explicit. Both the politics and the literary tastes of the *Dublin University Magazine* would have ensured a readership sympathetic to Le Fanu's story. The magazine's conservative ethos has already been noted and two of its editors published Gothic tales: Isaac Butt's *Chapters of College Romance*, serialized from November 1834 to November 1837, and Charles Lever's 'Carl Stelling – The Painter of Dresden' (1842).

If Le Fanu's use of the Gothic literary mode and his precise dating disassociate his narrative from the folk tale, so does his exploration of Sir Robert's character. If Griffin was beginning to portray characters of psychological complexity, Le Fanu specialized in conveying states of mind: in 'The Fortunes of Sir Robert Ardagh', he mixes in with the steadily deepening horror, psychological explanations for Sir Robert's behaviour that were likely to appeal to a modern readership. In his hands, the supernatural tale becomes transformed into a modern psychological thriller. 'The Fortunes of Sir Robert Ardagh' was later collected along with other Le Fanu tales from this period purporting to have come from the archives of Francis Purcell and published posthumously by Alfred Graves under the title *The Purcell Papers* in 1880. Some of these tales, despite their length, are more akin to anecdote and character sketches than to the tightly crafted stories of *In A Glass Darkly* (1872). In them, we see Le Fanu trying out a variety of styles – the folk tale, the horror story, the historical tale. Like 'The Fortunes of Sir Robert Ardagh', 'The Last Heir of Castle Connor', originally published in the *Dublin University Magazine* in June 1838, is set in Jacobite times and explores the psychology of a man facing up to the inevitability of his death and confronting the possibility of the soul dying along with the body. In Le Fanu's hands, short fiction was beginning to be a carefully crafted purveyor of tension and a sophisticated instrument for probing the dark recesses of personality. In this development, the existence of the *Dublin University Magazine*, a periodical sympathetic to Le Fanu's type of fiction, clearly played a crucial role.

All the problems posed by Ireland's turbulent times and the instability of the short story form came to a head in the work of William Carleton, whose vivid depictions of peasant life in *Traits and Stories of the Irish Peasantry* (first series 1830, second series 1833, definitive edition 1843–4) established him as the first major Irish Catholic writer in English. Carleton was closer to the lives he was describing than the Banims since he came of peasant stock, from small farmers in County Tyrone, and received his education in various hedge schools. It was a bilingual household and his father's storytelling and his mother's songs gave him another advantage over previous writers, providing a direct link back to the Gaelic culture that was even now passing away. Carleton's stories were crucial in capturing Irish identity at a moment of transition and dissolution, providing the most vivid portrait in Irish literature of pre-Famine Ireland, its hedge schools and chapels, its weddings and wakes, at the same time as illustrating how such a culture, its language and beliefs, was becoming unsustainable in the modern world.

The significance of Irish magazines in stimulating the writing and reading of short fiction is clearly seen in relation to Carleton, the first nineteenth-century writer of fiction to be published widely in Ireland. The stories in *Traits and Stories* appeared regularly during the 1830s in the Irish periodicals that had begun to be established in an outward sign of the emerging national consciousness: in his 1842 preface, Carleton mentioned the *Dublin Literary Gazette*, *The National Magazine*, *The Dublin Monthly Magazine*, the *Dublin University Review* and the *Dublin University Magazine* as places where he had published. In her seminal study of Carleton, Barbara Hayley argues that it was the atmosphere of renewed optimism created by these Irish periodicals that inspired Carleton to produce his best stories.[44] His originality was recognized almost at once by his contemporaries: 'Irish, intensely Irish indeed his stories are, but utterly unlike any thing that ever before then had been given to the public under the name of Irish stories.'[45] The pride with which Carleton speaks in his preface of his early success is corroborated by observations of his contemporaries: 'His works have commanded a rapid and extensive sale; and high indeed has been the praise bestowed upon them on both sides of the channel.'[46] *The Illustrated Dublin Journal* of 1861 noted the French and German translations of his work.

The pressing circumstances of Irish life meant, however, that non-literary matters often took precedence over the literary in Carleton's writing. In his 1842 preface, he positioned himself, like Griffin, as inheritor of an Irish literary tradition, citing as his predecessors, Maria Edgeworth, Anna Hall, the novelist Lady Morgan, John Banim, Samuel Lover and Griffin himself. Yet the larger part of the preface was taken up, not with discussing the establishment of an Irish literary tradition, but with a defence of the Irish peasant as 'a remarkably moral man', given his lack of education and the political and economic structures in which he lived. Like previous Irish writers, Carleton's primary aim was not to shape the Irish short story form but to counteract stereotypes about the Irish by portraying the people he had known in his youth: 'I found them, and only gave them a linked embodiment, some at school or at college, or amid the lanes and hill-sides of my native Tyrone. I found them at mass, in "stations", and pilgrimages, in the company of priests.'[47] This combination of the literary and the extra-literary, emphasized by Carleton's title, *Traits and Stories*, was highlighted in an admiring review published in the *Dublin University Magazine* in 1841: 'he stands alone as the portrayer of the manners and customs of our people...at once fiction and truth'.[48] What his readers looked for in Carleton's writing was not his handling of the short narrative form but a portrait of their country. 'To Mr Carleton, the Irish peasant – and when we say the Irish peasant, we include the great mass of the Irish people – is indebted for the only creditable vindication of the national character,' commented Samuel Ferguson.[49]

Carleton's initial readership in *The Christian Examiner* and the *Dublin Family Magazine* was composed of Dublin Protestants, a reminder that though Carleton was raised in a peasant community, he had been educated out of his class. In Dublin he was at pains to establish himself as a gentleman, even to the extent of joining the Church of Ireland and marrying a Protestant. Later, as his tales received an enthusiastic reception from English and Scottish readers, Carleton's audience shifted: as Declan

Kiberd describes it, Carleton became a sort of middleman between the peasants he understood so well and the English audience for which he was writing.[50] The strain of this dual aim – to make known the previously unknown world of the Irish peasant and to impress the English reader – shows in his writing. Although Carleton's stories are full of authentic details, strong characterizations and lively dialogue, his eye to an English readership meant that as much as his predecessors in the form he could not let a story tell itself but felt obliged to intervene and explain things to the reader. His constant revisions between editions, listed in detail by Barbara Hayley, reveal his uncertainty about his aims.

Traits and Stories originated as a sequence of stories told by peasants around the fireside at Ned M'Keown's pub but after the first five stories Carleton abandoned this device. In his preface to the 1842 edition, he gave two explanations for this, namely that overuse of Irish dialect might become tedious for the reader and that the convention of stories told around a fireside did not allow for comments by an omniscient narrator. This clearly important moment in the transition from the oral tradition to the written short story form in Ireland was thus brought about by a combination of artistry and snobbery, in which Carleton's artistic need to escape the confines of the oral tradition of storytelling was complemented by his increasingly middle-class equivocations about dialect. Under pressure of events in Ireland, Carleton sought to control and shape his readers' reactions, and for this he needed to abandon the oral storytelling tradition. Such was his determination to document his stories as factual and authentic accounts that by the 1842 edition the original story was often drowned in commentary and footnotes. In other words, Carleton made a deliberate choice to sacrifice spontaneity and lively storytelling for a desire to comment on Ireland. It may be argued, then, that the urgency of Irish circumstances was directly responsible both for the abandonment of the oral storytelling mode and for the instability surrounding the short narrative form in this period.

An examination of the drastic revisions undergone by just one of Carleton's stories illustrates his uncertainty over the purpose of short fiction. 'The Landlord and Tenant', which appeared in April 1831 in the *National Magazine* with the telling subtitle 'an authentic story', concerns Owen M'Carthy, a hard-working and relatively prosperous small farmer reduced to beggary by an indifferent landlord, a corrupt agent and Ireland's economic depression. The story is precisely dated: until 1814, Owen is able to struggle on despite high rents and the depressed agricultural prices, but as the national crisis deepens, he gradually gets into difficulties, despite his sober and industrious way of life. In this first version, the agricultural and financial details are not redundant but add to the authenticity of the story. The story is controlled with a single plot and a single theme (a combination of careless landlords and high rents was ruining small farmers, even hard-working ones like Owen). The dialogue is lively and the rural speech convincing. The omniscient narrator is not much in evidence and, where he is, he claims personal acquaintance with Owen and sounds more like a friend than someone outside the action. Short passages highlight the callousness of the landlord class and Owen's worthiness, but the story, for the most part, is allowed to speak for itself in a highly effective and realistic manner. The ending is realistic, too, as, despite their obvious qualities of industry, probity and charity, Owen and his family set out for a life of begging. In the portrayal of one family's ruin, Carleton's story marks the passing of an entire way of life.

In the 1842 edition the revised version of this story, now called 'Tubber Derg; or, the Red Well', is one and a half times the length of the original, taking up where the 1831 version left off. The narrator is no longer an intimate of Owen but omniscient and knowledgeable about political and economic affairs in a way that distances him from the lives and language of those he is describing. As Owen and his family set out to beg, the narrator delivers a four-page homily on the necessity of introducing poor laws into Ireland along the lines of those in Scotland and England. It seems as if, under pressure from the times, Carleton felt that fiction was not in itself sufficient to convince the reader of the urgency of the situation, so that what began as fiction turns into an illustrated essay on Irish life, complete with footnotes. Authentic details about peasant life are replaced with generalities, as much of Owen's experience of beggary is skipped over and illustrated in the most general of terms by means of a few typical responses of indifference from the gentry. Carleton's increasing need to please and influence an English audience results in a tone which is inconsistent and evasive: where one would expect the horrors of beggary to be dwelt on, Carlton makes the artistic misjudgment of inserting a comic dialogue between a farmer and his wife. The story's original message about careless landlords becomes transformed into something very much more optimistic and unrealistic: honest, hard-working Catholics can rise by their own efforts. In other words, with an eye on his English readers, what began as a story setting the ruin of a small farmer in its wider economic and political context with the emphasis on Owen's destitution as being no fault of his own, retreats into an analysis that puts the onus back on character. Because Owen remains the same upright, honourable, charitable man that he was at the outset he is, somewhat implausibly given the times, able to rise again in the world through his own efforts and those of his family. Owen's lack of psychological development may be acceptable in the shorter version and does make Carleton's point that none of his misery is of his making; the greater length of the revised version, however, and the change of fortune that Owen and his family live through, leads the reader to expect some psychological development on the part of Carleton's protagonist. As it is, the reflections of the narrator in the final paragraph simply turn him into a moral exemplum for his fellow countrymen. Carleton's revised tale reads as though it has become contaminated by the classic realist novel and its concern with progress and social harmony, a model that, as numerous scholars have pointed out, fits uneasily into the unstable circumstances of nineteenth-century Irish life.[51] Perhaps in the end Carleton's problem was, as Samuel Ferguson's perceptive review in the *Dublin University Magazine* pointed out, fiction's inadequacy to address Ireland's political problems.[52] Fiction, Ferguson argued, had the capacity to portray poverty and chaos; it also had the capacity to portray social regeneration, but what it could not do satisfactorily was describe the transformation from one state to another. It was a problem that Carleton's successors in the twentieth century, short story writers like John McGahern, William Trevor and Éilís Ní Dhuibhne who use the form to comment on social transformations, would attempt to get to grips with. For now, Carleton was demanding too much from his fictional form.

For none of this can Carleton be blamed. It was precisely the thematic content of his stories that was valued and praised by his contemporary readers: 'They are, under the guise of fiction, descriptions of the social state of Ireland, drawn from the life, and conveying more knowledge on the subject of the condition of Ireland – the feelings, the superstitions, and the virtues and crimes of our countrymen, than would be found in many a long and laboured political essay.'[53] With very little understanding from his contemporaries (one notice in the *Dublin University Magazine* even complained of his dilatoriness), Carleton was trying to forge an Irish literary tradition, developing his style as he went along, while at the same time endeavouring to present habits of thought and a way of life on the verge of extinction. His writing both reflects and is a product of the turbulent times he was trying to capture in his prose. Hence his constant experiments with language and form, his uncertain veering between narrative and his message to the reader. His writing demonstrates an often imperfect marrying of the conventions of the oral tale with European traditions of the Gothic, the sublime and the romantic. Such compromise between European formal influence and local material is, as Franco Moretti has argued in the context of the novel, inherently unstable.[54] As time went on, Carleton became more and more distanced from, and in a sense more judgmental of, the peasant life he was describing. From the neutral setting of the first four fireside tales, where the peasants are allowed to speak in their own voices, Carleton's narrator became increasingly concerned to explain, justify and control his peasant characters. Partly, of course, this was with an eye to his English readers, partly also from an increasing loss of confidence in the peasant world he was describing and a concomitant desire to create an Irish literary voice that would possess authority and dignity. As Barbara Hayley puts it: 'In striving towards his respectable voice, Carleton loses his wild Irish one.'[55]

The much anthologized story of agrarian violence, 'The Wildgoose Lodge', 'the most thrilling of his tales' according to a contemporary notice,[56] is an example of Carleton's power as a writer when he allowed a story to tell itself. The autobiographical impulse behind the story undoubtedly contributes to its effectiveness – Carleton was writing about what he knew, having been in his youth sworn into the shadowy agrarian underground movement named the Ribbonmen.[57] The story's force comes from Carlton's abandonment of an omniscient narrator in favour of a narrator who is directly involved in the incidents he recounts and therefore shares the reader's limited knowledge. In employing the subjective mode, Carleton moves the story away from a historical account of the events of 30 October 1816, in which he was not personally involved, into fiction.[58] The story's power derives from the carefully controlled build-up of tension during the Ribbonmen's secret meeting. Gothic elements increase the narrative tension with references to the narrator's 'dark presentiment', the foul weather, the captain's 'satanic expression' and the sacrilege of drinking whiskey at the altar. The choice of a parish chapel as the murderers' meeting place is factually accurate but the Ribbonmen's oath to commit murder taken on the prayer book adds to the impression that Christianity is being inverted, whilst the dark night illumined by occasional flashes of light aptly reflects the narrator's confused state of mind. It was not only Anglo-Irish writers who exploited the Gothic mode: in addition to Carleton, Catholic writers like John and Michael Banim and Gerald Griffin employed the Gothic to express Ireland's turbulent times. Carleton adds to the Gothic, however, elements of the sublime in order to highlight the demonic and irrational in the plotters' behaviour. In doing so he was, as a recent critic has pointed out, distancing himself and the reader not only from the Ribbonmen's violence, presented as satanic, but also from an investigation into the social and political realities behind the violence.[59] His account is deliberately slanted to gain approval from his upper-class Protestant readership.[60] What is lost in realism, however, is gained in artistry.

Carleton's tone falters only towards the end, where the narrator, momentarily forgetting his own involvement in the night's action, refers both to the perpetrators of the violence and the observers, of which he is one, as 'they' instead of 'we'. A didactic note, guaranteed to appeal to Carleton's Protestant readership, creeps in ('to such a scene they were brought by the pernicious influence of Ribbonism'[61]), together with a footnote attesting to the story's veracity: what had seemed to be a case of demonic possession in the Irish countryside turns out to be all too true. The ending is anticlimactic: instead of exploring the psychological effect on the narrator of witnessing such violence, there is simply a short paragraph pointing out that justice was served in the end as the captain and his cohorts were caught and hanged. The narrator, however, remains convincingly flawed and relieved to have escaped unpunished. Despite the weakness of the ending, 'The Wildgoose Lodge' effectively conveys the barbarizing effect of violence. Like Griffin, and in contrast with oral storytelling, Carleton introduced psychological development into his narrative. The narrator's progression from vanity at the outset to increasing horror at what he is becoming involved in is paralleled in the captain's evolution from calm leader in control of his men and his emotions to the unrestrained brutality he displays during the fire. Apart from the ending, consistency of tone and atmosphere is maintained throughout. Carleton's 'The Wildgoose Lodge' is a turning-point in the evolution of the Irish short narrative, moving it beyond representation, history and didacticism into art.

Carleton's tales belong to the world of pre-Famine Ireland and depict a rural culture that survived the repressive Penal Laws but could not survive the famines of the 1840s and their aftermath in the form of the minor famines that continued to plague the country until the end of the century.[62] In 1863, when starvation and emigration had all but swept the last remnants of that pre-Famine world away, when Griffin and John Banim were dead and he himself was nearly blind and almost destitute, Carleton predicted the silence that would fall upon Irish Catholic literature: 'The only three names that Ireland can point out with pride are Griffin's, Banim's, and – do not accuse me of vanity when I say – my own. Banim and Griffin are gone, and I will soon follow them – *ultima Romanorum*, and after that will come a lull, an obscurity of perhaps half a century.'[63] It was an exaggeration, but only just. The history of the Great Hunger (1845–9) in Irish short fiction became one of ellipsis: Carleton's portraits of pre-Famine Ireland were followed by the stories of Rosa Mulholland and Emily Lawless, in which the famines of the 1840s and subsequently were already depicted as a historical event.[64] Irish publishing, too, declined as a consequence of the economic upheavals following the famines and once again, Irish writers had to seek publication in England. In retrospect, the optimism of the writer in the *Dublin University Magazine* who in 1841 trusted to 'the humanising effects of extended education and improved literature' seems immensely self-deceiving.[65]

Rosa Mulholland, a Catholic writer born in Belfast, portrayed the effects of famine on the ten or twelve hundred inhabitants of the island of Innisboffin in 'The Hungry Death', published in 1891 in *The Haunted Organist of Hurly Burly*, and selected the same year for publication in Yeats' *Representative Irish Tales*. The story has been dated to the 1886 famine experienced by the inhabitants of Innisboffin.[66] This catastrophe is presented as the final act in the history of an island where civilizations have been made and unmade: from St Coleman's time, when the island was a seat of learning, through to Elizabethan times when Grace O'Malley reigned, to Cromwell's invasion, the history of the island is written into its landscape. From the first paragraph, themes of death and dissolution are present: this island, like Caliban's, is full of 'weird and appalling voices which have sung alike the lullaby and death-keen of all their race'.[67] An omniscient narrator sets the scene in the opening paragraphs, describing the appearance of the island and its inhabitants and providing precise and convincing details about the interior of Tim Lavelle's house with its earthern floor and heather-lined roof, its dresser and sacred pictures. It is taken for granted that the reader will be outside this community, as the narrator is, and therefore needs such details, yet the peasants are never condescended to. They speak in dialect but it is quiet and restrained, lacking the bombast found in earlier Irish writers, and their qualities are highlighted: the community may be poor but Judy's quilt is neat and clean; they may be anxious about the potato crop but they can sing and dance and enjoy themselves. The narrator, not as intrusive as some of Griffin's and Carleton's narrators, acts as a kind of Greek chorus, commenting on the unfolding of Brigid's tragedy and the gradual disintegration of a community as the crop fails and the islanders are reduced to eating Indian meal. Though the weather eventually becomes calm enough to allow entry to the vessel carrying the relief meal, the reader is left with the impression that a way of life has been irrevocably destroyed. Ending with the emigration of Coll and Moya to America, Mulholland's story captures a community at the moment of its dissolution. Mulholland's work was well received by her contemporaries, particularly by the Catholic *Irish Monthly*. *The Dublin University Review*'s verdict was more cautious but acknowledged her 'high and doubtless lasting reputation as a writer of prose'.[68]

The story of Irish emigration consequent on the famines was taken up on the other side of the Atlantic by Sarah Orne Jewett, the New England writer who was inspired by her visit to Ireland in 1882 to write eight stories dealing with the experience of Irish emigrants in New England. The stories were published in contemporary magazines like *Scribner's*, *The Cosmopolitan*, *McClure's* and *Lippincott's Magazine*. Described by their modern-day editors as 'the first serious treatment of the Irish in America', they remained uncollected in her lifetime.[69] Jewett's stories tend to present an idealized version of Ireland: in 'The Luck of the Bogans' (1889), the Bogan family must be unique in the period in leaving behind a prosperous farm and a good landlord in Ireland. However, her stories do acknowledge the importance of the tie to Ireland and her modern editors point out how much in advance Jewett was of contemporaries like Hawthorne, Emerson and Thoreau in her respect for Irish cultural otherness. Jewett resists the 'Paddy' stereotype by portraying the Irish as immigrants who adapt well to the American ethos of hard work and family values. The success of the Irish in some of her stories is balanced, however, by other stories where the Irish are either caught in a cycle of financial dependency (Nora in 'A Little Captive Maid', the mill workers in 'The Gray Mills of Farley'), or corrupted by their American environment (Dan Bogan in 'The Luck of the Bogans', Dan Nolan in 'Between Mass and Vespers'). Jewett's stories sensitively convey some of the pain and psychic disruption of the Irish immigrant experience.

If Irish Catholic short fiction of this period reflected the chaos following the dissolution of a way of life and a language, Anglo-Irish writers, for all their belief in their hereditary right to rule Ireland, were also left shaken by political events. The post-Famine era saw Catholic resurgency at home, the rise of Fenianism and the widening of the Catholic church's influence, while in England a Whig government rejected an identity of interests with the Anglo-Irish landlords. All these factors accelerated the decline of the Anglo-Irish Ascendancy class into political lethargy and despair. The 1869 Act disestablishing the Church of Ireland and the 1870

Land Act giving rights to tenants, were widely interpreted as marking the end of the Ascendancy: 'By 1870, the social and religious dominance of the "Ascendancy" outside Ulster was effectively broken; the power of Catholic nationalism was on the edge of realization.'[70] Emily Lawless' 'After the Famine', examined in the interchapter, portrays the impact of the post-Famine era on one Anglo-Irish family. Anglo-Irish anxiety in this period found its fullest expression, however, in Sheridan Le Fanu's stories of hauntings and guilty consciences that share with his Catholic contemporaries the theme of the disappearance of a way of life.

In Le Fanu's collection from this period, *In A Glass Darkly*, published in London in 1872, the Irish connections are less explicit than in *The Purcell Papers*. The stories are supposedly culled by an anonymous editor from among the case notes of a certain Dr Martin Hesselius, a German physician specializing in diseases of the mind. Nevertheless, there are Irish traces in this collection. The vampire tale, 'Carmilla', concerns female desire and loss of boundaries but it is also a political fable expressing Le Fanu's fear that the Anglo-Irish class to which he belonged was on the brink of dissolution. His portrait of Carmilla, who exerts such a fascination over the nineteen-year-old narrator, Laura, mingles Balkan vampire legend with the Irish tradition of the *sí* (fairy folk) and the *ban sí* (fairy woman); but Carmilla is not only a vampire, she is a dispossessed Catholic noblewoman and, as such, represents those peasants and tenants whose estates had been appropriated by the Anglo-Irish and whose presence in the Irish countryside remained an uneasy reminder of the latter's inherited political guilt.

Though 'Carmilla' is set in Styria, there are, as critics have pointed out, many Irish echoes.[71] The castle Laura and her father inhabit is isolated from the surrounding neighbourhood, suggesting the social isolation of the Anglo-Irish Big House. The indigenous population dying of fever brought on by vampire attacks recalls the famine fevers suffered by the Irish peasants. When Carmilla makes clear the religious divide between herself and Laura, ostensibly the division is between vampire and Christian, but behind that lies the Irish religious divide between Catholic and Protestant. Carmilla embodies Le Fanu's fear that Catholic Ireland would never be laid to rest and that its inheritors, the Fenians, would rise and dispossess the Protestant gentry as the latter had dispossessed the Catholic gentry after 1690. By 1872, as we have seen, these fears were very real. Though Carmilla is apparently killed off, she may yet return to haunt the narrator, in the same way as the dispossessed Irish Catholic tenantry, beginning to mobilize during these years, was haunting the

Anglo-Irish. Laura's passivity and later death suggests that Le Fanu feared his class would not have the courage to resist. By employing themes of the Gothic mode, the subconscious, dreams and vampires, Le Fanu used the short narrative form to indicate anxiety around the themes of identity, both personal and political.

There are other Irish traces in his collection: in 'Green Tea', first published in 1869 in Dickens' *All the Year Round*, the increasingly aggressive and malevolent spirit-monkey that haunts the Reverend Jennings may represent the animal side of himself suppressed by his lengthy studies but, as Robert Tracy points out, the monkey had a political resonance, picking up on the simian cartoons of the Irish common in the period, and indicating Le Fanu's anxiety about possible Fenian violence.[72] The monkey possesses 'an air of menace, as if it was always brooding over some atrocious plan'.[73] 'The Familiar', set in Dublin 'somewhere about the year 1794', captures a period of transformation when the building boom of the 1790s, prompted by Grattan's Parliament, was developing Dublin into a capital city. Through Captain Barton's wanderings around Dublin pursued by a spectre whose haunting eventually causes his complete psychic collapse and death, Le Fanu gives a vivid portrait of a city under construction.[74] Alongside the realism of this precise moment in Dublin's history is the psychological study of a man confronting his own death. As in 'Green Tea', several explanations are provided for Captain Barton's demise, which, while psychologically plausible, do not quite rule out the supernatural element. 'The Familiar' is followed by 'Mr Justice Harbottle' and together the first three stories of this collection portray, respectively, representatives of the church, the navy and the law as haunted and uneasy, suggesting that Le Fanu regarded the great institutions underpinning the British Empire, of which the colonizing Anglo-Irish were a crucial part, as on the brink of collapse.

'The Familiar' is not much altered from its first version, 'The Watcher', published in the *Dublin University Magazine* in November 1847. 'Mr Justice Harbottle', on the other hand, is a virtually rewritten version of 'An Account of Some Strange Disturbances in Aungier Street', published in the same magazine in December 1853. The later story is set in London rather than Dublin in keeping with Le Fanu's increasing tendency to please his English publishers by removing Irish references in order to make his work more saleable. Again the story is precisely dated. We are told that Judge Harbottle's death took place in 1748 and that the events described in the story occurred in 1746. The previous year Bonnie Prince Charlie had landed in Scotland intending to capture the English throne for the Stuarts: Judge Harbottle's fears of a Jacobite plot are entirely plausible and represent Le Fanu's own political anxieties. The gruesome mock trial Judge Harbottle undergoes suggests a fear on the author's part that he and his class were about to reap the consequences of their administration of Ireland. The portrayal of Judge Harbottle contrasts with that of the helpful antiquarian, Baron Vordenburg, in 'Carmilla', suggesting that Le Fanu believed the way forward for the Anglo-Irish was to ally themselves not with the forces of empire but, anticipating the Revival, with those who showed commitment to Ireland and to Irish culture. Indeed, Le Fanu returned to traditional Irish material in tales such as 'The White Cat of Drumgunniol', 'The Child That Went with the Fairies' and 'Stories of Lough Guir', all published in 1870 in *All the Year Round*. Like the American writer, Edgar Allan Poe, Le Fanu used the tale to portray psychological states, revealing minds on the brink of collapse at those moments when the barrier between the mortal and the spirit world seems to dissolve. Like Poe's work, the tightly constructed tales of *In A Glass Darkly*, exploring the psychological consequences of suppressed guilt, fear of death and, in 'Carmilla', suppressed sexual anxiety, may be regarded as forerunners of the modern short story.

Terry Eagleton has argued that the Gothic was a mode perfectly adapted to nineteenth-century Protestant Ireland with its decaying gentry isolated in their crumbling castles, conscious of hereditary political guilt, and burdened by debt.[75] The influence of Le Fanu's tales on fellow middle-class Protestant, Bram Stoker, is apparent, not only in Stoker's vampire novel, *Dracula* (1897), but in his short fiction. Stoker's horror story, 'The Judge's House', for example, published in 1891, is a reworking of 'Mr Justice Harbottle'. The Antrim-born writer, Charlotte Riddell, was also inspired by Le Fanu's example to explore the possibilities of the Gothic in some of her stories set in Ireland: indeed, in 'Diarmid Chittock's Story', published in her collection, *Handsome Phil and Other Stories* (1899), Cyril Danson picks up a copy of Le Fanu's *House by the Churchyard* in his bid to get acquainted with Ireland. 'Conn Kilrea' in the same collection starts off in Gothic mode with a description of the strangely morose Private Kilray, serving in an English regiment. The story is precisely dated 1892 and portrays Kilray haunted by his glimpse of the ghost of Lord Yiewsley, murdered over a hundred years previously by one of his ancestors and who, in true *ban sí* tradition, appears to members of the family before their death. However, what begins, in Le Fanu fashion, as the psychological portrait of a man facing up to his own death, declines into a moralizing tale of how fright over Lord

Yiewsley's appearance prompts the hitherto wild and irresponsible Conn Kilrea to get his life in order. The story ends happily with Conn reinstated as his grandfather's heir.

If these stories are definitely sub Le Fanu, Riddell's collection does contain one story that interestingly anticipates later Irish women writers in its portrayal of a woman who maintains her writing career against the odds. Bearing the apt title, 'Out in the Cold', the story depicts Miss Annabel Saridge, who persists secretly with her writing despite her mother's admonitions that it will kill her scholarly father to learn that his daughter wishes to be an author. The story has distinctly autobiographical overtones. Annabel writes under the pseudonym 'Anna Bell', as Riddell had earlier employed the gender-free pseudonym F.G. Trafford, and, like Riddell, Annabel finds a publisher for her work in London after being turned down by Dublin publishers. Contemplating the secret writing life of her heroine, who eventually dies from exhaustion and poverty, Riddell is unable to refrain from the kind of impassioned outbursts that Virginia Woolf was later to criticize as marring the artistry of nineteenth-century fiction by women. Nevertheless, 'Out in the Cold' is a useful reminder of the psychological and material obstacles that Irish women writers faced in the nineteenth century and of the waste of their potential. Riddell cannot resist pointing out what her country is losing by its discouragement of women writers: 'What might she not have done for Ireland and herself had the fates been kinder?'[76] It is worth noting, however, that after her move to England, Riddell went on to publish nearly fifty volumes of novels and stories.[77]

Another author who points towards the twentieth century is May Laffan Hartley. Her two stories set in the Dublin slums, 'Flitters, Tatters and the Counsellor' and 'The Game Hen', published in *Flitters, Tatters and the Counsellor and Other Stories* in London in 1881, are small gems almost lost to literary history, though in 1895 the collection was included by Yeats in his 'List of Best Irish Books' for *The Bookman*.[78] In the title story, Laffan depicts the lives of three orphaned street children struggling for survival on the Dublin streets. The dialogue is lively, the Dublin speech is plausible and though the story is recounted through the voice of an educated narrator, there is none of the overt sentimentality and heavy-handed moralizing characteristic of much nineteenth-century short fiction. Laffan's second story, 'The Game Hen', concerning the lives and quarrels of adults in a Dublin slum, is again told without sentimentality and without either condemning or idealizing the poor, its urban realism anticipating stories by Frank O'Connor and James Plunkett.

After the Great Famine, short fiction writers continued the lengthy nineteenth-century tradition of presenting Ireland through the eyes of English outsiders but with the crucial difference that now it was the English visitors who were the object of satire. The English writer, Anthony Trollope, began writing short stories as a result of a combination of his travels abroad as civil servant for the Post Office and his discovery, while in America, of a growing and lucrative market for short fiction. In 'The O'Connors of Castle Conor, County Mayo' (published in *Harper's*, May 1860) and 'Father Giles of Ballymoy' (published in the *Argosy*, May 1866), Trollope, like Emily Lawless, reverses the usual nineteenth-century trope of the superior English visitor who laughs at Irish foibles. These two entertaining stories, set back in the early 1840s, the time of Trollope's arrival in Ireland, reflect, as Trollope explains in chapter 4 of *An Autobiography*, his own experiences as an Englishman encountering Ireland for the first time. Archibald Green (green in more senses than one) comes into contact with a range of Ireland's social classes from servants and village policemen to the parish priest and the local hunting squirearchy, but remains essentially an outsider in the country. In making the English outsider, rather than the Irish, the target of his humour, and in his description of the fox-hunting set in 'The O'Connors of Castle Conor', Trollope points forward to Somerville and Ross, who in their stories about the adventures of an Anglo-Irish Resident Magistrate in the wilds of West Cork portray the Irish in a humorous light but reserve their sharpest satire for the English authorities.

In 1889, Violet Martin returned to her family home in County Galway and commenced a series of sketches and short stories of her native Connemara. As in the stories of Anna Hall and other visitors to Ireland in the earlier part of the century, the narrator, though engaging in dialogue with the peasants, remains an outsider to their lives, and Martin's Unionist sympathies are evident. 'The Dog from Doone' (undated) is significant in that the wry voice of a bumbling Sandhurst officer recounting his tragi-comic adventures with the eponymous dog anticipates the tone of the *Irish R.M.* stories. The final story, 'At the River's Edge', dates from 1914, the year before Martin's death, and through the words of Anastasia, an illiterate, bilingual Galway woman, gives an insight into the pragmatic basis on which peasant courtship was necessarily conducted. Its description of the mission priest preaching against young men and women walking out together foreshadows by thirty years Mary Lavin's short story 'Sunday Brings Sunday'. 'Two Sunday Afternoons' is also worthy of note, anticipating Joyce in its account of a

Dublin servant girl seduced and used by a gallant. These stories, mid-way between fiction and fact, were later collected by Edith Somerville and published in 1920 under the title *Stray-aways*.

The *Irish R.M.* stories of Edith Somerville and Martin Ross (Violet Martin), published in three volumes by the London publisher, Longmans, *Some Experiences of an Irish R.M.* (1899), *Further Experiences of an Irish R.M.* (1908) and *In Mr Knox's Country* (1915), have been described by Gregory Schirmer as 'the last cry of the nineteenth century'.[79] Schirmer argues that by the date of the last volume of Major Yeates' adventures, writers like Moore and Joyce had moved the Irish short story in a radically different direction from Somerville and Ross's depiction of an already vanishing world of obtuse Protestant landlords and wily Catholic tenants. Yet, artistically, the tight formal structure of the *Irish R.M.* stories, first serialized in *Badminton Magazine* (1898–9), provides a marked contrast to the rambling, unwieldy tales of the early part of the nineteenth century. The authors' use of recurring characters and a consistent narrative voice points forward to the thematic unity of collections such as Moore's *The Untilled Field* and Joyce's *Dubliners*. Their ear for dialogue is acute and their observation of the Irish scene detailed. If their characters lack depth and if their preference seems to be to perpetuate stereotypes about the wily Irish rather than to interrogate the political and economic structures within which the Irish had to operate, a recent study by Julie Anne Stevens has opened up our appreciation of their artistry by emphasizing their alertness to contemporary artistic developments and by linking their writing to European traditions of pantomime, carnival and harlequinade.[80] In this reading of the *Irish R.M.* stories, stereotypes about the Irish character are challenged by the authors' emphasis on the performative nature of Irish identity. Viewed in this way, the writing of Somerville and Ross seems markedly more modern, its European dimension pointing forward to developments in the twentieth century when the Irish short story would open up to such outside influences as Chekhov, Flaubert, Maupassant, Turgenev and Ibsen.

Traditionally, Somerville and Ross's stories of fox-hunting and yachting in County Cork have been viewed as entertainments written, as Gifford Lewis has suggested, to earn their authors sufficient money to enable them to stay on in their native land when so many of their class were leaving.[81] Certainly the commercial aspect was important. The authors' knowledge of the expectations of the British popular press, in which most of these stories first appeared, allowed them to exploit to the full the comic potential of presenting Irish identity as a performance.

They experimented with a variety of styles from pure farce in stories such as 'The House of Fahy', 'Occasional Licences', 'The Pug-Nosed Fox' and 'A Royal Command', through to Gothic in 'The Waters of Strife' (where the person haunted by his past misdeeds is not Anglo-Irish as in Le Fanu but native Irish) and tales of ghost hauntings in 'Harrington's' and 'Major Apollo Riggs'. The linking narrative voice of Major Yeates, who is of Irish extraction but, as resident magistrate, represents the British authorities in Ireland, is reliable, unimaginative, wryly self-deprecating, and susceptible to women's charm, and thus nicely calculated to appeal to the English reader. Yeates' willingness to admit when he has been gulled shows up the obtuseness of English outsiders like Leigh Kelway in 'Lisheen Races, Second-Hand', Mr Tebbutts in 'The Aussolas Martin Cat' and Maxwell Bruce in 'The Last Day of Shraft', all of whom retreat from Ireland, baffled. In stories such as these, Yeates finds himself allied with the native Irish, and even, in the latter story, on the wrong side of the law in a way that would be inconceivable for a member of the colonial class in Anna Hall's stories. At other moments, Yeates' easy tone jars on the modern reader: his snobbishness over the 'boundary-crossing' McRory family, whose newly acquired wealth allows them grudging acceptance into Anglo-Irish circles, for instance, or his conversation with Mrs Courtney about the emigration of her children, where, in what seems like a deliberate diversion of the reader's attention from the unpalatable aspects of British rule, the focus shifts from the underlying tragedy in order to exploit the comic potential of Mrs Courtney's picturesque turn of phrase.

The tendency in recent critical writing has been to look for veiled political meanings in the *Irish R.M.* stories. Bi-Ling Chen reads the fox as a device by which Somerville and Ross, despite their Unionism, show their sympathy with Ireland as the wily fox demonstrates the survival skills of the colonized race in contrast to the incompetent English huntsmen.[82] In a subtler reading than Chen's, Julie Anne Stevens sees Somerville and Ross' fox as a figure that evades ideology, and reads the *Irish R.M.* stories as lampooning romanticized versions of the past in order to present Ireland as a country of multiple and shifting narratives. In this reading, 'Lisheen Races' and 'The Last Day of Shraft' mock idealizations of Ireland espoused by the Celtic Revival; 'The Waters of Strife' satirizes popular nationalist propaganda, particularly in relation to the Wexford rebellion of 1798; 'Holy Island' presents the rising Irish middle class employing the Catholic religion as a weapon in their bid to weaken British authority; and 'The Whiteboys' parodies nationalist idealizations of the Irish landscape that conceal what is really going on in the countryside. Stevens argues that the final collection, *In Mr Knox's Country*, takes on added political meaning when viewed against the backdrop of debates over Asquith's Home Rule Bill of 1912. She detects such themes as the prolongation of Anglo-Irish power (by the wiles of the arch-manipulator Mrs Knox), the rise of the Dublin middle-class woman (Larkie McRory, who so impresses the Major) and the subversion of romantic ideologies of the land. Read in this way, Somerville and Ross' stories seem decidedly less backward-looking and more like an active intervention in current debates about Ireland's future at a time of transition, though for Stevens, their message remains deliberately ambivalent, an attack on all those whose romantic ideologies of Ireland blind them to the realities of Irish life.

Somerville and Ross' stories portray the fractures and uncertainties of Irish life in the first decade of the new century. In the end, perhaps the real question raised by the *Irish R.M.* stories is who has the moral right to tell Ireland's story? The English's utter incomprehension of Irish life rules them out: 'Ah, these English,' says McCabe in 'The Shooting of Shinroe', 'they'd believe anything so long as it wasn't the truth.'[83] Major Yeates usually finds the story wrested from his hands by the manoeuvrings of Flurry Knox, the half-sir, who in turn is outmanoeuvred by the rightful heir to the Whiteboy hounds, Lukey O'Reilly. In 'The Comte de Pralines', where, for once, the fox is cornered, the Anglo-Irish hunting party is beaten to the post by a Catholic priest, a Frenchman (albeit fake), the rising middle-class Irishwoman, Larkie McRory, and a crowd of country people. Yeates' comment as he retreats ignominiously from the hunting-ground, 'We were all quite outside the picture, and we knew it', seems, from the Anglo-Irish point of view, grimly prophetic.[84] There is no comforting conclusion to the *Irish R.M.* stories: in an ending which must have given their English readers pause for thought, the final story, 'The Shooting of Shinroe', leaves Major Yeates blundering fruitlessly around the Irish countryside on an appropriately wet and dark night.

Though the rise of indigenous literary periodicals from the 1830s onwards clearly did much to promote Irish short fiction in its transition from the oral to the written form, particularly in the case of the careers of William Carleton and Sheridan Le Fanu, the typical nineteenth-century short narrative, sprawling, didactic with one anxious eye always on its English readership, would seem to have little in common with the modern short story. Nomadic both in theme and structure, nineteenth-century Irish short fiction reflects the dissolution of a way of life for both the Gaelic-speaking peasant and, in the end, their Anglo-Irish rulers.

Nevertheless, despite the strain of an increasingly turbulent political situation, as the century wore on, Irish authors began to pay attention to structure, tension and psychological development in a way that intermittently foreshadowed the short story of the twentieth century. Somerville and Ross anticipated the Irish short story's openness to European influences, Gerald Griffin has been seen as a precursor of Moore and Joyce, whilst Le Fanu's tales of political and psychological hauntings were to inspire Elizabeth Bowen, and his portrait of Dublin streets, Joyce. Comparing William Carleton and Samuel Ferguson, Peter Denham posits that if Ferguson's writing recuperating Irish history and legend prepared the way for the Irish Literary Revival, Carleton's observations of the contemporary social scene establish him, however remotely, as a precursor of John McGahern.[85] The history of the development of the Irish short story form in the twentieth century would be incomplete without an acknowledgment of its nineteenth-century predecessors.

READINGS: WILLIAM CARLETON AND EMILY LAWLESS

William Carleton, 'The Poor Scholar' (1833)

'The Poor Scholar', one of Carleton's best-known stories, illustrates the difficulties that beset the short story form and Irish national identity in the nineteenth century, both struggling in this period to take shape. 'The Poor Scholar', singled out alongside 'Tubber Derg' as 'excellent' by Samuel Ferguson in the *Dublin University Magazine*,[86] gains much of its force from the fact that Carleton drew on his own brief experience of setting out to study for the priesthood at Maynooth. The theme was treated in burlesque mode in another of Carleton's stories, 'Going to Maynooth', but in this story his aim was to convince English readers that virtue would emerge in the Irish peasant if he was given a chance. This characteristic nineteenth-century use of short fiction for extra-literary purposes elevates the tone of Carleton's story but hampers his artistry. Carleton's vivid descriptions of the bleak Irish countryside and the famine-stricken peasants, together with patches of lively peasant dialogue, are interrupted by lengthy disquisitions on absentee landlords and the character of the Irish peasant, complete with explanatory footnotes. As in the case of many other nineteenth-century writers, Carleton's fictional framework became distorted by the pressure of living in a society under stress.

'The Poor Scholar' begins promisingly with a vivid description of the icy Tyrone hillside on which Jemmy M'Evoy and his father, having been evicted from their farm by the machinations of Colonel B's agent, Yallow Sam, are labouring to scratch a living from their miserable patch of land. The dialogue is lively and captures the fractured language of a community in transition between Gaelic and English. The story then breaks off to allow the omniscient narrator to address the reader in standard English and point out that this story will have a specific purpose, namely to demonstrate that the Irish are as capable as the English and Scottish of perseverance in the attainment of a goal. Carleton's story is an active intervention in the struggle to forge an Irish national identity equal to that of her neighbours, but the explanatory passage reveals his lack of confidence in fiction as adequate to get his point across.

Such precautions were unnecessary: Jemmy's determination to go to Munster and get an education as a poor scholar in order to train as a priest and raise up his family comes across sufficiently clearly in the narrative itself. Carleton's mutually contradictory aims of, on the one hand, presenting peasant life in all its vividness and, on the other, satisfying his English readers, are clearly illustrated when he allows Jemmy to use the highly appropriate word 'slavery' to describe the toil of his father and himself on the icy hillside, but controls the meaning of the word in an anxious footnote explaining that when Jemmy speaks of 'slavery' he means 'toil-labour' (as opposed to the spectre of rebellion that might arise in the minds of English readers).

The story maintains this inconsistency of tone. There are vivid passages of storytelling in the description of the domestic life of the M'Evoy family, in the comic vignette of the priest's well-judged mixture of flattery, pathos and humour in his sermon to raise a collection for Jemmy and in the portrait of the tyrannical schoolmaster, which Carleton assures us in his preface is drawn from life. But there is also much sentimentality, as in the scenes of Jemmy's leave-taking. Sometimes this sentimentality has a didactic purpose: by showing the peasants' consistent kindness towards Jemmy as he journeys down to Munster, Carleton aims to illustrate the respect in which learning is held in Ireland. After Jemmy's arrival in Munster, the vivid schoolroom scenes and the description of the countryside during a period of famine and fever are undercut by the lengthy disquisitions against ignorant landlords put into the mouth of Jemmy's friend, the curate. Even the famine scenes with their detailed anthropological descriptions of what the peasants ate – chickweed, nettles, seaweed, cows' blood – seem explanatory rather than integral to the plot. They feature because Carleton felt the need to explain to English readers the full horrors of the situation in Ireland. Once again the fictional framework of a nineteenth-century story was coming under pressure from the political and economic situation in Ireland.

The rich linguistic layers of speech in 'The Poor Scholar' represent the three languages of Ireland – Gaelic for moments of deep feeling, English for everyday use, and Latin to impress with one's learning. As Jemmy's education advances, he learns to speak in standard English, though without the pompous and meaningless Latinisms favoured by the schoolmasters in the story, retaining his ability to drop into Gaelic when speaking to his mother. Barbara Hayley speaks of Jemmy's character development, but arguably it is not so much psychological development that Carleton gives us as development in Jemmy's circumstances. Not only does his education lead him to speak in standard English, but a new suit of clothes gives him added self-confidence and dignity, so that when he enters the Lanigans' house he is received with all the respect due to a priest.

Like the McCarthys in 'Tubber Derg', the M'Evoys are an idealized peasant family, but the ending of 'The Poor Scholar' adds a touch of realism missing from the former story in the narrator's brief, almost laconic aside that Jemmy died shortly after being reunited with his family. The discourse of improvement and social progress underpinning the classic nineteenth-century realist novel is undermined. Irish Catholics may have the determination to raise themselves up, but the economic and political structures of this society are so weighted against them that the effort exhausts them.

The ending comes, however, after the momentum of the story has been interrupted by a lengthy side plot during which Colonel B investigates the allegations against Yellow Sam and restores the fortunes of Jemmy's family. This episode, whilst fulfilling one of Jemmy's aims, namely to raise up his family again, not only interrupts the narrative flow but obliges Carleton to skip over Jemmy's years in Maynooth. With a clumsy sleight of hand, the narrator shifts the focus of the story from the poor Irish scholar to Colonel B's transformation into a responsible and caring landlord, a more pressing theme for the attention of English readers. Such forays into the higher social classes did not always go down well with his fellow countrymen, who, at the same time as they criticized him for coarseness, preferred Carleton to remain among the peasants: 'Carleton shines forth in the fields and the thatched cabins. He is no longer himself upstairs or in a slated house. If he gets you into the drawing-room, you are ready to jump out of the window to escape from him.'[87] In this case, the reviewer may have had a point: Carleton's eye to his English readership robs us of a potentially interesting insight into contemporary life at Maynooth.

With all its flaws and momentary flashes of brilliance, 'The Poor Scholar' presents both Irish national identity and the short narrative form at a difficult moment of transition. Carleton can scarcely be blamed if both identity and form collapse under the weight of the times.

Emily Lawless, 'After the Famine' (1897)

As in the case of Carleton, middleman between Irish peasant and English reader, Emily Lawless' national identity was somewhat fluid: she was a member of the Ascendancy but her family was a fairly recent recruit and sometimes despised on account of this.[88] Lawless was highly critical of British policy in Ireland, though she did not go so far as to favour Home Rule. The fluidity of her national identity is matched by the hybrid nature of the collection in which 'After the Famine' was published. *Traits and Confidences* is a mixed bag of genres, including, among other things, an autobiographical essay on a girlhood moth hunt, a historical short story and a medieval romance. 'After the Famine' is prefaced by 'Famine Roads and Famine Memories', Lawless' reflections on a famine village in Connemara. The village and the surrounding countryside are vividly and knowledgeably evoked and Lawless is sharply critical of the British administration. This device of a preliminary essay not only establishes Lawless' credentials as a writer on the Famine but also has the distinct artistic advantage of siphoning off the author's own comments from the story proper.

In 'After the Famine', Lawless looks back on the Famine of 1845–8 as a historical event, employing the mediating memories of a fictitious unnamed elderly English gentleman who visits Ireland in 1848 and sees the effects of the famine for himself. As often in Lawless' fiction, the male narrator is used in order to lend her account authority. At the same time, also characteristically, she undermines that authority by presenting him as an unreliable narrator, class-bound and ignorant of the country he is about to exploit.[89] The post-Famine stories of Trollope and Somerville and Ross share this device of the naïve and ignorant English visitor to Ireland, indicating that after the Famine the figure of the English tourist who laughs fondly at Irish eccentricities was no longer acceptable, even to an English readership. In Lawless, the gentleman's ignorance about Ireland is damning: he knows, but does not want to face up to, just why land in Ireland is so cheap at present. 'Somehow from the first I had not relished the errand. I knew nothing of Ireland. As for Cashla Bay it might have been in Kamscatka for anything I knew to the contrary. Still I knew what every one else knew; what the newspapers had told us, and – In short, I did not fancy the errand.'[90] The ellipsis used to cover over the realities of Irish suffering during the Famine effectively conveys Lawless' condemnation of English attitudes. The insistence of the narrator's more senior colleagues that he should be the one to go over to Ireland indicates that they share his reluctance to have an intimate acquaintance with the country they are about to exploit with a quick land deal.

The Englishman's observations of the dismantled rooms in Castle d'Arcy, the servant's patched livery and the skeletal humans who inhabit the barren, stone-covered land, serve to portray a society on the brink of collapse. Encountering the Anglo-Irish Eleanor d'Arcy, so traumatized by the Famine that she cannot fully grasp the fact of the deaths of her father and her sister, even this obtuse narrator is forced to admit: 'Although wholly innocent, of course, of having had any share in producing her troubles, I felt for the moment as if I had been guilty of them all.'[91] Elly's 'paralysis of the mind' is a highly effective way of conveying the trauma of the Famine, even on the class generally regarded as having been the least affected. This last damaged childlike remnant of the d'Arcy family pre-figures Elizabeth Bowen's 'last of the line' Anglo-Irish heiresses, but Elly's psychological state is also emblematic of Ireland in general after the Famine: 'It was as though so much that was heartrending and confusing had passed before her eyes that they could never become natural again; could never lose that expression of vacant misery; could never cease to see something – I did not know what – that haunted them.'[92]

Elly's household, and therefore the narrator as their guest, is reduced to eating the same food as the peasants, and Elly has to choose between penury and the hand of Henry O'Hara, who in the eyes of the biased narrator is not 'what is commonly known as a gentleman'.[93] Henry's brother, a bad land agent, is partly to blame for the d'Arcys' destitution, but Lawless' story refrains from the usual didacticism against corrupt agents, as if the damaging effects of the Famine were so great that they had relegated even corrupt agents to second place in the history of Ireland's ruin.

The story concludes, like Mulholland's, with emigration. After lengthy rivalry between the Englishman and Henry O'Hara for Elly's hand, the Englishman concedes Henry's moral claim to Elly (and to Ireland?) when Henry rescues her from the waves. Henry and Elly set out for America and are never heard of again. The story ends with the narrator staring down 'a long stretch of empty road, which seemed to be stretching dully away to all infinity',[94] evoking both the long journeys embarked on by starving emigrants and the silent Famine roads, built by hungry tenants, that led nowhere. The final mention of the creeper tapping against the wall recalls the small ghost hand that disturbs Lockwood in *Wuthering Heights* (1847) and suggests that the dead souls of the famine victims linger on in the silent Irish countryside.[95]

CHAPTER THREE

Fin de siècle *visions: Irish short fiction at the turn of the century*

In the *Dublin University Review* of 1886 W. B. Yeats quoted an acquaintance as saying: 'I would gladly lecture in Dublin on Irish literature, but the people know too little about it.'[1] Six years later Yeats was complaining that: 'In the small towns of Ireland are few book shops and few books.'[2] The situation was to improve. In *Dana*, a monthly review founded by Frederick Ryan and 'John Eglinton' (W. K. Magee) in 1904, the proposal by the novelist, Jane Barlow, that Ireland introduce a circulating library scheme, similar to one she had seen operating in Wales, for people living in remote country areas, prompted a response from the Secretary of the Rural Libraries Association to the effect that rural councils now had the power to establish libraries in their districts and what was needed was good lists of books.[3] This correspondence reflected the fact that the number of available readers in Ireland was increasing: between 1850 and 1900 the number of National Schools doubled and attendance was stimulated by the Education Act of 1892, rising to over 60 per cent in the 1890s and 75 per cent by 1908. This in turn led to a sharp decrease in rates of illiteracy: whereas in 1851, 45 per cent of the Irish population had been illiterate, by 1911 the rate was down to 12 per cent.[4] In the same year, T. Coulson writing in *The Irish Review* was able to say: 'No one acquainted with Irish life needs to be informed of the new vigour which has been imparted to the Irish nation during the past two decades. Slumbering phases of national life have awakened under the new influence, and no change is more worthy of admiration than the achievements in literature.'[5]

The urge to transform – society, politics, gender relations, art – was dominant at the turn of the century in Ireland. In the 1880s, under the leadership of Charles Stewart Parnell, the Irish Party had been able to unite the warring factions within Irish nationalism to the cause of Home Rule. After Parnell's fall in 1890 and his death the following year, the nationalist cause split into different political factions again and broadened to embrace literary and cultural revival. Despite its stated desire to retrieve an ancient culture, the impetus behind the Irish Literary Revival may be described as essentially a modernizing one: Yeats and his colleagues in the revivalist movement were intent on reviving the Celtic past but also reshaping it to suit their own vision of Ireland in the future. The tension in this period between modern literary impulses, often influenced by foreign models, and the impulse towards the past and the local inspired by the Gaelic Revival, is complicated by the fact that in turning back to the Irish folk tale, Irish Revivalist writers anticipated modernist writers in abandoning the nineteenth-century realist mode that in any case had mostly failed to take purchase in Ireland. The anti-mimetic tendencies of the Irish folk tale reinforced the overlap between the Revival and the modernist movement and the search for the Celtic past itself has been linked to modernism's interest in the primitive.[6] Traces of the modernist short story may sometimes be spied in the writing of the Irish Revivalists, who used the short narrative, as earlier writers had done, to express Irish identity in transition, but eschewed realism in favour of the visionary mode. Nadine Gordimer has argued that the brevity and intensity of the short story form makes it especially suited to conveying visions and fantasies: 'Fantasy in the hands of short story writers is so much more successful than when in the hands of novelists because it is necessary for it to hold good only for the brief illumination of the situation it dominates.'[7] The use of short fiction as a vehicle for transformation was not confined to writers of the Irish Revival but was a thread that ran through *fin de siècle* authors as diverse as Oscar Wilde and George Egerton.

The Irish Literary Revival was inspired by the general urge to strengthen Irish identity after the long depression following on the famines of the mid-nineteenth century. It was part of the movement that saw the founding of the Gaelic Athletic Association in 1884 to revive ancient Irish sports like Gaelic football and hurling, and the establishment of the Gaelic League in 1893 to preserve and promote the Irish language. Post-Famine nineteenth-century antiquarians and collectors of folklore sought to retrieve authentic folk tales from oral sources.[8] Between 1888 and 1920 many folk tales were collected by such figures as Jeremiah Curtin, Douglas Hyde and William Larminie. Their concern for accuracy distinguished them from earlier writers like Croker and Lover whom Douglas Hyde criticized for manipulating their sources to suit their own literary ends. By contrast, Hyde aimed to provide accurate information on the sources and classification of his stories. In 1890 he published *Beside the Fire*, a collection of folk tales in Irish with English translations. In

1884, under Hyde's influence, William Larminie started to collect the tales in Irish that were published in 1893 as *West Irish Folktales and Romances*. Folklore began to be used to reinforce a sense of ethnic identity: in a new Irish Ireland the Gaelic storyteller would be a sacred figure. One of the activities that took place during the visits of Gaelic League members to the Gaeltacht to learn Irish was to listen to tales. Storytelling competitions were held during *feis* (festivals) and the League's periodicals included versions of folk tales.

However, as John Wilson Foster has argued, the mere fact of writing down these tales changed them into a different thing. No longer oral but printed, they ceased to convey the manner in which they were recounted, omitting the gesture and the somatic element so vital to the whole experience of storytelling.[9] As Walter Ong points out: 'the oral word . . . never exists in a simply verbal context as a written word does. Spoken words are always part of a total existential situation, which always engages the body.'[10] Moreover, collectors often had their own agenda. Even Jeremiah Curtin, a trained ethnographer, had an ulterior motive beyond the recovery of Irish folk tales: he wished to prove their connection with myths from other cultures in order to shed light on theories of universal human knowledge. In this period, as much as in the earlier part of the century, writers and collectors continued to exploit the folk tale for their own ends.

The writers of the Irish Literary Revival participated in the effort to rescue the folk tale from its nineteenth-century accretions. Lady Gregory started learning Irish in order to collect oral material in her County Galway neighbourhood, J. M. Synge spent four and a half months in the Aran islands listening to the islanders' tales and 'AE' (George Russell) cycled the Irish countryside, conversing with Irish peasants. Inspired by long holidays spent in his mother's native Sligo, an area particularly rich in fairy and folk tales, Yeats edited *Fairy and Folk Tales of the Irish Peasantry* (1888) and *Irish Fairy Tales* (1892), and in 1893 published *The Celtic Twilight: Men and Women, Dhouls and Fairies*. This was subsequently expanded and for the 1902 edition Yeats had the help of Lady Gregory, who brought Yeats with her on her collecting trips in County Galway. Under her influence, Yeats took a more scientific interest in folklore, presenting himself as a field collector and claiming, in his preface to *The Celtic Twilight*, to have 'written down accurately and candidly much that I have heard and seen, and except by way of commentary, nothing that I merely imagined'.[11] However, *The Celtic Twilight*'s hybrid status as part collector's book, part spiritual autobiography, highlights a common problem with these collections: the writers of the Irish renaissance took from peasants' tales what they wished to find in order to bolster their own literary efforts. AE may have conversed with Irish peasants but he adapted his material to support his visions of the emerging Irish nation. Georges Zimmermann comments:

> Each writer was likely to find what he wished to see: Yeats expected the storyteller to be a visionary, or the embodiment of instinctive passion, or both; Lady Gregory and Synge looked for people who were materially poor but endowed with the power of inventing richness through words . . . for AE, avatars of ancient gods were hiding among Irish peasants.[12]

George Moore was later to satirize the Revival's reverence for the *seanchaí* (storyteller) in *A Story Teller's Holiday* (1918), whilst Pádraic Pearse rejected both the Revivalists' English language and their use of folk narrative in favour of an Irish-language literature that would reflect modern Irish experience and look outward to European models.

Yeats' attitude to fairy and folk tales always remained primarily creative rather than scholarly. He used folk themes to explain and justify his belief in the spiritual qualities of the Irish landscape and peasantry and to demonstrate that the Irish peasant was not the comic buffoon who featured in the writings of Croker and Lover but a figure of deep and heroic passions. To this end, he attempted to uncover links between Irish folklore and a mainstream European ancient heritage of wisdom such as Dante, Shakespeare and Blake might have drawn on, insisting that 'The root-stories of the Greek poets are told today at the cabin fires of Donegal.'[13] As time went on, Yeats' researches into Irish folklore overlapped with his interest in occultism and spiritualism until he was using folk tales only in order to borrow ideas and symbols to work into his own personal mythological scheme. For, simultaneous to his investigations into Irish folklore, Yeats was becoming aware of artistic developments in Europe. As early as 1902 he complained, in his preface to Lady Gregory's *Cuchulain of Muirthemne*, that tellers of folk tales 'did not think sufficiently about the shape of the poem and the story'.[14] In his pivotal essay, 'The Celtic Element in Literature' (1898), writing against Matthew Arnold's portrait of the dreamy Celt in *The Celtic Element in Literature*, Yeats allied the developing interest in Irish legends and folklore with the emergence of the Symbolist movement in Europe, seeing both as part of a general reawakening of the imagination after the rationalism of the eighteenth century and the materialism of the nineteenth. In 1894, with the help of his friend, Arthur Symons, he had the opportunity during his stay in Paris to come into direct contact with the French Symbolists.[15] The Symbolists' belief in the power of a word or symbol to conjure a hidden reality chimed in with his own wish to evoke an occult tradition in his writing.

In Yeats we see a tension between the demands of the Irish Revival and the quest for artistic form that has implications for our understanding of the development of the Irish short story. His unease is demonstrated in his introduction to *Representative Irish Tales*, his influential collection of short fiction by Carleton, Griffin, Croker, Lover, the Banim brothers and others, published in 1891, where he lays stress on the fact that, with a few exceptions, these tales are limited by their lack of artistry. He concludes: 'No modern Irish writer has ever had anything of the high culture that makes it possible for an author to do as he will with life.'[16] Whereas in Hall and Carleton, for different reasons, the story form all but collapsed under the weight of the times, in Yeats, the need to present his vision for Ireland was always balanced by his concern for artistic form. Contemporary reviewers, however, continued to judge not on aesthetics but on themes, in particular the way in which an author presented the Irish nation to a foreign audience. In the *Irish Monthly*, the anonymous reviewer of *Representative Irish Tales* disliked Yeats' collection, commenting: 'the rollicking, savage, and droll elements are much too largely represented. We are far nicer people than the American or English reader will gather from these samples.'[17]

In London, Yeats frequented avant-garde literary circles and was instrumental in getting the Rhymers Club started in 1890.[18] The Rhymers were influenced by Walter Pater's attempt to move prose closer to the rhythms of poetry, an admiration that Yeats shared without, however, espousing Pater's doctrine of 'art for art's sake'. Despite the name of the club, some members, like Ernest Dowson, ranked prose above poetry and five of the Rhymers published short fiction in the early 1890s.[19] The Rhymers' espousal of the short narrative reflects the fact that, on the international scene, the short story was very much the modern artistic form of the 1890s. The collapse of the three-volume novel and the establishment of new periodicals on both sides of the Atlantic created a market for short fiction. Writers not only began to adopt the form in large numbers but also to reflect on the principles of short story writing: 'People talked about them tremendously, compared them, and ranked them. That was the thing that mattered,' H. G. Wells explained in 1911.[20]

Irish periodicals such as the *Irish Homestead* (1895–1923), *The Irish Review* (1911–14) and, later, *The Irish Statesman* (1919–30) played an influential role in the development of the modern short story, publishing work by writers associated with the Irish Revival and thereby providing a new readership for short fiction. *The Irish Review*, subtitled 'a monthly magazine of Irish politics, literature and art' and edited at various stages by Pádraic Colum and Joseph Plunkett, published, among others, tales by James Stephens and Lord Dunsany. A new type of story was developing, one less concerned with a remarkable incident or a plot recounted by an omniscient narrator but focusing rather on mood and psychological exploration. Writers were influenced by the psychological realism of Flaubert and Maupassant, by Ibsen's naturalism and by the newly translated Russian writers, Tolstoy, Turgenev and Chekhov. Between November 1885 and September 1886, *The Dublin University Review* serialized a translation of Turgenev's *On the Eve*. Some of Chekhov's stories appeared in translation in America by 1891 and in England by 1897.[21]

In London, the *Strand Magazine*, founded in 1891, began to publish single short stories, while the aim of *The Yellow Book*, founded in 1894, was to feature modern short fiction that focused on psychological intensity and formal innovation. George Egerton published her short story, 'A Lost Masterpiece', in the first volume, which also included work by Henry James, Arthur Symons and George Moore; James, in particular, welcoming the magazine's emphasis on artistic experimentation and freedom from length restrictions.[22] *The Irish Times* waxed lyrical over this volume: 'Those who can revel in the consummation of artistic expression, and in the most restrained and refined language of English modernity, will find here a sumptuous feast.'[23] *The Yellow Book*, published by John Lane at the Bodley Head, was edited initially by Henry Harland and Aubrey Beardsley and was therefore associated with the 'decadent' and 'aesthetic' movements of the *fin de siècle* of which both Yeats and Oscar Wilde were a part. Yeats was not so much interested in the technical innovations of the short story but he was interested in Wilde, who made occasional appearances at the Rhymers Club and whose reputation as an author dated from publication of *The Happy Prince and Other Tales* in London in 1888.

There were many lines of connection between Yeats and Wilde, not least in the area of folklore. In his *Irish Fairy and Folk Tales of the Irish Peasantry*, Yeats acknowledged his debt to Lady Wilde's *Ancient Legends, Mystic Charms and Superstitions of Ireland*, published the previous year (1887), compiled and expanded from her husband's recordings of folk tales. Her son's favourable review of Yeats' *Irish Fairy and Folk Tales* in *Woman's World* (February 1889) demonstrated his familiarity with the world of this material, on which he too was to draw for some of his stories. Indeed, Wilde had been brought into direct contact with the world of the Irish-speaking peasants in the late 1870s, when he accompanied his father to the west of Ireland. Deirdre Toomey has connected Wilde's reputation in London drawing rooms for storytelling with the tradition of the *seanchaí* and argues that in this it is possible to see Wilde's identification with Irish culture and its privileging of the oral over the written.[24] Yeats himself recognized that much about Wilde was 'Irish of the Irish' and in his 1923 introduction to *The Happy Prince and Other Tales* revealed his admiration for Wilde the talker, expressing his preference for *The Happy Prince* stories over *The House of Pomegranates* on account of the former's oral qualities.

Recent critical writing on Wilde's fairy stories has emphasized their connections with the world of Irish folklore. Richard Pine argues that Wilde set his fairy stories back into the world of folklore from where they originated, the subversive, largely oral lore directed at adults, which had become sentimentalized into storybook narratives for the moral improvement of Victorian children.[25] Pine traces several Irish folk motifs in Wilde's stories: the changelings in 'The Star-Child' and 'The Young King', the deserted soul in 'The Fisherman and His Soul', and concludes that Wilde's fairy stories are a hybrid mixture of sources. 'The Fisherman and His Soul' echoes stories in Lady Wilde's *Ancient Legends of Ireland* and in Yeats' *Fairy and Folk Tales*, but also uses motifs from Hans Andersen's 'The Little Mermaid'.[26] At the time when he was composing *The Secret Rose*, Yeats may well have found inspiration in Wilde's incorporation into the fairy tale of social, political and religious themes connected with modern life, described by Wilde in a letter to Amelie Rives Chanler as 'an attempt to mirror modern life in a form remote from reality'.[27] Neil Sammells has argued that Wilde's use of the fairy tale was a deliberate choice of a stylized form over realism, a mode about which Wilde remained unconvinced. Sammells connects this choice with Declan Kiberd's association of Wilde's anti-realist strategies with his nationalist sympathies and critique of British imperialism. In his full-length study of Wilde's fairy tales, Jarlath Killeen too reads these strategies in the light of Wilde's nationalism but adds in his interest in the occult and his sympathy for folk-Catholicism.[28] Readings such as these draw Wilde's fairy tales close to Yeats' alliance of mysticism and nationalism in *The Secret Rose*.[29]

Wilde's use of short fiction to convey a moral vision of the world may have attracted Yeats' attention. In the general context of Wilde's influence on Yeats, Terence Brown comments: 'He would remember how Wilde in his person and in his critical writings had espoused a doctrine which made the aesthetic a force for the spiritual transformation of human consciousness.'[30] If Yeats' vision in his stories combined, as we shall see, Irish nationalism and occultism, Wilde used his fairy tales, his prose poems and his social parables both to subvert his audience's expectations and to critique society's values, carrying into his short fiction 'the art of elegant inversion' on which Declan Kiberd regards him as having based his life.[31] If the essence of the colonized Irishman was childishness as opposed to the hypermasculinity of the colonizers, Wilde chose to stylize that childishness into sophisticated fairy tales that critiqued the values of Victorian society from the margins. Descriptions of the urban poor in 'The Happy Prince' or the effects of famine in 'The Young King' underline the fact that, as Jerusha McCormack has argued, 'It is from the margins of society, from the perspective of the poor, the colonized, the disreputable and dispossessed, that these stories must be read.'[32] It was precisely this element that puzzled Wilde's contemporaries. Reviewers in *The Athenaeum* (1 September 1888) and the *Saturday Review* (20 October 1888) noted that Wilde's satire differentiated his fairy tales from those of Hans Andersen and felt that it made them unsuitable for children. The comparison with Hans Christian Andersen must, however, have encouraged Wilde, who had had a hard time trying to place his fairy tales. Rejected by Macmillan as unlikely to be popular, surely one of the most stunning literary misjudgments of all time, the manuscript was eventually accepted by David Nutt, a minor publishing firm in London.

The themes of redemptive love and social critique link Wilde's other short narratives with his fairy tales for children, where the traditional fairy tale happy ending is avoided, where selfless love is contrasted with society's materialism, treachery and cruelty and is often defeated by them: the nightingale who dies to create beauty, the swallow who perishes performing acts of charity, little Hans who sacrifices his life for friendship, the dwarf who dies of a broken heart. In *Lord Arthur Savile's Crime and Other Stories* (1891), Wilde took the popular genres of the ghost story ('The Canterville Ghost') and the detective story ('Lord Arthur Savile's Crime') and reversed his readers' expectations. Rather than the status quo being restored at the end, as is usual in these essentially conservative forms, in Wilde it is society that turns out to be the villain. In the case of 'The Canterville Ghost', society's corrupt values are revealed and juxtaposed to the love and exercise of imaginative sympathy shown by Virginia.[33] Some contemporary commentators, including Yeats, found these stories disappointing compared with his fairy tales.[34]

Wilde's interest in exploiting the popular market for short fiction that had developed in England during the second half of the nineteenth century, as a result of cheaper book production and the spread of adult literacy following John Forster's 1870 Education Act, may have been dictated by personal financial necessity. He was nevertheless too great a writer, and perhaps too much of an Irishman, to adhere to the conventional formula for fairy tales, ghost stories and detective fiction. In an interpretation that may have been more apparent to Yeats than it has been to intervening commentators on Wilde, Jarlath Killeen has extended the reading of Wilde's fairy tales as social critique to a specifically Irish context, and argued that they may be viewed as criticizing British imperialism from the perspective of the colonized Irish, portrayed in the tales as children ruled by wrong-headed giants and princes.[35] Less didactically than Maria Edgeworth, Wilde used the children's story to convey to the English reader a message about Ireland. His fairy tales reverse the usual nineteenth-century mode of inculcating children into the values of the adult world: the role of the child in 'The Selfish Giant' is essentially to educate the giant into the art of good parenting (and the Anglo-Irish landlord into the art of good rule). Fairy tale paganism is replaced by a Christian framework: at the end of 'The Selfish Giant' the child becomes transformed into an image of Christ offering his hand to lead the giant to heaven. Like the stories in Yeats' *The Secret Rose*, Wilde's fairy tales in Killeen's reading cross the boundary between this world and the next, using secret codes and symbols clear only to readers familiar with Ireland's history, Irish folk and fairy lore, and the evolution of Irish Catholicism. Hence the similarities between Yeats' marginal magi and ascetics and Wilde's Christ-like figures who embrace poverty, shame and social ostracism: as Declan Kiberd has pointed out, 'Wilde's is the outcast Christ celebrated in the popular spirituality of the rural Irish tales and proverbs heard from peasants in Wilde's youth.'[36]

The dominant theme of both *The Happy Prince* and *A House of Pomegranates* (1891) is one that also preoccupied Yeats, namely the conflict between society's materialism and the spiritual and artistic life. Wilde's story of the professor's daughter in 'The Nightingale and the Rose', who prefers material objects to a rose, portrays both society's materialism and the cost of the spiritual/artistic quest in a way that would surely have interested Yeats. The fact that the Student eventually turns his back on love anticipates Yeats' *Secret Rose* stories, where the spiritual quest often fails due to the flaws and fears of the seeker (Red Hanrahan, Michael Robartes). Across several different genres – fairy tale, detective story, ghost story – Wilde used the short narrative to express a coherent moral vision and one that would have appealed to Yeats. Yet a distinction remains: Yeats used his short fiction as a vehicle to express his ideas on nationalism and the spiritual quest, whereas, for Wilde, the choice of artistic form came first: 'I like to think that there may be many meanings to the Tale – for in writing it . . . I did not start with the idea and clothe it in form, but began with a form and strove to make it beautiful enough to have many secrets and many answers.'[37]

If Wilde's vision in his tales was primarily aesthetic, incorporating along the way his sympathies for the poor and the colonized and his interest in folk-Catholicism, Yeats used his short fiction first and foremost to transmit his occult and nationalist vision. As he wrote to Olivia Shakespear in 1895: 'I am now trying to do some wild Irish stories which shall be not mere phantasies but the signatures – to use a medieval term – of things invisable [*sic*] and ideal.'[38] As in the case of his nineteenth-century predecessors, literary magazines did much to aid Yeats' career in short fiction: Richard Finneran has assessed that between 1889 and 1905 Yeats published forty-eight stories in various periodicals such as the *National Observer, The New Review, The Savoy,* and *The Speaker.*[39] In this chapter I shall be concerned mainly with the stories from the 1890s that Yeats collected and revised for his 1897 volume, *The Secret Rose,* published in London with illustrations by his father, with a glance at his revisions of them in collaboration with Lady Gregory for the 1905 edition, *Stories of Red Hanrahan,* published in Ireland by the Dun Emer Press. Critics are divided about these revisions, finding in them gains and losses. Richard Finneran believes the revised Hanrahan stories are more cohesive. G. J. Watson disagrees, arguing that though the focus of a story is sometimes made sharper in the 1905 edition, the impact generally of the psychological and sexual themes is diminished and the overall coherence lessened, while the increased use of dialect under the influence of Lady Gregory's Kiltartanese adds little to the stylistic effect.[40] To all intents and purposes Yeats' career as a short story writer came to an end with *The Secret Rose,* the 'Stories of Michael Robartes' which he produced in 1930 being essentially a prolegomena to *A Vision* and, as such, a vehicle to expound his philosophical interests rather than demonstrating continuing commitment to prose fiction.

Yeats' short stories belong, then, to his formative years as an artist and were part of a process by which he was elaborating his quest for enlightenment and exploring the tension between the material world and the world of the occult imagination. If it is possible to highlight a theme in Yeats' stories it is this question of borders – between this world and the supernatural, between the material world and the world of the imagination, the kind of liminal space that is experienced by the half-asleep John Sherman: 'He was at that marchland between waking and dreaming where our thoughts begin to have a life of their own – the region where art is nurtured and inspiration born.'[41] Added to this sense of liminality is the theme of dissolution: throughout *The Secret Rose*, particularly in the 1897 edition, readers have a sense of historical periods forming and dissolving before their eyes.

It was Yeats' father who in 1887, worried that his son's creative energies were being diverted into journalism, suggested he write a short story that might earn him some money. In the autumn of 1887, therefore, Yeats embarked on 'Dhoya', a story about the interaction between the mortal world and the world of spirits, in which Dhoya's passion and energy draw a fairy woman to him. The story is analogous to many Irish tales in which fairies desire humans and it has a localized Sligo setting. However, it is not told in the style of a folk tale but in Paterian language with opening references to the Buddha and Japanese art. Despite its overwritten, sentimental manner and creaky structure, 'Dhoya' is significant in that it signalled Yeats' interest in border states, in the interaction between the material and the spiritual world and thus pointed forward to the stories of *The Secret Rose*. It was published in London in 1891, together with 'John Sherman', analysed in the interchapter. Reviewing the volume in the *Irish Monthly*, Matthew Russell praised 'John Sherman' for 'the quaint little touches of very subtle observation' in its descriptions both of scenery and character but worried what 'Saxon critics' would make of 'the wild Celtic phantasy, *Dhoya*'.[42] However, the book sold quite well, vindicating John Yeats' advice.

The 1897 edition of *The Secret Rose* followed a chronological order that emphasized the continuing conflict between the spiritual and the material world through different historical periods, 'the war of spiritual with natural order' as Yeats described it in his dedication to AE. *The Secret Rose* thus had a unity of design almost unknown in Irish story collections until Joyce's *Dubliners*. It spanned twenty centuries of spiritual warfare leading to a modern-day apocalypse which Yeats envisaged occurring in Ireland as prelude to a new spiritual age. Unity was also provided by the tight geographical focus on the west of Ireland, particularly Yeats' native Sligo. Folk tale was only part of the equation, however, as the stories combined an emphasis on the spirituality of Gaelic Ireland, manifested through its folklore, with Yeats' personal interest in the occult quest. Despite his use of Irish folklore and legend, Yeats was by no means addressing a popular audience in this collection. Rather, he was writing in a style heavily influenced by Pater for an intellectual elite whom he hoped would understand and profit by the esoteric and occult meanings in his stories. He thus moved the folklore tradition away from its oral and popular roots into the realms of the literary and the occult. His description of the book in a letter to John O'Leary in May 1897 as 'an honest attempt towards that aristocratic esoteric Irish literature, which has been my chief ambition' indicated that it would be a far cry from a collection of popular anecdotes about the Irish peasant.[43] Not all of the stories are drawn from folklore, some being invented by Yeats to illustrate this quest: 'The Curse of the Fires and of the Shadows' is a wonder tale taken from Sligo folk history but supplied with an artistic dimension through Yeats' invention of a recurring dance motif, and given a nationalist colouring by the addition of the *sí* (fairy folk) who lead the Puritan despoilers of the monastery to their death. The dedication of the volume to AE marked Yeats' intention to employ Irish myth in pursuit of his highly personal vision of the life of the artist and visionary, during the course of which he hoped to transform both himself and those readers who were capable of grasping the secret meaning of his work. As Terence Brown points out, Yeats' introductory poem, 'To the Secret Rose', made his book not merely an exploration of a literary theme through the ages, but an act of magical conjuration.[44]

The collection deals with such themes as the defeat of romantic passion by the material world ('The Binding of the Hair'), the incompatibility between the spiritual and the mortal world ('The Wisdom of the King'), and ambivalence about the spirit world ('The Rose of Shadow'). In 'The Rose of Shadow', Oona's invocation of her dead lover's spirit through Hanrahan's song, points forward to the dread of encounter with the spiritual found in the Hanrahan stories and in the later occult tales. 'Out of the Rose', a tightly written and compelling tale of a medieval knight whose dreams have dwindled under pressure from the modern world, illustrates Yeats' move away from popular peasant tales. It was invented by Yeats to marry the occult with an Irish setting, for the knight is the last of the Order of the Rose, the rose operating throughout the collection as a symbol of beauty and of mystic rapture, and representing the spiritual life to which Yeats' heroes try and often fail to gain access. Early reviewers of the collection, accustomed to the heavily plotted stories of Stevenson and Kipling, castigated stories like these for having too little plot and relying instead on mood and atmosphere. Mood and atmosphere were, however, precisely the qualities that were to become characteristic of the modernist short story and it is at moments like these one spies the overlap between the writing of the Irish Revival and the modernist movement.

Only occasionally does a dreamer, like Angus in 'Where There is Nothing, There is God', succeed in both preserving his dreams and surviving in the world. This story is unusual in that the dreamer is a Christian in a collection where Christians are more often portrayed as suppressing ancient pagan wisdom. In 'The Crucifixion of the Outcast', the wanderings of Cumhal, last of the gleemen, whose life has been devoted to his art, are contrasted with the comfortable bourgeois existence of the friars who persecute him. Clearly identifying with the heroic and passionate nature of Cumhal, whose pagan songs so infuriate the friars, Yeats called this story 'the nearest to my heart', and in the 1908 and subsequent editions put it first in his collection. Perhaps because of its sympathy with the outcast against the established powers, Wilde declared this story 'sublime'.[45]

In 'The Heart of the Spring', set in seventeenth-century Ireland, the gentle magus' willingness to forgo earthly passions contrasts with the Hanrahan stories, where Hanrahan accepts mortality in order to enjoy them. George Moore praised this story, and William O'Donnell observes that as Yeats moved further away from folklore and closer to the occult, his style became more polished.[46] 'Of Costello the Proud' is more of a straightforward folk tale like those in *The Celtic Twilight* but it fits the general theme of *The Secret Rose* of heroic passions defeated by the modern world. Like Red Hanrahan, Costello's passions cannot be accommodated in this unheroic modern age and in the 1897 edition of *The Secret Rose* this story led on to the Red Hanrahan stories to which it is thematically linked, thus underlining the coherence of the collection.

The Red Hanrahan stories are based on the eighteenth-century Kerry poet, scribe and hedge schoolmaster, Eoghan Rua Ó'Súilleabháin. Yeats' willingness to manipulate his historical sources for his own artistic purposes is demonstrated by the fact that he combined the stories of Eoghan Rua Ó'Súilleabháin, whose passion for women was the undoing of him, with another Gaelic poet, Timothy O'Sullivan, who repented of his early dissipation by turning to religious poetry. For the 1897 edition, Yeats changed the name O'Sullivan to Hanrahan and by 1905 he was claiming that Hanrahan was an invented figure. This was not entirely misleading since, as William O'Donnell points out, though there were historical precedents for Hanrahan's debauchery, his spirituality was Yeats' invention, allowing him to create his favourite character: the Irish peasant as dreamer and man of action.[47]

In the 1897 edition, the first Hanrahan story was 'The Book of the Great Dhoul and Hanrahan the Red'. Hanrahan is presented as someone who, like Dhoya, lives on the borders between the natural and the supernatural world. He uses a book rumoured to have been written by the Devil to conjure up the fairy queen, Cleena of the Wave, whom he later rejects when she appears to him in mortal form. The story is weak and was dropped in the 1905 edition but it nevertheless provided, in Cleena's retaliatory curse, an explanation for Hanrahan's doomed search for the spiritual in the following stories.

'The Twisting of the Rope and Hanrahan the Red' is one of the strongest of the Hanrahan stories in its juxtaposition of a Gaelic Ireland that still honoured visionary poets like Hanrahan with modern bourgeois society, which has no place for ancient Irish heroes. Hanrahan inhabits the liminal space between the supernatural and the mortal world and as he journeys westwards he finds his imagination stirred by visions of beauty and memories of the old Gaelic myths, so that when he meets a young peasant girl, he compares her to 'the beauty of white Deirdre'.[48] The bourgeois world cannot accommodate passion on Hanrahan's scale and his desire for them both to be transported into the ancient heroic world of passion is thwarted by the machinations of the girl's mother and her crony. Cleena of the Wave's mockery of his sadness unites this story thematically with the first Hanrahan story. 'The Curse of Hanrahan the Red' and 'The Death of Hanrahan the Red' are both invented stories, underlining Yeats' shift of the Hanrahan stories away from historical legend into the realms of the mystical. The former emphasizes the theme of mortality, to which the ageing Hanrahan comes to realize he is subject, while in 'The Death of Hanrahan the Red', as Cleena's curse is lifted, Hanarahan achieves spiritual marriage in death. Its placing in the 1897 edition enhanced the unity of the collection through its internal references to other Hanrahan stories as well as to earlier stories in the collection.

Originally Yeats intended *The Secret Rose* to end with three stories held together by a single narrator, Owen Aherne, and dealing with visionary moments in a contemporary setting presaging the end of the Christian era and the birth of a new dispensation. Yeats explained: 'Presently Oisin and his islands faded and the sort of images that come into "Rosa Alchemica" and "The Adoration of the Magi" took their place. Our civilization was about to reverse itself, or some new civilization was about to be born from all our age had rejected.'[49] In the event his English publisher took fright at their unorthodoxy and only one of the stories, 'Rosa Alchemica', appeared in *The Secret Rose*. Later, A. H. Bullen changed his mind and published 'The Tables of the Law' and 'The Adoration of the Magi' separately.

Despite the fact that these three occult stories turn away from folk tale, the artistic unity of *The Secret Rose* was maintained by the stories' Irish settings and their themes of dissolution (of historical periods) and of borders (between the natural and the spiritual worlds, the flesh and the soul, the material life and the visionary). Like Hanrahan, Aherne fatally hesitates on the borders between the material world and the spiritual and thus remains blocked in his spiritual quest. The stories reflect Yeats' range of influence, from Joachim of Fiore, to Blake and Huysmans. The influence of the Parisian millennialist fringe culture hangs over them together with, as Roy Foster has pointed out, Yeats' experiments with drugs.[50] The stories make use of Pater's langorous rhythms, not as an end in themselves, but to reveal the trance-like progress of the narrator on his quest for spiritual enlightenment and to underline his liminal state, poised between two worlds. Faced with the necessity of abandoning the self in his spiritual quest to be initiated into the Order of the Alchemical Rose, Aherne hesitates, misinterprets the ceremonial dance as a sexual orgy and finally retreats into religious orthodoxy, all of which demonstrate his unfitness for the quest. 'The Tables of the Law' underlines the link in Yeats' mind between the occult quest and the Irish Literary Revival, the narrator commenting on 'the fermentation of belief which is coming upon our people with the reawakening of their imaginative life'.[51] It reminds us that at this time Yeats was planning, with Maud Gonne, AE and William Sharp, to establish a cult in Ireland with the aim of reawakening both Ireland's spirituality and her national identity.[52] The final story, 'The Adoration of the Magi', highlights Yeats' desire to link the Irish Revival with ancient European wisdom in the mingled references to Virgil and Homer as well as to ancient Gaelic writers 'who expounded an heroic and simple life'.[53]

Contemporary critical reception of *The Secret Rose* ranged from praise for Yeats' philosophy by George Moore in the *Daily Chronicle* (24 April 1897) to a review in *The Dial* (16 April 1898) which admired the volume's charm but pronounced 'the pseudo-serious ideas shadowed forth in these stories' 'silly'. An anonymous reviewer in *The Speaker* found the stories too high flown and plotless, remarking caustically: 'few will deny to Mr Yeats the possession of genius, yet it were well that he should strive to make himself intelligible to the plain people'.[54]

Why did Yeats abandon prose fiction? Richard Finneran gives several reasons, among which must rank highly Yeats' failure to complete *The*

Speckled Bird, the novel he was working on between 1896 and 1902 and in which he hoped to combine the occult, fairy tale and realism. As his financial pressures lessened, Yeats' belief that prose ranked below poetry and drama and that others (Douglas Hyde, Lady Gregory) were more skilled collectors of folklore, was also a powerful persuader against continuing with short fiction. Finally, if his stories did function as disguised autobiography, the record of his artistic evolution became diverted into the diary he began in 1908.[55]

The Secret Rose is valuable for the insight it grants us into Yeats' early artistic vision, as well as into his doubts at this period about whether art is ever served by magic. More than that, for all its flaws and uncertainties, *The Secret Rose* provided a model for an Irish story collection that was unified thematically and artistically. In the 1897 edition the sense of chronology is strong as the war between the physical and spiritual worlds is portrayed being waged down the ages. Yeats' examination of his subject from different angles avoids creating an overly schematic collection: the quest is not always a failure ('Where There is Nothing, There is God'), Christianity is not always portrayed in a negative light ('Old Men of the Sea'). The continuing conflict between the material and the spiritual world is genuinely moving and persuades the reader to empathize with such characters as Angus, the knight and Red Hanrahan. The high stakes involved – loss of selfhood and even death – add to the dramatic impact. Yeats' rapidly changing ideas and his constant rewriting and reordering of his stories, often for extra-literary reasons, should not obscure the genuine artistic achievement of the 1897 edition of *The Secret Rose*.

George Egerton, too, used short fiction as a vehicle for her visions, in her case about the nature of women. As a New Woman writer she was, like Wilde and Yeats, initially allied to London's decadent and aesthetic literary circles and some of her stories were, as we have seen, published in *The Yellow Book*. Born Mary Chavelita Dunne, she spent part of her childhood in Ireland and it was there that she later worked on her two collections of stories, *Keynotes*, published in 1893, and *Discords*, published a year later. In *Keynotes* and *Discords*, Egerton set out to use short fiction to portray the female unconscious and female sexuality, drawing on the subversive qualities inherent in the short story form to do away with 'masculine' conventions of plot, linearity and discursive explanation in favour of dreams, associations and symbols.

Elaine Showalter has argued that New Woman writers were especially attracted to short fiction because it offered freedom and flexibility from the traditional plots of the Victorian novel, as well as affording the opportunity to focus on moments of psychological intensity and the possibilities for formal innovation necessary for exploring the new subject of women's consciousness.[56] Lyn Pykett positions Egerton as a self-consciously innovatory writer, committed to the development of a female aesthetic.[57] Sally Ledger, too, regards Egerton as a forerunner of the modernists, employing dreams, fantasy and psychoanalysis in the sort of fluid writing that lends her work to being analysed in the light of theories of *écriture féminine*.[58] In view of the fact that her short stories are a psychological exploration of women's inner lives, using dreams, symbolism and stream-of-consciousness, it might be argued that Egerton continues the Irish tradition of writers using short fiction to free themselves from the psychological subjugation of colonialism, only this time the subjugation takes the form of a masculinist society's domination of women.

Neither a suffragette nor a feminist, Egerton explored female sexuality in works that argue that women should enjoy the same sexual freedoms as men. Inspired by her reading of Ibsen, her stories portray women who disdain conventional morality, which, Egerton believed, had been constructed by men and imposed on women, narrowing their lives: 'the untrue feminine is of men's making, whilst the strong, the natural, the true womanly is of God's making' comments the narrator in 'Now Spring Has Come'.[59] Her heroines refuse to be contained by male definitions of womanhood: in 'The Regeneration of Two', the heroine's recognition of the falseness of her society's views of women and marriage leads her to propose entering into a free union with her lover. In stories where women do cave in to convention ('An Empty Frame', 'Her Share'), they are portrayed as leading emotionally sterile lives. The daughter in 'Virgin Soil', married off at seventeen to a wealthy older man, returns to berate her mother and opts for a solitary life over the 'legal prostitution' of an unhappy marriage. 'Virgin Soil' is a forerunner of Mary Lavin's story, 'The Nun's Mother', in depicting the disaster that follows a mother keeping her young daughter ignorant about sexual matters. Lavin, though, was more sympathetic than Egerton to the social and psychological constraints on the mother figure.

Though *The Yellow Book* was, as we have seen, the subject of an admiring review in *The Irish Times*, across the water the association between the New Women writers and the male decadents was judged to be an alliance of degenerates, threatening marriage, gender boundaries and social stability. *Keynotes* had been an immediate success, twice reprinted in the first six months of publication and subsequently translated into seven languages. Partly this was the result of clever marketing on the part of John Lane, who published them with an Aubrey Beardsley design on the dust jacket and opened the collection with 'A Cross Line', the most sexually frank story. The success of *Keynotes* led, however, to a backlash among the more conservative elements of the British press. *Punch* published endless cartoons and parodies of the New Woman, including in 1894 'She-Notes' by 'Borgia Smudgiton' (Owen Seaman), parodying 'A Cross Line'.[60] An attack in *Blackwood's Magazine* in 1895 seems likewise specifically targeted at the sexual radicalism of Egerton's writings: 'Emancipated woman in particular loves to show her independence by dealing freely with the relations of the sexes. Hence the prating of passion, animalism, "the natural workings of sex", and so forth, with which we are nauseated. Most of the characters in these books seem to be erotomaniacs.'[61]

Egerton was by no means an equal rights feminist, however. Her writing displays indifference towards women's education and equal opportunities in professional life. 'The Spell of the White Elf' portrays a professional woman who supports her husband and herself financially but has suppressed her maternal instincts to the extent that she is depicted as an 'unnatural' woman until the appearance of 'a white elf' in her life reawakens her emotions. In its suspicion of the life of the professional woman, 'The Spell of the White Elf' anticipates Mary Lavin's story, 'A Memory'. For Egerton, women's capacity for feeling was the key to the female self and the source of women's moral superiority over men. Rather than being co-opted for feminism, Egerton's belief in the superior spiritual powers of women may be regarded as characteristic of 1890s *fin de siècle* circles generally.[62]

Notwithstanding Egerton's cultural fluidity (born in Australia to an Irish father and a Welsh mother, Egerton lived at various times in Ireland, New Zealand, Wales, Chile, Germany and New York), the neglected topic of Irish themes in her work has come under recent critical scrutiny. In a letter dated 1926, Egerton described herself as 'intensely Irish'[63] and Mary O'Donoghue has argued that Egerton's Catholic upbringing in late nineteenth-century Ireland was a formative experience that had a huge impact on her writing.[64] Egerton's correspondence with Terence de Vere White is shot through with references to Ireland, most of them critical: 'They blather about political freedom. "Cutting the bonds that bind them to England, etc. etc." They evade the real issue – their own spiritual, mental and moral bondage.'[65] Irish traces in her work include references to Irish peasant beliefs in 'The Spell of the White Elf', the Irish cook in

'Virgin Soil', the quotation from Mangan that prefaces 'An Ebb Tide' and one from Wilde prefacing 'A Little Grey Glove', as well as various Irish phrases scattered through the stories.

Like Yeats, Egerton used the story form to record her emotional and spiritual development: the stories grouped together under the title 'Under Northern Sky' are a thinly veiled account of her life with the alcoholic Henry Higginson. Of direct interest to the Irish short story are the three stories published in her collection *Discords* under the title 'A Psychological Moment at Three Periods'. Tracing the development of a young woman from her childhood in Dublin, to a convent school in Germany, to mistress in Paris, they mark a strong protest against Irish society and the dependent position of Irish women. As the title suggests, psychological exploration of the inner consciousness of her heroine is favoured over a wider ranging linear narrative. In this, Egerton was aided by the nature of the short narrative that lends itself to focus on single, crucial moments in the life of the protagonist. In the fragmented sketches of 'A Psychological Moment at Three Periods' we may spy an emerging modernist aesthetic.

'The Child' opens in Dublin, where the child, already trained in the spirit of self-sacrifice, gives up the pleasure of reading her book in the belief that this will be pleasing to God. Her conscience, as punishing as that of a George Eliot heroine, compels her to confess to her schoolmates that the story with which she entranced them is not true. In this first story, the latent storywriter is presented and the social snobberies and hierarchies of the Dublin school she attends are laid bare. In the following story, 'The Girl', set in Germany, Isabel has turned into a wild-spirited and truth-loving convent schoolgirl, indifferent to the nuns' rules and compassionate to the poor and the marginal. In 'The Woman', the truth-telling child and the girl who defied the nuns has grown up into a woman who braves convention by living in Paris as the mistress of a married man. If eventually Isabel feels ashamed of her situation, it is not because society regards her as a 'fallen' woman, but because she has lived with this lustful, predatory man under compulsion; in effect she was blackmailed into becoming his mistress against her instincts.

'The Woman' may seem to present an easy distinction between the innocence of the heroine's Irish childhood and the evils lurking beneath the sophistication of life in Paris. This too facile distinction is complicated both by the fact that Isabel's predatory lover is Irish and by the presence of Mr Aloysius Gonzaga O'Brien, a vulgar, fawning Irishman who, resembling a nineteenth-century land agent, acts as middleman between the woman and her lover, emphasizing her colonized state. Though she eventually achieves independence, Isabel has effectively been ruined by her married lover's brutally casual behaviour, as references to the Finn legend make clear. Isabel's marginal position allows her to sympathize with her schoolfriend, who, with the collusion of the Catholic clergy, has been compelled by her socially ambitious parents to give up her love for an impoverished Protestant in order to marry a wealthy Catholic. Years before *Dubliners*, Egerton's story contains a lengthy indictment of the snobbery and materialism of Dublin society, its shallow piety and the dependent position of Irish women. Isabel's advice to separate from her husband is accepted by her friend and, in line with the emerging modernist aesthetic, the story evades closure, leaving Isabel's fate, and that of her friend, open-ended.

Egerton's third volume of stories, *Symphonies*, came out in 1896 but neither this volume nor *Fantasias*, which was published in 1898, abstract fables on the Yeatsian theme of visionaries at odds with a materialistic society, was a success. By this time, Oscar Wilde's trial and conviction in 1895 had led to an increased caution on the part of publishers of New Woman writing and John Lane's request that Egerton tone down the sexual content of her work produced an angry reaction on her part and may have contributed to the weakness of these subsequent volumes. Egerton's critique of Irish society, in particular its treatment of women, continued in a lesser-known collection, *Flies in Amber*, published in London by Hutchinson in 1905, where the central image of flies trapped in amber aptly reflects her portrayal of women's lives. The volume was favourably reviewed in *The Irish Times* as 'a collection of powerfully-written stories . . . They are of extraordinary observation and insight into character, and sometimes are so striking as to be painful.'[66]

In the two stories in the collection with Irish settings, Ireland is depicted as a dirty, disorderly place, both in the provincial town of Millroad (actually Millstreet) in County Cork in 'The Marriage of Mary Ascension' and in Dublin, 'at all times the most narrow of provincial towns', in 'Mammy'.[67] 'Mammy' centres on a brothel in Mecklenburgh Street run by the eponymous Mammy, Mrs Sylvester. As one would expect, Egerton's sympathies are on the side of the streetwalkers. In her portrayal of Mrs Sylvester carrying one of her dying girls to church after the priest has refused to give her the Last Rites, Egerton complicates assumptions about prostitutes by likening the Mammy bearing her burden through the streets of Dublin to Christ carrying his cross. The story ends on the suggestion that Christ's view of these women might be different from that of his priests. If the dying prostitute has been trapped by economic circumstances, convent-educated Mary in 'The Marriage of Mary Ascension' is constrained both by the power of the priests who, as in 'Woman', collude with her relatives to prevent her from marrying the Protestant man she loves, and by her religious upbringing, which has suppressed her natural sexual instincts. The stories in *Flies in Amber*, though continuing Egerton's theme of women's sexual lives, abandon the use of dreams and the psychological explorations of *Keynotes* and *Discords*. With their urban realism and their depiction of Ireland as a shabby, backward place under the control of priests, they point forward to Joyce.

Though Egerton is not generally admitted to histories of the Irish short story, her stories have many links with other Irish writers. She shares with Yeats the use of the form to convey her artistic and spiritual visions. Her stories anticipate Joyce in their critique of Dublin's narrow-minded materialism and in their use of the Orient as a place of imagined liberation and sexual fantasy. Many of her themes are recognizably Irish – her scorn for the middleman in 'The Woman', her treatment of Irish emigration in 'Gone Under'. Sally Ledger points out that only Egerton among the New Woman writers extended her range to portray women from social groups other than the middle class.[68] This sympathy with the underprivileged may well be an Irish trace in her work.

Sarah Grand, pseudonym of Frances McFall, also has a claim to be considered an Irish writer since she was born in Ireland in 1854 and spent the first seven years of her life there. She shared Egerton's vision of equality between the sexes, though with an emphasis not on women's sexual freedom but on women's sexual purity, and the necessity for men to live up to the same sexual standards as women. 'The Undefinable: A Fantasia', published in *Cosmopolitan* (1894) and later collected in *Emotional Moments* (1908), employs the voice of a self-satisfied male narrator to expose male constructs of womanhood as dependent and inferior. Since this is a New Woman story, a female muse appears to instruct him about the 'free woman, a new creature, a source of inspiration the like of which no man has even imagined in art or literature'.[69] Grand's most significant work, however, was in the novel form.[70]

Other writers of the early twentieth century who used the story form as a vehicle for visions include Pádraic Pearse, whose two collections of short stories in Irish, 'Íosagán agus Sgéalta Eile' (1907) and 'An Mháthair agus Sgéalta Eile' (1915), provide a glimpse into the lives of the people of the Gaeltacht and his hopes for the end of English rule ('An Bhean Chaointe').[71] The four stories in the first collection were written for children, and 'Íosagán' ('Little Jesus') has parallels with Oscar Wilde's 'The Selfish Giant' in portraying an adult led to redemption by the Christ child. The later collection contains stories for adults that fall between two stools in being too complex for children and not complex enough for adults. Quite at odds with New Woman writing, the stories reveal Pearse's distrust of the marginal woman ('An Dearg-Daol') and warn of the fate in store for rebellious girls ('Na Bóithre'). Pearse's espousal of the short story as the modern literary form sits oddly with the essentially conservative nature of his subject matter and his portrait of peasant life is often idealized, glossing over the hardships of their lives.

It would be incorrect, however, to state that all or even most of the short fiction by writers connected with the Irish Revival resisted realism. Jane Barlow's *Irish Idylls* presents the daily life of impoverished Connemara peasants in a series of interlinking stories that, in their detailed observations, approach travelogue and social documentary. The illustrations that appeared by the time of the eighth edition in 1898 add to the documentary feel of this collection. Published in London in 1892, *Irish Idylls* was written with an eye for the English reader but it treats the peasants with seriousness, by and large rejecting the attitude of moral superiority found in earlier nineteenth-century accounts. It was possibly for this reason that Yeats included Barlow's volume in his list of 'Best Irish Books'. Despite the title, Barlow does not downplay the hardship of the peasants' lives: in 'One Too Many', Larry Sheridan is forced to quit his family and try his fortune in America but dies along the way. Two stories by Pádraic Colum published in *The Irish Review* (January and February 1912), likewise connect the preoccupations of the Irish Revival with the realist mode. 'A Meeting on the Road' and 'A Country Marriage' portray rural life with a detailed eye, particularly in the latter story, where the economic realities behind country marriages are laid bare.

Katharine Tynan shared Yeats' commitment to the Literary Revival, and sketches she published in 1894 under the title, *A Cluster of Nuts*, depicting the suffering of the Irish peasants, have been described as 'an early minor, ground-clearing work of the Irish Literary Revival'.[72] Tynan's stories in *The Handsome Quaker and Other Stories*, published in London in 1902, have a nationalist colouring, the title story recounting an episode from Lord Edward Fitzgerald's career. Most of the stories portray the lives of ordinary Irish men and women and deal with such subjects as rural poverty ('The Widower', 'The Cry of the Child'), rural politics ('The Politician'), marriage in rural Ireland ('A Ridiculous Affair', 'A Childless Woman') and emigration ('A Benefactor'). All these stories are set within a realistic framework and aspire to little more than to entertain and instruct the reader on the conditions of life in Ireland. In 'The Enemy of God', Tynan's attempt to move beyond realism into Yeatsian visionary mode simply lapses into conventional piety.

A more successful rupturing of the realist mode is found in the prose of James Stephens. Stephens published two collections of stories with Macmillan in London, *Here Are Ladies* (1913) and *Etched in Moonlight* (1928), at the same time as he was reworking saga material in *Irish Fairy Tales* (1920), *Deirdre* (1923) and *In the Land of Youth* (1924). Taken together, these volumes illustrate the overlap between Irish Revivalist preoccupations and modernist tendencies. Despite their later publication dates, the fact of his friendship with Joyce and the positioning of his stories by some critics as urban counterparts of Moore's,[73] Stephens' work has much in common with *fin de siècle* writers. Like Egerton, Stephens used his short fictions to portray the breakdown of communication between the sexes. Like Wilde, he blended the mythical and the fabulous with the everyday, social critique with moral fable. Like Yeats, he believed fairy tales had universal significance and he was interested in the borders between the mortal world and the spiritual. Stephens aimed to be as careful a stylist as any of these writers, declaring that: 'One can polish a short story just like a poem.'[74] Some of the stories in *Here Are Ladies* were originally published in Arthur Griffith's newspaper, *Sinn Féin*. Stephens later reworked them for his collection, removing the more nationalistic references and giving them a more European feel.[75]

Here Are Ladies is a collection of interlinked poems, sketches and stories circling around the theme of the lack of communication between men and women. The first section is prefaced by a poem, 'Women', criticizing the unkindness of women. This is followed by three sketches ('Three Heavy Husbands') portraying three marriages unhappy for different reasons (unfaithful wife, shy husband, controlling husband). The sketches and the poem prepare the reader for the story that ends this section, 'A Glass of Beer'. Akin to one of Poe's tales, 'A Glass of Beer' portrays a heightened psychological state, straining against realism in a manner that, Augustine Martin has argued, displays 'the author's fundamental unease with the limits of the realist short story itself'.[76] The story opens realistically enough with a foreigner having a drink in a Paris bar and feeling hampered in his Paris life by the difficulty of making himself understood. As the story gradually moves into describing the man's thoughts, it takes on a less realistic, more obsessive tinge. The man's recall of intense hatred for his wife rises to a crescendo as, in his loneliness and isolation, he gives way to generalized misogyny: 'Women went past in multitudes, and he knew the appearance of them all ... Raddled faces with heavy eyes and rouged lips. Ragged lips that had been chewed by every mad dog in the world ... Lips of a horrid fascination that one looked at and hated and ran to.'[77] The hypnotic rhythms of this passage express an obsessive disgust and loathing for women that disrupts the realist mode and gives an insight into a mind bordering on madness. The man's isolation and existential despair are explained in the final paragraph where it is revealed that, though his wife's death has granted him freedom, it is a freedom he can no longer take advantage of since as an artist he is burned out. 'A Glass of Beer' is a well-crafted tale, rather than short story, just contained within the bounds of realism, yet allowing the reader to enter into an extreme state of mind. The psychological exploration, the hypnotic prose rhythms and the theme of the conflict between the sexes, all have parallels with Egerton.

The stories in the rest of *Here Are Ladies* reveal Stephens experimenting with a variety of modes, from the realism of 'The Triangle', another portrait of an unhappy marriage, to fable in 'The Threepenny-Piece', a comic tale of the afterlife. Like 'A Glass of Beer', 'The Horses' disrupts the realist mode, moving from the portrait of a marriage in which a husband has been trained into domesticity by his wife, into fairy tale when the husband empathizes with a horse that is being beaten. As we enter into the consciousness of the horse and his dreams of exchanging his life in the city for green fields, a change comes over the husband and he takes on aspects of a wild horse charging towards freedom. The story is lifted on to another plane and ends inconclusively in modernist vein as Stephens forbears to give us the inevitable return to reality.

Stephens' later volume, *Etched in Moonlight*, also displays a variety of styles, including social critiques of modern urban life that verge on fable ('The Boss') or approach the simplicity of parable ('Hunger'). In others, such as 'Desire' and 'Etched in Moonlight', he stretches the boundaries of the story form, like Egerton using dreams to express emotions suppressed by his characters in their daily lives. 'Etched in Moonlight' explores the theme of obsessive sexual jealousy and the effect of guilt on the psyche, in a mode far removed from realism. Dreams are, the narrator argues, phenomena in which time, place and identity become dissolved, and to prove this, he recounts a dream in which he assumed an entirely different personality: 'I was not this I, either physically, mentally, or temperamentally.'[78] Stephens' tale approaches Elizabeth Bowen's use of the short story to portray obsessive states of mind that threaten the dissolution of identity. The world is seen through the grip of an obsession and the moral ambivalence of the protagonist is suggested in the darkness that shadows him after his release from the keep. Psychology and morality blend into a powerful fable about the fragility of human identity.

Here Are Ladies was the subject of a warm review in *The Irish Times* (21 November 1928) but *Etched in Moonlight* was much less favourably reviewed, the reviewer singling out 'Hunger' and 'Desire' as the most successful but commenting: 'the rest all are in the same grim, if not morbid, tone. All are introspective, uncanny, dismal.'[79] As a storyteller, Stephens was acceptable to his contemporaries in his Irish Revival mode but not when he used the form to explore states of mind, as a later commentator made clear: 'we all admired Mr James Stephens when he was giving us those delightful fantastic tales and those charming poems, but there were few reviewers who showed any great enthusiasm over his last volume'.[80] Yet it is in stories like 'Etched in Moonlight' that Stephens leaves the Irish Revival behind and edges towards modernism.

Fin de siècle writers' use of fairy tales, dreams, symbolism and visions underlines the distinction Charles May has drawn between the novel which 'exists to reaffirm the world of everyday reality' and the short story's role, which is, he believes, to 'defamiliarize the everyday': 'the field of research for the short story is the primitive antisocial world of the unconscious, and the material of its analysis are not manners but dreams'.[81] This chapter may have begun with the story's link to Irish folklore but foreign influences were also starting to shape Irish short fiction in this period: the French Symbolists, the Russians and, in the case of Egerton, Scandinavian writers like Strindberg and Ibsen. Study of Irish short narratives in this period reinforces the notion gaining critical currency that, far from being antithetical to modernism, Ireland was a place that lent itself particularly well to modernist sensibilities.[82] Not only in Stephens' tales but also in the earlier work of Egerton and Yeats, we see the beginnings of the modernist short story – impressionistic, concentrated, resisting narrative closure and using dreams to probe the inner psychology of their characters. It is to that modernist short story we now turn.

READINGS: W. B. YEATS AND GEORGE EGERTON

W. B. Yeats, 'John Sherman' (1891)

Yeats' story, 'Dhoya', written at his father's behest, failed to meet his father's criterion for what a story should be: 'my father was dissatisfied and said he meant a story with real people'.[83] To please his father, Yeats embarked on 'John Sherman', a long story usually classified as a novella on account of its length and changes of scene. Realism was not a mode that came naturally to Yeats, as he somewhat cynically underlines in the excessive precision of dates and place in the opening paragraphs. After these opening shafts, characteristic of a son rebelling against the paternal edict, Yeats settled down to portray in John Sherman his own youthful difficulties in establishing himself and his determination to preserve his imaginative world at all costs. Nothing decisive comes of Sherman's rejection of an advantageous marriage to Margaret and a job in his uncle's office – there is no suggestion that he will become a poet or a writer – but he remains true to himself and to his love for the west of Ireland. The novella's necessary thematic unity is provided by the ending's ironic reversal of the opening scene in which Howard declares he will never marry for money because he seeks sincerity in all things and Sherman's insistence that he needs to marry a wealthy woman since he will never be able to sustain an occupation. The novella has been read as a reversal of the traditional nineteenth-century *Bildungsroman* with Yeats' hero learning to resist, rather than explore, the world of ambition.[84] In all this, despite such flaws as reliance on authorial commentary rather than dialogue to convey character, Yeats' story fits into the realist mode approved by John Yeats. A contemporary reviewer writing in *United Ireland* in 1891 observed: 'Mr Yeats has fashioned his style after the serious Russian model'[85] and Deirdre Toomey has noted traces of Yeats' reading of Turgenev, a writer who was to have a crucial influence on the development of the Irish short story in the following decades.[86]

However, there is a way of reading this story that suggests Yeats was less influenced by the views of his rationalist and sceptical father in writing it than by a wish to recapture his mother's world of Sligo and storytelling. The novella contains celebratory and evocative depictions of Ballah, the town in the west of Ireland where Sherman lives with his mother, in reality Sligo, where Yeats spent many youthful holidays with his maternal grandparents. In a letter to Katharine Tynan, Yeats commented: 'I have studied my characters in Ireland and described a typical Irish feeling in Sherman's devotion to Ballah. A West of Ireland feeling I might almost say . . . I remember when we were children how intense our devotion was to all things in Sligo and still see in my mother the old feeling.'[87] Sherman's withdrawn, recalcitrant mother shares characteristics in common with Susan Yeats: her solitariness, her knitting, her dislike of London, which she passed on to her son, and her corresponding love of Sligo.

Yet Yeats' relationship with his undemonstrative, depressed mother was never close, and in this context, 'John Sherman' may be read in the light of Melanie Klein's theories of art as repairing the relationship with the mother. In her paper, 'Infantile Anxiety-Situations Reflected in a Work of Art and in the Creative Impulse' (1929), Klein argued that in art both children and adults seek to make good the damage seemingly done in attacking the mother. Janet Sayers comments: 'Klein's discovery of the child's early internalization of its first relation with the mother led ... to an important shift in psychoanalytic perspectives on art, now understood as stemming not from sublimation of instinct but from a wish to repair relations with others, in the first place with the mother.'[88] This reading slightly redeems the sentimental ending, where Mary Carton, Sherman's childhood love, consents to marry him, prompted by feelings that are presented as maternal rather than sexual. A weak ending gains in significance if we read it with an understanding of Yeats' desire to maintain connection with his own silent, reserved and, since 1887, stroke-ridden mother and her imaginative world of Sligo folklore.

'John Sherman' may be written in the realist mode, as Yeats' father wished, but the underlying impulse suggests a break with realism. When Yeats told Tynan in March 1891 that 'There is more of myself in it than in any thing I have done',[89] he may have been referring not only to the celebration of the west of Ireland and Sherman's rejection of the bourgeois working world, but to his personal alignment with his mother's world of storytelling and folklore. Read in this light 'John Sherman', as much as 'Dhoya', points towards the dominant themes of *The Secret Rose*.

George Egerton, 'A Cross Line' (1893)

The presentation of the relationship between the sexes in 'A Cross Line' has to be read in the context of the *fin de siècle* decadent movement that positioned men as aesthetic and women as earth-bound and materialistic.[90] In 'A Cross Line', Egerton reverses this positioning: her heroine's appreciation of nature leads her into aesthetic reverie, whereas her lover and her husband are preoccupied with more material questions. The lover believes he is adept at classifying women and wants to embark on a sexual relationship with Gipsy, whilst her prosaic husband, preoccupied with farming his land, thinks of his wife primarily in her reproductive role. Neither man is capable of comprehending the power and complexity of Gipsy's sexuality, revealed to the reader in her eroticized reveries.

The opening of the story makes explicit the contrast between the stranger's jaunty singing of a music-hall song and Gipsy, whose thoughts, inspired by her reading, are filled with aesthetic images of beautiful maidens. Whereas the stranger's vulgar ditty is incongruous in the Irish countryside, Gipsy is presented as at home in the wildness of nature in a way that anticipates the writings of Hélène Cixous and Luce Irigaray aligning women and nature. There are specifically Irish touches in the references to her 'scarlet shawl' and the 'speckled red "fairy hats"' that form part of the undergrowth. Gipsy is no objectified Mother Ireland figure, however: the stranger's shallow reference to the natural setting as a place to prompt a fellow to thought earns him an amused glance from Gipsy, whose imaginative capacities far exceed his own.

Men and women meet on terms of equality in 'A Cross Line': Gipsy is as knowledgeable as the stranger about fly fishing, whilst her husband, on account of her liberal approach to his sexual past, looks on her as 'a chum'. For Egerton, however, equal rights feminism took second place to exploring women's psychology and their secret sexual desires. The stranger is checked by being unable to classify Gipsy; Gipsy is inhibited in her flights of fancy by her husband's dullness; her husband is unable to penetrate Gipsy's imaginative life. The title, 'A Cross Line', underlines the difficulty of achieving communication between the sexes as the two men and the woman remain at cross-purposes.

The daringly erotic passages describing Gipsy's dreams and sexual fantasies in terms of the Oriental other may be read in the light of French feminist notions of *écriture féminine*, where, inspired by female bodily energies, the semiotic breaks into the symbolic and reveals a submerged woman's world running beneath the male symbolic order. Dreaming of erotic power over men, the heroine mocks male constructs of femininity: 'They have all overlooked the eternal wildness, the untamed primitive savage temperament that lurks in the mildest, best woman.'[91] Decades before Mary Daly, Egerton positions woman as a witch, outside society's conventions.[92] In the context specifically of the Irish short story, the use of the Orient as a place of liberation and sexual fantasy anticipates Joyce's *Dubliners*.

Nevertheless, women are easily trapped in Egerton's stories – by convention, by their need for affection, or by motherhood. At the end of 'A Cross Line', the realization of her impending motherhood leads Gipsy to exchange her wild freedoms and her sexual desires for childbearing. Egerton's writing has often been interpreted as essentialist for presenting motherhood as the fulfilment of womanhood.[93] A story like 'Gone Under' reveals the dangers of thwarted maternity. Seduced at sixteen and forced to give birth in the sort of establishment that makes sure the baby is registered as a stillbirth, the heroine thereafter turns to drink. Listening to her tale, the young Irish girl comments: 'I think the *only divine* fibre in a woman is her maternal instinct.'[94] 'Wedlock' likewise portrays the danger of unfulfilled maternity: when a mother is forcibly separated from her daughter she declines into alcoholism and, after her daughter's death, kills her three stepchildren in revenge. Years before she encountered Freud, Egerton was probing the psychological cost of repression. In her essay on *Keynotes*, she commented: 'If I did not know the technical jargon current today of Freud and his psycho-analysts, I did know something of complexes and inhibitions, repressions and the subconscious impulses that determine actions and reactions. I used them in my stories.'[95]

In 'A Cross Line', however, motherhood is presented as only one of a range of identities open to the heroine and, indeed, until the closing paragraphs, it is her reluctance to mother that is underlined. Repulsed by the baby chicks her husband cherishes, Gipsy strains against the domestic role, imagining herself in turn as a sexually powerful Cleopatra, an Arabian rider, an Oriental dancer. These different fantasies suggest the instability of her self-identity, 'the untamed spirit that dwells in her', as the narrator puts it.[96] Even Gipsy's gender seems nomadic: when her husband remarks that being married to her 'is like chumming with a chap', her reply is, 'Perhaps I was a man last time.'[97]

'A Cross Line' ends on a characteristic Egerton note of sisterhood. Gipsy's maid has in the past borne a child out of wedlock. By revealing her grief over its death, Liz initiates her mistress into the emotions of motherhood. Egerton follows earlier nineteenth-century women writers like Christina Rossetti and Elizabeth Barrett Browning in rejecting society's arbitrary division between respectable and 'fallen' women.[98] Story after story by Egerton probes the reasons behind women's 'fall' in order to challenge society's judgments. When the Irish girl in 'Gone Under' befriends an older 'fallen' woman, both are shunned by the rest of the women on the ship. Behind the woman's 'fall', however, Egerton reveals a story of thwarted maternity. The heroine of 'The Regeneration of Two', previously a rich, spoiled widow, turns her house into a self-sustaining community for unmarried women and their illegitimate children.

'A Cross Line' has a conventional plot– a woman married to a dull man seeks excitement in contemplating an adulterous affair – but within that conventional story line, Egerton uses fantasy and dream sequences to evoke the energy and power of women's feelings and to protest against society's limiting and entrapping roles for women.

CHAPTER FOUR

The modern Irish short story: Moore and Joyce

The Irish Literary Revival returned cultural energy and optimism to Ireland and, though the Revival is mainly associated with drama and poetry, this period was also responsible for beginning the transformation of Irish short fiction into the modern Irish short story. However, as we started to see at the end of the last chapter, it can be argued that the modern Irish short story was being shaped, not, as the Irish Revivalists proclaimed, by the indigenous folk tradition, but by foreign influences, including the Russian writers, Turgenev and Chekhov, the French writers, Flaubert and Maupassant, and, prefiguring James Joyce, Scandinavian writers like Ibsen. The turn of the century debates on the aesthetics of the short story were no doubt a factor in attracting Joyce, a writer unusually alert to international developments, to the form. Joyce believed that Yeats was on the wrong track with his obsession with folk themes, but he did appreciate his stories of the occult addressed to an educated elite: Stephen Hero is so impressed by Yeats' portrayal of wandering magi that he learns by heart 'The Adoration of the Magi' and 'The Tables of the Law',[1] and traces of the card-playing Red Hanrahan have been detected in 'After the Races'.[2] There is a connection, too, with George Moore, who claimed, with uncertain veracity, to have helped Yeats solve a problem with one of his stories in The Secret Rose.[3] Unlikely as it may seem, accustomed as we are to neat divisions between Revival and Counter Revival, in the context of the Irish short story there is a thread of continuity leading from Yeats to Moore and Joyce. The continuity lies, however, not so much in the specific aims and aspirations of the Irish Revival, as in all these writers' dedication to the shape of a story and their openness to foreign influences. Joyce praised Yeats' occult stories for being 'Russian' and, by a telling coincidence, it was the Russian quality of Dubliners that Yeats was later to admire.[4]

What did Irish writers learn from French and Russian writers? From Flaubert they learned the importance of attention to style and to sentence rhythm. From Maupassant, they learned brevity and concentration.

Constrained by the requirements of the newspapers in which he published, Maupassant focused in his stories on a single, revelatory, often life-changing moment that breaks up everyday routine, clearly differing in this from the episodic nature of the nineteenth-century Irish short story in the hands of writers like Griffin and Carleton. Edith Wharton described the short stories of the Russians and the French as combining 'a great closeness of texture with profundity of form. Instead of a loose web spread over the surface of life, they have made it, at its best, a shaft driven straight into the heart of experience.'[5] Rather than plot, Chekhov relied on mood, feeling and tone to achieve unity in his stories and he was not afraid to give his stories anticlimactic endings or ones that simply petered out, in order to convey a sense of life endlessly continuing.

There was a move, too, away from authorial comment. Flaubert's free indirect style presented events through the consciousness of his characters while Chekhov's stories depicted an experience encountered rather than explained, a change from nineteenth-century Irish short fiction where even a writer as skilled as Le Fanu employed an imaginary editor to pull his tales together. A change, too, from the stories of Yeats and Egerton: Chekhov's stories might deal with moments when the veil over reality lifted to reveal a deeper truth, but this truth was never part of a specific message he wished to convey, about the artist in a philistine society or the relations between the sexes; instead, it was portrayed in such a way as to appear to arise organically from the situation of his characters. The necessary objectivity and impartiality of the artist is insisted on by Chekhov in letter after letter on the art of short story writing: 'You see, to depict horse-thieves, in seven hundred lines I must all the time speak and think in their tone and feel in their spirit, otherwise, if I introduce subjectivity, the image becomes blurred.'[6]

Like Flaubert's psychological explorations, Chekhov's revelations of character always occur within a specific social setting and this was something that Irish writers, intent on reflecting Irish experience, could appreciate. Indeed, Valerie Shaw has maintained that the specific socio-historical context of Irish writers' stories permitted them to gain in focus, in comparison with the stories of Katherine Mansfield that often lack force, Shaw argues, because of their indeterminate settings.[7] Charles May pinpoints Chekhov's stories as marking the beginning of a new kind of short fiction precisely because of this combination of 'the specific detail of realism with the poetic lyricism of romanticism'.[8]

Constance Garnett's thirteen volumes of translations of Chekhov appearing between 1916 and 1922 were particularly influential in the

English-speaking world.[9] Chekhov's portrayal of the tedium and philistinism of provincial life and his belief that the everyday provided the best material for fiction were to inspire Frank O'Connor, but it was his style that attracted the modernists. For them his stories, constructed around images and sense impressions and conveying the randomness and open-endedness of life, were perfect vehicles to express the restlessness and fragmentation of the modern age. Maupassant's stories, too, suggested a view of the world that was disjointed, fragmented and partial, and his work, like that of Flaubert and Chekhov, was informed by irony. Irony, complexity, ambiguity and a way of looking at the short story as a self-consciously stylized work of art rather than as a mimetic portrayal of life – all these the Russians and the French bequeathed to Irish short story writers. Greater demands were placed on the reader, who was now required to participate actively in the construction of meaning. However, a caveat must be entered concerning Chekhov's influence on the Irish short story at this stage. Joyce stated that he had not read Chekhov before he wrote *Dubliners*, though he had certainly read Flaubert, Maupassant, Lermontov, Tolstoy, as well as the American writer, Bret Harte,[10] and it was Turgenev who influenced Moore.

The tension between modernity and the past, the local and the foreign in this period is exemplified by the remarkable genesis of George Moore's groundbreaking collection, *The Untilled Field*. As far as foreign influences are concerned, Moore's lengthy residence in Paris during the 1870s acquainted him with the social realism of writers like Balzac, Flaubert and Zola and culminated in his novel in this vein, *Esther Waters* (1894) and the three novellas published as *Celibates* (1895). Subsequently, he moved away from social realism to concentrate on psychological realism, learning much from Flaubert's indirect style of narration.

In 1901 Moore returned to Dublin and went through a period of artistic renewal as he became involved in the Gaelic League and the beginnings of the dramatic movement that would lead in 1904 to the founding of the Abbey Theatre. Richard Cave points to the influence of the theatre in tightening up the dialogue in Moore's fiction during these years.[11] The theatre may also have stimulated Moore's interest in the short story form. A later writer, V. S. Pritchett, discussing his time in Dublin during the civil war, attested to the influence of the Abbey Theatre on his own career as a short story writer: 'In Ireland, there was a link with the Abbey Theatre where they produced a large number of one-act plays . . . such plays are of course a step to the writing of short stories: it's adjacent to it. That was my beginning.'[12]

Even amongst these local influences, the foreign continued to stimulate Moore artistically. Through his relationship with the artist Clara Christian, Moore came to understand the techniques of the impressionist painters – how they captured moments in the flux of time and evoked mood without explanation or judgment, achieving in paint what Chekhov aimed for in his writing. In her study of the short story, Suzanne Ferguson has argued that the modern short story is not a discrete genre at all, but part of the impressionist movement.[13] All these influences, both local and foreign, led Moore to seek to pare away authorial commentary in his writing and replace his previous artifice with suggestion and understatement. He was already on his way to developing a style suited to the modern short story.

The genesis of *The Untilled Field* is described in Moore's autobiography, *Hail and Farewell*. Eager to contribute something to the Gaelic Revival, despite not having Irish himself, Moore proposed that international masterpieces of fiction be translated into Irish for students. However, he was unable to find works that would be acceptable to the Catholic hierarchy, and a Jesuit acquaintance, Father Tom Finlay, suggested that Moore himself should write a work of fiction that could be translated into Irish and published in his brother's Jesuit journal, *The New Ireland Review*. If successful, it could be turned into a school textbook to be used in Irish classes. In accordance with the aims of the Irish Revival, Moore wanted to write on the west of Ireland peasantry, and the librarian, 'John Eglinton', suggested Turgenev's portrayals of Russian peasants as a model.[14]

The social context of Ivan Turgenev's *Sketches from a Hunter's Album* (1852), a collection of observations about the suffering and exploitation of the Russian serfs narrated by a compassionate and intelligent landowner as he moves around the countryside, had particular resonance for Irish readers. Turgenev himself recognized that the exploitation of Russian peasants by a repressive landlord class had an affinity with the Irish situation and he gained some of his inspiration from reading Maria Edgeworth's stories about Ireland. His many evocative descriptions of the Russian landscape chimed in with Irish nationalist feeling for the land. His respect for the lives of the peasants and his portrayal of their intellectual and spiritual potential bear an obvious thematic comparison with the stories of William Carleton. Stylistically they are very different. Turgenev eschews didacticism and proceeds through understatement and suggestion. His stories reflect the rhythms of everyday life and are relatively plotless.

Moore had long been fascinated by Turgenev's work (indeed he had written an essay on him ten years earlier) but until now he had never conceived of him as a literary model. However, the development of his own style under local and foreign influences as described above, meant that he was now open to Turgenev's manner of proceeding through suggestion and evocation. Though Moore's stories present a rural Irish parish that seems unchanged since the stories of Carleton and Mulholland, his literary technique, inspired by Flaubert as well as by Turgenev, moves his stories into the modern period. Through a remarkable intertwining of the local and the foreign, the modern short story was born in Ireland.

The publishing history of the stories that make up *The Untilled Field* likewise reveals a mixture of the local and the international. Father Peter Finlay stipulated that Moore's stories should appear in his *New Ireland Review*, but in the event only three of Moore's stories were published as originally planned in that organ, 'The Wedding Gown', 'The Clerk's Quest' and 'Alms-Giving' appearing at intervals during 1902 in both English and Irish versions. All were revised versions of stories Moore had originally published in English magazines over the previous fourteen years, the earliest, 'The Wedding Gown', appearing in 1887.[15] The revisions were in line with Moore's new preoccupation of modelling himself on Turgenev's respect for the lives he was describing and his manner of suggesting states of mind without authorial commentary. *Hail and Farewell* records Moore's difficulty in finding stories suitable for a school textbook and his partnership with the *New Ireland Review* broke down as his writing became increasingly critical of Catholic Ireland.[16] Several of the other stories in *The Untilled Field* came out in English and American magazines during 1902. Six of them were published in Gaelic translations by Pádraic Ó Súilleabháin and Tadhg Ó Donnchadha in Dublin in 1902 under the title *An t-Úr-Ghort*, prior to the London publication of *The Untilled Field* in 1903.[17] Even after that date, Moore continued to rearrange and revise his collection, most notably omitting 'In the Clay' and 'The Way Back' from subsequent editions until in 1931 he added a new story, 'Fugitives', combining material from these two stories. Moore's uncertainty about how to shape his collection rivals Yeats' and makes Joyce's assuredness in *Dubliners* all the more remarkable.

Often acclaimed as the first modern short story collection in English, *The Untilled Field* displays unevenness in the handling of the short story form. To some extent, this reflects the uncertainties of Turgenev's *Sketches*, which, as the title indicates, vary from sketch to anecdote to fully rounded short stories but which also include the much longer and loosely structured 'The End of Chertopkhanov', as well as a concluding essay on the joys of hunting. Moore's own uncertainty about the short story form is revealed in his doubts about how to classify *The Untilled Field*, referring to it variously as 'a book about Ireland', 'no mere collection of short stories' and even 'A Novel in Thirteen Episodes', thereby conferring a unity on his collection which, in comparison with Joyce's *Dubliners*, it noticeably lacks. The lack of unity in *The Untilled Field* is both thematic and stylistic. Moore's collection omits Turgenev's unifying narrator. It does not confine itself to Irish rural life but also takes in the urban poor, as well as bohemians and artists. In three of the stories – 'Alms-Giving', 'The Wild Goose' and 'Fugitives' – Moore was unable to resist the impulse to didacticism, rendering them stylistically very different from the rest. Rather than an imaginative entering into the life of a blind beggar on the streets of Dublin, as in other stories Moore enters into the lives of the rural poor, 'Alms-Giving' is an account of the educated narrator's changing attitude towards the beggar. It reads less like a short story than an essay challenging Schopenhauer, complete with some final didactic sentences on the necessity of following instinct rather than reason.

Likewise, 'The Wild Goose' is too didactic, and also too lengthy, to qualify as a modern short story along Russian lines, although it does contain some fine lyrical evocations of the Irish countryside reminiscent of Turgenev's descriptions of the Russian landscape. Ned Carmady, returning from America, is so distanced from Irish life that many of his reflections echo the nineteenth-century traveller's stereotypical views of the Irish peasant (filthy, feckless, comic, picturesque). The story fails to put enough distance between the author and his protagonist as Ned, journalist and social reformer, becomes a mouthpiece for Moore's disillusionment with Ireland and his deepening anti-clericalism. In *Hail and Farewell*, he commented:

Each story in the volume entitled *The Untilled Field* had helped me to understand my own country, but it was while writing *The Wild Goose* that it occurred to me for the first time that, it being impossible to enjoy independence of body and soul in Ireland, the thought of every brave-hearted boy is to cry, Now, off with my coat so that I may earn five pounds to take me out of the country.[18]

'Fugitives', an amalgamation of 'In the Clay' and 'The Way Back', also disrupts the thematic and stylistic unity of the collection and for similar reasons. Like Yeats' outcast artists and seers, Moore's sculptor, Rodney, becomes a mouthpiece for the author's views on Ireland, in this case for

Moore's growing conviction that the Catholic clergy would thwart the cultural renaissance he had hoped for in Ireland. Together, 'The Wild Goose' and 'Fugitives' suggest that, abandoned by intellectuals and artists, Ireland's fields will remain untilled.

In addition to this didacticism, echoes of the oral tradition in some of Moore's stories reveal a local influence that disrupts the claims of *The Untilled Field* to be regarded as a unified collection of modern short stories. 'A Play-House in the Waste' contains many elements of the nineteenth-century tale modelled on the oral tradition. In the revised version, the story of Father MacTurnan's scheme to aid his poor rural parish by attempting to establish a play-house is a fireside tale recounted to the community by Pat O'Connor, who has himself heard it from a jarvey: 'As he told us this story, so it is printed in this book.'[19] 'A Play-House in the Waste' opens with a proverbial saying: 'It's a closed mouth that can hold a good story', which leads us into neighbourhood gossip over Father MacTurnan's various schemes to improve the lives of his parishioners. The story moves beyond folk tale in portraying Father MacTurnan as a visionary defeated by the circumstances of Irish life. Overcoming his anti-clericalism, if not his anti-Catholicism, Moore depicts MacTurnan as a tragic figure defeated in his attempt to improve his parishioners' lives by a combination of fate (the wind blows down his play-house), Catholicism (his parishioners' narrow piety is disturbed by the play-house) and superstition (his parishioners' belief that the ghost of Margaret Sheridan's murdered child has returned to haunt them prevents them from restoring the play-house). Moore's portrait of Father Mac-Turnan anticipates Frank O'Connor's description of the modern short story as dealing with alienated individuals, as well as pointing forward to O'Connor's own portraits of solitary priests. Rather than introducing us directly to the thoughts of Father MacTurnan, however, Moore paints the portrait of his priest from the outside, from the point of view of his community, which concludes that 'Father James is a very quare man.'[20] This focus on the community rather than the individual, the references to the jarvey's storytelling abilities, and the dwelling on the absurdities of Irish life, all look back to the nineteenth-century tale rather than pointing forward to the modern short story. The same might be said about the following story, 'Julia Cahill's Curse', where Moore likewise draws on folk material and Irish idiom in a manner that recalls the nineteenth-century tale rather than the modernist short story.

Nevertheless, many of Moore's stories do represent the beginning of the modern Irish short story. The opening story, 'Exile', is carefully controlled, moving adeptly between the outer and inner lives of his characters in a technique Moore borrows from Flaubert rather than from Turgenev. Turgenev's hunting sketches allow the peasants to speak for themselves but their recorded speech is always framed by passages of commentary from the educated narrator and his stories never really enter into the minds of his peasants, hardly surprising given the huge social divide between themselves and the author. By contrast, the opening paragraph of 'Exile' moves directly into the world of Pat Phelan and his two sons, portraying a quiet rural atmosphere akin to that in John McGahern's *That They May Face the Rising Sun*. Father and sons are sensitive of one another's feelings and know each other so well that they often do not need words to communicate: Peter, guessing that his father is in a dilemma as to whom to send with the bullocks to the fair, slips tactfully out of the room to allow James and his father to discuss the problem. As the story unfolds through dialogue between Pat and his sons, with the minimum of authorial comment, the reader has, like Peter, to learn to read the subtext of a conversation where what is left unsaid is often more important than what is voiced. Though the story is ultimately a tragic one of mismatched love and exile, all the characters behave with a quiet decency. Moore controls his anti-clericalism so that even the Reverend Mother behaves honourably in agreeing to release Catherine from the convent. In 'Exile', Yeats' desire for Irish fiction to portray the nobility of the peasant is fulfilled in the context of a modern short story which models itself on Turgenev's respect for the peasantry and adopts Flaubert's technique of entering directly into the minds of his characters.

The following story, 'Homesickness', indicates Moore's attempt to give thematic unity to his collection by continuing the theme of exile. Once again the story conveys the reader directly into the thoughts of the protagonist, James Bryden, who has returned to Ireland after working for thirteen years in America. The story delicately explores the central ironies of the exile's dilemma, namely a longing to return to Ireland, yet his dissatisfaction with Irish society when he does return. Moore's portrait of the exile's eternal restlessness would be picked up and explored by many later Irish short story writers, including Liam O'Flaherty ('The Parting', 'The Letter'), Frank O'Connor ('Darcy in the Land of Youth', 'Ghosts'), Mary Lavin ('Girders') and Edna O'Brien ('Cords'). By contrasting urban life in the United States with Irish rural life, 'Homesickness' vividly encapsulates the tension between modernity and the past, between the international and the local. Bryden's ambivalent state of mind is explored through evocation and suggestion. In its mixture of external details (the

Irish landscape) and psychological states of mind (the landscape alters according to Bryden's mood), 'Homesickness' is truly Chekhovian. Moreover, like many of Chekhov's stories, it tears the veil from the everyday by opening out in the end into a reflection on the universal longing for happiness. Its evocation of the human condition as one of exile and loneliness foreshadows Frank O'Connor's definition of the short story as representing 'the lonely voice'.

The next three stories in the collection, 'Some Parishioners', 'Patchwork' and 'The Wedding Feast', are unlike the modern short story in that they do not stand alone but portray the continuing clash (to which a fourth story, 'The Window', also makes reference) between Father Maguire, a bigoted priest, and his independent-minded parishioner, Kate Kavanagh, who is determined to choose for herself in marriage. Indeed, 'Some Parishioners' was initially intended by Moore to be the first chapter of a novel of that name. At the same time these stories, like the two previous ones, are told through dialogue with a minimum of authorial comment and share the modern short story's eschewal of incident in favour of concentration on the psychology of the characters. But it is Moore's portrayal of the poor old widow, Biddy McHale, first introduced to us in 'Some Parishioners' and then made the protagonist of the fourth story in this series, 'The Window', which most successfully conveys the inner thoughts of his character. 'The Window' gains in resonance by setting Biddy's artistic visions of the stained glass window she wants installed in Father Maguire's church in the context of the portrayal in the preceding three stories of a narrow-minded and materialistic rural society where even marriage is subject to economics. Through controlled use of irony and a careful manipulation of the tragi-comic tone, 'The Window' gives an imaginative insight into the visions of a simple peasant woman, in which she becomes completely absorbed by the sounds and colours evoked by her window, in a way that recalls Félicité's visions in Flaubert's short story, 'Un coeur simple'. Moore's poor widow succeeds, where Father MacTurnan had failed, in using art, albeit in an entirely conventional form, to transcend the constrictions of Irish rural society.

'The Wedding Gown' also centres on the consciousness of a woman, that of the young Molly O'Dwyer, and her gradual awakening, through tending to her aged great-aunt, Margaret Kirwin, to awareness of her own mortality. Molly's central epiphany, 'Yes, she is like me. I shall be like that some day if I live long enough',[21] is achieved with the minimum of authorial commentary. Like John McGahern's 'Oldfashioned', 'The

Wedding Gown' works from the external (the introduction of the O'Dwyer family, their relationship with the Big House, Margaret's past life) before gradually closing in to focus on Molly, initially through dialogue between her mother and Margaret, and then in the quickening rhythms of Molly's thoughts as she runs back home with the premonition that her great-aunt has died. 'The Wedding Gown' is the earliest story, published in 1887, but substantially revised by Moore so that both Molly's epiphany and Margaret's thoughts as she lies dying are beautifully understated.

'The Clerk's Quest' is another skilfully controlled story that manages to avoid mawkishness and sentimentality as we enter into a clerk's dreams of love for Henrietta Brown. The rural setting of the previous stories is exchanged for a Joycean urban lower-middle class milieu where the clerk, Edward Dempsey, has become trapped in a life of narrow routine. Moore's ending is more optimistic than the stories in Joyce's *Dubliners*, however, for, like Biddy McHale, Edward transcends the constraints of his life through his visions of love, to which he remains true, regardless of material considerations. He is rewarded with an ending that is almost Wildean in tone.

The Irish version of *The Untilled Field* seems to have caused relatively little stir. The English version was reviewed in London, Paris and New York but its stylistic originality passed largely unnoticed by contemporary readers, who tended to focus on Moore's pessimistic portrayal of Ireland rather on stylistics, though the *New York Times* (29 August 1903) praised its 'excellence of literary form' while disputing the label 'short story collection' for what it described as 'hardly more than detached incidents without formal beginning or ending'. In the modern period, Moore's volume has been hailed as a landmark for the modern Irish short story, though only some of the stories in *The Untilled Field* fit this definition. The collection may more appropriately be seen as a transitional volume, employing some traditional techniques while at the same time developing the sophistication of the Irish short story form through psychological insight, concision, allusiveness and understatement. A story like 'So on He Fares' perfectly illustrates the blend of old and new in Moore's collection. It is at once a psychological study of a child's awareness of his rejection by his mother and a folk tale in which the boy is saved from drowning by a bargeman, finds a substitute mother and embarks on a quest for adventure.

It may be that it was such lingering traces of the folk tale, together with the didacticism of stories like 'The Wild Goose' and 'Fugitives', which led Joyce to speak critically of *The Untilled Field,* calling it 'very dull and flat indeed: and ill-written'.[22] Or perhaps his criticisms were due to artistic rivalry: Joyce had already produced versions of three of the stories in *Dubliners* by the time *The Untilled Field* was published and he may have had a sense that his desired position, as an Irish writer influenced by developments in European literature, had already been taken by Moore.[23] Moore, however, did not continue his experiment with the modern Irish short story along Russian and French lines. *A Storyteller's Holiday* (1918), on which James Stephens collaborated, is a fictional autobiography featuring a storytelling contest between Moore and a *seanchaí*, during which Moore marries the folk tale with modernist stream-of-consciousness in a prolonged meditation on storytelling. *Celibate Lives* (1927), a revised version of *Celibates* (1895) and *In Single Strictness* (1922), is a collection of psychological tales of unequal length exploring lives lived outside heterosexual marriage. The best of them, 'Alfred Nobbs' (a striking tale of cross-dressing) and 'Sarah Gwynn', recall the realism of *Esther Waters* by portraying the constraints of women's lives as they struggle against poverty. If Joyce did at this point feel he had something to fear from Moore's achievement in the Irish short story, he was soon to surpass him.

Unlike many of the short story collections in this study, *Dubliners* has attracted a substantial body of criticism deriving from virtually all branches of literary theory. There have been structuralist readings,[24] poststructuralist readings drawing on Derrida and Lacan,[25] psychoanalytical interpretations,[26] Freudian readings,[27] postmodernist readings,[28] feminist readings,[29] cultural materialist readings[30] and postcolonial readings.[31] Such has been the ingeniousness of some of the interpretations of *Dubliners* that it has sometimes seemed as if these short, beautifully crafted stories by a writer still in his twenties have been all but buried under the weight of critical interpretation.[32]

Compared with Joyce's Irish predecessors in the short story form, *Dubliners* was an innovation: never before had there been such an artistically unified collection, nor one that in matters of style so clearly broke with the Gaelic tradition of storytelling. Yet *Dubliners* is not entirely without links to other Irish writing. The theme of the fragility of identity recalls Le Fanu, a writer whom Joyce admired, while the publishing history of the collection is linked to the Irish Revival. Early versions of three of the stories, 'The Sisters', 'Eveline' and 'After the Races', appeared in AE's *The Irish Homestead*, a context which in itself may have led his first readers to underestimate Joyce's originality in handling the short story form. Joyce also owed more to George Moore than he admitted, borrowing from Moore for the final part of 'The Dead'[33] and reworking

Moore's story of Edward Dempsey, Dublin clerk, in 'Counterparts'.[34] Nevertheless, in many respects Joyce's genius makes him look like an anomaly in the history of the development of the Irish short story. Years after the publication of *Dubliners*, writers like Daniel Corkery, Frank O'Connor and Seán O'Faoláin wrote realist stories that continued to be influenced to a greater or lesser extent by the oral tradition and lacked the unity, patterning and allusiveness of Joyce's collection. It was as if *Dubliners* had never existed. In many ways, O'Connor wished it had not and his suspicions of Joyce's achievement are outlined in *The Lonely Voice*.[35] With the exception of Samuel Beckett and Elizabeth Bowen, who, unlike her friend Virginia Woolf, never underestimated Joyce, it took several decades for Joyce's influence on the Irish short story to permeate. 'It took me years to identify Joyce's technique and describe it with any care, and by that time I realized that it was useless for any purpose of my own,' confessed O'Connor.[36] Later, O'Faoláin was to regret that they had not taken account of Joyce earlier. Not till we get to John McGahern's stories in the 1970s and 1980s do we find an Irish writer adopting Joyce's method of unifying a collection through symbolism, and handling language in a way that gestures beyond the framework of the form so that what is said is only part of the story.

Joyce himself, in a letter to his brother Stanislaus in 1905 outlining the pattern of his book, signalled the thematic and stylistic originality of *Dubliners*. It was to consist of stories about childhood followed by stories about, respectively, adolescence, maturity and public life, all set in the context of life in Dublin, a city that, he explained to his English publisher, Grant Richards, with more enthusiasm than accuracy, 'I do not think any writer has yet presented to the world'.[37] Both in terms of subject matter and unity of arrangement, *Dubliners* was to be unique. Too unique in some respects, for Grant Richards took fright at Joyce's realism in sexual matters and, although most of the stories were completed by 1905 and all by 1907, it was not until 1914 that *Dubliners* saw the light of day.[38] In the meantime, the Dublin publishing house, Maunsel and Company, had got as far as printing the text, only to destroy it at the last moment due to fears of libel action. The casual treatment of this groundbreaking work of literature is reflected in an anecdote told by an employee in Maunsel and Company, Joseph Hone. In 1908 Hone was given a manuscript of *Dubliners* 'written out in cheap notebooks in a copperplate hand that would have won for a schoolboy a prize in calligraphy' and for a month or two he left it lying around at home while he anguished over the references in 'Ivy Day' to Edward VII's private life.[39]

From Joyce's description, readers might expect to find a collection of short stories depicting in realist fashion the life of Dublin's citizens at the turn of the century. In one sense they would be right. *Dubliners* is deeply embedded in the historical fabric of Dublin: 'Araby' refers to a bazaar held in Dublin in 1894, 'A Mother' incorporates a concert that took place in 1904. In the Dubliners' wanderings around the city, they are shadowed by the monuments of the British colonial administration. Writing, like Moore, against the romantic nationalism of the Celtic Revival, Joyce portrays the reality of living in a decaying, depressed colonial backwater, 'an Ireland frozen in servitude' as Declan Kiberd calls it, 'a place of copied and derived gestures, whose denizens were turned outward to serve a distant source of authority in London'.[40] Stories of poverty, drunkenness, emigration and general lethargy reflect the enervation of Ireland after the Famine. The theme owes much to the influence of Ibsen's social realism and has been given fresh emphasis in the postcolonial readings of critics like Vincent Cheng, David Spurr and Luke Gibbons.

Dubliners is very far from being confined to a realist text, however. The figure of the 'gnomon' meaning, amongst other things, an incomplete parallelogram that, along with 'paralysis' and 'simony', so fascinates the young boy in the opening story, 'The Sisters', has been taken by many critics to be an organizing motif for the whole collection. If the gnomon has thematic relevance to the characters' lives in this decaying colonial city as thwarted and incomplete, it has even greater bearing on the style of the collection. *Dubliners* extends Moore's method of operating through suggestion and implication, using ellipses, hiatuses and silences in a way that obliges the reader to become an essential part of the equation in order to complete the story's meaning. The subject becomes decentred in a manner characteristic of modernism, or even postmodernism, and the gaps in the discourse demand that the reader work to supply the meaning of the incomplete parallelogram: another meaning of 'gnomon' is judge or interpreter. This participation of the reader in constructing the meaning of the text marks Joyce's break with the didacticism of nineteenth-century short fiction.[41]

Joyce enters directly into the thoughts of his characters by use of the free indirect style borrowed, like Moore's, from Flaubert, but extending beyond Moore's use of it to produce a text that is unstable. In 'Clay', where the character of Maria is entirely created through a simple, naïve style that echoes her simple-mindedness, the smooth surface of the story is undermined by the reader's recognition that what Maria is constantly suppressing is an awareness of her own marginality.[42] The instability of the surface text is signalled in the opening story, 'The Sisters', where the title disrupts the reader's expectations when the eponymous sisters turn out to be more peripheral than it suggests. L. J. Morrissey has outlined the metamorphosis of 'The Sisters' from a readerly narrative in the first version published in the *Irish Homestead* in August 1904 to the writerly narrative of *Dubliners*.[43] In the course of this process one might say that the modern Irish short story finally came to birth. Characters and plot are now implied, rather than stated, and the reader must work to supply the meaning. Subsequently, some of Joyce's readers, generally reading back from *Ulysses* and *Finnegans Wake*, were to take full advantage of their part of the equation to develop mythical and symbolic interpretations of the stories that verged, in their elaborations, on the absurd.[44] They had clearly not attended to Joyce's warning in his first story of the danger of investing an incident (here, the breaking of the chalice) with too much symbolic importance. Joyce's reliance on puns, ellipses and an ambivalence that disrupts the surface meaning of his text means that any single reading inevitably reduces the range of possibilities inherent in his stories.[45] Consequently the aim in a historical survey such as this must be to resist any kind of definitive summing up and simply indicate some of the varieties of ways in which individual stories have been interpreted, hoping to stay true to the overall unity of the collection that Joyce intended his readers to experience.

In limiting the narrator's consciousness in the first three stories by his youth, arguably the same youth in all three stories, Joyce provided the reader with a key as to how to approach his collection. In 'The Sisters', the young boy does not understand why Father Flynn's death gives him such a feeling of freedom, being only dimly aware that the religion the priest has taught him is narrow and ritualistic. It is the reader who supplies the indictment of a society that offers a sensitive young boy no greater choice than that between the hearty outdoor masculine pursuits advocated by his uncle, and the arid, stifling religion espoused by Father Flynn. It is the reader who interprets (or perhaps over-interprets) the priest's acknowledgment of paedophiliac desire in the boy's dream and who makes the link, explicit in the first version of this story, between Father Flynn's paralysis and tertiary syphilis. In this first story Joyce is guiding the reader into the way in which his stories should be read, while introducing key themes of the collection. Through the ellipses and hesitations in the conversation between the boy's aunt and the priest's sister, the paralysis of Dublin society is introduced. Linear time, in which all Joyce's Dubliners will be trapped, is emphasized in the first paragraph, while Father Flynn's paralysis introduces another leitmotif of the collection, namely, the close connection between the living and the dead. However, despite Joyce's guidance for the reader, 'The Sisters' remains one of the most mysterious stories in *Dubliners*. Writing in 1962, Frank O'Connor commented: 'The point of it still eludes me.'[46] The reader's uncertainty and confusion at the end of this first story is a preparation for reading the collection as a whole, where suspension rather than closure is to be the keynote and where in the final story the uncertainty becomes metaphysical.

'The Sisters' has given rise to readings that are biographical (Joyce discarding the notion of becoming a priest), feminist (the title focuses attention on the two sisters), and postcolonial (the boy's dreams of escape from the priest's stifling attentions to the exotic Orient are proleptic of the theme of the Orient throughout the collection as a place of imagined liberation and licence for the European self). Marian Eide accounts for the title through yet another meaning of 'gnomon', namely the upright marker of the sundial that casts a shadow.[47] In this reading, Father Flynn becomes the solid parallelogram of masculinity casting a shadow over his sisters' lives. The equation of solidity with masculinity is reinforced by the uncle's insistence that the narrator must learn to 'box his corner'. If masculinity is the restored parallelogram, women, like Eve formed out of Adam's rib, are the piece that is missing. Yet it is this missing piece that the title deliberately highlights. For Eide, the title reflects Joyce's desire to throw light on hitherto neglected lives: here, two Dublin spinsters, figures traditionally invisible and taken for granted, yet who have provided the environment that nurtures their brother. Florence Walzl has revealed the accuracy of Joyce's depictions of Irish women's restricted lives during this period, when employment opportunities were severely limited and marriages were relatively few and late.[48] Eide's reading of 'The Sisters' through the lens of feminist theory allows for one possible explanation of the title. Feminist and postcolonial readings come together in Vincent Cheng's suggestion that the boy's imagined Persia represents not only the orientalized other of Western imagination but the feminized self, which is suppressed in this very patriarchal, Catholic society.[49]

There is perhaps room, even in the crowded field of critical interpretations of *Dubliners*, for an extension of a feminist reading that may be pertinent to other stories in this collection. It was a phrase from Joyce, 'Father's time, mother's species', that inspired Julia Kristeva to develop her notion of the father's time as linear.[50] Reversing the process to read Joyce in the light of Kristeva, we may see Nannie's deafness, foreshadowing Queenie's in Bowen's 'Summer Night', as indicating how little she counts in the symbolic order. The sisters' tangential position in relation to the symbolic order of language is demonstrated when they require Father O'Rourke's aid to insert the death notice. Eliza's difficulties with language are highlighted in her references to the '*Freeman's General*' and 'rheumatic wheels'. It is interesting to speculate to what extent Moore's portraits of female characters in *The Untilled Field* influenced Joyce, particularly, in the context of this story, the marginalized Biddy.[51] Unlike Biddy, however, whose semiotic visions inspired by her stained glass window enable her to evade Father Maguire's control, Joyce's two sisters are powerless to articulate their perceptions of another world. Nannie retreats into silence and Eliza, despite her shrewdness, remains trapped in superstition and uncertainty. If the semiotic possesses the potential for inaugurating change, these two sisters show no sign of being able to evolve into Kristeva's 'truth outside time'. Nevertheless they signal a theme that will be taken up later in the collection, namely the possibility that in this masculinized society, women have access to a world beyond language and the everyday denied to men, and that that world is the missing part of the parallelogram in *Dubliners*: 'the other (sex) that torments and possesses him' is Kristeva's description of the repressed feminine of Western culture as it emerges in the work of male modernists.[52]

In the following two stories, the youthful narrator's quest for adventure turns sour and ends with sudden, bitter comments on his own nature. By the third story, 'Araby', the first readers of Joyce would have become aware that in contrast with earlier Irish collections of short fiction, with the possible exception of Yeats, they were encountering an author unusually attentive to patterning. The mention of the dead priest and the image of the chalice used to symbolize the narrator's romantic fantasies echo 'The Sisters', while his boyish games and snobbish wish to distinguish himself from 'the rough tribes from the cottages' recall 'An Encounter'.[53] Building on a suggestion in 'The Sisters', 'Araby' depicts the Orient as the focus of the narrator's romanticized desire for the feminine other in contrast with the paralysed masculinity of Dublin life. Recalling the orientalism of Egerton's 'A Cross Line', the semiotic enchantment of the word 'Araby' casts its spell over the narrator, but the boy's sensual and emotional wakening to another world through the attractions of Mangan's sister, foreshadowing Gabriel's emotional awakening through Gretta in 'The Dead', ends in a sense of shame. Observing the cheap flirtation between two Englishmen and an English female stallholder at the bazaar, the boy realizes that his idealized chivalric love masks only lust. If women are to hold the key for him to a world beyond the symbolic order, he will have to dismantle his idealizations of them. 'Araby' unpacks the mechanism of male idealizations of women: Mangan's sister remains the missing part of the parallelogram, a blank page on which the narrator writes his romantic and chivalric longings. The girl's surname recalls James Clarence Mangan's idealizations of Ireland as a young girl in his poetry. In Joyce, Ireland is not the Dark Rosaleen, however, but 'a cheap flirt selling her wares and her self for the coins of strangers'.[54] As the boy must abandon his idealization of women, so Joyce's fellow countrymen would have to relinquish Revivalist writers' idealizations about Ireland if they were to see the truth of themselves in his 'nicely polished looking-glass'.[55]

These opening three stories of childhood reveal a world that offers so little to the young narrator that he is constantly seeking ways to escape and yet that world gradually closes in on him until all his dreams of escape end in frustration. The boy's realization of the extent to which he has become implicated in the corrupt ideologies of the adult world marks the end of childhood. Henceforth the stories will be told in the third person, for their older protagonists have already become trapped by Dublin's paralysis.

The following four stories were intended by Joyce to denote adolescence, not in the chronological sense, but in accordance with the classical Latin meaning of someone who has not yet achieved maturity. The paralysis of the eponymous heroine of 'Eveline' is clearly indicated in the opening description, where she is seated at the window inhaling 'the odour of dusty cretonne',[56] a phrase repeated later in the story. The dust has been read as a metonym for Eveline's dead mother, who has become dust but whose presence remains pervasive in Eveline's life.[57] Joyce's story of a woman who, like so many of the women who were to feature in later writing by Irish women, desires to escape Ireland in order to avoid repeating her mother's thwarted life, clearly lends itself to being read through a feminist lens. On one level, there is little sense of liberation, for it is the internalized mother's voice that reminds her daughter of her duty to serve the family. The story portrays Eveline as trapped between two different versions of the patriarchy – her father's parsimony and brutality (reflecting so many of the fathers and husbands in this collection) and Frank's possible immorality.[58] Lacking subjectivity, she risks being defined solely in terms of the men to whom she belongs and her blankness at the end suggests that she will repeat her mother's self-sacrificing and self-effacing life. Like Nannie and Eliza in the first story, Eveline is the invisible piece of the parallelogram on which the patriarchy relies in order to function properly.

However, drawing on Lacanian theory, Garry Leonard has provided a different interpretation, focusing on the second memory Eveline has of her mother, not the patriarchal mother who demands she keep the family home together, but the mother who died babbling 'Deveraun Seraun! Deveraun Seraun!' This mother represents the buried mother of the patriarchy, described in the writing of Hélène Cixous and Luce Irigaray, whose strange semiotic babble indicates to her daughter a knowledge that cannot be inscribed in the patriarchy.[59] Leonard sees the text as resisting the masculine epiphanies of the preceding two stories and in the final scene inscribing Eveline as unknowable, her *jouissance* elsewhere, outside the framework of Frank's comprehension, to whom her expression appears simply as a blank. In this interpretation, foreshadowing the portrayal of Gretta in 'The Dead', Eveline and her mother experience a world of female desire beyond the patriarchy that can only dimly be glimpsed in the symbolic world of language and culture.

The following three stories lend themselves to postcolonial readings. 'After the Race', generally acknowledged to be the weakest story in the collection, moves into the world of the wealthy upper classes and portrays Dubliners who, in their depressed condition, are too easily impressed by Continentals, particularly the French, a reference perhaps to French aid in Irish nationalist struggles of the past. The next two stories of adolescence, 'Two Gallants' and 'The Boarding House', reveal how Dublin's depressed economic climate affects both men and women as Joyce balances two males' exploitation of a servant girl in the first story against the scheming of a mother and daughter to trap an available bachelor into marriage in the second. The long shadow of colonial exploitation is evident in the desperate and base stratagems of the mostly unemployed Lenehan and Corley to scrape together some money in a city dominated by the Ascendancy buildings that form a background to the two gallants' wanderings.[60] In postcolonial readings, Irish national identity becomes the missing part of the parallelogram, illustrated by the gold coin with the British sovereign's head that the servant girl, at Corley's bidding, steals from her employer. As Ireland was forced to pay in taxes for a colonial relationship imposed upon it, so the skivvy is manoeuvred into paying for her own seduction. A feminist reading, on the other hand, might note that what is missing here is the story of the silent servant girl who, like Eveline and Mangan's sister, is objectified and preyed upon by males.

In 'The Boarding House', Mrs Mooney is, like Corley and Lenehan, teetering on the edge of respectability. Separated from her alcoholic husband and with her boarding house gathering an unsavoury reputation, Mrs Mooney is understandably anxious, given the limited opportunities available to women at that time, to marry off her daughter and therefore allows Polly 'the run of the young men'.[61] The discovery that one of them is sufficiently naïve to have compromised himself with Polly precipitates Mrs Mooney into action. Dublin's depressed economic climate is on her side, for she calculates correctly that Mr Doran, who has a respectable job with a Catholic wine-merchant, cannot afford to jeopardize his situation by having sexual impropriety attached to his name. Mrs Mooney may be seen as a woman who, unlike many of the other female characters in *Dubliners*, has succeeded in gaining a certain independence and control over her life to the extent that she is able to manipulate the male gaze to her advantage.[62] This comes, however, at the cost of colluding with the patriarchy, and her treatment of marriage as a business transaction represents an approach to love that Joyce in *Stephen Hero* characterizes as moral 'simony'.[63] Accustomed to dealing with moral problems 'as a cleaver deals with meat', Mrs Mooney has forfeited any access to that other world beyond the symbolic order to which some of the female characters in *Dubliners* have access. The point is underlined in the portrayal of Polly, a 'little perverse madonna'[64] who, it is suggested, seduced her mother's celibate lodger and is well aware of her mother's machinations. Polly's semiotic musings come to an abrupt end when her mother, having concluded her negotiations, calls her downstairs. Compliance with the patriarchy cuts off Polly's access to any other world.

The following stories of maturity are lengthier than those in the previous group, allowing Joyce, in a technique adopted from Flaubert, to explore in greater depth the inner consciousness of his characters in styles appropriate to each. 'A Little Cloud', like 'Two Gallants', portrays a weak, immature male, Little Chandler, attracted by a more ebullient friend, Ignatius Gallaher. Like the boy in 'Araby', Little Chandler substitutes for genuine escape a cheap exoticism in which the Orient features as the unknown other, filled with the sensuous delights from which his job and his marriage exclude him. His melancholy meditations on his unachieved life as a poet give Joyce the opportunity to satirize the poetasters of the Celtic Twilight. Little Chandler's reverie is so romanticized and self-interested that he hardly notices the slum children moving like vermin beneath his feet. He returns to his lowly home and vents his frustration by yelling at his baby in the same way as Farrington at the end of the following story, 'Counterparts', expresses his rage by beating his son. By contrast, Annie's calming babble to soothe the child expresses an emotional truth from which Little Chandler with his half-baked literary pretensions is exiled. As in 'Eveline', there is a suggestion that Annie has access to a world beyond language and the everyday denied to men. As in 'Two Gallants', it is the reader who is left to supply Annie's missing story of domestic entrapment.

If 'A Little Cloud' is recounted in a wistful, poetic tone recording the shifts in Little Chandler's mood from melancholy to admiration to envy to rebellion and then remorse, 'Counterparts', as befits the central character, employs a more robust style. The slang, the curses and generally vigorous masculine style reflect Farrington's character as much as the repeated use of 'nice' sums up Maria in 'Clay'. Farrington searches for the maternal in the illusory comforts of a warm pub where, like Little Chandler and Maria, he tries to disguise to himself the fact of his own insignificance. Trevor Williams' Marxist reading of this story sets this insignificance in the wider political context of Ireland's colonized state, arguing that the ending portrays Farrington reproducing in the domestic sphere the counterpart of the oppressions he himself has suffered in public from, consecutively, his Northern Irish employer, a London lady and an English arm wrestler.[65]

Like Moore's 'The Window', 'Clay' may owe something to Flaubert's portrayal of the consciousness of the servant woman, Félicité, in his short story, 'Un coeur simple'. Joyce goes further, though, than Moore in penetrating the consciousness of his character. 'Clay' is a perfectly finished example of Joyce's gnomic style, the seemingly objective third person narration describing Maria only in terms she herself would use. As Margot Norris' perceptive reading makes clear, 'Clay' reveals how much may be left out of a narrative yet still understood by the reader, as Maria tries to gloss over the disappointments in her life in order to present a surface appearance of happiness.[66]

Maria's disappointments are obvious to the reader. Her difficulty, as a small, impoverished spinster, in getting herself noticed is underlined by her emphasis on those few occasions when people do single her out. Her thwarted maternity is suggested when she allows the drunken man on the train to assume that she has children. Her pain at remaining unmarried is implied by her instinctive avoidance of the second verse from Balfe's aria, 'I Dreamt that I Dwelt in Marble Halls'. The aria itself expresses Maria's sense of class displacement. Despite Maria's insistence that she has refused Joe's offer of a home, doubts are raised in the reader's mind about the sincerity of that offer when we know that she has ended up as a scullery maid in a Protestant institution for reformed prostitutes and alcoholics, a setting which undermines, as Norris points out, Maria's genteel presentation of herself. Maria's thwarted desires for a home, for social status, for the significance of being wife and mother, chime in with patriarchy's relegation to the margins of the woman who does not fit in with the prescribed female role. 'Clay' demonstrates that someone regarded by the symbolic order as of no significance does not thereby automatically have the consolation of access to that other world beyond the symbolic. Maria's constant insistence on her own significance reveals a temperament as ego-bound as any of the male characters: her initial choice of the saucer of clay, a portent of death in Halloween games, is marked by a sudden pause in the narrative, underlining Maria's fear of the final dissolution of the self in death. Full of illusions and psychological repressions, Maria's narrative illustrates a capitulation to the patriarchy that blocks off access to the semiotic as effectively as the knowing collusion practised by Mrs Mooney.

If Maria is excluded from the life she desires, Mr Duffy in 'A Painful Case' excludes himself through intellectual pride, living at a Nietzschean distance from his fellow citizens. His high-minded contempt for the life around him has killed, it is implied, any artistic or intellectual endeavour he may have been capable of, a theme underlined by the manuscript of Hauptmann's *Michael Kramer* that lies on his desk.[67] Though Duffy feels he has found his soul's companion in Mrs Sinico, who provides a silent and admiring mirror for his narcissism, he takes alarm when, in a moment of sympathy, she expresses her feelings by taking hold of his hand and pressing it to her cheek. Like other male Dubliners, Duffy cannot cope with the expression of female subjectivity. Unlike previous protagonists, though, Duffy does achieve a brief moment of insight. The newspaper account of Mrs Sinico's death jolts him out of his self-absorption and in a moment of empathy, before the walls of solitude close around him once more, he has an insight into her state of mind: 'Why had he withheld life from her? Why had he sentenced her to death? He felt his moral nature falling to pieces.'[68] Duffy's repression of the body and the life of the emotions caused him to reject Mrs Sinico's maternal world, represented by her room where the couple sit in the dark, united by the concert music still echoing in their ears. His moment of empathy leads him to an awareness of another world beyond the symbolic and this is also marked by sound, that of the goods train that connects with Mrs Sinico's death. As the rhythm of the engine passes away, however, so does his insight. Nonetheless, Duffy's momentary clear-sightedness paves the way for Gabriel's more penetrating vision, prompted by empathy with Gretta, at the end of 'The Dead'.

In the following three stories of public life the narrative style, as befits their subject, is distanced and impersonal with only occasional forays into the consciousness of the characters. 'Ivy Day in the Committee Room', Joyce's depiction of Dublin political life, proceeds almost entirely through dialogue and external description of the characters. The tone is largely satirical, highlighting the absence of ideas and the petty self-interest of the speakers, who are chiefly concerned with whether they will get paid for their canvassing. When we do get a glimpse into the thoughts of one of them, Mr Crofton, we discover that they are a mixture of blankness and contempt for his fellow canvassers. 'Ivy Day' aptly conveys Joyce's belief that everything had gone downhill in Irish politics after Parnell, whose absence dominates the story, as the absent Michael Furey will dominate 'The Dead'. The satire is complicated and deepened by the genuine pathos of Hynes' sentimental poem on 'The Death of Parnell', based on Joyce's own juvenile composition, which momentarily silences the speakers. Crofton's condescending and erroneous comment that it is 'a very fine piece of writing' prepares us for Joyce's attack on Dublin's second-rate artistic life in the following story, 'A Mother'.

The portrayal of Dublin's artistic circles in 'A Mother' picks up the theme of the commercial self-interest underlying Dublin's public life and points forward to the following story, 'Grace', where even Dublin's religious life is revealed as corrupted by materialism and worldliness. In critical readings of 'A Mother', the tendency has been for critics to focus on its echoes of previous stories – Mrs Kearney's manipulations on behalf of her daughter recalling 'The Boarding House', the materialism underlying the pretensions of the Irish Revival recalling Little Chandler's self-interested daydreams. Jane Miller's feminist reading places the story in its historical and cultural context as only secondarily a satire on the cultural pretensions of the Irish Revival movement, but first and foremost a study of a woman venturing outside the domestic sphere to interact with men in a business setting.[69] Mrs Kearney is motivated both by the need to establish her daughter in the public eye so that she achieves either a career or a husband, and by her own romantic dreams, which she has not quite relinquished. Her romanticism, like that of other Dubliners, comes up against the realities of Dublin life, namely the inferior quality of the city's artistic life and the fact that men control access to the public sphere. Mrs Kearney is caught in a double bind by her society's gender prescriptions: she needs to speak up for her daughter's rights but knows that a lady should never complain in public. When she does, Mr Holohan's insult effectively silences her, turning her into 'an angry stone image' that recalls Eveline's blankness. It becomes clear that women are the missing piece of the parallelogram in these stories of Dublin's public life: 'A Mother' portrays the artistic world as one to which women may have entry only if they stay in the background and conform to the code prescribed for 'a lady'; in 'Ivy Day', women are conspicuous by their absence; and in 'Grace', Dublin's ecclesiastical world is portrayed as an opportunity for male bonding, leaving Mrs Kernan marginalized, her religion confined to the domestic sphere.

If Joyce's collection had ended with 'Grace', as he originally intended, there would have been a certain balance between the opening story (religion in its private aspect as ritual and superstition) and the closing story (the public aspect of religion dominated by social respectability), but the picture of Dublin would have been bleak. Using a variety of comic styles – satire, social comedy, farce – the three final stories indict the politics, culture and religion of Dublin life as shallow, materialistic and hypocritical. Moreover, if the collection had ended here, the world of women would have remained almost entirely submerged: from Nannie and Eliza, to Mangan's sister, to Eveline and Annie Chandler and the servant girl in 'The Two Gallants', their stories would have stayed largely untold. Or where they are told (Maria, Mrs Mooney, Mrs Kearney), belong to women who reflect, or are defeated by, the patriarchal system. Set against this, Mr Duffy's moment of empathy with the world of Mrs Sinico seems very slight indeed.

However, in exile in Italy, Joyce began to feel that he had been too severe on his fellow countrymen, writing to his brother, Stanislaus: 'Sometimes thinking of Ireland it seems to me that I have been unnecessarily harsh. I have reproduced (in *Dubliners* at least) none of the attraction of the city for I have never felt at my ease in any city since I left it except in Paris. I have not reproduced its ingenuous insularity and its hospitality.'[70] Accordingly, he added as appendix to his collection a story that develops the notion of a world beyond the symbolic to which women, especially, have access. 'The Dead' combines both the public and private aspects of the previous stories, while moving Joyce closer to finding the voice of Leopold Bloom. In length and number of characters already a novella rather than a short story, 'The Dead' shows Joyce straining to express more than the form can contain. Writing to the secretary of the Royal Literary Fund in the hope of securing a grant for Joyce, Yeats noted: 'his book of short stories *Dubliners* has the promise of a great novelist and a great novelist of a new kind'.[71]

Though we have detected forerunners of Joyce's modernism in the stories of Yeats, Egerton and Moore, with these authors the reader often has the impression that their visions of Irish life are dictating the story, whereas Joyce's artistry in the short story form is such that his vision, like Chekhov's, arises organically from an often sordid and grim reality. In *Dubliners*, the reader does not need to be told the point of a story; s/he experiences it directly. The unity of the collection derives from its patterning rather than from its subject matter, leading to Joyce's paradoxical achievement of aesthetic unity in a collection reflecting so many fragmented lives. If he had never written another word after *Dubliners*, Joyce's contribution to Irish, and indeed world, literature through the development of the short story into an art form would still have been enormous. He transformed the Irish short story through his adaptation of tone, style and form to the character of his protagonists, his use of patterning, epiphany and symbols, his intertextuality and his 'writerly' texts that compel the reader's active participation in determining meaning. The irony is that for many years, Irish short story writers failed to get to grips with his achievement and went on writing short stories as if Joyce had never happened.

One obvious factor in this neglect was the eventual date of publication, 1914, by which time the world had other things on its mind. Four hundred and ninety-nine copies of *Dubliners* were sold in 1914, one below the number when Joyce could start to earn royalties, and in the first six months of 1915 only twenty-six were sold.[72] In a letter to Harriet Weaver, dated July 1916, Joyce complained that *Dubliners* had sold only seven copies in the preceding six months.[73] The efforts of Joyce's earliest supporters, like Ezra Pound, who was eager to disassociate Joyce from the Irish Literary Revival and promote him as a European writer (and even Pound thought *Dubliners* uneven), may also have played some part in this neglect by Irish writers. By 1914 also, *A Portrait of the Artist as a Young Man*, serialized in *The Egoist*, had begun to attract notice and for many years critical attention focused on Joyce's use of the novel form. Ignoring the implications of Joyce's modernist experiments, the Irish short story of the following decades turned back on itself and attempted to pin down the realism that had, by and large, eluded it in the nineteenth century.

READING: JAMES JOYCE

James Joyce, 'The Dead' (1914)

Despite the fact that 'The Dead' was not part of Joyce's original conception for his collection, the parallels between it and earlier stories in
Dubliners are numerous: the elderly Misses Morkan recall the two sisters
of the opening story, Aunt Julia's inappropriate song about bridal love
echoes Maria's song in 'Clay', the dinner table discussion of religion
recalls the errors of the speakers in 'Grace', and the portrait of Miss Ivors
extends Joyce's satire on the Celtic Revival found in 'A Little Cloud' and
'A Mother'. As in the preceding stories, Dublin's artists are portrayed as
second rate (Mr D'Arcy's voice is hoarse, Mary Jane's playing is too
academic) and women are excluded from public life (the Pope's dismissal
of women from church choirs is discussed). Gabriel's sense that he and
Gretta are about to embark on 'a new adventure'[74] recalls the youthful
protagonists of 'An Encounter' and 'Araby'. However, 'The Dead' far
extends the technique of the other stories in its exploration of Gabriel's
consciousness and his relationship with Gretta.

In 'The Dead' Joyce perfected his technique of moving flexibly from
external narration into the thoughts of his protagonist. The story opens
with the narrator's emphasis on the ritual nature of the Misses Morkan's
annual dance. It is the voice of someone who has clearly known the
Morkans a long time and shares the class-consciousness of many of the
Dubliners in Joyce's stories. Even here, the narration is not quite external.
The redundant adverb in the phrase 'was literally run off her feet'[75] must
belong to the caretaker's daughter, Lily, rather than to Joyce, reminding
us of the technique he used in previous stories of describing characters
through language appropriate to their consciousness. Lily's clumsiness
with language (Gabriel smiles at the three syllables she gives his surname)
recalls the two sisters of the first story while her distrust of men's words is
justified in the reader's mind by recollection of 'Two Gallants'. The
theme of women being excluded from the world of language is underlined when Aunt Julia admits that she does not understand the word
'goloshes'. However, there is a development on the earlier stories as
Gretta's casual dismissal of her husband's pretentious language signals
that she is not overawed by men's apparently greater access to the world
of language and culture.

Gradually the story moves from external description, through dialogue,
into the consciousness of Gabriel Conroy. Gabriel is established from the

outset as someone clumsy in his relations with women yet, unlike many of the other male Dubliners, well meaning and capable of being profoundly affected by them. The fact that Gabriel's identity is no longer entirely determined by his environment caused Frank O'Connor to remark that Joyce moved beyond the short story form in 'The Dead'.[76] Another reading would regard 'The Dead' as completing Joyce's collection: because of Gabriel's responsiveness, the world of women, previously so marginalized in the consciousness of male Dubliners, takes on greater significance in this story as the missing part of the parallelogram begins to emerge.

In the opening pages, Lily's bitter retort about men startles Gabriel into an awareness of the realities of her world and instinctively he offers her a coin. The patriarchal overtones of this offer, which Lily initially refuses but is eventually obliged to accept (she may after all be pregnant), are coloured by the way in which coins have been used in previous stories both to exploit women and to denote Ireland's colonized status. Gabriel's mishandling of Lily leads him into a downward spiral of self-criticism until he feels that the speech he has prepared will be an utter failure. Confusion over his tactlessness with Lily foreshadows the greater self-criticism following his realization that a whole area of his wife's experience has remained invisible to him until now.

Gabriel's failure with women is underlined in the first part of the story and parodied in the figure of Mr Browne, who believes he is a hit with the ladies but whose language, significantly, offends them. Gabriel is the protective patriarch, laying down rules for Gretta and his children, and offering to accompany Miss Ivors home. His dismissal of his aunts as two ignorant old women echoes the other males in *Dubliners*, who take women and their nurturing role for granted. In the university-educated Miss Ivors, however, Gabriel comes up against a woman he cannot so easily dismiss. Molly Ivors resists colonization as much by men as by the British. Gabriel is unsettled both by her nationalism and by the fact that her professional standing equals his. 'The girl or woman, or whatever she was'[77] troubles his gender categories to such an extent that eventually he reduces her in his mind to a rabbit. Molly's exclusion from the meal is strangely prophetic of the invisibility of Irish women, despite their prominent part in the struggle for Irish independence, in the public life of the Irish state after 1922.

Gabriel's sentimentality about women is underlined when he tries to transform the sight of Gretta standing on the stairs listening to a song into a mawkish symbol. In describing Gabriel's thought processes here,

Joyce anticipates the resistance of writers like Eavan Boland to male objectification of women in art. The episode recalls the youthful narrator's adoration of Mangan's sister in 'Araby', but Joyce extends his perception of the way in which male idealizations of women fail to capture the truth of their lives when Gabriel later learns that the reality behind Gretta's attitude, which he endows here with such 'grace and mystery',[78] is that the song reminds her of a figure from her Galway past, her dead lover, Michael Furey.

It is this theme of the past that ties together the public and private elements of the story. Through the conversation at the dinner party, Dublin is portrayed as a city living on times gone by. The guests dwell on great singers of the past who visited the city and Gabriel's speech is full of nostalgia for the traditions of Dublin hospitality. As the story moves further into the private world of Gabriel and Gretta, it becomes apparent that their marriage has, unbeknown to Gabriel, been shadowed by Gretta's memories of Michael Furey. The story tracks Gabriel's gradual entry into his wife's feminine world.

Gabriel's vision of Gretta on the stairs as a motif in art makes him aware of another world calling to him. Misreading her feelings in the light of his own, he associates this world with sensual pleasures now long past in his marriage but which he hopes to recapture this night with Gretta. His desire to rekindle past joys soon turns into straightforward lust and a masculinist desire for control over Gretta's 'strange mood'.[79] Her explanation of her thoughts, like Lily's words earlier, jolts him into an awareness of the extent to which he has misinterpreted her attitude and provokes him into a similar downward spiral of self-criticism. It is this ability to stand outside himself which sets Gabriel apart from other male Dubliners and recalls Mr Duffy's moment of empathy with Mrs Sinico in 'A Painful Case'. Unlike Duffy, however, Gabriel does not retreat from this moment but uses it to enter further into Gretta's world. Reflecting on her love affair with Michael Furey, Gabriel is forced to recognize that, unlike Gretta, he has never known what it is to love.

Under Gretta's influence and signalled by the increasingly semiotic rhythms of Joyce's prose, Gabriel's solid masculinity starts to crumble as he penetrates into the world beyond the social structures which trap the other Dubliners until he finally acknowledges the facts of his own death and dissolution: 'His own identity was fading out into a grey implacable world: the solid world itself which these dead had one time reared and lived in was dissolving and dwindling.' The snow, 'general all over Ireland',[80] completes the dissolution of the boundary between the living and the dead, uniting Gabriel in Dublin with the churchyard in the west where Michael Furey lies buried, in a development of the theme of the interrelationship between the living and the dead that had long pre-occupied Joyce.[81]

Joyce's use of snow to represent Irish life starts an image that will run through the Irish short story (given the rarity of snow in Ireland, this represents a triumph of fiction over meteorology). In 'The Dead', snow imagery has been signalled from the outset as something natural which bothers Gabriel (he enters scraping the snow off his goloshes), but which Gretta embraces (she would walk home in the snow 'if she were let'[82]). It becomes a many-sided symbol, representing both Gretta's adventurous spirit in comparison with her husband and her greater awareness of the realities of life and death, which until now he has tried to evade.

In the context of Gabriel's liminal state between waking and sleeping, the reference to his 'journey westward'[83] has been interpreted as Gabriel finally giving in to Molly Ivors' demand that he learn something of his own country. At the very least it may indicate his belated acknowledgment, in the light of the passion between Gretta and Michael Furey, that the west represents all that is instinctive and vital in his country's life, in contrast to the paralysed lives of his fellow Dubliners. The portrayal of the west in this way recalls Yeats' 'The Twisting of the Rope and Han-rahan the Red', where Hanrahan journeys to the west of Ireland and in 'that Celtic twilight' finds his mind opened to visions of beauty. 'John Sherman' also celebrates the west, and the realism of that story together with the fact that, like 'The Dead', it is more of a novella than a short story, may well have tempted Joyce to look at it again. Sherman, nodding off in his mother's drawing room, experiences a liminal state similar to Gabriel's here. Tellingly revealing of the differences between the two writers, in Yeats such a borderline space is where imagination is nurtured; in Joyce, Gabriel's sleepy state expands his capacity for imaginative empathy. Though resisting Yeats' romantic nationalism as another of the paralysing mechanisms weighing on his Dubliners' lives, the ending of 'The Dead', with the lyrical beauty of its prose and its themes of limi-nality and dissolution, begins to read like Joyce's tribute to Yeats' imaginative world.[84]

There are differences. 'The Dead' opens into the metaphysical as Gabriel recognizes that 'One by one they were all becoming shades',[85] recalling Molly O'Dwyer's sudden awareness of her mortality at the end of Moore's 'The Wedding Gown'. The hypnotic rhythms of Joyce's prose invite the reader, as well as Gabriel, into this shadowy world where living and dead meet. Yet in contrast to 'The Twisting of the Rope', where Hanrahan lies down to sleep and is borne away into the realm of the supernatural, there is no attempt in Joyce to describe the afterlife. The collection that began with our doubts about Father Flynn's sanity ends on uncertainty, and this time the missing part of the parallelogram cannot be supplied by the reader. We can know nothing more than Gabriel about this other world shadowing us. Joyce's final short story implicates the reader in his Dubliners' limitations.

CHAPTER FIVE

1920–1939: years of transition

'They pay for politics in this country but they refuse to pay for literature,' complained Liam O'Flaherty in a letter of 14 March 1924 to his editor, Edward Garnett.[1] 'Literature is a poor trade in Ireland,' Lennox Robinson remarked in the first volume of the newly established magazine, *The Irish Statesman*, 'and it is difficult to think of any man or woman over here who lives entirely by writing.'[2] In *The Irish Times*, 1932, Brinsley Mac-Namara summed up this period succinctly: 'The outlook for literature in Ireland at the beginning of the Free State was not so promising as it had been ten or even twenty years earlier.'[3] The years of fighting ending in partition of the country, a stagnant economy, the decline of the Irish language and a repressive religious ethos were just some of the factors that contributed to shape the depressed cultural, economic and social climate of post-revolutionary Ireland, so prominent a theme in the Irish short story of the 1920s and 1930s.

One attempt to keep the literary torch alight in the exhausted years following the war of independence and the civil war was *The Dublin Magazine*, founded in 1923 and edited by Seumas O'Sullivan until his death in 1958. In defiance of Ireland's stultifying post-revolutionary cultural climate, O'Sullivan proclaimed his aim of 'making a definite and practical effort towards reawakening in Ireland the unifying spirit of art, towards fostering the creative side of the national individuality in order that the country may gain the power of expressing her nobler values in the world'.[4] The stress on art as 'unifying' and on the purpose of art as giving expression to a set of national values is entirely in keeping with the homogeneous society that emerged in Ireland after independence, an Ireland that was to be rural, inward-looking and dominated by a con-servative Catholic ideology. *The Dublin Magazine*'s solid and conservative approach was never going to encourage creative innovation nor, in an era of censorship, artistic risk-taking. During the 1920s and 1930s, it did provide an outlet for stories by James Stephens, Margaret Barrington,

Pádraic Colum, Dorothy Macardle, Brinsley MacNamara, Pádraic Fallon, Frank O'Connor and Liam O'Flaherty, but it also published several undistinguished stories by a certain George Manning-Sanders. The stories it tended to prefer were either reworkings of Revival themes or sentimental stories about childhood. After *The Dublin Magazine* changed from a monthly magazine to a quarterly, the volume of short stories it published declined in proportion to poetry, possibly for reasons of economy. Liam O'Flaherty was reluctant to place his stories there because of the low rates of pay offered by O'Sullivan.[5] The magazine responded by labelling his work 'flashy'.[6]

   The Irish Statesman, which AE edited from 1923, was also committed to renewing Ireland's moribund intellectual and cultural life in an era of social and religious conservatism. Having merged with the *Irish Homestead*, *The Irish Statesman* was not primarily a literary magazine but, in a period not noted for its proliferation of Irish literary magazines, it did provide another outlet for the Irish short story, publishing work by Frank O'Connor, Seán O'Faoláin, Liam O'Flaherty, Margaret Barrington and James Stephens. It was committed to diversity within Ireland and attempted to counter Irish insularity by drawing comparisons with other small nations. In 1930, however, *The Irish Statesman* foundered over a libel case.

   The dearth of new literary magazines in this period is a sign of Ireland's exhaustion. In a country still struggling to find its feet, where bookshops were scarce and the Irish reading public small, foreign magazines and publishing houses remained crucial for Irish writers. Frank O'Connor's stories of this period found homes in *The Irish Statesman*, *The Irish Tribune* and *The Dublin Magazine* but also in the United Kingdom and the United States in such outlets as *Harper's Bazaar*, the *Yale Review*, *Criterion*, the *London Mercury* and the *Atlantic Monthly*. Seán O'Faoláin's stories were published in *The Irish Statesman* but also in the *London Mercury* and *Harper's Bazaar*. Edward Garnett, editor with Jonathan Cape in London, played an influential role in shaping the Irish short story of the period, acting as mentor to both Seán O'Faoláin and Liam O'Flaherty early in their careers. O'Flaherty's correspondence reveals the extent of Garnett's guidance: in addition to practical and monetary aid, Garnett advised O'Flaherty to read the Russians, sending him volumes of Chekhov and Turgenev translated by his wife, Constance. Garnett also wrote an introduction to O'Faoláin's first collection, *Midsummer Night Madness and Other Stories*, published by Cape in 1932. O'Faoláin's alliance with overseas publishers was to continue throughout his career. The favourable reception of *Midsummer Night Madness* amongst British reviewers, leading to reviewing work, talks on the BBC and, eventually, an advance from Cape, played a vital part in O'Faoláin's ability to give up teaching in London and return to Ireland to establish himself as a professional writer.[7] Likewise, the positive reception of *Guests of the Nation* in America laid the foundations for Frank O'Connor's later, highly successful, career in the United States.[8]

O'Flaherty's own attempt in 1924 to establish a monthly literary magazine, *Tomorrow*, foundered after two issues due to objections by the Jesuits to a story by Lennox Robinson, 'The Madonna of Slieve Dun', considered blasphemous. This experience of censorship disillusioned O'Flaherty with the Irish literary scene and led him to quit the country for a time, a pattern repeated in the lives of O'Faoláin and O'Connor, both of whom spent substantial periods pursuing their careers outside Ireland. O'Flaherty's stories continued to be published in a variety of UK and American outlets, including the *Manchester Guardian, The Tatler* and *Harper's Bazaar*. The economic uncertainty of these decades and the depressed social and cultural life of a nation exhausted by prolonged colonial mismanagement, the fight for independence and the civil war, had practical consequences for the lives of Irish writers and postponed the full flowering of the Irish short story as a national form.

General uncertainty about the short story form itself also played its part, as L. A. G. (Leonard Alfred George) Strong pointed out in his lecture on the short story to a packed audience in the Abbey Theatre in 1935: 'Mr Strong, in the course of his lecture, said that it was difficult to deal with the subject, because there was not general agreement as to what was, or was not, a short story – the people offering these productions to the public were all the time disputing among themselves on this point.'[9] This uncertainty was not to be allayed until the following decades, when writers like O'Connor and O'Faoláin began to publish critical writing on the short story. Strong was sure, however, that the short story 'was particularly suited to the Irish genius. In the field of the modern short story the contribution of the Irish nation would stand comparison with that of any other in grace, power, and above all, in imaginative passion.'[10] In these unpromising years the short story began to be regarded as the paradigmatic Irish prose form.

Though a writer like Stephens might continue in the visionary mode while Elizabeth Bowen, as we will see, explored the modernist vein, in general the Irish short story during the post-revolutionary period abandoned Yeats' romanticism for a realism shorn of the modernist experiments of Moore and Joyce. International debates on realism, inspired by the novels of Balzac, Flaubert and Zola and gathering momentum during the 1880s and 1890s, had influenced Moore and Joyce, but it was in post-independence Ireland that the classic realist short story came to general prominence. In the Irish language, Pádraic Ó Conaire, an important influence on O'Flaherty, had begun to treat realistically the lives of the Gaeltacht inhabitants. In the English language tradition, the establishment of an independent Ireland prompted Irish writers to portray the life of contemporary Irish Catholic society and the emerging Catholic middle class. An uncertain relationship between modernity and tradition, between the international and the local, is evident and these writers' relationship to their country is complex. Since many of them had participated in the nationalist movement they did not want to turn their backs on their country; at the same time, they felt that independence had been only partly achieved and they became disenchanted with the political rhetoric they had imbibed and acted upon. The civil war, censorship, a deep social conservatism, a puritanical religion and the narrowly defined nationalism that marked the newly independent state, were all deeply disillusioning for these writers. As the energies sparked by the Literary Revival and by the 1916 Rising and the war of independence faded in the more repressive and provincial atmosphere of the 1920s and 1930s, the short story in this period often reflected a realistic awareness of the limitations of the Irish nation as embodied in the Irish state.

Despite the fact that the short story developed into the characteristic Irish prose form of these difficult years, several writers were not to reach full maturity as artists until after these decades, and what most strikes the reader is the transitional nature of the Irish short story of this period, both in theme and style. An early, minor example of this is the collection by the County Down writer, Hugh MacCartan, *Silhouettes*, published in Dublin in 1918. On one level, *Silhouettes* continues the nineteenth-century sketch used by writers like Anna Hall and Jane Barlow: the subtitle is 'some character studies from North and South'. The difference from those earlier volumes is that MacCartan transfers his character studies from a rural to an urban setting, with the result that his collection becomes an uneven blend of Revivalist fairy and folk motifs and an urban realism in which one critic has spied the influence of Joyce.[11] In 'Life: a Study in Timidity', the dull routine of John Waters, 'confidential clerk in the firm of Messrs. Watts, Cooke, Brokers', recalls Little Chandler. When the timorous Waters decides to break out of his routine, his wanderings take him from Westmoreland Street to Grafton Street to a music hall in

George's Street and a pub on the Docks in what seems like an effort on the author's part to imitate Joyce's mapping of the city. This is very far from being a modernist collection, however; in fact there is a distinct impression of the author trying out a variety of styles to see which one will fit. There are touches of Wildean decadence ('A Gentle Sybarite') and of Le Fanu's Dublin ghosts ('Survivals'). MacCartan's curious mixture of Yeatsian Revivalism with urban realism is at its most pronounced in 'Exiled: a Fantasy', which contains a vivid description of O'Connell Street a week after the Easter Rising: 'the deformed and crumbling buildings, the lacerated girders, the pathetic remnants of what had once been chimneys and windows, the pungent smoke issuing from the burning wreckage, the fluttering wisps of charred paper that darkened the air like ants on a summer's day'.[12] Mixed in with this realism are passages likening Irish prisoners on their way to English jails to the legendary mythological heroes favoured by the Irish Revivalists.

MacCartan's collection is a minor but telling example of the uncertainty facing the short story form in these years; by contrast, Seumas O'Kelly's 'The Weaver's Grave', also transitional, is a masterpiece. 'The Weaver's Grave', published posthumously in 1919, was republished in 1922 by Dublin's Talbot Press in a handsome presentation edition with eight illustrations by Jack Yeats. The Talbot Press, founded in 1912 by W. G. Lyon, made efforts to promote Irish fiction, publishing, among others, Daniel Corkery. The tragi-comic tone and earthy dialect of 'The Weaver's Grave' recall the nineteenth-century short narrative; in form, it is as lengthy as a tale by Carleton. The young widow's first appearance, with her 'palely sad face' obscured by a black shawl, links her with the invisibility of female characters in Carleton's work, in contrast to the centrality of females in Joyce and Moore. The two elderly men, Meehaul Lynskey, a former nail-maker, and Cahir Bowes, a former stone-breaker, physically deformed by their trades, underline the link with Carleton's peasants, resembling elemental creatures only half-emerged from the earth. Like Carleton, O'Kelly wished to portray the peasants to the outside world, but he did so in a manner that reveals affection for his peasants, who have been moulded into eccentricity by their occupations and their environment. Aware that this is their last chance for the limelight, the two old men are none too eager to resolve their dispute as to the whereabouts of Mortimer Hehir's grave. Like Yeats' ancient heroes, they know that they represent the last of a line, possessing skills no longer needed in the modern world. The two old *seanchaí* tell each other romanticized stories of the past, finding their counterpart in Malachi

Roohan, another fiercely independent old man, who lives in a world of fable and magic. The decaying graveyard, the Gothic tombs belonging to aristocratic families who 'locked up their dead as if they were dangerous wild animals', as well as echoes of fairy tales in the description of the broken slabs of tombs at which 'goblin-like' guests might sit, are all elements in 'The Weaver's Grave' that represent the pull towards the past.[13]

This is not a peasant story, however, despite echoes of the oral tradition; instead it is narrated in standard English for an educated and literate readership, as the references to Gray's 'Elegy' and to *Hamlet* indicate. The elderly men may represent a dying culture but their quarrel takes place in the presence of Hehir's young widow, his fourth wife, and she comes to the fore as a love affair blossoms between herself and one of the young gravediggers. In contrast to the focus on death and the past for most of the story, the gravedigger's youthful energy in jumping across the grave to embrace her represents the future and suggests that a new way of life is beginning. The focus shifts from the elderly men's tale-telling and use of repetitions characteristic of the oral tradition, to modernist stream-of-consciousness with the widow's gradual realization that after a loveless marriage she is falling in love: 'the widow thought that the world was strange, the sky extraordinary, the man's head against the red sky a wonder, a poem, above it the sparkle of the great young star'.[14] What seems like a tale of peasant life ends on a modernist epiphany, perhaps one of the reasons why Joyce admired this story. 'The Weaver's Grave' simultaneously insists on the value of the past while showing that that past is about to be transformed. A comparison may be drawn with John McGahern's novel, *That They May Face the Rising Sun*, celebrating the value of a way of life at the point of its dying. Contemporaries were not slow to recognize the quality of O'Kelly's tale, the *Manchester Guardian* judging it 'the most promising thing that has come out of Ireland for some time'.[15]

'What Barrie and Ian Maclaren have done for Scotland, Daniel Corkery has done for the South of Ireland,' proclaimed the blurb for Corkery's volume of short fiction, *A Munster Twilight*, published in Dublin in 1916 by the Talbot Press. From the outset, Corkery's collection was placed within a national, if not nationalistic, context, a connection compounded by the later equation of the author with the narrow form of Irish nationalism promoted in his non-fiction works such as *Synge and Anglo-Irish Literature* (1931). This damaged Corkery's literary standing: 'he is not a real short story writer as Liam O'Flaherty is,' sniffed Brinsley MacNamara.[16] Yet Corkery's stories make him an acknowledged early influence on Frank O'Connor, Seán O'Faoláin, Michael McLaverty and, in a later period, John McGahern, as well as an important transitional figure, not only in terms of theme but also of style.[17] Despite his propaganda for Irish nationalism, Corkery's best stories bear witness to the stresses and strains of an emergent Irish nation unsure of the way forward and of how much of the past to jettison.

Corkery's alliance with tradition is evident in the many traces of oral storytelling in his work.[18] His series of stories in *A Munster Twilight* under the general heading 'The Cobbler's Den' draw on the oral tradition as neighbours assemble in John Ahern's shop to gossip. However, his stories are more usually set within a literary framework, using an educated narrator to introduce and explain the setting, a reminder that Corkery, who grew up in the back lanes and alleys of Cork described so vividly in his work, was himself an outsider to rural life and to the Gaelic tradition. As Paul Delaney has pointed out, Corkery's stories did not seek so much to reproduce oral techniques as to combine them with modern literary forms.[19] In the previous chapter we saw that Russian writers had an important impact on the development of the short story form in Ireland, and even Corkery, given to monitoring the frontiers of Irish literature, recommended Turgenev, Chekhov and Gogol as models for the young O'Connor and O'Faoláin.[20]

The fact that the Irish folk tale often draws attention to its own artifice is one reason why modernism has been seen to sit easily within the Irish tradition, but when Corkery drew on older forms – the oral, the Gothic – he did so in stories where the dominant mode was realism, rapidly becoming the characteristic style of this period. In a decade when more than half the Irish population continued to live in rural areas, a quarter of that number on farms of less than fifteen acres, Yeatsian romanticism, useful for inspiring a revolution, no longer seemed adequate to portray the realities of Irish life. In the 1920s, as in the nineteenth century, the pressing circumstances of Ireland had its consequences for the short fiction form. 'Solace' takes the Yeatsian subject of the last of the line in the portrayal of the eighteenth-century Gaelic poet, Eoghan Mor O'Donovan, but avoids Yeats' romanticism by placing O'Donovan in a realistic and detailed setting. Although a group of Irish peasants is described as listening spellbound to O'Donovan's Gaelic recitation, the reader is given only two lines of the poet's 'vision-song'. The emphasis is on the harsh realities of O'Donovan's life, his inability to make a living from his stony patch of land and his imminent eviction. The educated voice in which the story is told distances us again from the oral tradition and the story is rounded off with a description of an eighteenth-century English traveller's reactions. By employing realism to describe the lives of the peasants, Corkery's story resists both Yeats' idealization of the lost world of the Gael and the patronizing tone of earlier accounts, like Anna Hall's, written from the point of view of the English observer. Corkery has already brought us into the thoughts and struggles of O'Donovan, so that by the time the Englishman expresses his amused contempt for the Irish peasants' impractical preference for a story over ploughing, his lack of understanding of the conditions of their lives strikes the reader as grotesque. Corkery reclaims the dignity of the Irish peasant from his status in early English travellers' tales as an occasion for comedy and moralizing.

The Stormy Hills, published in London in 1929, is Corkery's strongest collection. 'The Rivals' challenges Yeats' idealization of the heroes of Irish folk tales by placing the tale of rival storytellers, Murty the road-mender and Dreoilin the cobbler, in a realistic setting. Shedding their quasi-mythical status, these storytellers prosaically provide respite and entertainment for weary city dwellers like the narrator, who has escaped to the Gaeltacht for a vacation. The peasants' faith in heroes is set against the realism of Murty's funeral and 'The Rivals' reveals how the everyday can become transformed into the legendary as the peasants, watching the four pall bearers struggle up the hill with Murty's coffin, believe that 'a heroic deed was being wrought out in their presence.'[21] There is no attempt to create a Yeatsian sense of awe; instead the city-dwelling narrator, revealing the extent of the distance between himself and the peasants, feels obliged to explain away their reverence for heroes: 'To understand it, one must recollect that the people of that countryside, fed mentally on folklore and the heroic literature of the sagas, are possessed of an instinctive reverence for physical size, prowess, energy, endurance.'[22] Whatever Corkery's personal adherence to the Gaelic tradition, the realistic mode he adopted for his stories could not help but record its vanishing.

The tension between tradition and modernity is present in many of Corkery's stories and several depict the psychological and emotional price of progress, a theme that was to become prominent in the Irish short story of the 1940s and 1950s. 'The Emptied Sack' portrays the old ways disappearing as a modern furnace puts Tadhg Kinnane, the furze-gatherer, out of business. Tadgh's cry, ' "Vo! Vo! Vo! Vo!"– the traditional Irish cry of sorrow', evokes a sense of ending without suggesting a way forward, a paralysis that has been likened to that which grips Joyce's *Dubliners*.[23] 'The Wandering Spring' suggests that Ireland's future lies in farming, and Dick Donovan's realization that his wife is pregnant, ensuring a new generation to inherit, gives him a renewed zest for working the land. Like most of Corkery's women, Donovan's wife is virtually invisible: she merely whispers news of her pregnancy in his ear, her role as the almost silenced bearer of new life reflecting Irish women's marginalized position in the new Irish state. Stories like these have to be balanced against stylistically superior ones such as 'Carrig-an-Afrinn' and 'The Priest', which are much less certain about how the new Irish state will develop.

In Corkery's earlier story, 'The Ploughing of Leaca-na-Naomh', Gothic and folk tale are employed to depict the punishment following on the contravening of ancient tradition for material gain. By the time of 'Carrig-an-Afrinn', folk tale and horror have been dropped, the mode is realistic and sacred sites are seemingly destroyed with impunity. Michael Hodnett's endeavours to raise his family in the world – symbolic of the struggle to bring the Irish state into being – have resulted in a model farm, Dunerling East, but have exhausted his energies and those of his family, and led to important traditions being discarded. By abandoning his old farm, Carrig-an-Afrinn with its mass rock, Michael has seemingly brought down a curse on himself. After the move his wife and four of his children die, and Ellen, Michael's eldest living child, has had to be mother to her young siblings. The cost to Irish women of the struggle to bring the new Irish state into being is suggested in Ellen's fate: she has never married and now, at sixty, she is mentally drained. Yet Corkery's story is perfectly poised between past and present: Dunerling East has prospered, as have Michael's younger children, who have known nothing of the hard labour that has worn out their older siblings. The old mass rock has been destroyed to widen the road, with apparent impunity. Knowledge of that would kill Michael and is kept from him, but the younger generation accepts its destruction as a necessary part of progress.

'The Priest' recalls George Moore's portraits of priests who try to aid their communities by enlarging their vision. Corkery gives an uncompromising portrayal of peasants moulded by the cold, bare landscape into harsh, materialistic beings, very different from Yeats' romantic view of the peasant and O'Kelly's affectionate portraits. Scratching a living in a desolate landscape has hindered any growth of community spirit and focused the inhabitants' energies on the lust for property. Father Reen despairs of being able to change them and Corkery suggests that the Irish nation faces a bleak future if its fate rests in their hands. Seán O'Faoláin will pick up this theme in 'A Broken World'.

Echoes of George Moore in the stories of Corkery and O'Kelly point towards a desire for modernity but, unlike Moore, these writers opposed emigration, stressing instead the value of traditional bonds with the land and the community. In Corkery's 'Storm-Struck', first published in *The Irish Review* (1914), John Donovan's emigration to America and subsequent blinding in a mining accident put an unbridgeable rift between himself and the community on his return. In O'Kelly's 'Both Sides of the Pond', Denis Donohoe is entirely in tune with his exacting life on the verge of the bog until news of Agnes Deely's emigration to Australia causes a division between himself and his environment. When we next see him he is singing in some tawdry bar in America. 'Both Sides of the Pond' invites comparison with Moore's 'Homesickness' while refuting Moore's suggestion that the emigrant may find fulfilment abroad. Corkery's story, 'Nightfall', also prompts comparison with Moore in its portrait of a returned Irishman finding himself suddenly attracted by the old country but, as in O'Kelly, the point Corkery is making is very different from Moore's, for Corkery took a dim view of those Irish men who deserted their country. Reen's years in New Zealand have allowed him to prosper but have rendered him out of touch with his country's developments. Nicknamed the Colonial, Reen's best linen and polished boots contrast with the shabby clothes of the Renahans and their neighbours who have endured years of guerrilla warfare, suffering for their country rather than enriching themselves in exile. Mat belongs to a family who have continued farming the land and so far resisted the temptation to emigrate; for this he is rewarded with the girl, though the story is not without compassion for Reen. Emigration from Ireland had been constant since the famines of the 1840s: Reen is simply part of a huge Irish diaspora which, by the early 1920s, had resulted in over 40 per cent of Irish-born men and women living abroad.[24]

'Nightfall' illustrates Corkery's move towards the modern short story being tightly narrated, in standard English, by someone slightly distanced from the community he describes. For all his insistence on the Irish tradition in his non-fiction works, Corkery clearly absorbed lessons from his reading of Turgenev and Chekhov: another story, 'The Awakening', employs epiphany to depict a Munster fisherman, Ivor O'Donovan, who in the course of a long night has a sudden insight into what the life of a fisherman means. The story ends, quite convincingly, on a moment of transcendence. However, not all of Corkery's moves towards the modern short story were successful: his attempt to construct a story around a central irony in 'Cowards?' is heavy-handed.

The stories of Corkery and O'Kelly are transitional, combining oral storytelling methods with echoes of Moore, Gothic with realism. Both writers ignored Joyce's focus on the solitary, rebellious individual, choosing to highlight instead, in stories such as O'Kelly's 'Nan Hogan's House' and Corkery's 'Nightfall' and 'Storm-Struck', the necessary interdependence between individuals and the community. Yet Corkery's stories, in particular, reveal awareness that the old communal way of life was breaking down, either as a result of emigration or of new ways of working. In 'Carrig-an-Afrinn', only Ellen and Nicholas remain with their father on the land; Michael's younger sons have moved away to earn their living in cities, a reflection of the contemporary situation where those family members outside the line of inheritance were obliged either to seek jobs in towns or to emigrate. In 'A Looter of the Hills', Mrs Donaghy is the last of her family to remember the land, her memories of it sustaining her through her final days in an urban slum. The story points to a theme that would become prominent in Irish writing in the following decades, namely the psychological cost of the transfer from the countryside to the towns.

Several Irish short story collections published during the early 1920s endeavoured to capture the atmosphere of the war of independence. *Tales of the R.I.C.*, published anonymously in 1922, is a series of popular tales set in the west of Ireland and recounting the struggles of Blake, a First World War veteran, now District Inspector in the Royal Irish Constabulary, against the local Sinn Féin. The viewpoint is pro-unionist, and towards the end of the collection, fiction gives way to polemic against the British Government for agreeing the truce: 'The sacrifice of the southern Loyalists will form one of the most disgraceful chapters in the history of England.'[25] Like Elizabeth Bowen's stories from this period, *Tales of the R.I.C.* is directed at an English readership and critical of the British government's handling of their withdrawal from Ireland.

On the nationalist side, characteristic features of these war stories are gunmen on the run, a house of refuge, a romantic encounter with a beautiful woman, all set against the backdrop of a romanticized Irish landscape in an atmosphere of heightened tension and excitement. Corkery's collection, *The Hounds of Banba*, published by the Talbot Press in 1920 and written in a spirit of romantic nationalism to celebrate the Irish struggle for independence, is generally regarded as his weakest, with its crude portrayal of the British as villains and Irish republicans as heroes. The most successful of the stories, 'Colonel Mac Gillicuddy Goes Home', combines Gothic mode with what we would now call post-traumatic stress disorder as the Colonel becomes haunted by Britain's imperial crimes in India and Ireland. Corkery's story is typical of the way in which the Irish short story dealing with the violence of this period repeatedly strains beyond the bounds of realism into horror, as if the realist mode were insufficient to cope with events in Ireland. In Dorothy Macardle's collection, *Earth-bound: Nine Stories of Ireland*, published in 1924 in Ireland and the USA, the dominant realist mode frequently shades into ghost story, Irish legend and horror in order to convey the violence of Irish life during the war of independence.

Earth-bound derives its unity from being supposedly composed from tales recounted by Irish exiles who have been involved in various ways in the war of independence and turn up in the Philadelphia studio of Una and Frank O'Carroll, editors of the republican newspaper, *Tri-Colour*. Macardle wrote the stories while she was imprisoned by the Free State forces in Mountjoy and Kilmainham for her support of the anti-treaty side during the civil war, and her stories share Corkery's romantic nationalism, depicting Ireland as an enchanted place that draws men gladly to sacrifice their lives for her. Hugo Blake's portrait of Róisín Dhu expresses 'that wild, sweet holiness of Ireland for which men die'.[26] Later Irish women writers were to challenge this kind of yoking together of women and the nation and in 'The Portrait of Róisín Dhu' Macardle anticipates this by revealing the human cost behind such idealizations of women in art. Nuala, the original of Róisín Dhu, wastes away from unrequited love of Hugo. Macardle's stories are not immune, though, to the glorification of war: one of her spokesmen, Father Martin, dreads the deterioration that peace may bring, believing that 'Ireland struggling, praying, suffering persecution, is holy.'[27] Such attitudes as these were to become a decided inconvenience in peacetime Ireland.

Macardle's stories do, however, illustrate the stresses of the times by constantly dissolving their realistic settings in a way that not only demonstrates Macardle's interest in the occult, but suggests that the violence in Ireland led to nightmarish, hallucinatory states on the part of its participants.[28] In 'The Prisoner', Liam, on hunger strike in Kilmainham, hallucinates that Lord Edward Fitzgerald's messenger boy is sharing his cell. In the title story, Michael recounts his escape from Mountjoy prison and the way in which the Black and Tans were drawn away from discovery of his hiding place by a mysterious figure whom Michael and his listeners believe to be the reincarnation of Aodh Ruadh O'Donal or Red Hugh. The boundaries between the living and the dead collapse in these stories, as if all of Ireland's past is coming to the aid of the country's struggle for independence. In 'By God's Mercy', portraying the war of independence from the point of view not of the gunmen but of the women who sheltered them, there is a vivid account of Black and Tans raiding Nannie's home and setting fire to it. The story shades off into the supernatural as Nannie hears the voice of her dead brother telling her to run to the bridge and warn the Irish fighters of the presence of British soldiers. *Earth-bound* portrays Ireland as a liminal place where the barrier between the living and the dead is thin: the theme is signalled in the opening of the first story, where Una elaborates on 'that sense one has everywhere in Ireland – in the glens, and in Dublin – the old squares on the north side, and the quays – of the companionship of the dead'.[29] Like the tales of Sheridan Le Fanu, Macardle's stories, though coming from a very different political standpoint, belong in a line of Irish writing displaying a tendency in times of acute strain to look back into Irish history and break up the realist mode.

Corkery and Macardle express little of the scepticism towards war apparent in other writers of the period. Liam O'Flaherty's first published story, 'The Sniper' (1923), which brought him to the attention of Edward Garnett, is a simple but effective tale highlighting the futility of the civil war by depicting a Republican gunman shooting his Free Stater brother. In its disillusionment with violence and atmosphere of betrayal, 'The Sniper' points forward to later stories by O'Connor and O'Faoláin.

O'Flaherty grew up on the Aran islands in an Irish-speaking community where the oral tradition was still very much alive. In his autobiography, *Shame the Devil*, O'Flaherty acknowledged his debt to his mother's storytelling: 'Even when there was no food in the house, she would gather us about her at the empty hearth and weave fantastic stories about giants and fairies, or more often the comic adventures of our neighbours.'[30] The influence of both the oral tradition and the Aran islands is evident in O'Flaherty's three major collections of short stories published by Cape during the 1920s: *Spring Sowing* (1924), *The Tent* (1926) and *The Mountain Tavern and Other Stories* (1929). In 1953 he was to publish *Dúil*, a collection of eighteen short stories generally regarded as one of the most outstanding collections of stories in the Irish language. Some ('The Cow's Death') were written first in English and translated into Irish; others, like 'Poor People', were written first in Irish and then reworked in English.[31]

Many of O'Flaherty's stories in *Spring Sowing* and *The Tent* are seemingly timeless evocations of nature, the animals and the peasants among whom he spent his childhood. The title story of his first published collection, 'Spring Sowing', is a lyrical and moving portrayal of the lives of peasants tied to the seasons in an almost Tolstoyan manner. Writing about the peasants from the inside, as Tolstoy could not, O'Flaherty was able to present their way of life as hard but dignified, in marked contrast to nineteenth-century tales presenting Irish peasants for the entertainment of English readers. His realism provides a contrast, too, with the idealizations of the Irish Revival, as a contemporary review of *Spring Sowing* pointed out: 'Following Synge in modern Irish literature, he should, with Mr Joyce, give the quietus to the Celtic Twilight.'[32]

Some of his stories are plotless sketches, simply painting a word picture of nature's energy ('A Wave') or the primitive struggle for life ('The Rockfish'). Others portray brief moments of sympathy between humans and animals, as in 'The Cow's Death', one of O'Flaherty's personal favourites, where the farmer's wife empathizes with the cow's grief for her dead calf. Yet others, like 'The Blackbird', are animal fables in the manner of La Fontaine, with animals taking on human traits. Conversely, humans may be likened to animals. In 'The Tramp', the comparison of the eponymous tramp to 'a graceful wild animal'[33] celebrates the tramp's independence over the timidity of petty clerks like Deignan, and reflects O'Flaherty's belief that cities were alien, destructive environments for human beings.

At other times, the resemblance between humans and animals indicates a loss of humanity. In 'Lovers', Old Michael Doyle has lost not only all physical strength, a crucial virtue in O'Flaherty's world, but charity as well, with the result that he fails to respond to Mary Kane's touching account of their youthful love affair. Age has dehumanized him: 'His withered countenance seemed to have lost all traces of human consciousness. It was apelike. His rheumy eyes, wrinkled like those of a gorilla, had no light in them.'[34] 'Lovers' is a simple and perfectly controlled story of old age recounted through the device of a single encounter between Michael and Mary and the dialogue that follows. There is very little narrative; all we know of Michael we learn through his conversation with Mary and his crotchety gestures. The ending avoids the kind of summing up that often mars Frank O'Connor's early stories: instead Michael fades gently into the landscape, in a manner appropriate to one whose physical and mental energies have vanished.

Other O'Flaherty stories remain confined to social realism. In 'The Caress', fifty-year-old Bartly Delaney is dehumanized by age and sexual frustration, having been tied for too long to his mother and to his land, a situation not uncommon in a period when economic necessity led to a high proportion of Irish people remaining unmarried till late in life, and a puritanical Catholic church frowned on sexual activity outside marriage. In 1929, Brinsley MacNamara published a collection of stories, *The Smiling Faces*, which combined the traditional voice of the storyteller with contemporary social realism to portray a series of bachelors and spinsters in the Irish countryside. In the title story, Thomas Weldon has had to wait for his sisters to marry before he can think of bringing a wife to his farm. MacNamara highlights the resulting emotional damage: 'it was the waiting, more than anything else, that had made him so timid, speaking no word to any girl, thinking of no girl until now'.[35] O'Flaherty's story is much more sexually explicit: when Bartly decides he must marry a young girl who will give him children, he fixes on Mary Madigan and becomes animal-like in his lust, likened to 'a rampant goat'.[36] In contrast to the drunken exploits and sordid bargaining indoors, the young lovers, Martin and Mary, consummate their passion out of doors in a scene full of lyricism and natural imagery which, as often in moments of charged emotion in O'Flaherty, dissolves the barrier between humans and nature.

Heightened lyricism pervades 'The Mermaid', in form as classically simple as a fable. Michael McNamara resembles an idealized fairy tale figure, possessing enormous physical strength and beauty and famed for his skill at sailing and taming animals. Innocent until he falls in love with Margaret, Michael experiences love as violent and elemental, like 'the frenzy of a wild hurricane'.[37] Again the barrier between the human and the natural world is dissolved as Margaret's eyes are likened to sun shining through rain and her hair to light playing on the sea. Their love is passionate and physical but doomed: a month after their marriage, Margaret dies. A grief-stricken Michael, hearing his dead bride calling to him over the sea, rows out to meet her. The story ends with Michael's vision of Margaret as a sea goddess or mermaid rising up to meet him at the door of a cave in the cliff face. On the surge of a wave he enters her embrace, achieving death and love simultaneously. The mixture of violence and lyricism in the narrative style lifts the story to the level of a prose poem, the richness of the language recalling Oscar Wilde's fairy tales.

The comparison with Wilde is not inappropriate for, however much O'Flaherty's stories seem written out of a particular community, using phrases such as 'our island women' or 'our Western land', O'Flaherty had been educated out of that community from an early age and was influenced by the portrayal of peasant life in Maupassant and Gorky, as well as by the naturalism of writers like Zola and Jack London. In a typically impassioned review in *The Irish Statesman*, O'Flaherty wrote: 'Would that we Irish could exchange a whole shipload of our political martyrs for a genius like Guy de Maupassant.'[38] His correspondence with Edward Garnett is filled with praise for the Russians, particularly Turgenev and Chekhov ('the greatest genius ever born').[39]

Unlike O'Connor and O'Faoláin, O'Flaherty left no study of the short story, but comments scattered through his correspondence suggest that he saw the form as poetic and instinctual: 'The modern short story or sketch seems to have become a poem and where ideas and images attain lordship over poetry it ceases to be elemental and universal.'[40] His stories are at once traditional and modern, combining the oral tradition's respect for physical courage with D. H. Lawrence's admiration for the instinctual life. A similar balance is achieved in stories that mark the transition between peasant beliefs and the modern age by juxtaposing folk beliefs with the voice of an educated narrator or outsider. In 'The Salted Goat', set in the remote village of Kilmillick on the island of Inverara (Aran), the fact that Mick Hernon's red cow gave birth to a calf with a fish's tail may only mean, the educated narrator explains, that the calf was born prematurely. A newborn child falling out of old Mrs Derrane's arms into the fire may not have been the work of malevolent fairies but the result of Mrs Derrane's drunkenness.

The themes of O'Flaherty's stories may seem timeless, but many of them mark change, even in these rural communities: in 'The Caress', published as a postscript to *Shame the Devil*, Mary has saved enough money from working in America to be able to choose a suitor for herself. Despite frequent criticisms of O'Flaherty's misogyny,[41] what is noticeable in these stories of the Western Isles in terms of gender relations is the equality between women and men as they work the land together. In 'Spring Sowing', Martin and Mary work side by side to sow their crops in a way that is quite different from Corkery's invisible women or the trapped, idle, middle-class wives in Seán O'Faoláin's stories of the period. 'Spring Sowing' is shot through with Mary's moments of rebellion against the hardship of being a peasant's wife and the unremitting hard work and poverty that will be her life from now on: 'there is a grim realism about Mr O'Flaherty's works,' observed an anonymous reviewer of *Spring Sowing*, adding, 'He also has a notable mastery of the technique of the short story.'[42] This is one of the few cases of a contemporary reviewer singling out the form as well as the content of a story; unfortunately the reviewer did not go on to elaborate on what those techniques might be.

Emigration was the biggest threat to the traditional way of life of these peasant communities. 'Going into Exile' presents a paradigmatic moment in their lives as two of Patrick Feeney's children are given a farewell party on the eve of their departure for the United States. Again there is equality between the sexes: both a son and a daughter are emigrating. There are, however, subtle differences in their attitude. Michael is looking for adventure and is glad that he will be earning money to support his family back home. Mary thinks of the men she might meet – and in this context it is suggested that she may be pleased to escape her father's restricting presence. This simple but beautifully controlled story about the emotional cost of emigration in an inarticulate people who can barely find the words to express their sorrow is one of O'Flaherty's finest stories. Unlike Moore's 'Homesickness' or O'Kelly's 'Both Sides of the Pond', it focuses on emigration not as the experience of one individual but in its effects on an entire community. 'Going into Exile' perfectly illustrates O'Flaherty's own comment on his stories: 'I don't think I exert any judgement whatsoever in my writing at the moment of writing but seem to be impelled by the Aran Islanders themselves who cry out dumbly to me to give expression to them.'[43]

Liam O'Flaherty's later volume, *The Mountain Tavern and Other Stories*, was published at the end of a decade during which O'Flaherty had become gradually disheartened both by his failure to inaugurate a literary movement and by the general stifling of intellectual and artistic life in Ireland. It presents a bleaker picture of peasant life than his two earlier collections. 'The Letter' opens with a description of the innocence and simplicity of peasants' lives, comparable to 'Milking Time' and 'Spring Sowing', but a letter from a daughter in America shatters this atmosphere, raising questions in her family's mind as to how Mary's much-needed money has been earned. The hints in O'Flaherty's earlier story, 'Going into Exile', that Mary may become preyed upon abroad because of her beauty, are here confirmed in what is suggested has happened to this other Mary (pregnancy perhaps, or prostitution). The repetition of names in O'Flaherty's stories reveals that, unlike O'Faoláin, he was less interested in portraying individuals than types. In this later collection, the picture of the peasants as prone to hysterical superstitions ('The Fairy Goose') or degenerate through intermarriage ('The Strange Disease'), suggests a distance on the part of the author and a more critical stance towards the peasants than in his earlier volumes. Two stories in particular, 'The Child of God' and 'Red Barbara', contain echoes of George Moore in their portrayal of the suspicion and hostility of the peasant community towards artists and anyone else who does not fit into their *mores*.

Once again we see the urgency of Irish circumstances shaping the Irish short story. During this period, O'Flaherty abandoned his earlier lyricism in favour of a realist mode that would better highlight his disillusionment with peacetime Ireland, but it is arguable that his distinctive artistry is most evident in his earlier poetic and lyric stories. O'Flaherty's anti-clericalism comes to the fore in stories such as 'Offerings', where a priest pockets money brought to the wake of a child of poor parishioners, or 'The Outcast', where the priest harshly dismisses a young unmarried mother, who drowns herself in consequence. These types of themes point forward to the stories of O'Connor and O'Faoláin in the following decade. O'Flaherty's 'A Public Scandal', first published in the *Manchester Guardian* in September 1925, highlights corruption in public places, while stories like 'Blackmail' and 'Proclamation' reveal the deep divisions running through Irish society in the aftermath of the civil war. 'Proclamation' portrays the career of John Considine, who, like O'Flaherty himself, fought in the First World War and later joined the nationalists, fighting in the war of independence and for the Free Staters during the civil war. Put into the form of a document signed by Considine, O'Flaherty's story presents Ireland as a society in which practically everyone is jockeying for power and position. O'Flaherty's skill is such that, through the words of Considine's self-serving document, without authorial explanation or comment, he succeeds in conveying the turmoil in Irish society. Considine particularly resents the fact that: 'Young scuts that never fired a shot and other fountain-pen warriors that served on the so-called staff are now up in Dublin drinking the champagne that men like me earned for them, while good men like myself are hiding in dugouts with a price on our heads.'[44] The resentment of former fighters that their country failed to acknowledge their valour will continue to make its appearance as a theme in the Irish short story as late as the work of John McGahern.

If O'Flaherty's stories, like those of O'Kelly and Corkery, reflect the Irish short story in a transitional state, combining oral techniques with literary, fable with social critique of rural life, the debate over the future direction of Irish literature continued when Yeats founded his Irish Academy of Letters in 1932 to encourage young writers, and to show solidarity against the anti-literary activities of the Catholic church and the Censorship Board. Corkery refused an invitation to join the Academy, believing that it should be confined to Irish language writers, but members included such major figures from the Literary Revival as AE and George Moore, as well as younger writers like O'Flaherty, Frank

O'Connor and Seán O'Faoláin. Though Irish Irelanders like Corkery were eager to break with the Anglo-Irish past, the link with the earlier generation was maintained in the Sunday evening gatherings in AE's Rathgar home, to which O'Connor was invited, as well as Yeats' Monday evening get-togethers where O'Connor mingled with people like George Moore and Lady Gregory.[45] O'Connor was much aided in his early career by AE, who, from 1925 onwards, published his translations from Old Irish and his stories in *The Irish Statesman*. AE was instrumental in getting O'Connor's first volume of short stories published when he recommended him to his own London publisher, Macmillan.[46] In 1926, he helped O'Faoláin secure a two-year travelling fellowship to the USA, and the positioning of the younger generation as heirs to the Irish Revival was underlined in a letter AE wrote to O'Faoláin, congratulating him on the publication of his first collection, *Midsummer Night Madness*: 'Your generation must create its own ideals as the generation to which I belonged . . . Frank O'Connor is full of vitality and out of your discussion with him and others you may do for your generation what Yeats and others did for my generation.'[47]

Frank O'Connor's collections from this period, *Guests of the Nation* (1931) and *Bones of Contention* (1936), are transitional volumes in which traces of the oral tradition, and an emphasis like Corkery's on the community rather than the individual, make these stories less characteristic of his style than his later work. In his autobiography, O'Connor describes how, in the early years of his career as a writer, he participated in the literary circles around Corkery, who taught him Irish and encouraged him to join the anti-treaty side during the civil war. The view of Corkery as a narrow nationalist becomes nuanced in O'Connor's account of how Corkery urged him to study Russian authors. O'Connor duly read Chekhov, Turgenev, Babel and Gogol, describing himself as 'an aspiring young writer who wanted to know Ireland as Gorky had known Russia'.[48] 'They had all read the Russians,' V. S. Pritchett was later to remark after meeting Irish writers in Dublin.[49] Certainly by this date, references to Turgenev in particular were cropping up frequently in the pages of literary magazines such as *The Irish Review*.[50]

O'Connor's reading of the Russian masters led him to wish to imitate Turgenev's *Sketches* by producing a volume of stories that would be unified thematically, an ambition he only partially achieved in *Guests of the Nation*. His reading also influenced him towards Chekhov's conception of the short story as a tightly controlled form focused on a single situation that provokes a crisis. He endorsed Chekhov's belief that ordinary life provides the best material for fiction. In other respects, the oft-repeated description of O'Connor as the Irish Chekhov is misleading (indeed, to this day, lazy reviewers are fond of sticking the handy label 'an Irish Chekhov' on any new collection of Irish short stories). O'Connor's insistence on the primacy of life, and his resistance to artistic experiment (witness his criticisms of Joyce in *The Lonely Voice*, his study of the short story form) meant that whilst the setting of his stories was often Chekhovian (dull, provincial life), he neglected Chekhov's emphasis on mood and feeling, his impressionistic characterizations, his lyricism and open-endedness. O'Connor early found a structure and form for his stories that served him well, and which he passed on to his students: 'He virtually defined a theme as an incident in which the people involved become basically changed' was a student's comment on his teaching.[51] A characteristic O'Connor story opens with narrative, then proceeds to relate, by means of action and dialogue with minimum descriptions of landscape or physical characteristics and little symbolism, a crisis that changes a person's life.

In O'Connor's earliest stories, however, Chekhov's influence was less apparent than that of the indigenous oral tradition, reflecting O'Connor's preoccupation with the speaking voice and his efforts to recreate in the modern short story the human warmth and vigour of oral storytelling. Stories like 'The Late Henry Conran' are related almost entirely through dialogue in a way that is uncharacteristic of O'Connor's later work: ' "I've another little story for you," said the old man. "I hope it's a good one," said I.'[52] In other respects, 'The Late Henry Conran', with its tale of poverty, emigration to America and Henry's come-down from his heady days of political activity to being offered a job as 'a walking advertisement for somebody's ale',[53] captures the atmosphere of post-revolutionary Ireland, where, as O'Connor observed in *My Father's Son*: 'This was no longer the romantic Ireland of the little cottages and the hunted men, but an Ireland where everyone was searching frantically for a job.'[54] The portrait of Henry Conran's deserted wife is characteristic of later O'Connor stories in which widows or elderly women who cling to the old ways constitute one of O'Connor's submerged population groups. A story like 'The Late Henry Conran' is thus transitional. The later O'Connor would have taken it out of its oral framework and tragi-comic mode and explored the situation in greater psychological depth. The stories of his second collection, *Bones of Contention*, also published by Macmillan, continue to display traits uncharacteristic of the mature O'Connor, indicating that he was still feeling his way towards the modern short story.

In the 1930s both Frank O'Connor and Seán O'Faoláin published stories illustrating their disenchantment with the romantic nationalism of their former mentor, Corkery. Published over ten years after the fighting, their war stories embody their mature reflection on their youthful involvement with the republicans and reveal their disillusionment with the way the Irish state had subsequently developed. Wryly commenting on his part in the revolutionary violence, O'Connor said: 'what we were bringing about was a new Establishment of Church and State in which imagination would play no part, and young men and women would emigrate to the ends of the earth, not because the country was poor, but because it was mediocre'.[55] These writers' embrace of realism was not only inspired by French and Russian literary influences but had personal roots, in their reaction against their own early romanticization of violence.

'Guests of the Nation', set during the war of independence, was O'Connor's most successful story of this period, pointing the way in which his later style was to develop. It is analysed in the interchapter. Other stories in *Guests of the Nation* draw on O'Connor's experiences during the civil war, but their jaunty tone, a residue of the oral story-teller's art, whilst aptly emphasizing the naïve 'Boys' Own' attitudes of the revolutionaries, often sits uneasily with the genuinely tragic subject matter. In 'Jumbo's Wife', a naturalistic tale of a government informer's violent end and his wife's grief at her betrayal of him to the republicans is too glibly rounded off by the concluding sentence. More characteristic of the mature O'Connor is 'September Dawn', where physical courage in pursuit of a political cause is juxtaposed with the private world of ordinary human ties that was to become a central theme of his work. Turgenev's influence is evident in the description of two republican officers, Hickey and Keown, escaping through a romanticized Irish countryside after being forced to disband their column. Realism dissolves into horror as Keown awakens in a drunken nightmare, fearing that the Tans are surrounding the house. Generally, however, the story keeps within the bounds of realism, and the loneliness and despair of the gunman on the run are vividly conveyed as Hickey reflects on the war which has compelled him to drop out of college and break most of his ties with the past. If his side loses, he envisages having to emigrate to America, as many republicans in fact did. As he contemplates a life ending in failure, his longing for some human warmth leads him to kiss the servant girl who becomes, momentarily, a symbol of the Ireland for which he is fighting. O'Connor's adoption of Flaubert's technique of conveying the internal consciousness of his characters ensures that 'September Dawn' avoids the kind of glib summing up by an external narrator that mars some of the other stories in this collection. The ending stays instead with the mood of the story, perfectly capturing Hickey's emotional state in the early morning.

'September Dawn' bears resemblances in theme, if not style, with 'Fugue' by Seán O'Faoláin, indicating the close collaboration between the two writers at this time.[56] Written earlier than O'Connor's story, in 1927, 'Fugue' portrays two ill-matched gunmen on the run from the Black and Tans. Rory's hedge-school chatter recalls Carleton's bombastic schoolmasters, but the story is narrated by the more sensitive of the gunmen, who, like Hickey, is becoming disillusioned by the futility of the war and whose longing for a home and a settled way of life leads him to seek comfort with a young woman in the house where he shelters. Unlike O'Connor's story, 'Fugue' does not end with the kiss but with the gunman again fleeing for his life, the narrator observing, in Yeatsian manner, that 'life begins once more its ancient, ceaseless gyre'.[57] Both stories underline the allegorical association of Ireland and womanhood but they are very different in style, O'Faoláin's being more lyrical, subjective and bleak, O'Connor's more detached and, by ending with the embrace, more consolatory. O'Faoláin's is much the most complex: Deborah Averill has noted his use of recurring motifs and counterpointed voices to convey the musical patterns of a fugue.[58]

'Fugue' was included in O'Faoláin's collection, *Midsummer Night Madness and Other Stories*, published by Cape in 1932, and immediately banned under the 1929 Censorship of Publications Act. The collection also angered the IRA since stories like 'The Patriot' made clear O'Faoláin's disillusionment with the republicans, whose leaders, he felt, had deceived him. Many of the stories in *Midsummer Night Madness*, a collection that brought O'Faoláin literary, if not commercial, success, were based on his own experiences with the republicans. They depict bomb-making revolutionaries and rebels fleeing the Black and Tans in the mountains around Cork but, despite the romantic style characteristic of the early O'Faoláin, war is not glamorized. In 'The Bombshop', the potential heroism of the revolutionaries is undermined as one by one they leave the house and the only person who dies as the result of their efforts is an elderly woman whom they all admired. O'Faoláin highlights the loneliness of gunmen who sleep in a different place every night and, like Bernard in 'The Patriot', become disillusioned by the apparent futility of the war. The dehumanizing effect of this way of life is such that it almost brings about Bernard's disintegration as a human being until he is saved by his love for Norah. This, the final story of the collection, suggests a clear break with the past as abstract love of Ireland is replaced by the warmth of a human relationship.

Many of the stories in *Midsummer Night Madness* are as much about current debates on the nature and direction of Irish society in the 1930s as they are about the revolutionary fighting. By the 1930s, O'Faoláin had broken with his former teacher, Corkery, over his decision to write in English and what he saw as Corkery's narrow-minded patriotism. Donal McCartney writes: 'Corkery had disapproved of O'Faoláin's angry criticisms of republican politics, whereas Corkery's continued interest in such "folly" was regarded by O'Faoláin as the peak of unrealism.'[59] The portrayal of the fanatical Sinn Féin propagandist, Edward Bradley in 'The Patriot', borrows several traits from O'Faoláin's former mentor.

The title story of the collection is a paradigmatic O'Faoláin story of this period in which romantic nationalism is replaced by an ironic realism appropriate to his loss of belief in republican violence: rather than attacking the Black and Tans, his anti-hero, Stevey Long, resorts to bullying the elderly Anglo-Irish man, Henn, in whose house he is sheltering. In terms of the characteristic Irish short story of this period, 'Midsummer Night Madness' marks a shift of focus from concentration on incidents, such as the burning down of the Blakes' house, to a skilful exploration of the narrator's psychology. A gunman himself, he has been brought up to hate Henn as representative of a class that has exploited his people, yet his hatred changes to pity when he arrives at Henn Hall to find the old man being coerced by Stevey into marrying Gipsy, whom Stevey has almost certainly made pregnant. Henn's ruined physique is matched by his ruined house, but O'Faoláin avoids what had become a cliché in writing about the Anglo-Irish, namely their lack of energy and vitality, by portraying Henn as a man whose ideas for improving the Irish economy have gone unheeded. The conversation between the narrator and Henn complicates the definition of a patriot and O'Faoláin eschews the kind of neat endings O'Connor favoured. Henn's effort to greet the Blakes with civility contrasts sharply with the coarseness of Stevey Long and our attitude to him remains a complex mixture of disapproval, pity and unwilling admiration. O'Faoláin aligns himself with Yeats and his associates against Corkery and the Irish Irelanders; Henn's marriage with Gipsy, however incongruous, suggests a Yeatsian alliance of peasant and Anglo-Irish, and their flight to Paris indicates the direction O'Faoláin believed Ireland should take to renew its cultural and literary life.

O'Faoláin's stories are more extended than those of O'Connor and O'Flaherty and shift the short story more firmly towards modernist techniques of irony, indirection and suggestion used to probe the inner consciousness of his characters. A story like 'Midsummer Night Madness' becomes shaped not by external forces but by the narrator's partial consciousness, as the speaking voice of oral tradition becomes transformed into the perspectivalism of the modernist narrator. Other modernist traits in this collection include the musical counterpointing and inconclusiveness of 'Fugue' and the snatches of stream-of-consciousness techniques in the portrayal of Bella and Denis in 'The Small Lady'. Such modernist traces point forward to O'Faoláin's next collection, *A Purse of Coppers*, where the fractured dialogues of stories like 'Admiring the Scenery' and 'A Broken World' oblige the reader to supply the meaning.

In the 1930s, the Monaghan writer, Michael McLaverty, started to gain a reputation for himself as a short story writer, publishing in magazines like the *Irish Monthly* and *Ireland Today*, although it was not until the following decade that collections of his stories appeared. A story from this period, 'Pigeons' (1936), echoes the interrogation of violence found in O'Connor and O'Faoláin. Recounted by Frankie, younger brother of Johnnie, who in the course of the story is killed fighting for the republican cause, 'Pigeons' is a simple story told in straightforward language, as befits a story told from a child's viewpoint. Nonetheless, it is effective in contrasting Johnnie's death for an abstraction, Ireland, with Frankie's loving care for the pigeons. The ballad-like refrain, 'our Johnnie died for Ireland', comes to sound increasingly ironic.

The disillusionment with the fighting apparent in stories by O'Flaherty, O'Connor, O'Faoláin and McLaverty reflected the more general disillusionment with Irish society found in the Irish short story from the late 1920s onwards. In his second collection from this period, *Bones of Contention*, Frank O'Connor, like O'Flaherty, interrogates the values of peasant communities in stories such as 'The Majesty of the Law', 'Peasants' and 'In the Train', where the peasants' distrust of legal institutions recalls the work of Griffin and Carleton but is also characteristic of postcolonial societies where suspicion of the authorities often takes years to fade. In 'Peasants', the rural community defends Michael John Cronin, preferring to see him sent to America for stealing the club's funds rather than disgrace his family and the community by being brought before the law. The portrait of Father Crowley, the priest who stands out against the community and insists Michael John be tried in the proper way, anticipates O'Connor's later stories of isolated individuals who are often, ironically enough given his anti-clerical views, priests. Father Crowley with his stiff-necked insistence on doing the right thing is a less attractive character than O'Connor's later clerical portraits, and the community is correspondingly more hostile to his failure to realize that what they really want is to get rid of Michael John without bringing scandal on themselves. O'Connor's story operates through irony as the community's traditional values backfire on them: far from expressing gratitude to them for setting him up in business, Michael John marries a rich girl and holds his neighbours in thrall through his money-lending. 'Peasants' reveals O'Connor, unlike Corkery, questioning the enclosed, restrictive nature of a society clinging to deep-rooted attitudes. The tragi-comic tone militates, however, against the psychological exploration O'Connor would bring to his later tales.

Other stories in this period, notably 'The Majesty of the Law' and 'In the Train', mark a move towards O'Connor's later style. 'The Majesty of the Law' seems at first entirely traditional, being concerned less with the alienated individual of O'Connor's later stories than with the community that turns out to bid farewell to old Dan on his journey to prison. The story portrays the traditional Irish qualities of hospitality, of tactfulness on both sides during the conversation between the sergeant and Dan, and of indirection as the sergeant introduces, almost as an aside, the question which will lead to Dan's going to prison. Yet the structure is characteristic of the later O'Connor with its introductory narrated paragraph evoking sympathy for Dan's way of life, the central part conducted through dialogue between the sergeant and Dan, and the return to narrative at the end. The conclusion, which avoids any glib summing up, is characteristic of O'Connor's mature art. In the suggestion of something Christ-like about old Dan making his way to prison on his donkey, there is an obvious parallel with Gogol's story, 'The Overcoat', discussed by O'Connor at the beginning of *The Lonely Voice*. Both stories portray the Little Man in a mock-heroic setting but impose over him the image of the crucified Christ in order to highlight the heroism of the everyday.

In 'In the Train', as in 'Peasants', the community bands together against the authorities to protect one of its own. At Helena Maguire's trial for poisoning her husband, the peasants lie for Helena, feeling that to bear witness against one of their own would be tantamount to turning informer, an attitude left over from their habit of resisting the British. Through the various conversations on the train a picture of the closed, materialistic, prejudiced village environment that has contributed to Helena's crime is built up. The villagers would understand killing for land or money, but to kill for love seems to them an unnecessary luxury. In *The Bell*, O'Faoláin praised this story on account of the controlled narrative perspective, which is indeed so skilful that it is only towards the end of the story that the reader realizes that Helena is also on the train.[60] At this point, the theme of community gives way to the more characteristic O'Connor theme of the alienated individual since it is clear that Helena is returning only to be ostracized by her community. Though its use of Joycean symbolism was something O'Connor would swiftly abandon, 'In the Train' illustrates his move from stories based around traditional communities to the modern short story focused, like Joyce's writing, on the alienated individual. O'Connor's stories from the 1930s display some characteristics of his later work but he had not yet developed the psychological exploration and multiple layers of irony characteristic of the stories he was to publish in the following decades.

As in the case of stories by O'Flaherty and O'Connor, Seán O'Faoláin's second collection, *A Purse of Coppers*, published by Cape in 1937, contains several penetrating analyses of the chaos and diminishment of life in postrevolutionary Ireland, where individual aspiration was thwarted. The election of de Valera's Fianna Fáil party in 1932 heralded an era of deepening conservatism shaped by an economic nationalism, a Catholic social policy increasingly enshrined in the country's legislation, and a religious and cultural protectionism stimulated by the activities of the Censorship Board. On his return from the United States in 1933, O'Faoláin quickly became disillusioned by what he felt was the stifling of intellectual life in Ireland by such forces as the Gaelic League and the Catholic church. In a letter dated 28 September 1934, he complained of being 'not only insulated from world ideas but isolated and icebound'.[61] The Joycean imagery is echoed in his story, 'A Broken World', portraying Ireland as a country exhausted, not only by the recent fighting, but by centuries of struggle to wrest a living from the land. The Ireland that emerges from the conversation on a train between the priest, a prosperous farmer and the narrator, is a land made up of separate nations: the gentry who used to rule the country, strong farmers and the 'mountainy' people. In the Irish short story of this period, from Frank O'Connor's 'In the Train' to Mícheál Mac Liammóir's impressionist sketch, 'The Journey', the train becomes something of a feature as a setting, providing as it does a ready-made environment for assembling characters from different walks of life.[62] In 'A Broken World', the narrator's complacent belief that the 'mountainy' people will come into their own now that the gentry have gone is challenged by the priest's despairing laughter. The narrator is forced to recognize the truth of the priest's words: 'under that white shroud, covering the whole of Ireland, life was lying broken and hardly breathing'.[63]

That 'A Broken World' is still an apprentice piece is evidenced both by the second-hand imagery and by the technique used before in 'Midsummer Night Madness' of conveying ideas in the form of a dispute: the pressing circumstances of Irish life were still, as in Carleton's day, impinging on the shape of the short story. Nevertheless, if the conversational device is clumsy, by describing it from the perspective of the narrator O'Faoláin shifts the emphasis of his story from the external to the internal and in modernist fashion obliges the reader to look beneath the surface dialogue for the meaning. The significance of 'A Broken World' lies in its reflection of the fractured nature of Irish society at this time, made up of disparate classes that had not yet found a common identity and seemingly lacked the energy to do so. The peasants' ignorance of how to work the land, having been deprived of it for so long, their submissiveness as a result of years of being treated as second-class citizens in their own country, and the ever-present threat of emigration, are summed up in O'Faoláin's striking image of a people 'huddled over the embers of their lives'.[64]

In general, the stories in *A Purse of Coppers*, portraying a Chekhovian world of petty clerks and hopeless peasants, are less lyrical in style, more compressed and concentrated than those in *Midsummer Night Madness* and there is greater use of dialogue. Some of the stories are slight and indicate O'Faoláin's uneven adherence to the modernist techniques he was beginning to explore in his first collection: 'One is always searching for different forms,' he wrote in his foreword to *The Finest Stories*.[65] O'Connor's influence is evident in 'The Confessional', a story of three children aping a priest hearing confession, as well as in 'The Old Master' and 'My Son Austen', which employ O'Connor's technique of narration through a speaking voice arising out of the community. There are wide divergences in tone, from the tragic portrayal of the way Ireland's provincialism blocks an individual's bid for artistic fulfilment in 'A Born Genius' to the comedy of 'The Old Master', depicting the puritanical attitudes of the new state, and the satire on de Valera's isolationist economic policies in 'Sullivan's Trousers'.

Women cast off the cloaks and shawls that render them invisible in Corkery to take centre stage in O'Faoláin's writing. Several stories in *A Purse of Coppers* deal with the isolation of women who, like the young girl in 'Kitty the Wren', fail to fit into the prevailing mores. In 'There's a Birdie in the Cage', the plight of the unmarried daughter at home is portrayed as vividly as any inter-war women's writing dealing with this subject (Radclyffe Hall's *The Unlit Lamp*, for instance, or Lettice Cooper's *The New House*). The story skilfully suggests Helen's consciousness of her entrapment: in comparison with the movement of the 'dumb gulls' wheeling freely over the house, Helen recalls the blankness of characters like Eveline and Mrs Kearney in *Dubliners*, reduced to paralysis by the patriarchy. She stands like a statue, 'without moving either eye or head', before going down to pour tea for her father.[66] This focus on women's lives contributes to the modernity of the collection: 'A Meeting', for instance, with its tragic insight into the retreat into domesticity of Irish women who had previously participated in the struggle for independence, anticipates later writing by Irish women.

Women are central in the writing of Norah Hoult and Olivia Manning. Hoult's collection of short stories, *Poor Women!*, was published by Heinemann in London in 1930 and, like O'Connor and O'Faoláin, Hoult employed the realist mode to express her deep disenchantment with Irish life during this period: her obituary for AE in 1935 described Dublin as a city 'lacking in charity and charged with cynicism'.[67] A story from this collection is discussed in the interchapter. Hoult's disillusionment with Ireland is echoed in the work of Olivia Manning. Manning's mother came from a prosperous County Down family and Manning spent much of her childhood in Bangor, but Ireland is not glamorized in her stories from the 1930s, where warring parents, hostile Catholic neighbours and the decline in her family's status are all portrayed through the eyes of a child. 'The Children' and 'Two Birthdays', both dating from 1938, foreshadow later Irish women's writing in their depiction of difficult mother–daughter relationships, while 'A Case of Injury' (1939) is notable for the rare glimpse it gives into the lives of young, professional women in Dublin during this period. These stories already convey the sense of displacement and alienation that would become Manning's great theme in her novels based on her wartime experiences. 'A Visit' (1939) vividly portrays poverty-stricken Belfast through the eyes of a child displaced from England:

The black river crawling under the drizzle of rain; the wet cobbles; the dirty pavements; the stale fishy smell from the docks; the women with starved and bitter faces beneath their shawls; the cold – the irritating chilliness of summer and the knife-edged winter cold; and the harsh-voiced school-children whom we, the aliens, were always fighting.[68]

The back streets of Belfast also feature in Michael McLaverty's stories. An admirer of Chekhov, McLaverty is a quiet writer who sought exactness of observation in a series of beautifully controlled stories portraying everyday life on the farms of Northern Ireland, in the slums of Belfast and on Rathlin Island, where he spent part of his childhood. McLaverty's writing on the short story always emphasized the importance of writing out of a known environment, and Seamus Heaney has praised his 'fidelity to the intimate and the local'.[69] Several of his stories echo O'Connor in being recounted through the eyes of a child, and 'The White Mare' recalls O'Flaherty in its description of the intense bond between an old man and his aged mare. Like many of Corkery's stories, McLaverty's stories often evoke the dying of rural communities: in 'The White Mare', Paddy and his sisters are childless, and in 'Stone', Jamesy, the last Heaney left on the island, seeks immortality through his gravestone. The parallels between McLaverty's work and that of other Irish writers reveal that, even after partition, there was a similarity of themes in the Irish short story of this period from both sides of the border.

Though McLaverty adopted a realist vein, his stories frequently rise to poetry as they record the rhythms of country life and celebrate the local and everyday. The same feature may be observed in many short stories of this period where realism is often tempered by a lyricism that, in contrast to the pragmatic, constricted petit-bourgeois or rural society portrayed, is intensely personal, private and romantic. In the brief epiphanies that momentarily transcend the bleak conditions of everyday life the boundaries of realism are undermined or dissolved: in Liam O'Flaherty's lyrical descriptions of nature, in Frank O'Connor's celebration of the variety of human nature, in Seán O'Faoláin's moments of psychological insight. The emphasis is no longer on plot but on what O'Faoláin termed 'the adventure of the mind'.[70] In this way, short story writers sought to mark a protest of the individual, imaginative, creative spirit against the oppressive, authoritarian environment of the period.

Notwithstanding the disenchanted critique of Irish society in stories by O'Flaherty, O'Connor and O'Faoláin, at least one contemporary believed that Irish short story writers were not outspoken enough in their criticisms: in his vote of thanks to L. A. G. Strong for his lecture on the short story, Walter Starkie argued that short story writers 'suffered from moral cowardice in their writing in this country. He would like to see a good deal more of criticism of their own period.'[71] He suggested they follow George Moore's example, though conceded that they would probably have to leave the country in order to do so. Starkie's remarks indicate that, for all their criticisms of Irish society, Irish writers found it hard to resist the conservative ethos of the period. For the modern reader, though, this conservatism is arguably most striking, not in their choice of themes, but in the realist mode in which they mostly chose to work. This sometimes gives a dated feel to their writing that may account for their relative critical neglect in the latter years of the twentieth century and the fact that many of their short story collections are out of print. Starkie's observations reveal, however, that what even comparatively sophisticated contemporary readers sought in the form was not stylistic innovation but a reflection of the state of their country.

At the same time it should not be forgotten that other Irish writers of the period were working more centrally in the modernist mode. Elizabeth Bowen began her writing career in the 1920s and her short stories prolonged into this period the nineteenth-century Anglo-Irish preoccupation with the supernatural and with what could not be expressed out loud, using these themes now to suggest the unease and insecurities that lay beneath modern life. Many of her stories are set in countries other than Ireland but two from this period take as their subject the situation of the Anglo-Irish after the war of independence.

In 'The Back Drawing-Room', first published in *Ann Lee's* in London in 1926, an Anglo-Irish story is set in the framework of a discussion about immortality among a group of English sophisticates: if this is a story drawing on the oral tradition of telling ghost stories around a fireside, the conversation proceeds on a level far removed from the popular, embracing Ancient Greece and Hellenism, spiritualism and telepathy. The interlocutors combine to try to silence the odd little man who insists on bringing the conversation down from these heady abstractions to the level of a ghost story based on mere personal experience. Undeterred, the man proceeds to recount his Irish adventure in a manner that reveals nineteenth-century English attitudes of condescension still lingering: Ireland's recent wars are downplayed by the Englishman as 'these civic disturbances'.[72] Describing how, in search of somewhere to repair his bicycle, he came across a large demesne, he at last succeeds in attracting the attention of his listeners, who attempt to add literary touches to his story from their reading of Gothic literature, all of which are refuted by the determinedly prosaic narrator. When he entered the back drawing room of the house, he found a young lady sobbing as if her world had ended. Knowing he could do nothing for her, he retreated, as the English had recently retreated from Ireland, leaving the Anglo-Irish to their own devices. Later the narrator learned that the house was Kilbarran, an Anglo-Irish house burnt by the rebels two years previously. A familiar Bowen theme, namely the rootlessness of the dispossessed, is introduced: the

Barran family may be still alive in Dublin or England, but it hardly matters where they are since they can no longer be 'at home'. The dissolution of the Anglo-Irish identity, signalled in the nineteenth century by Le Fanu, has now become a reality. The narrator is quietly bundled away and the room falls silent, suggesting English guilt at having abandoned the Anglo-Irish to their fate. 'The Back Drawing-Room' is a story written to alert the English to this guilt and to suggest possible punishment in the shape of ghosts from the Anglo-Irish past returning to haunt them.

Bowen's other Irish story from this period, 'Her Table Spread', first appearing as 'A Conversation Piece' in *The Broadsheet Press*, May 1930, presents another Anglo-Irish house on the brink of dissolution. If Valeria Cuffe, the statuesque, simple-minded Anglo-Irish heiress and last of her line, fails to marry, her aunt fears that the Castle will have to be sold and the family scattered. To prevent this, an Englishman, Alban, has been invited over to make a match with Miss Cuffe. Alban, like Thomas in 'Foothold' or St Quentin in *The Death of the Heart*, is one of Bowen's Jamesian hangers-on, a detached observer who remains negative about women and is convinced that the Anglo-Irish are all mad. The intensity and isolation of the Anglo-Irish way of life, remarked upon by Bowen in *Bowen's Court*, is revealed in the fantasy Valeria has woven around English officers who once visited the Castle in her absence. Valeria takes little notice of Alban, her imagination being absorbed by these English officers whose arrival she expects at any moment due to the presence of an English destroyer in the estuary. In *Bowen's Court*, Bowen likened life in the Anglo-Irish Big House to 'a continuous, semi-physical dream', remarking that their way of life was largely built on fantasies of power.[73] In 'Her Table Spread', the huge, deluded Anglo-Irish heiress, who relies on the English to save her, sums up in her person the hopeless political situation of the Anglo-Irish. As in 'The Back Drawing-Room', the English disappoint: the English officers do not turn up, Alban is not attracted to Valeria, though momentarily he does abandon egocentricity to acknowledge the splendour of Valeria and her relatives: 'Close by, Valeria's fingers creaked on her warm wet satin. She laughed like a princess, magnificently justified. Their unseen faces were all three lovely, and, in the silence after the laughter, such strong tenderness reached him that, standing there in full manhood, he was for a moment not exiled.'[74] Taken together, Bowen's two Irish stories from this period suggest that the English should both acknowledge their guilt towards the Anglo-Irish and, like Alban, appreciate the bravado of a social performance sustained through a time of crisis.

In 1934, there appeared an apprentice work by another writer from the Protestant minority, Samuel Beckett. *More Pricks Than Kicks* is a series of ten interlocking stories recounting the life of Belacqua from student to corpse.[75] The use of interlinked stories may recall oral storytelling, but Beckett moved his stories away from folk tradition by announcing his adherence to the European masters. Belacqua is named after Dante's Florentine lutemaker, who appears, carefree and indolent, in the fourth canto of Dante's *Purgatory*, lazily postponing repentance until the last possible moment. Beckett's Belacqua is similarly 'bogged in indolence'.[76] As this echo of Dante suggests, *More Pricks Than Kicks* is written in a self-consciously literary style stuffed full of literary allusions. Nevertheless these stories are recognizably Irish for, bucking the trend of the Irish short story of the period, one of the masters Beckett follows is Joyce. Unsurprisingly, given its title, the collection was immediately banned in Ireland. It received a grudging review in the *Dublin Magazine*: 'a book that glitters and will make holiday for the highbrow', an assessment that highlights both the cultural conservatism of that magazine and the general suspicion of modernist experimentation among Beckett's compatriots.[77]

Set in Dublin, *More Pricks Than Kicks* displays Joycean attention to the precise locations of Belacqua's wanderings and continues, through parodic imitation, the satire of Dublin life found in *Dubliners*: 'A Wet Night' satirizes Dublin's provincial intelligentsia, substituting rain for the snow of 'The Dead'. Like Stephen Dedalus, Belacqua desperately seeks to break free of the structures in which he has been raised. The difference from *Dubliners* lies in the noticeably Protestant colouring of Beckett's stories. Belacqua describes himself as 'a dirty low-down Low Church Protestant high-brow' fleeing the world of work and other people's expectations of him, much like Beckett himself, who, at the age of twenty-five, resigned his lectureship in French at Trinity College, Dublin, preferring, he said, to lie on his back and think about Dante.[78] Nevertheless, Belacqua finds it difficult to shake off his Protestant upbringing. Phrases like 'There was always something to do next' or 'if a thing was worth doing it was worth doing well' swirl around in his mind, together with a certain ingrained Protestant gloom: 'he must just hope for the best. And expect the worst.'[79]

Despite the apprentice nature of these stories, many deal with recognizably Beckettian themes. 'Dante and the Lobster' is a tragi-comic meditation on pain, not only of the eponymous boiled lobster, but of McCabe, due to be hanged at dawn. The story opens out into a general disquisition on suffering, ending on the sentence 'It is not', identified by one critic as an authentic Beckettian line confronting us with the stark realities of life.[80] Beckett was already depicting a profounder, more universal sense of alienation and isolation than can be found in the stories of O'Connor and O'Faoláin. Belacqua's alienation is not just from a particular society but from all society and, in the end, from life itself: in 'Love and Lethe', Belacqua makes a suicide pact with Ruby Tough.

In *More Pricks Than Kicks* Beckett began tackling his characteristic themes, though in a display of linguistic exuberance that differed sharply from his later minimalist style. This was soon to come. If the Belacqua stories were indebted in style, if not theme, to Beckett's reading of *Ulysses* and *Work in Progress*, 'A Case in a Thousand', published in *The Bookman* (1934), revealed Beckett turning back to the example of *Dubliners* and experimenting with Joycean realism in what one critic has seen as an ironic reworking of Joyce's 'A Painful Case'.[81] Shortly after the publication of *More Pricks Than Kicks*, a letter written to Axel Kawn indicates that Beckett was already working on a pared-down language very different from the verbal excesses in those stories: 'more and more my own language appears to me like a veil that must be torn apart to get at the things (or the Nothingness) behind it'.[82] In *More Pricks Than Kicks*, Belacqua is aware of the nothingness, but he has not yet found the language to express it.

Like Bowen, Beckett employed modernist techniques in his short stories to express the unease and insecurities that lay beneath Irish life. The fact that Bowen and Beckett – one Anglo-Irish, the other Protestant middle class – pursued a literary path different from the realism embraced by their Catholic contemporaries, raises the question as to how the Anglo-Irish/Protestant minorities situated themselves in the new state. By 1926, the Protestant population in the South of Ireland had declined by about a third, reduced by the Great War, the burning down of their Big Houses and a general feeling of social isolation in the new Ireland which often positioned them as strangers in their own land.[83] Bowen famously declared that home was somewhere in the middle of the Irish Sea; Beckett's restless hero, Belacqua, feels that his true home is 'nowhere so far as I can see'.[84] On the surface, the stories of Bowen and Beckett do not easily fit in with the preoccupations and interests of the new inheritors in Ireland. Behind them we sense the doom of an entire way of life and thought: 'It is suicide to be abroad. But what is it to be at home, Mr Tyler, what is it to be at home? A lingering dissolution.'[85]

And yet on further investigation, perhaps these writers from the Protestant tradition were not so very different from their Catholic contemporaries. Modernist traces can be discerned within the ostensibly realist stories of O'Kelly, O'Flaherty and above all O'Faoláin. Moreover, at a time when a new Irish state had at last come into being the irony is that, rather than looking to the future, the Irish short story from its different traditions focused on last of the line figures and on ways of life coming to an end, an illustration of Declan Kiberd's telling observation: 'in Ireland everything must first seem to die before it can be reborn as something slightly different'.[86] This dying is as much a theme in the stories of O'Kelly, Corkery and McLaverty as it is in the modernist stories of Bowen and Beckett, while the work of O'Flaherty, O'Connor and O'Faoláin portrays the identity of the new Irish Catholic state as much less secure and more transitional than its rulers liked to claim. O'Connor's vote of thanks to L. A. G. Strong on the event of his lecture on the short story in the Abbey Theatre summed up the uncertainty felt by many Irish people during these decades: 'Mr Frank O'Connor said that it seemed to him that they had not really begun to find themselves in literature, and he did not think they would do so for a long time.'[87]

READINGS: FRANK O'CONNOR AND NORAH HOULT

Frank O'Connor, 'Guests of the Nation' (1931)

'Guests of the Nation', first published in the *Atlantic Monthly* in January 1931, is characteristic of the transitional nature of the Irish short story in this period. O'Connor's wish to recreate the speaking voice of oral tradition in the modern short story form in order to forge a bond with his readers similar to that between the *seanchaí* and his audience is reflected in his use of direct narration to the reader. There is an interesting reversal of nineteenth-century travellers' tales in which an English narrator, visiting an outpost of the empire, is amused by the curious behaviour and Hibernicisms of the natives. In 'Guests of the Nation' it is the Irish narrator who, while using some Irish idiom, employs language closer to standard English than the two Englishmen. In O'Connor's original version, the Englishmen speak in Cockney dialect and display marked eccentricities of behaviour. Rather than any native expression, it is the English slang word 'chum' that resonates through the story. In contrast to nineteenth-century tales of wily Irish natives observing and imitating their English masters, here the uninvited English are the observant ones, learning Irish dances, a cross-cultural gesture that is not reciprocated by their Irish guards: 'our lads at that time did not dance foreign dances on principle,' records the narrator, whose inflated patriotism is suggested by his nickname, Bonaparte.[88]

At the same time, despite these echoes of the oral tradition and of the nineteenth-century short story, 'Guests of the Nation' exemplifies several traits that were to become characteristic of the modern short story form, namely precision of language, economy and careful attention to tone, imagery and structure. The focus on a moment of crisis in the narrator's life makes this a paradigmatic O'Connor story, though in his later work the turning-point in his protagonist's life would be conveyed more subtly, through the narrative itself, without the need for the overt statement that ends this story. In *The Lonely Voice*, O'Connor quotes from Gogol's 'The Overcoat' in order to illustrate his view of the short story as pivoting on a central crisis: 'If one wanted an alternative description of what the short story means, one could hardly find better than that single half-sentence, "and from that day forth, everything was as it were changed and appeared in a different light to him".'[89] It was a view of the short story that O'Connor never departed from. His widow, Harriet O'Donovan Sheehy, quotes him as saying towards the end of his life that the short story 'is about a moment of change in a person's life. It's a bright light falling on an action in such a way that the landscape of that person's life assumes a new shape. Something happens – the iron bar is bent – and anything that happens to that person afterwards, they never feel the same about again.'[90] The echo here of the ending of 'Guests of the Nation' indicates the centrality of this story to O'Connor's oeuvre.

'Guests of the Nation' is important in the canon of the Irish short story not only stylistically but also thematically. O'Connor provides an early interrogation of Irish nationalism, presenting, through the voice of the narrator, disillusionment with the violence exercised in the name of the Irish nation and, in the disapproval expressed by the elderly woman of the house, anticipating the time when the Irish people would turn against the gunmen and refuse to provide them with shelter. The personalities of the garrulous Hawkins and the silent, clumsy Belcher are so vividly captured in gesture and dialogue that the wrong-headedness of a war where fighters make friends with their English captives before having to shoot them has a powerful emotional impact on the reader. The story reveals how far O'Connor had travelled from the influence of his former teacher, Daniel Corkery, both in style and subject matter, romantic nationalism being replaced by an ironic realism that becomes transmuted at the end into tragedy. 'Guests of the Nation' may be compared with 'The Martyr', published posthumously in 1981 from papers preserved by

O'Connor's widow. 'The Martyr' focuses on a violent incident during the civil war that leads the narrator to become similarly disillusioned by the actions he is compelled to take. Like Bonaparte in 'Guests of the Nation', he finds himself making friends with those who are supposed to be his enemies and enemies of his friends.

The autobiographical impulse behind 'Guests of the Nation' is revealed by the fact that the narrator's admission at the end that 'anything that ever happened to me after I never felt the same about again',[91] is echoed in O'Connor's memoir of his early years, *An Only Child*, published in 1961. The autobiography recounts a slightly different incident that took place at the time of O'Connor's internment in Gormanstown during the civil war by the Free State government. Describing an IRA boy beaten up and then executed by his Free Stater captors, O'Connor remarks: 'Certainly that night changed something for ever in me.'[92] O'Connor's 1923 internment marked a turning-point in his life after which he doubted 'if I should ever again be completely at ease with the people I loved, their introverted religion and introverted patriotism'.[93] This alienation from his own people was to shape O'Connor's life as an artist. It lay behind his later belief that the short story addresses itself to the solitary reader and takes as its subject marginal and submerged population groups. 'Guests of the Nation' marks the narrator's abrupt turning away from his companions, not only implying a questioning of the violent nationalism he has previously espoused but opening out to a wider sense of alienation and loneliness, as the deaths of the two Englishmen lead him to realize how easily a home and human affections can be betrayed and destroyed. It was in this tension between the outsider and the traditional ties of family and community that O'Connor was to write his best work.

Norah Hoult, 'Bridget Kiernon' (1930)

The interaction between the Irish and the English is given a female angle in Norah Hoult's story, 'Bridget Kiernon', published in Hoult's collection, *Poor Women!* in London in 1930. Like Frank O'Connor and Seán O'Faoláin, Hoult worked in the realist mode and, in harnessing the short story form to depict the lives of women on the margins of society, she may be said to be claiming for women membership of a submerged population group. In *The Lonely Voice*, O'Connor argues that, in contrast with the novel's focus on a single protagonist, such submerged population groups provide the central subject matter of the short story, adding: 'That submerged population changes its character from writer to writer, from generation to generation.'[94] Hoult's stories are set mainly in England and deal with themes common to inter-war women's fiction, such as the mother–daughter relationship and spinsterhood. 'Bridget Kiernon', however, draws on Hoult's Irish background to provide a rare glimpse into a day in the life of an Irish Catholic maid in England. Like 'Guests of the Nation', 'Bridget Kiernon' portrays the rupturing of community ties, this time through the paradigmatic Irish theme of exile. In the insight it provides into an Irishwoman's experiences in a foreign country, 'Bridget Kiernon' may be regarded as complementary to Liam O'Flaherty's stories in this period of young women leaving their rural communities to seek work abroad, as well as to Sarah Orne Jewett's earlier accounts of Irish emigrants in America.

Hoult's story paints an acute psychological portrait of Bridget's sufferings as she makes the transition from Ireland to England, from rural life to urban, from Catholicism to Protestantism, and as she encounters anti-Irish prejudice in the household of her English Protestant mistress, Mrs Fitzroy. Hoult draws out the cultural differences between the employer and her maid: whereas Mrs Fitzroy prizes efficiency, economy and cleanliness, Bridget values personal contact and human warmth above all else and feels she is being asked to 'work in new ways that no one had ever heard of before'.[95] Even their notions of time are different. Bridget, from the country, works too slowly for Mrs Fitzroy, whose urban day is strictly regulated by clock time. Mrs Fitzroy's English voice makes Bridget feel alien: 'She listened to the precise English accent which made her feel she was dealing with someone she could never approach as an ordinary human being; one who must be an inhabitant of a quite different world from herself.'[96] (The heroine of *Sarah's Youth*, a novel by Somerville and Ross published in the 1930s, experiences similar alienation in London. Sarah Heritage-Dixon is an Anglo-Irish heiress and therefore of a completely different class from Bridget, but she also feels a stranger in London: 'The smart clothes and the high English voices antagonised and scared Sarah. This was enemy country.'[97])

Using precise and telling detail, Hoult builds up a grim picture of Bridget's daily life at the constant beck and call of her employer. Bridget is homesick, confused by cultural differences and blamed for her dirtiness, inevitable when her tasks involve laying fires and hauling coal up from the cellar. Running through the story is Bridget's fear that she may be pregnant. If she is, she knows that she will not be able to return home 'bringing scandal into the parish and disgrace on her poor mother'.[98] Throughout the story Bridget observes her employer's behaviour with the envy and rage of the dispossessed, and a comparison may be drawn with the Irish maids in Herbert's Retreat, a wealthy fictional community outside New York depicted in Maeve Brennan's series of stories published in the *New Yorker* in the 1950s. By the end of 'Bridget Kiernon', as often in Brennan's stories, power shifts from the mistress to the maid as Bridget discovers she is not pregnant and realizes that, given the shortage of domestic labour, she will be able to find another job more easily than Mrs Fitzroy will be able to hire another maid. The optimistic ending reflects the popular market for which Hoult was writing but it does not outweigh her previous emphasis on the harsh reality of this Irish maid's daily life.

CHAPTER SIX

1940–1959: isolation

'This place is a backwater', grumbles one of Olivia Manning's characters.[1] Isolation is a key theme in the Irish short story of this period, it being the widespread view of Irish fiction writers that the Second World War, or the Emergency as it was known in Ireland, had the effect of making an already inward-looking society even more isolated from the rest of the world. This was not necessarily the whole story. As Clair Wills has argued in *That Neutral Island*, Ireland's isolation paradoxically allowed for a new vitality in Irish culture. Neutrality encouraged the development of Irish artistic and cultural life as wartime censorship kept out rival foreign material. The number of art exhibitions and theatrical performances increased during this period and the indigenous film industry was given a boost due to restrictions on imports of foreign films. Moreover, the influx of refugees from Europe included artists, musicians and poets, swelling the ranks of Dublin's intelligentsia and giving the city a more cosmopolitan feel.[2] Nevertheless, the view of Ireland's wartime writers, cosmopolitan and often European in outlook, was that neutrality had increased Ireland's isolation from the rest of the world.

For an Anglo-Irish writer like Elizabeth Bowen, by now, as *The Irish Times* noted, 'accepted as a master of the short story form',[3] the war posed a conflict of loyalty. Whilst feeling it was her duty to support the war effort by spending the majority of the war years in London, Bowen understood that Ireland's neutrality was, as she observed in her reports for the British Ministry of Information in 1940, necessary for that country's sense of identity. Nonetheless, her short stories of this period portray Ireland as an unreal, unchanging place, cut off from what was happening in the rest of Europe. A central argument of W. J. McCormack's pioneering study, *Dissolute Characters*, is that nineteenth-century writers like Le Fanu anticipated the psychic dislocations characteristic of modernist writers. Elizabeth Bowen was a perceptive reader of Le Fanu, as her preface to *Uncle Silas* demonstrates. During the Second World War, influenced by Le Fanu's use of the ghost story to articulate social and psychological anxieties, she drew on the ghost story to express unease about the self and the self in relation to society. In many of her stories Bowen shares with Le Fanu a sense of the imminence of chaos and the threat of annihilation and, as with Le Fanu, her anxieties are exacerbated by membership of the rapidly vanishing Anglo-Irish class. Of Bowen's nine short stories set in Ireland, four belong to the war period and provide an insight into the fragmented, heightened feelings of those years or, as one contemporary reviewer of Bowen's war stories put it: 'our need to place our hearts in some security which cannot yet be found or called secure'.[4]

Bowen's wartime writing presents the fracturing of identity brought about by the war, when homes and with them entire ways of life were blown up during the Blitz. She portrays people trying desperately to preserve a sense of self by clinging to what personal possessions still remained, thereby filling, 'the vacuum for the uncertain "I"'.[5] Under these circumstances personality became peculiarly porous. Bowen describes living 'with every pore open . . . Sometimes I hardly knew where I stopped and somebody else began . . . Walls went down.'[6] Bowen is speaking here of life in London but many of these themes become transposed to Ireland in her story 'Summer Night', where the Second World War is the backdrop for an exploration of the breakdown of language and the fracturing of individual and political identities. The Irish countryside through which Emma is speeding on the way to meet her lover is strangely insubstantial in the evening light and even the car in which she travels is unstable, lacking boundaries and open to the evening air. The instability, the sense of boundaries collapsing, even Emma's febrile impatience to be with her lover (Bowen described the Second World War as a time when, not knowing whether they would survive another day, people were more than usually promiscuous) are all themes common to Bowen's wartime writing, but there are elements in the story that more particularly reflect the Irish situation. Emma, for example, would seem deliberately drawn to represent traits Bowen thought characteristic of neutral Ireland. In her essay, 'Eire', Bowen commented that Ireland's neutrality and isolation from the war resulted in 'a national childishness, a lack of grasp on the general scheme of the world'[7] and in her story Emma embodies this 'childishness', her bare legs and crumpled coat conveying an impression of a 'childish, blown little woman'.[8] Her excitement is only possible in someone who, unlike her husband, the Major, has shut out all thoughts of the war. With her foolish romantic fantasy about a man as pragmatic and practised in love as Robinson, Emma displays that 'inhibition of judgement' Bowen feared would result from Irish neutrality.[9] In Vivie, the daughter who resembles her mother, Emma's uncivilized behaviour comes home to roost. Vivie's pre-pubertal sexuality breaks out in a series of anarchical scenes correctly associated by Aunt Fran with the outbreak of some evil in the house. Emma's implied failure to inculcate moral standards into her children is a portent of the next generation's barbarism: Emma represents all that Bowen feared Ireland would become as a consequence of its policy of neutrality.

Other characters in the story embody attitudes Bowen thought characteristic of Ireland during the Emergency. Justin experiences that feeling of entrapment and claustrophobia which Bowen saw as a particular threat to Ireland's intellectual life during the war, resulting from the suspension of travel between Ireland and Britain. Justin's feeling that language is breaking down and must be renewed brings with it a concomitant observation that personal identity is also dissolving and will need to be remade: 'On the far side of the nothing – my new form. Scrap "me"; scrap my wretched identity and you'll bring to the open some bud of life. I *not* "I".'[10] In such, almost Beckettian, passages, Bowen catches the nomadic Irish identity at a moment of change and for at least one contemporary reviewer, Bowen's wartime stories demonstrated 'a very great advance in their author's power over her medium'.[11]

'Unwelcome Idea', published in the same collection, *Look At All Those Roses*, in 1941, observes the combination of claustrophobia and restlessness in Irish life during the Emergency. A sense of stasis is conveyed: in Dublin on a sunny July morning, only the tram is in motion. The conflicted attitudes of the Irish to the war become apparent in the conversation on the tram between Miss Kevin and Mrs Kearney, during which opinions range from that of Miss Kevin's father, who displays ambivalent support for Hitler, to Mrs Kearney, who sees the war chiefly as an obstacle to her social life (the Horse Show has been cancelled) and whose sister has scurried off to County Cavan in fright. Bowen satirizes a country that does not know whether to treat the war as a major threat or a minor inconvenience. The accuracy of Bowen's portrayal of Ireland at this date is confirmed in the reactions of Seán O'Faoláin and his wife:

His English friends told him London would soon be under threat. He himself thought that Ireland might be invaded. In Dublin there was a lot of scare talk: the Americans would take the ports, there would be an Allied fleet in the Irish sea, and dog fights over Killiney. Eileen was so frightened that she ran down to Dunloghaire [*sic*] and bought two tins of corned beef and half a stone of flour.[12]

This was in 1940. A similar combination of claustrophobia and rest-lessness is portrayed in Bowen's 'A Love Story, 1939', set in Ireland, most probably in County Cork. The opening description of the mist's 'muffling silence'[13] conjures up a country where energy is paralysed and prepares us for the claustrophobic relationship between Clifford Perry-Dunton, an Englishman stranded in Ireland since the outbreak of war, and his wife, Polly, who holds the purse strings and has no intention of letting him return to the dangers of England. In contrast, Mrs Massey's self-dramatizing restlessness due to her lover's death in the war incom-modes them all. *Look at All Those Roses* was given a generally favourable review in *The Irish Times*, though the reviewer was suspicious of some of Bowen's more modernist touches.

In 'Sunday Afternoon', also set in wartime Ireland and published in the same year as 'Summer Night', in *Life and Letters of To-day*, the general collapse in language and civilized standards of behaviour is juxtaposed to the Anglo-Irish way of life. Henry Roussel, who has lost all his possessions during the bombing of his London flat, is on a brief visit back to old friends in Ireland. All now elderly, their Anglo-Irish way of living has not been altered by the war and their lives have for Henry 'an air of being secluded behind glass'.[14] They are horrified, in a Jamesian way, to hear of the loss of 'his beautiful things', but would really prefer him not to enter into details about life during the Blitz. Their moral indifference to the war is portrayed as deplorable, yet Henry cannot help contrasting the civilized manners of the Anglo-Irish with the breakdown in language and identity experienced by those living through the Blitz in London. Only the young girl, Maria, is energized by Henry's description of life in London. Maria, whom Henry in a clear reference to *The Tempest* insists on calling Miranda, is eager to leave her enchanted home (neutral Ire-land) to participate in the war effort in London, ruthlessly dismissing the Ivy Compton-Burnett type dialogue of her elders, who wish her to stay in Ireland. Though recognizing the paralysis of the Anglo-Irish, Henry refuses to aid Maria's getaway, telling her that the brave new world she envisages is one where the brutality of war has caused language, and even personal identity, to all but disappear. In contrast with the stylized civilities of the Anglo-Irish in neutral Ireland, life in London has been reduced to the mere will to survive. Depersonalization and the brute struggle for survival are all that await Maria, this world-weary Prospero warns: in London, she will have an identity number but no identity. The story has an autobiographical resonance. Like Henry, Bowen felt she had an obligation during the war to stay in London, where she worked as an

ARP warden. The reference to the bombing of Henry's flat reflects the fear with which Bowen lived daily during the Blitz and in fact, in July 1944, a bomb blew apart her house in Clarence Terrace. Her story may be based on one of several trips Bowen made back to Ireland during the war, gathering information for the British government.

Olivia Manning's stories from the 1940s provide a postscript to Bowen's wartime writing. In particular, her postwar story, 'Twilight of the Gods' (1947), resonates with Bowen's 'A Love Story: 1939'. Ireland is portrayed as a place of refuge where the English, traumatized by the war, find themselves amazed by the friendliness of strangers and by the quantity of food in the shops. The relationship between Clifford and Polly in Bowen's story finds its echo here in that between Flora and Ralph, an English deserter who has been relying on Flora's finances to keep him afloat. A similar atmosphere of claustrophobia and restlessness is conjured up as Ralph's receipt of a legacy frees him at last from Flora but leaves him trapped in provincial Ireland. Alienation and migration, which one critic has characterized as the predominant themes of Manning's trilogies, based on her wartime experiences, *The Balkan Trilogy* and *The Levant Trilogy*,[15] feature in 'In a Winter Landscape' (1941), where a group of English intellectuals in central Europe see in the plight of a Polish refugee intimations that they too might soon be forced to exchange their privileged cosmopolitan status for that of political refugees. Manning's own sense of displacement was, as Eve Patten has pointed out, both an anxiety and a source of creative inspiration.[16] Arguably, it had its roots in her childhood, during which, like Bowen, Manning found herself moving between England and Ireland and never quite belonging in either country.

If Ireland was isolated from the rest of Europe during this period, within Ireland there were many varieties of loneliness. Frank O'Connor's trenchant criticisms of Irish life led to his unofficial blacklisting during the Second World War and the drying up of his work with Radio Éireann.[17] So suspicious did government authorities become of his journeys to England to work on broadcasts for the BBC that they banned him from travelling for a time and he was obliged to earn his living during these war years writing articles for the *Sunday Independent* under the name of Ben Mayo. Partly as a consequence of the financial hardship he suffered during the 1940s, O'Connor spent most of the 1950s outside Ireland, in the United States, where his career flourished. In his influential discussion of the short story form, *The Lonely Voice: a Study of the Short Story*, published in 1962 after his return to Ireland, O'Connor identifies loneliness as a central distinguishing theme of the modern short story: 'there is in the short story at its most characteristic something we do not often find in the novel – an intense awareness of human loneliness'.[18] This formulation, too often taken as the definitive description of the Irish short story, arose not only from O'Connor's study and practice of the form, but was also prompted by O'Connor's personal disillusionment with Irish society post-independence. He believed there should be an organic link between the life of the individual and that of the community but that the restrictive social conditions prevailing in Ireland (censorship, the influence of the Catholic church) had increased the number of lonely and alienated individuals. For this reason, he thought the modern short story suited the Ireland of his times better than the novel for, whereas the novel generally deals with entire societies, the short story, he argued, portrays marginal or isolated individuals and what he termed 'submerged population groups': 'always in the short story there is this sense of out-lawed figures wandering about the fringes of society'.[19]

In contrast with oral storytelling drawing on a sense of community, the modern short story O'Connor judged to be a solitary art: 'the short story remains by its very nature remote from the community – romantic, individualistic, and intransigent'.[20] We may identify with the characters in a novel but we do not really see into the minds of anyone in a short story, he reasoned. 'Which of us can feel, let alone describe, another's interior world?' the narrator enquires at the end of 'The Ugly Duckling'.[21] O'Connor's argument that the short story does not allow the reader to enter into the minds of its characters might already be disputed by stories such as Moore's 'Homesickness', 'The Window' and 'The Clerk's Quest' or Joyce's 'Eveline', 'Clay' and 'The Dead', and it does not always hold water, either, for the Irish short story of later periods. Nevertheless, as a description of the way in which the modern short story presents isolated or eccentric characters and prevents the reader, on account of its brevity, from being drawn into identifying with them, it conveys an important insight into the way in which the short story, as distinct from the novel, operates.

The emphasis on storytelling as a solitary art makes it plain that O'Connor's attempt to incorporate the warm human voice of the oral tradition into the modern short story was being challenged by the con-ditions of modern life. Indeed, the dying out of the oral tradition is the subject of several Irish short stories from this period. From the 1930s onwards, radio had begun to be a widely available and popular form of entertainment, and in Bryan MacMahon's 'The Good Dead in the Green

Hills', the narrator recalls the moment in his youth when he saw the community storyteller, Peadar Feeney, driven out by the advent of radio: 'Small as I was...I had the good grace to appreciate that I had been witness to the end of an epoch.'[22] After his departure, the community gradually tires of the radio, but is unable to revive the art of conversation. In 'The Silence of the Valley', Seán O'Faoláin's tribute to Tim Buckley the Tailor, the tourists fail to understand the significance of the cobbler's death but the priest, a mediator between the outsiders and the locals, recognizes the silence that has fallen over the valley after the old story-teller's death. 'The End of the Record' portrays an effort to preserve the last dying traces of the oral tradition as a recording van makes a tour of the poorhouses to collect the stories of the elderly inmates. The lonely cry of the bittern inadvertently recorded by the engineer becomes a keen for a dying tradition.

Nevertheless, traces of the oral storytelling tradition of his native Cork are still present in O'Connor's first collection of this period, *Crab Apple Jelly*, published in 1944 and banned in Ireland. Many of the stories had originally been tried out on radio and retain their vocal quality. 'The Grand Vizier's Daughters' features a storytelling uncle, whilst several, such as 'The Long Road to Ummera', 'The Cheapjack' and 'The Luceys', have openings that suggest a story arising out of a community, and 'Public Opinion', a comic tale of the claustrophobia of Irish society, is set in an oral framework appropriate to convey small town gossip. Unlike the storyteller of the oral tradition, however, these narrators cannot be straightforwardly equated with O'Connor's own voice. They frequently turn out to be unreliable or limited in their point of view and so enmeshed in their narrow-minded, repressive communities that by the end of the story the reader is led to reject their conclusions. O'Connor's view of the short story in this period was being shaped, not only by personal disenchantment with Irish life, but also by his study of French and Russian authors. In *The Lonely Voice*, in addition to chapters on Joyce, Lavin and contemporary English and American writers, O'Connor writes on Turgenev, Maupassant, Chekhov and Isaac Babel. He distinguishes sharply between the modern short story, drawing on Russian and French models, and the oral storytelling tradition, insisting that 'the short story, like the novel, is a modern art form'.[23] The oral story is a public art and the *seanchaí* assumes a shared outlook with his audience, he argues, whereas the short story is 'a private art intended to satisfy the standards of the individual, solitary, critical reader'.[24] Just as the short story features lonely or marginalized individuals, so the writer is 'a lonely voice' speaking both from within and outside the community. In contrast with the diffuseness of the oral tale the modern short story, in O'Connor's reading, is tightly controlled. Unlike the oral storyteller, who piles up incidents, the modern short story writer aims for a single, life-changing incident. Here O'Connor is formulating what writers like himself and O'Faoláin had already begun to put into practice in the previous decades. As O'Faoláin explained in an interview in 1946: 'We Irish writers went to the French for technique and to the Russians for passion. The great inspiration of our writing came from reading Tolstoy, Gogol, Gorki because in the lives and books of those men we saw the similarity to life in Ireland.'[25]

O'Connor's evolution in his understanding of the short story form was influenced, not only by his study of foreign authors, but also by his link with the *New Yorker* magazine. James Alexander has traced the way in which O'Connor's 'first reading agreement' with the *New Yorker* from 1945 onwards caused him to alter the form of his short stories, moving away from narratorial intrusion into a more complex literary story suited to his new reading public.[26] O'Connor reduced or ironized the role of narrator and, despite his doubts as to whether the short story was suited to complex characterization, focused on character development, producing a series of stories (series were popular at the *New Yorker*) centred on particular characters, such as Father Fogarty and Larry Delaney. All these elements distanced O'Connor from the oral tradition and Alexander argues that his association with the *New Yorker* was favourable to developing and deepening his style.

The prevailing view of Irish writers' isolation during this period is challenged by the fact that many of them, like O'Connor, had links with the *New Yorker*. Several, including Brian Friel, had a 'first reading agreement' with the *New Yorker* whereby they received an annual bonus if they agreed to let the magazine see their work first. Others, such as Mary Lavin and, later, Edna O'Brien, Benedict Kiely and William Trevor were published regularly there. The number of Irish writers published with the magazine raises the question of the extent to which the editorial policies of the *New Yorker* affected the shape of the Irish short story during this period. Founded in 1925, the *New Yorker* began to get serious about its short fiction from the 1930s onwards. The word limit for short stories gradually expanded until by the late 1930s stories published in the magazine approached 4,000 words. The word limit was restricting for authors, obliging them to concentrate on setting, mood and character rather than plot: the fiction editor, Katharine White, disliked plot and wished to distance the *New Yorker* story from the surprise endings of the still popular O. Henry stories. There had to be a fair amount of dialogue and the preferred tone was understated irony with few flights of fancy or displays of emotion. 'Short character studies' was how F. Scott Fitzgerald, who rarely published in the *New Yorker*, defined that magazine's short story.[27] Experimentation was frowned upon: precision, detail and, above all, clarity were the qualities sought after.

It is clear that O'Connor's stories would fit easily into the mould of the ideal *New Yorker* short story but that O'Faoláin's more diffuse, detached and intellectual stories would not. Indeed the latter jibed, in a reference to the *New Yorker*'s notoriously fussy editing, that he preferred to write his stories himself rather than have them written for him by editors. O'Connor's relationship with the magazine therefore had pluses and minuses. The tight editorial control exercised meant there was a danger of stories becoming formulaic: stating the theme, in one of those cryptic generalizations favoured by the *New Yorker*, introducing the characters, telling the story, then restating the theme. It was a formula that suited the O'Connor story all too well, and contemporaries like O'Faoláin, Daniel Corkery and Patrick Kavanagh tended to pour scorn on his connection with the magazine. This was slightly unfair as the editors were prepared to be persuaded, and O'Connor's stories were not only deepened as a consequence of his association but, in turn, his complex narrative voice expanded the range of *New Yorker* fiction, dealing as his stories did with failed marriages, infidelity, prostitution and illegitimacy.

However, the 1950s was a decade during which the magazine went through a particularly bland phase. The fact that the Irish short story, with its characteristics of subdued realism and subtle irony, suited the *New Yorker* ethos suggests, at the very least, that the Irish short story was not at the cutting edge of literary experimentalism. Its absence of overt sexuality, violence and general literary radicalism suited a magazine that was turning down work by, among others, William Styron, Jack Kerouac, Saul Bellow and Philip Roth. Though the link with the *New Yorker* might seem to suggest cosmopolitanism, this relationship could actually be regarded as reinforcing the image of Ireland as a stagnant society since it was the conservatism of Irish writers that fitted in well with the blandness of the *New Yorker* during this period. Writing out of a depressed and introverted society, Irish writers could do understated irony but tended to avoid the more extreme emotions and any hint of the radical.

Magazine outlets were all the more vital given the state of Irish publishing: 'Since the firm of Maunsel and Roberts went out of existence, none of our Irish firms have done anything to assist our writers who have to depend on British publishers for the production of their works,' complained an editorial in *Envoy*.[28] It reiterated the point in the following issue, lambasting the Irish publishing industry as 'backward and antiquated' and claiming that Irish writers went to London publishing houses not only because they paid better but also because they could be sure their work would be marketed properly: 'The vast bulk of our serious book-publishing is done from English publishing houses...Yeats, Russell, Synge, O'Faoláin, O'Connor, O'Casey, Lavin *et al*. Practically all our writers whose names, abroad, represent Irish literature, have their works produced in London.'[29] This was certainly true for the short story collections of Frank O'Connor, Seán O'Faoláin, Liam O'Flaherty and Mary Lavin in this period. *The Irish Times* lamented Irish publishers' reluctance to take a risk on short story collections, complaining that in Ireland 'the short story writer is forced into the novel form' and blaming this on

the fault of the public and of its servant, the publisher, who see little good in the short story except when it appears in a magazine, so that a book of short stories is seldom undertaken without a promise that a novel is on the way; indeed the majority of publishers view the short story with some of the suspicion and distaste which they normally reserve for verse.[30]

In popular magazines, stories continued to flourish, so much so that one reviewer felt impelled to issue a warning that: 'Short story writing is a grass-covered bog into which many writers rush without first making sure where the few safe paths are. The result is that, of the hundreds of short stories written every year, only a very small percentage is worth reading.'[31]

As concerns the literary short story, indigenous as well as foreign magazines played their part in shaping the genre during these years. *The Dublin Magazine* continued under the editorship of Seumas O'Sullivan and, after the war, *Irish Writing* was founded under the editorship of David Marcus and Terence Smith. It ran from 1947 until 1956 and published work by Frank O'Connor, Liam O'Flaherty, Seán O'Faoláin and Somerville and Ross. The most influential periodical of these years, however, was *The Bell*, founded in 1940 by Seán O'Faoláin in an effort to combat Ireland's isolationism and raise the level of intellectual debate in the country. Frank O'Connor became poetry editor. O'Faoláin's editorials severely criticized what he saw as the prevailing ills of Irish society, namely censorship, provincialism, middle-class complacency, the power of the clergy and de Valera's isolationist economic policies. In an editorial of 1941, 'The Gaelic and the Good', he expanded on AE's arguments in

The Irish Statesman twenty years previously and anticipated those of the 'new nationalists' by insisting that Irish culture was made up of many diverse strands, Catholic, Protestant, non-conformist, urban, rural, the cottage and the Big House. Here, as elsewhere in his editorials, O'Faoláin saw the drive towards everything Gaelic as leading inevitably to censorship and isolationism.[32] In the September issue of 1943, he lambasted Ireland's intellectual stagnation: 'We are not really wide-awake at all, not keeping pace at all with the irresistible movement of life.'[33] In November of the same year, he thundered: 'A clamp was put down on all intellectual activity here almost from the first day that the Free State was set up.'[34] In December 1944 he enquired, through obviously gritted teeth: 'Can we seriously hope to develop a dynamic industrial future with a system of education which is based on an uncritical adoration of Finn MacCool?'[35] In his December 1943 editorial, 'Past Tense', he pointed forward to the wider canvas of his own short stories in later decades when he declared: 'The truest Irish patriot of today is the man who can look at Ireland as a modern man, and as a Citizen of the World, who happens to be resident in this corner of it.'[36] Eventually, overburdened by his task and discouraged by the lack of change in Irish society, O'Faoláin resigned his editorship and from 1946 Peadar O'Donnell took over.

As well as using his editorship of *The Bell* to promote his political views, O'Faoláin provided an opportunity for younger writers to publish and he spent a lot of his time helping other writers revise their work, turning this aspect of his editorship into what amounted virtually to a creative writing course on the short story. Through his comments on the short story form and by his selection of authors, O'Faoláin shaped the Irish short story of this period in a particular direction, rejecting Yeatsian romanticism and de Valera's rural idyll in favour of realistic portrayals of contemporary urban and rural life. Some of the names published in *The Bell* represented the best in Irish short story writing of the period, including O'Connor, Bryan MacMahon, James Plunkett and Mary Lavin. Writing from Northern Ireland was a particularly strong presence, featuring work by Sam Hanna Bell, Mary Beckett and Michael McLaverty.

James Plunkett's resolutely urban realist short stories, portraying the restrictive and controlling society that had developed after independence, chimed in particularly well with O'Faoláin's views of what the Irish short story should be doing. 'Weep for Our Pride' recalls Joyce's *Portrait of the Artist* as the Irish language fanatic, Mr O'Rourke, hammers Irish and patriotism into his charges whilst Brother Quinlan beats in religion. In 'The Wearin' of the Green', a new schoolmaster who desires a more democratic Ireland is driven out by the combined forces of religion, nationalism and the Gaelic League, as embodied in Father Finnegan, Lacey, a fanatical Gaelic Leaguer, and Murphy, whose wealth has been achieved by profiteering during the war of independence. 'Janey Mary', published in *The Bell*, February 1945, depicts, through the consciousness of a starving child, the grinding effects of urban poverty.

O'Faoláin published his views on the short story form in a series of articles in *The Bell* that appeared between January and July 1944 and were eventually incorporated into his study, *The Short Story* (1948). Eilís Dillon has attested to its impact on an aspiring young writer in a period when there was precious little in the way of advice or encouragement: 'I remember it the way an outcast member of the Foreign Legion would remember his first drink after he had crossed the desert on foot,' she wrote. 'So lacking in confidence we were then...Books were being banned wholesale, until almost the whole corpus of world literature was represented on that list. Shakespeare escaped but not Stendhal, nor Flaubert, nor Maupassant, nor Zola, nor indeed O'Faoláin himself, nor Frank O'Connor, nor Liam O'Flaherty nor Kate O'Brien.' For Dillon, O'Faoláin's study was simply 'the best I have ever read on the art and craft of writing'.[37]

Like O'Connor, O'Faoláin endeavoured to distinguish the modern short story from the diffuse and loosely structured tale of oral tradition: 'We have come to expect from the short story much more than a series of incidents.'[38] In his view, the modern short story was a highly compressed form and achieved its best effects through suggestion and implication. He offered O'Connor's 'In the Train' as a model in this regard. Like O'Connor, O'Faoláin believed the short story should be based around a significant incident and argued that there could be no room for major character development or lengthy time lapses. In later years, O'Faoláin moved away from the compact short story to what he called, in his preface to *The Heat of the Sun*, the 'tale', a longer, more digressive form with more incidents and more changes of mood. This was not always successful.[39]

O'Faoláin anticipated O'Connor also in his argument that the short story form was particularly suited to Irish life because, unlike England, where the way of life was more social and therefore suited to the novel form, Ireland was a country made up of a collection of individuals, each with their own way of looking at life. These unique insights could be better conveyed, he believed, in the short story form, where 'tiny bits of life speak for the whole of life'.[40] He was perhaps on surer ground when he moved away from national stereotypes to define the modern short story as chiefly 'an adventure of the mind', an emphasis on psychological exploration that contradicted O'Connor's assertion that the short story was not suited to portraying the interior life of its protagonists.[41] Just as O'Faoláin's political views did not make much headway during this period, so his theories of the short story were challenged by more conservative readers, as the following letter from a 'Lowbrow' printed in *The Bell* in March 1944 attests: 'Many of the alleged "short-stories" printed in THE BELL seem to me to possess no qualities at all: they are certainly all distinguished by a complete absence of plot. They may be adequate descriptions of persons, or of personalities, or of the reactions of a particular mind to a particular situation – but is that a "story"?'[42] Despite O'Faoláin's best efforts to modernize the Irish short story, there was evidently still a public appetite for traditional stories based on incident and plot.

There were differences, then, in this period, between O'Faoláin and his readers, and between O'Faoláin and other Irish writers, as to what the short story should be doing. Posthumously published excerpts from Michael McLaverty's journals reveal disenchantment with O'Faoláin's theories of the short story, regarding them as tailored to his own particular style of writing: 'it seems to me that he is formulating a critical analysis to justify his own "romantic" products'.[43] If O'Faoláin had had access to McLaverty's private diaries and letters, he might have been less eager to publish him in *The Bell*, for McLaverty makes clear his dislike of O'Faoláin's stories. Calling them a 'falsification of life', he compares them unfavourably with the truth of Joyce's *Dubliners* and even some of Corkery's stories.[44] McLaverty makes similar criticisms of O'Connor, judging that only a handful of his stories will survive, among them 'Uprooted', 'The Road to Ummera' and 'Guests of the Nation'. This was two more than for O'Faoláin: of his entire short story oeuvre McLaverty thought only 'Admiring the Scenery' would last. If all this sounds unduly tetchy, McLaverty's journals and letters display perceptive critical insights into the short story form and deserve to take their place among the better-known writings of O'Connor and O'Faoláin. His was a voice that became increasingly out of tune with a changing Ireland but worth listening to despite, or perhaps because of, that. He gave early encouragement to John McGahern, on whom McLaverty's belief in the importance of depicting 'the ordinary in life' and of a writer taking time to immerse himself in his environment was surely not lost. 'Be artists of the normal... it is the normal that survives, and it comes from exploring the resources of your own people and your environment – no matter how small the latter is, if it is deeply pondered the resultant work will overleap its boundaries.'[45] McLaverty's words, published in 1952, sound like a blueprint for McGahern's later work.

Envoy: a Review of Literature and Art, which ran from 1949 till 1951 under the editorship of John Ryan and published work by, among others, Joyce, Flann O'Brien, Francis Stuart and Mary Lavin, shared O'Faoláin's frustration with the current state of Irish literary life. *Envoy* constantly had to defend itself against criticisms that it was not Irish enough because of its commitment not only to publish Irish writers but also to bring international writing, art and culture to the attention of the Irish public. It ceased publication after the twentieth volume, blaming rising costs but still defending its international perspective: 'We tried to rid the Irish literary scene of a number of the more depressing aspects of provincialism by introducing a European outlook.'[46] Unlike *The Bell*, *Envoy* directed its criticism not at the reading public but at writers themselves. After initial editorials proclaiming its dual aim of presenting Irish writers' work to the world and bringing international writing to the attention of an Irish audience, by 1950 it was complaining that: 'It is a difficult thing to perform our first function, that of sending native talent abroad. We now sell more copies of ENVOY overseas than in Ireland, yet it is difficult to discover writing of "exportable" quality.'[47] It hoped that a short story competition sponsored by the *Times Pictorial* and offering prizes of £150 for the two winning entries would stimulate Irish writers to set higher standards for themselves. 'Remember,' it admonished, 'you will be writing not only to win a Prize for yourself but to uphold the great literary traditions of Ireland.' A running 'Diary' column by Patrick Kavanagh adduced one reason for Irish literary life being in the doldrums, namely 'the difficulty of making a living by writing'.[48] A letter to *Envoy* from a certain Matthew Morgan of Trinity College, Dublin, suggesting that if contemporary authors felt discouraged in the face of great literary talents like Joyce and Yeats there was nothing wrong with aiming for the good second-rate, probably failed in its attempt to cheer up Irish writers of the day.[49]

What, then, were the characteristic themes and preoccupations of the Irish short story during the 1940s and 1950s? In *The Backward Look*, Frank O'Connor speaks of Irish literature in these years being 'diverted' by the realities of Irish life,[50] and the strains and stresses of the period are often reflected in the Irish short story. Seán O'Faoláin's resentment, expressed in his *Bell* editorials, at the claustrophobic nature of Irish life, surfaces as a theme in many of his stories. In 'Lady Lucifer', three representatives of the intelligentsia, a priest, a bank clerk and a doctor, debate whether they should stay in a country where so many lead lives of despairing self-sacrifice. Borrowing a technique from Bowen's 'A Love Story, 1939', O'Faoláin conveys the paralysis afflicting Irish life through his opening description of the stillness of the Irish countryside: 'They were secluded, lost, tucked-away. The world had died.'[51] Malachy, the bank clerk, is berated by the doctor for writing sleepy books: ' "All your stories," and his voice was not amiable now, "are about little spurts of passion. Faint gestures. You should call your next book *Faint Gestures.*" '[52] O'Faoláin here pinpoints a theme regarded by one critic as a general characteristic of much Irish writing during this period, namely buried emotion, 'recognized but rarely acted upon', due to the constraints of Irish society.[53] In Frank O'Connor's story, 'The American Wife', Ireland strikes Elsie, the eponymous American wife, as similarly backward and lacking in energy.

For some in this period, their energies were absorbed by the shift from country to town and the effort of adapting to a new rhythm of life. The move created a new type of loneliness in those suddenly uprooted from rural surroundings where their families had lived for generations. O'Connor's portrait of his Irish-speaking grandmother in 'The Long Road to Ummera' bears comparison with Daniel Corkery's 'Carrig-an-Afrinn' with its description of the emotional cost of uprooting an older generation from their birthplace. Abby resists her son's efforts to pull her into his upwardly mobile town life, retaining her country customs and displaying a fierce determination to be buried back home rather than 'among foreigners in the town'.[54] Her lapse into Irish as she is dying reminds the reader of another loss she has suffered in moving to the town. O'Connor's 'Uprooted', one of his finest stories, portrays the in-between position of the first generation to move to the city. Ned Keating discovers life as a schoolteacher in Dublin to be more constricting than he had envisaged. At the same time a trip home, where he finds everything going on as usual in his absence, confirms that he can never return. 'Uprooted' follows a structure characteristic of O'Connor's stories, namely, an introductory narrative that moves from the externals of Ned's life in the first three paragraphs to his thoughts, and then proceeds to tell the rest of the story mostly through dialogue and action, with a return to narrative in the final paragraph. It exemplifies O'Connor's belief that the short story should focus on a turning-point in an individual's life, his visit back home prompting Ned's realization that he is an outsider in both environments.

This theme of the exodus from the countryside is one that crosses political boundaries. A decade after O'Connor's 'Uprooted', *The Dublin Magazine* published a story with the same title by the Ulster writer, Michael McLaverty. In McLaverty, the theme is given a specifically Northern Irish twist since it is the British Army that precipitates the O'Briens' move by requisitioning their land. McLaverty's 'Uprooted' opens in idyllic countryside, describing, in a manner that recalls O'Flaherty's 'Spring Sowing', a rhythm of life that has gone on for centuries. Working the land, the O'Briens are a family in harmony with their surroundings and with each other. The story marks the dissolution of this way of life as their farm is requisitioned in order to build an aerodrome, and the son, Jim, opens a shop in town. Though the younger generation adapts easily to life in the town, Jim's elderly father, Tom, like Abby in O'Connor's story, experiences a yearning for home that will end only when death allows him to return to the land of his ancestors. Another story from Northern Ireland, Sam Hanna Bell's 'The Broken Tree', published in *Summer Loanen and Other Stories* (1943), presents a move to the town similarly precipitated by wartime regulations. Hans contravenes these regulations when he allows a dead cow to be cut up. Bell's story depicts the precarious living made by tenant farmers in rural Ulster: when Hans is prosecuted he has no choice but to relinquish the land. Like other representatives of the first generation to move into the towns, Hans has difficulty settling and longs to be back on his farm. The Irish short story has by no means finished with this theme of the emotional cost of the transfer from rural to urban living. In the following decade, John McGahern will publish 'The Slip-Up' on precisely this subject.

The shift from country to town often meant that those left behind in the countryside also experienced loneliness and isolation. The 1940s was the decade in which the country as a whole began to show signs of disenchantment with the conditions of rural living, and Liam O'Flaherty's stories from this period, collected in *Two Lovely Beasts and Other Stories* (1948), present a less lyrical view of peasant life than his earlier work. In contrast with the images of fertility in 'Spring Sowing', 'The Wedding' portrays village life as stagnant, with the youngest and most energetic emigrating. The wedding between Anthony and Barbara is the first in the community for five years and since both are middle-aged the emphasis is not on love and fertility but on Anthony's materialistic reasons for marrying. Barbara has returned from America with money and this gives her status over the other two middle-aged women in the story, the sexually frustrated Nuala and the alcoholic Peggy. The fact that the entire story takes place in Peggy's house adds to the claustrophobia and contrasts sharply with earlier O'Flaherty stories, such as 'The Caress', portraying sexual love in a natural setting. Peggy's illegitimate daughter, Girleen, is likely to be the next to leave for America, leaving Nuala and Peggy alone and unwed.

Another story from this collection, 'The Lament', opens with a thrillingly observed description of the sea that draws us in like tourists to admire its beauty. Part of the point about O'Flaherty's story, however, is that while visitors like the journalist might admire the beauty of the west of Ireland, for inhabitants life there can be lonely and oppressive. The young Connemara woman, Sheila Manning, is, like Nuala in the previous story, mentally unstable and sexually frustrated. To the journalist's remark about the beauty of the harbour, she responds acerbically: 'The sea is lovely . . . but the land is awful. I don't think it's lucky for anybody to live here in poverty.'[55] When the journalist expands didactically on the new houses that have been built and the energy of a new generation, Sheila questions the use of new houses 'when the spirit of the people is broken? They have new houses, but they live on the dole and, what's more, they don't believe any more in the old fairy tales.'[56] An entire community's loss of cultural self-confidence lies behind Sheila's remarks; moreover, by revealing her loneliness and frustration to the stranger, she loses her last chance of love and of escape. The story returns to a description of the sea at the end, but now the reader sees it through Sheila's eyes, as menacing and claustrophobic.

1942 marked the publication of *The Great Hunger*, Patrick Kavanagh's classic poem on sexual starvation in rural Ireland, and the theme was picked up in many of the short stories of this decade. In 'The Wedding', Nuala's sexual frustration is suggested by her immature body and by her constant scratching at her bosom. Other short stories used nature imagery to present the theme of sexual frustration in the Irish countryside. O'Flaherty's 'The Touch', a Lawrentian story about the suppression of natural instincts, tells of the physical desire between Kate Hernon and her father's hired labourer, which is thwarted when Kate's father virtually sells her to a prosperous neighbour. The imagery of hailstones on which the story ends expresses the life of sexual frustration to which Kate, like Nuala and Sheila in the previous stories, can look forward. 'Village without Men . . .' by Margaret Barrington, who was married to O'Flaherty for a time, takes up this theme of the sexual frustration of rural women as an entire village is robbed of its menfolk during a fishing accident. The subject is treated with a pathos that shades into humour when the war eventually brings them replacement males in the form of Danes whose boat has been torpedoed.[57]

Themes from the Northern Irish short story continued to overlap with writing from the Republic. In Michael McLaverty's 'Six Weeks On and Two Ashore', published in *Irish Writing* in the same year as O'Flaherty's collection appeared, the 'cold sea' reflects the loneliness of Mag's marriage to an elderly and exhausted lighthouse keeper, in the same way as the hailstones beating against the rocks announced Kate's future loveless marriage. Mag's sexual yearning, an unusual subject for McLaverty, is conveyed in her reaction to the soft wind that blows on the shore, as she looks towards the lighthouse, waiting in vain for a sign of communication from her husband: 'If only it were strong, blowing against her with force she would delight in it. But there was no strength in it – it was indolent and inert, as tired as an old man.'[58] The Irish short story of the period shows sexual desire continuing to be thwarted in the Irish countryside and marriages of necessity made more often for materialistic reasons than for love.

The desertion of the countryside for the towns by the youngest and best educated created problems for the educated left behind. In 'The Lament', part of Sheila's loneliness arises from the fact that her training as a teacher has turned her into an outsider in her rural community. Seán O'Faoláin's 'A Letter', published in *Teresa and Other Stories* (1947), is a Chekhovian story of a teacher isolated in a rural area and torn between love of the Irish countryside and the feeling that life is passing her by. It is a beautifully controlled mood piece reflecting not only O'Faoláin's ambivalence towards Ireland but also, in its concentration on psycho-logical exploration rather than social commentary, his view that the modern short story should be 'an adventure of the mind'.

Like teachers, priests were part of an educated minority that often found itself stranded in the countryside. The loneliness of the priest in a rural community is the subject of O'Connor's Father Fogarty stories. By creating a series of stories around Father Fogarty, O'Connor was able to explore his characterization in greater depth than the short story form usually allowed and in this respect, the *New Yorker*'s liking for story series may have helped deepen his art. O'Connor's treatment of the priest figure evolves in this period from the satire of 'The Shepherds', where the narrow-minded Father Whelan makes a fool of himself trying to police the morals of local girls, to the more sympathetic portraits of Father Fogarty and his fellow priests in stories like 'The Frying-Pan', 'The Wreath' and 'An Act of Charity', which reveal a sensitive understanding of the nature of priesthood and the sacrifices involved. Seán O'Faoláin's stories about religion are bleaker: in 'The Man Who Invented Sin', a curate's interference in an innocent friendship between a group of monks and nuns on holiday forces them into a lifetime of self-suppression. Though the tone of the story is light-hearted, dwelling on the innocent gaiety of the monks and nuns and, humorously, on Lispeen's satanic character ('his elongated shadow waved behind him like a tail'),[59] the message is sombre: the people now in authority in the church are destructive and narrow-minded.

O'Flaherty's autobiographical story, 'The Parting', portrays a boy's lonely start on the road to priesthood as he leaves his native island to enter a seminary on the mainland. As so often in O'Flaherty, the boundary between animals and humans dissolves when thirteen-year-old Michael feels pity for the young bullock which, like himself, is being taken away from its native island in order to serve other people's material interests. The parallel is strengthened when his mother, unable to express her maternal feelings directly, transfers them into a lament over the bullock. As the bullock is going to the mainland to be slaughtered, so for Michael the seminary represents a kind of death, cutting him off from the life of marriage and childrearing that his elder brother Martin will enjoy. The harsh reality is that the farm will support only the eldest son: Michael is being sacrificed to Martin as, in 'The Touch', Kate was sold by her father in marriage.

In stories like 'The Parting' and 'The Touch', O'Flaherty underlines the materialistic attitudes that generate much of the loneliness in the Irish short story of this period. The intrusion of the modern consumerist world into traditional rural life is given detailed treatment in his story, 'Two Lovely Beasts', in which Colm Derrane's rise from small farmer of twenty acres of stony land to successful shopkeeper separates him from his community. As in stories by Michael McLaverty and Sam Hanna Bell, it is the Second World War that precipitates the change, when Colm, after a prolonged mental struggle, is persuaded by Kate Higgins' argument that the war will raise the price of cattle and does what no one in the village has ever done before, namely, buys a second calf. The community provides a chorus on Colm's activities through the voice of the elderly Andy Gorum, who berates him for going against the traditions of their community. Though Gorum would seem to have right on his side here (and the story has been read as an anti-capitalist text), he later degenerates into a malicious and envious old man at odds with the rest of the community, who admire the success Colm is making of his life. O'Flaherty maintains a careful balance between the necessity of preserving tradition and the impossibility of continuing in the old, poverty-stricken ways. 'Two

Lovely Beasts' is a detailed study of the social and psychological costs of material progress and the rise of individualism over the life of the community. Colm Derrane may have prospered materially but O'Flaherty makes plain the emotional cost: 'His pale blue eyes stared fixedly straight ahead, cold and resolute and ruthless.'[60] Materialism is a theme that straddles both country and town life: in O'Faoláin's story, 'Up the Bare Stairs', Francis Nugent's heroic struggle out of urban poverty likewise exacts an emotional price. If 'The Man Who Invented Sin' reveals the life-denying qualities of those in authority in the church, 'Up the Bare Stairs' portrays the destructive characteristics of Irish school life, where even the best teachers like Brother Angelo become involved in petty political factionalism and take their spite out on their pupils.

Materialism is a prominent theme in the stories of Mary Lavin, who began her writing career in the 1940s, publishing four collections in this decade alone: *Tales from Bective Bridge* (1942), *The Long Ago and Other Stories* (1944), *The Becker Wives and Other Stories* (1946) and *At Sallygap and Other Stories* (1947). *The Irish Times* noted that Lavin 'received universal praise for her first book, *Tales from Bective Bridge*'.[61] Many of her stories feature a Catholic middle class so consumed by the need to earn a living that the death of the heart ensues. The theme encompasses both urban stories like 'The Little Prince' and those that have a rural setting, such as 'Lilacs'. 'The Little Prince' records Bedelia's gradual death of the heart as she puts material interests above affection for her brother, driving him out of the family business and out of Ireland. After years of scheming to advance in the world, she journeys to America to view what may be her brother's corpse, only to discover that she is no longer capable of expressing emotion. 'The Little Prince' ends in a stuffy and claustrophobic cab, aptly symbolizing Bedelia's life trapped in materialism.

In *The Lonely Voice*, O'Connor describes the discomfort he felt on reading Lavin's stories because they seemed to him to bear no relation to the central Irish themes of nationalism and war: 'an Irishman, reading the stories of Mary Lavin, is actually more at a loss than a foreigner would be. His not-so-distant political revolution, seen through her eyes, practically disappears from view.'[62] He confessed himself disorientated by the emphasis on the domestic and the female: 'All through Mary Lavin's stories one is aware of a certain difference in values.'[63] The mention of the word 'diapers' in one of her stories seems to drive him over the edge: 'the point of view is perhaps too exclusively feminine'.[64] O'Connor's bewildered comments on Lavin's work substantiate Woolf's famous statement in 'A Room of One's Own' that the values of a male reader differ from those of female readers.[65] Lavin herself highlighted gender differences in 'A Story with a Pattern', where she defends her view of the short story form against a male interrogator who urges her to get more plot into her work. This rather Woolfian story (we may recall that Lavin began a doctoral thesis on Woolf before abandoning scholarship in favour of creative writing) portrays an ill-educated, male reader seeking to demolish the female writer's view of her art, much as Charles Tansley in *To the Lighthouse* insists to Lily Briscoe that women cannot paint. O'Connor naturally misses the gender point of this story, regarding Lavin simply as 'guying her audience'.[66] As often in Woolf's writing, the male interrogator in Lavin's story constantly interrupts the woman, insisting on his point of view that her stories are limited because they lack plot and conclusive endings. For the woman writer, to give more plot and pattern to her stories would be to distort the truth, as she explains: 'Life in general isn't rounded off like that at the edges; out into neat shapes. Life is chaotic; its events are unrelated.'[67]

'A Story with a Pattern', written very early in Lavin's career in the late 1930s, though not published until 1945, signalled her artistic intention of abandoning the well-made short story packed with incident for a looser structure, more suited to probing beneath the surface and exploring, like O'Faoláin, states of mind. Lavin later famously defined the short story as 'an arrow in flight', having no definite beginning or end, being a revelation rather than an explanation.[68] She was a meticulous worker, often spending three or four months on a story which in its original form might be as long as a hundred pages. These she then edited down to create tightly woven stories that nevertheless convey something of the unpredictability and randomness of life of which she speaks in 'A Story with a Pattern'.[69] She later formulated her artistic credo in a preface that challenges O'Connor's view of the short story based on a single epiphany:

Because of this conviction that in a true story, form and matter are one, I cannot attach the same importance as the critics to brevity and relevance. It is surely significant that the great short stories of the world have often been studded with irrelevancies. It is to the magical risks that have been taken with the short story that we often owe their most magical embellishments.[70]

It was for just this quality of risk taking that Michael McLaverty crossed gender boundaries to admire Lavin's writing: 'She goes her own way unhampered by any short story formulae; it seems to me she can do anything she likes with the short story, entering into it with a freshness and freedom that are instantly compelling.'[71]

Although 'A Story with a Pattern' might indicate that Lavin adopted a gendered approach to her writing, she later rejected gender as an explanation of her work: 'I write as a person. I don't think of myself as a woman who writes. I am a writer. Gender is incidental to that.'[72] Nevertheless, Lavin has been an important trail-blazer for Irish women writers. Widowed early, she had to support herself and her three daughters by her work. In contrast to many of her female literary predecessors who remained childless – Maria Edgeworth, Somerville and Ross, Elizabeth Bowen, Kate O'Brien – Lavin illustrated in her daily life that writing and motherhood could be combined, often writing at the kitchen table while at her side her daughters did their homework. Later writers like Evelyn Conlon have claimed Lavin as a role model for Irish women writers and regretted that her works were not more widely available when they were growing up: 'young femalehood in Ireland in the sixties would have been greatly illuminated by the voice that examined the wars of relationships rather than those of countries'.[73] The extent to which Lavin's stories portray women enmeshed in a variety of social restrictions, whilst not classifying her automatically as a feminist, nevertheless highlights her awareness of the severe constraints on Irish women's lives.

V. S. Pritchett characterized Lavin's stories as 'long gazes into the hearts of her people'[74] and, despite O'Connor's misgivings, stories like 'The Little Prince' join a recognizable body of Irish short story writing of this period, atomizing a petty bourgeois Catholic society trapped in materialism and afraid of losing whatever hard-earned status they possessed. In 'The Becker Wives' (1946), a story qualifying as a novella on account of its length, the Beckers' stolid materialism is represented by their heavy furniture and stout, placid wives. For a while Flora, Theobald Becker's new wife, seems to offer the possibility of a different, more imaginative way of living, but she turns out to be schizophrenic. As a recent critic has pointed out, Lavin's outsiders, like Flora, reveal an 'inability to live positively and imaginatively in post-independent Ireland'.[75] 'The Becker Wives' is a surreal, but ultimately bleak, story suggesting that choice lies between conformity and insanity. Lavin's idealistic characters resist the materialism they see around them but often end either destitute, like Bedelia's brother Tom in 'The Little Prince', or forced to capitulate, like Stacy in 'Lilacs', a story in which Lavin follows, quite literally, Chekhov's precept about making literature out of dung-heaps.[76] In 'The Widow's Son', a story that draws on the folk tale tradition, Lavin depicts the constraints of a harsh economic climate that creates a world where, as in

O'Flaherty's stories, emotions cannot be articulated. Ironically, given the emphasis on the family during this period in Ireland by both church and government, in Lavin's stories the harsh economic climate and resultant materialism are portrayed as pitting family members against one another in a way that destroys the family unit and isolates both idealists like Stacy and materialists like Bedelia and the widow.

In 'The Will' (1944), one of Lavin's finest stories, Lally is distinguished from the rest of the Conroy siblings by her capacity for love, symbolized by the two blue feathers she wears in her hat on her wedding day and which so discomfort her mother. Lally has made an impractical love match and has accepted the consequence of a harder life than that experienced by her comfortable bourgeois siblings with their heavy furniture and their stiff black mourning clothes. In contrast to their materialism, Lally is genuinely grief-stricken at her mother's death and anguished that she has arrived too late for reconciliation. While Lally's siblings worry over the material consequences of their mother's refusal to forgive Lally for her inferior marriage, Lally's concern is for her mother's soul. Yet Lavin's story complicates any neat division between materialists and idealists by presenting Lally, too, as shaped by the constraints of the materialistic society in which she lives: her thoughts on the train home are entirely caught up with calculating the cost of the masses she will offer for her mother to lessen her time in purgatory.

Lally has dropped into a lower class by her marriage, and class often causes disunity among family members in the Irish short story of this period. As in O'Flaherty's 'The Touch', where Kate's father refuses to allow her to marry their hired labourer, so in Lavin's 'A Gentle Soul' (1951), Rose's love for the hired hand is opposed by her elder sister, Agatha, from reasons of spite and social snobbery which Rose is too weak to resist. The theme is given comic treatment in Frank O'Connor's 'Legal Aid', where the social disparity is between a farmer's son and a maid-servant. Religious differences accentuate class divisions and often get in the way of love, as in O'Connor's 'My First Protestant', 'The Cheat' and 'The Corkerys'. In all these stories, the theme of love is inextricably linked to the characters' material circumstances and frequently defeated by them, underpinning the central theme of loneliness in the Irish short story of this period. In 'The House that Johnny Built', Johnny's attitude to love is distorted by materialism and sexual naïvety, both attitudes inculcated into him by the society around him. Stories like these anticipate William Trevor's anatomizing of thwarted love in small-town Ireland.

The short story of this period also highlights the isolation of the eld-erly, discarded or neglected when they are seen to stand in the way of progress. In O'Connor's 'The Long Road to Ummera', Abby's son is reluctant to visit his mother while she keeps to her country ways and he opposes her wish to be buried in her home village. The casual treatment of the elderly is a theme of O'Flaherty's later stories: Girleen's contempt for her mother and for Nuala in 'The Wedding', Martin Joyce elbowing his father aside in 'The Parting', the family's neglect of the grandfather in 'Life' in favour of an equally dependent but more selfish and demanding baby. 'Galway Bay' is an insightful portrait of an angry old man, Tom, whose only remaining strength resides in his eyes, likened to 'the eyes of a captured hawk'.[77] However much Tom tries to assert his independence in the face of old age by keeping hold of his stock, the ending reveals him walking into town to sell his aged cow. Characteristic of O'Flaherty's stories of this period, there is little authorial comment, the poignant portrayal of an old man who knows his time has passed being conveyed through the final striking visual image of Tom and his cow: 'He walked beside her with downcast head, one hand on her high hip-bone, the other leaning heavily on his stick.'[78] At the other end of the spectrum, children also suffered from exclusion and isolation. At a time when the Catholic church was emphasizing the evils of sexuality outside marriage, Frank O'Connor, in such stories as 'The Babes in the Wood' and 'The Weeping Children', gives several heartbreaking portrayals of illegitimate children farmed out to often indifferent carers. In *The Backward Look*, O'Connor cites this theme in his work as an example of the Irish short story being shaped by the urgent realities of Irish life.[79]

Maeve Brennan's early short stories also deal with childhood. Brennan was born in Dublin in 1917, moving with her family to the United States when she was seventeen and staying on when the rest of her family returned to Ireland in 1947. In exile Brennan, like Joyce, endlessly recreated the petty social constraints and spiritual discontents of the Dublin of the 1920s in which she had grown up. For nearly thirty years she worked at the *New Yorker* and it was there that her stories began to appear in the 1950s. The genre that predominated at the *New Yorker* in the 1950s was reminiscence. Brennan's early short stories dealing with her Dublin childhood suited the *New Yorker*'s emphasis on realism and setting, as well as the personal interest of Brennan's editor, William Maxwell, in autobiographical fiction. Maxwell's encouragement was crucial to Brennan's career as a short story writer and his editorial pref-erences influenced the shape of her work: the detailed emphasis on place in her stories, for example, may have been prompted by an autobiographical impulse, but it also fitted in well with the *New Yorker*'s insistence that the setting of a story be clear from the opening paragraph.

'The Morning after the Big Fire' was one of a series of seven stories about her Dublin childhood that Brennan published between February 1953 and January 1955 in the *New Yorker*. As with O'Connor's Larry Delaney stories, the *New Yorker*'s preference for series must be seen as having played a part in the genesis of these stories, in which Brennan recreates her childhood home in Ranelagh, a red brick house with a tennis club and garage beyond the garden wall. As much memoir as stories, they are written in the first person and borrow characters and names from Brennan's own family. 'The Morning after the Big Fire' describes an incident that actually happened, namely the burning down of a neighbouring garage. The story is recounted through the eyes of a child anxious not to be excluded by adults from this exciting event. Since the new garage is 'garish and glaring' and 'cut off more of our view than the old building had', the story has been read as a political allegory of the Irish state.[80] Indeed, many of Brennan's stories of childhood convey the repressive nature of Irish society at this time. 'The Devil in Us' portrays a child internalizing the guilt-filled religion inculcated by the nuns into their charges. In 'The Clever One', when the young Maeve fantasizes about becoming an actress, her younger sister Derry responds with a chilling imitation of adult repressive reactions: 'Don't go getting any notions into your head.'[81]

'The Old Man of the Sea' introduces a characteristic Brennan theme as Maeve observes her mother's inability to refuse food or money to the poor men and women who come calling at her door. The theme was expanded in Brennan's 'The Poor Men and Women', published in *Harper's Bazaar* in 1952. This story inaugurated Brennan's series about the Derdon family, published during the 1960s and 1970s in the *New Yorker*. In 'The Poor Men and Women', Rose Derdon's sympathy with the down and outs is partly compensation for lack of emotional satisfaction in her marriage, partly a result of her financial dependence on her husband, which allows him to assert his authority in petty ways. The portrait of the tyrannical husband and the martyr mother recreates in some respects the marriage of Brennan's parents, and her interest in the socially marginalized may partly have stemmed from her fractured childhood. Brennan's early years were disrupted by her father's lengthy absences, either in prison or fighting first against the British and then on de Valera's side during the civil war. The autobiographical 'The Day We

Got Our Own Back' describes, through the eyes of the child Brennan then was, the intrusion of political violence into the domestic sphere as Free Staters raid the house in Ranelagh while their father is on the run. 'The Lie' suggests another reason for Brennan's later identification with marginal characters: Maeve's destruction of her younger sister's sewing machine is prompted by her feelings of abandonment when her mother insists that, while Derry is still small enough to sit on her lap, Maeve has grown too big. Sibling rivalry and maternal abandonment recur as themes in Brennan's American story, 'The Bride', where the Irish maid, Margaret Casey, reflects bitterly on the fact that her younger sister was her mother's favourite.

Brennan's feelings of exclusion from the Ireland that developed after independence – introverted and xenophobic with a narrow definition of femininity that had no place for the sophisticated professional woman she had now become – are, it has been suggested, reflected in her novella, 'The Visitor', published posthumously in 2000, but completed some time in the 1940s.[82] Anastasia has chosen to follow her timid and sorrowful mother to Paris rather than stay behind in Dublin with her father and grandmother. After her mother's death, when Anastasia returns to the family home, she is punished for this choice by her patriarchal grandmother, Mrs King, who gives her granddaughter a chilly welcome and replicates with Anastasia the campaign of cruelty she waged against Anastasia's mother. In the final scene of the novella, Anastasia is left standing outside the family home singing, as if in a dream, a scrap of a once-remembered song about a happy land 'Where we have eggs and ham / Three times a day'.[83] As so often in Irish women's writing, food is a replacement for the absent mother's nurturing. Brennan's novella is an extraordinarily resonant reflection of Irish women's position during this period when many young single women chose emigration over the limited opportunities available to them in Ireland. Its depth and complexity indicate what Brennan might have been capable of had she broken away from her association with the *New Yorker* and tried her hand at longer fiction. Whilst the *New Yorker* undoubtedly gave Brennan editorial advice and access to a market, as well as encouraging her in the kind of autobiographical work that suited her artistic purpose, in the end it may have limited her range as a writer.

'The Visitor' portrays Ireland as a chilly repressed place where Norah Kilbride, the lonely spinster who befriends Anastasia, has been forced to suppress her sexuality, and the Irish short story of this period frequently describes a society where its members are unable to articulate or act on sexual desire. In Frank O'Connor's 'The Cheapjack', Sam is too repressed to express his love; in 'The Sorcerer's Apprentice', the Irish lover is rejected because he is inhibited about sex; and in 'Judas', Jerry is condemned to a life of loneliness and sexual immaturity because he interprets his single experience of love for a woman as a betrayal of his mother. Several women writers of this period explore issues surrounding the suppression of female sexuality, foreshadowing a theme that was to become dominant in the Irish short story after the rise of the feminist movement in the 1970s. In 'The Rose Garden', Mary Lambert, one of Brennan's unglamorized outsiders, cannot fully articulate the yearnings prompted by the secret pleasure she takes in her annual walk in the nuns' rose garden. For the reader, however, the rose garden is described in terms that suggest female sexuality:

It was altogether a stirring place, warm red, even burning red, the way it filled the nostrils and left a sweet red taste in the lips, red with too many roses, red as all the passionate instruments of worship, red as the tongue, red as the heart, red and dark, in the slow-gathering summertime, as the treacherous parting in the nuns' flesh, where they feared, and said they feared, the Devil might yet enter in.[84]

Significantly, the garden dates from before the founding of the puritanical Irish state. A powerful portrayal of sexual hunger in an ungainly and spiteful Irish working woman, 'The Rose Garden' was published in 1959 in the *New Yorker* after being heavily edited by William Maxwell in the interests of concision but in ways that arguably robbed it of even greater depth.[85]

Mary Lavin's story, 'Sunday Brings Sunday' (1944), contains early and outspoken criticism of the sexual repressions of rural Irish life that could leave a young girl dangerously ignorant about her own body. The curate preaches against 'company-keeping' but this term is not precise enough for Mona, who sees many young people around her keeping company without running into danger. Inevitably, without quite knowing how it has happened, Mona becomes pregnant. The confusions and narrative delirium at the end of 'Sunday Brings Sunday' anticipate Edna O'Brien's stories by linking thwarted female sexuality with madness. One of Lavin's most forceful indictments of the censoring of Irish women's bodies comes in 'The Nun's Mother' (1944), in which Mrs Latimer's convent training induces her, even on her wedding night, to undress under her dressing gown. Mrs Latimer's prudery affects her relationship with her daughter, Angela, to the extent that when Angela announces that she wishes to enter a convent her mother is unable, despite her husband's urgings, to talk to her daughter about the sexual pleasure her daughter will be missing out on. Lavin's story portrays a mother–daughter relationship so entangled in Ireland's normalizing discourse concerning women's bodies that they are prevented from speaking openly to one another. It ends with Mrs Latimer, now the mother of a nun, training herself to suppress her thoughts 'with regard to – how should she say it – with regard to the pleasures of the body'.[86] The suppression of the female body in convent life recurs in Lavin's 'Chamois Gloves' (1956), in which Mabel's liberated talk about labour pains and breastfeeding causes several embarrassed silences in the convent parlour.

In addition to these varieties of isolation within Ireland, the loneliness of the emigrant is a theme in many Irish short stories of the period, reflecting the fact that from the 1940s onwards emigration steadily increased, prompted not only by economic necessity but by a real dissatisfaction with what life in Ireland, particularly rural Ireland, had to offer. Frank O'Connor's autobiographical 'Darcy in the Land of Youth', a satire on the difference between Irish and English girls, portrays Mick Darcy's isolation and alienation in England but, like Ned in 'Uprooted', a visit back home makes Mick realize the extent to which he has become detached from his roots. O'Connor's 'Ghosts', which belongs to this period but remained unpublished until 1972, sensitively reveals the emotional cost of emigration to the United States as the wealthy Jer Sullivan, returning to Ireland for a visit, becomes haunted by his ancestors' sufferings.[87] In 'Girders', an unusual story for Mary Lavin, a countryman who moves to the city feels homesick for the countryside but, when an accident forces him to return, he finds himself unable to settle there either. George Moore's example continued to inspire variations on the theme of the eternally restless exile.

As the daughter of the Secretary to the Irish Legation in Washington, Maeve Brennan would seem to have occupied a more secure social position than most Irish emigrants; nevertheless she was not immune to being patronized as an Irish woman by her American colleagues.[88] Between November 1953 and April 1956 the *New Yorker* published six stories by Brennan set in Herbert's Retreat, a wealthy community outside New York based on Snedens Landing, where Brennan lived for a time. Her Herbert's Retreat stories arguably reflect Brennan's own sense of exclusion from this society by portraying the American inhabitants through the eyes of their Irish maids. They present a topic of anxious interest among liberal middle-class readers of the *New Yorker* in this period, namely the relationship between employers and their live-in help. Brennan's focus on Irish maids would have been all the more welcome at the *New Yorker* since, for reasons of political sensitivity, references to African-American maids had become erased from stories set in the North.[89] Brennan's maids, given to observing their employers' behaviour with satirical eyes, are altogether more formidable than the eccentric and obtuse live-in helps that featured in the pages of the *New Yorker* during these years. Moreover, unlike the majority of these stories, Brennan's enter into the maids' interior lives.

The theme of the power play between these wealthy Americans and their Irish maids, reminiscent of that between Bridget Kiernan and her English employer in Norah Hoult's story, begins with an earlier Brennan story, 'The Joker', published in the *New Yorker* in 1952 and originally set in Bronxville but later changed to Herbert's Retreat to fit in with the other stories. 'The Joker' satirizes the wealthy American, Isobel Bailey, who firmly shuts her door to beggars but, in an elaborate display of condescension largely designed to show off her splendid home, invites certain waifs and strays of her acquaintance to Christmas dinner. Money is the source of Isobel's power over her guests, as it is the source of the American employers' power over their Irish maids. Leona's maid, Bridie, may fantasize about being invited to sit down and have a chat with her employer, but she knows that nothing will ever really alter her status. She will always be patronized as 'that splendid Irish woman of Leona's'.[90] Yet, illustrating Hegel's argument that slaves have no choice but to know their masters better than their masters know themselves, Brennan's submerged population group gains a certain power over their employers by observing their shallow lifestyles with a satirical eye and swapping stories about their employers' greedy, snobbish behaviour.[91] Revenge of the marginal on the wealthy and secure is as much a theme of Brennan's work as it is of Jean Rhys'. In 'The Anachronism', the desire of Liza's mother, Mrs Conroy, to continue her Irish habit of drinking tea by an open fire is thwarted by Liza's carefully designed American household but, by entering into an arrangement with Liza's new maid, the elderly, impoverished Mrs Conroy is able to outmanoeuvre her daughter. In 'The Joker', when the tramp who suffers Isobel's condescension turns the tables on his patron by leaving his cigar butt in her pudding sauce, Delia, Isobel's 'bony Irish maid',[92] can barely contain her laughter. Isobel becomes the one to endure her guests' pity, a reversal of power to which she reacts badly.

Unlike the characteristic *New Yorker* story of the period that tended both to praise and patronize the ethnic other – Hispanics, Arabs, Native Americans – for their simplicity, virtue and poverty, Brennan's portraits of Irish maids do not flatter. In her writing, as in Rhys' work, poverty distorts the character, making people distrustful, spiteful and full of envious rage: descriptions of servant girls clumping into rooms with heavy trays and darting poisonous glances at their employers are frequent. Her story of Mary Ramsay, the Irish ladies' room attendant, is a powerful depiction of malice and spite in operation, whilst the portrayal of Mary Lambert in 'The Rose Garden' points to the rage and shame felt by women who failed to fit into prevailing standards of femininity. Clothes underpin the gender theme. Brennan did a spell as a fashion writer for *Harper's Bazaar* and her fiction displays a detailed interest in clothes and make-up. The theme of female appearance being controlled by the male gaze appears in her Herbert's Retreat stories, notably in 'The Stone Hot-Water Bottle', in which Charles exercises power over Leona by playing on her insecurities about her appearance. But Brennan moves away from gender and makes clothes a more general economic indicator. The clothes of the Americans living in Herbert's Retreat are carefully chosen as part of their social performance, to impress their peers in a society caught up in an obsession with images and simulacra. By contrast, the clothes of the Irish maids are cheap and garish, emphasizing their inferior status.

Brennan presents society as a Darwinian struggle for survival, where power is retained by the wealthy inhabitants of Herbert's Retreat through their polished social performance. Yet because it is a performance, these stories recognize that ultimately anyone can feel like a waif. Even wealthy Americans like Leona Harkey and Liza Frye are not as socially secure as they at first appear. Coming from lower down the social scale than the other residents, both are obsessed with the necessity of surrounding themselves with the right furniture and décor for fear of losing status. They partly reflect anxieties felt by the readers of the *New Yorker* during these years, many of whom were newly arrived in the middle class and desirous of emulating the lifestyle of the very rich.[93] The theme of waifs and strays in Brennan's writings is developed in precise social contexts but opens out into a generalized loneliness so that being a waif comes to seem an inescapable part of the human condition. 'What makes a waif?' wonders Isobel Bailey. 'When do people get that fatal separate look?'[94] Isobel's comment expresses Brennan's own unease as an Irish woman living in the United States. Nor did she feel she could easily return home: on trips back to Ireland as, consecutively, an unmarried, professional woman, the wife of a three times divorced man, and finally as a divorcee herself, Brennan recognized that her country's version of femininity could not easily accommodate the woman she had become. Her Irish maid stories reflect this sense of otherness that increased as time went on until Brennan felt at home neither in Ireland nor America, writing in a letter: 'The most I ever knew was that I "didn't know where I was".'[95]

Brennan's stories, like many Irish stories in this period, were written to appeal to an international audience. Some Irish writers, however, continued to use the short story to portray regional customs. Sam Hanna Bell's stories in *Summer Loanen* are mainly set in rural Northern Ireland with occasional forays into Belfast and, as the title indicates, they make deliberate use of local dialect. Michael McLaverty's first two collections, *The White Mare* (1943) and *The Game Cock* (1947), portray urban and rural life among Northern Ireland's Catholics in a style that begins in realism but in his best stories expands into the lyrical and the elegiac in a manner reminiscent of O'Flaherty. In *The Bell*, John Hewitt described McLaverty as 'the best short story writer in Ulster'[96] and *The White Mare* was the subject of an approving, though sectarian, review by Robert Greacen, who argued that McLaverty's stories were livelier than those of his Ulster Protestant counterparts because his subjects (Northern Catholics) were livelier.[97] McLaverty was criticized, though, by Denis Ireland, in what sounds like a generalized attack on the limited range of the Irish short story in the hands of writers like Frank O'Connor: 'Like so many Irish Catholic writers McLaverty writes exquisitely about children and old men and women, but seems to avoid that (to me) much more enthralling chapter of human life, from thirty-five to fifty-five, when passions still smoulder and the mind has deepened and matured.'[98] In the following decades, writers like Seán O'Faoláin, William Trevor and John McGahern were to remedy this omission.

The regional short story was not the preserve of Northern Irish writers. In the 1940s, Walter Macken was writing his light-hearted, sentimental, slightly didactic stories of everyday life in Galway, aiming perhaps to do for Galway what Frank O'Connor had done for Cork. The difference between Macken and O'Connor lies not only in the quality of the prose but also in the narration: unlike O'Connor's stories, there is no distance between author and narrator in Macken's stories. They arise out of a particular community and assume a shared set of values, which O'Connor's often do not. Macken popularizes themes that had been treated by more literary authors: the disillusionment of former gunmen in 'Deputy Johnny', Irish neutrality in 'Homecoming', social isolation in 'Ambition' and 'New Clothes for the Giolla', and the exclusion of the elderly in 'The Passing of the Black Swan'. 'Dad' reveals the public silence surrounding domestic violence, anticipating Edna O'Brien's treatment of this theme, but the position of women in Ireland is largely reflected in Macken's stories by their absence. In 'The Passing of the Black Swan', the generations are represented by grandfather, father and son. Where they do feature, women are marginal figures, widows or forgotten lovers of gunmen. Their role is limited to the domestic and even there they are portrayed as unreliable: in 'Tale of a Kid' the mother commits suicide and it is Uncle Tom who heals his nephew of his trauma. The unity of these stories, published as *City of the Tribes* in 1997, is emphasized in 'The City', a sub-O'Flaherty story of a seagull flying over the city, uniting all the different lives.

Many of the stories in Bryan MacMahon's collection, *The Lion-Tamer and Other Stories* (1948), though ostensibly following the O'Connor mould of realistic stories set in a precise locality (Listowel, County Kerry in this case), turn out to be meditations on the role of storytelling in Irish society. This is perhaps what O'Faoláin, who published many of MacMahon's stories in *The Bell*, was getting at when he wrote: 'You have written short-stories based on common life in the mood of a prose-poet . . . the wonder of it to pedestrian prose writers like me . . . is that you have created as a result an extra art dimension.'[99] The title story of MacMahon's collection, drawing on the tradition of the *seanchaí* as teller of tall tales, tells us something about the fictive nature of storytelling as the listener is beguiled, through a series of authentic-sounding details, into believing a story revealed at the end to be untrue. MacMahon adopts the realist mode of a writer like O'Connor but spins away at the last moment to subvert it so that his story becomes a reflection on the classical adage that art is a lie that tells the truth. The importance of a storyteller to a community's sense of pride in itself is revealed in the publican's admiring words at the end. In 'The Glitterin' Man', such is the power of Micky Doyle's transformation of the well-worn folk tale of the gambler who plays cards against the devil into a revenge tale in which the sneering farmer, Edmond Heffernan, is incorporated as the devil, that his listeners stare down at the farmer's feet to see if they are cloven. For this powerful retelling of an old tale, they offer the storyteller a 'communal glance of pride'.[100] 'The End of the World' portrays the power of stories to enhance the everyday: the narrator knows he is being conned but willingly goes along with the pretence that the world is going to end at two in the morning because it momentarily enriches his too placid life. 'The Egotists' likewise pays tribute to the life-enhancing qualities of story-telling: the rival storytellers, Silver and Boy Hero, and the narrator who meditates a future as a short story writer, may be egotists but their storytelling warms them all for a while, protecting them from 'the widening cold', an evocative phrase suggesting a larger dimension to MacMahon's story.[101]

In all these stories, MacMahon validates the tradition of Irish storytelling as necessary to the life of a community. For MacMahon, storytelling was a vital part of the educational process and education was the force that would drive the Irish nation forward. Several stories in the collection underline the transforming power of art generally. In 'The Dancer's Aunt', a disparate community is united by a little girl's dance. In 'Sing, Milo, Sing!' the life of a flawed individual is redeemed, at least in his wife's eyes, by his singing. 'The Clarinet' ends on a surreal vision of a sleepy Irish town transported by the clarinet player to a foreign land. The story is both a comment on the power of art to transform everyday life and an implicit criticism of Ireland as a place where art is not appreciated: all the members of the 'B-flat clarinets' have been forced to take up other occupations. If MacMahon believed in the importance of the storyteller's art, he also knew that the modern literary short story had different requirements: the point of these stories lies not in the incidents they recount but in the way they become transformed into a series of meditations on art so that, paradoxically, his stories about Irish storytellers echo the folk tale's narrative reflexiveness while at the same time revealing the distance between the oral tradition and the modern short story form.

The stories of writers like Bryan MacMahon, Sam Hanna Bell and Walter Macken, writing out of a community and valuing that community's life and traditions, are exceptions to Frank O'Connor's view of the short story writer as 'a lonely voice' on the margins of a culture. Notwithstanding these examples, though, what is most marked in this period is the intrusion of the modern world into Irish traditional life. Frank O'Connor writes less about peasant life and more about love in small town settings. O'Flaherty's stories move away from lyrical descriptions of life in the Irish countryside to emphasize the loneliness, poverty and sexual frustration of its inhabitants, themes taken up by Seán O'Faoláin and Michael McLaverty. James Plunkett's short stories concentrate on the working classes in the cities ('Plain People', 'A Boy') and lower-middle-class insurance clerks and librarians, and anticipate the 1990s in tackling Irish racism ('A Walk in the Summer').[102] In portraying the material constraints and restrictions of Irish life, the short story of this period reveals a generation of writers moving away from the rigid positions of the civil war period and becoming more critical of the state than the previous generation had the freedom to be.

Whereas O'Connor continued to write stories focused around an emotional turning-point that changes the life or perception of a character, the drive of the Irish short story in the hands of writers like O'Faoláin, Mary Lavin and Maeve Brennan was towards greater sophistication and psychological complexity. Consonant with this move towards greater length and complexity, Liam O'Flaherty's stories of this period are also more elaborate in construction. Even where the local is present, as in Bryan MacMahon's work, the stories often explore complex themes such as the nature of storytelling. New topics enter the Irish short story. Stories by Lavin and Brennan anticipate later women writers in their exploration of female sexuality, whilst James Plunkett's 'The Half-Crown' deals with teenagers, a category, with the exception of some stories by O'Connor, not much explored in the Irish short story but which will be picked up in a later period by writers like Julia O'Faolain, Neil Jordan, Desmond Hogan and Kate Cruise O'Brien.

This period marked one of the heydays of the Irish short story, its success in American markets helping to consolidate the view that it was the predominant Irish literary form: 'With few exceptions it would appear that the Irish writer of to day is a master of the short story rather than the novel' remarked *The Irish Times* in 1946.[103] This success was not without its drawbacks, constraining writers like O'Connor and Brennan to work within a particular set of guidelines. Perhaps, too, Irish American readers' expectations of the Irish short story encouraged writers' conservatism in the form during this period. Irish writers can hardly be blamed for eschewing experimentalism, however: they had, after all, to make a living in a country where, as we have seen, very few publishers were willing to take a risk on a volume of short stories.

The conflict between tradition and modernity continued to impinge on attitudes to the Irish short story in these years. Notwithstanding the clear distinction he was to draw between the oral tradition and the modern short story in *The Lonely Voice*, in a radio broadcast on the short story later published in *The Bell*, O'Connor expressed the hope that radio would become the medium for reviving the art of storytelling:

I think the radio story-teller will get back what the modern story-teller was losing little by little in the elaboration of his forms; the delight in his own personality, the gusto, the intimacy, the pure emotion, and I think, when we begin to discover the resources of the spoken word again, that we shall recapture the vivid speech and fantastic incident which are the joy of the medieval romances.[104]

O'Connor's focus on the voice of the narrator speaking directly to the reader led him to undervalue the kind of in-depth psychological exploration O'Faoláin was to attempt in his later stories, as well as the formal experiments of writers like Mansfield, Hemingway and Joyce. During the course of the same broadcast, O'Connor argued that Joyce's 'The Dead' would be ineffective on the radio because the elaborate patterns Joyce built up in what O'Connor termed 'his rather cold and formal mind', would be undetectable to the listener. By contrast, O'Faoláin lamented that his generation had not studied Joyce enough.[105] In these conflicting arguments over the way in which the short story should develop by two writers whose names dominated discussions of the Irish short story during the period, the tension between tradition and modernity is visible. In advocating the retention of the speaking voice, O'Connor was going against the evolution of the short story in this period; O'Faoláin's preference for a detached narrator and increasingly complex psychological exploration signalled the way in which the Irish short story would evolve in the following decades.

READINGS: MARY LAVIN AND SEÁN O'FAOLÁIN

Mary Lavin, 'A Cup of Tea' (1944)

'A Cup of Tea' is one of three mother–daughter stories Mary Lavin published in her collection, *The Long Ago and Other Stories* (1944), the other two being 'The Will' and 'The Nun's Mother'. Characteristic of writing by Irish women during this period, the latter stories portray fraught mother–daughter relationships embedded in and shaped by the petty constraints and restrictions of Irish middle-class society of the time. In 'The Will', the relationship between Lally and her mother is fractured by considerations of class, whilst in 'The Nun's Mother' sexual constraint comes between Mrs Latimer and her daughter. 'The Cup of Tea', although also deeply embedded in Irish middle-class society, portrays the rift between Sophy and her mother as arising largely out of their disparate temperaments. 'The Cup of Tea' is partly autobiographical: Sophy's mother's high-handed treatment of her servant and jealousy of her daughter's close relationship with her father reflect characteristics of Lavin's own mother. Sophy's father is an amateur entomologist and Sophy is presented as more in tune with his scholarly world than with her mother's domesticity. In real life, Lavin's father, though highly encouraging of his daughter's school and university career, was barely literate.[106]

The story exemplifies Lavin's artistic credo, set out in 'A Story with a Pattern', in that it is relatively plotless, resists the dramatic and focuses on the evening of Sophy's return from university and on a single, symbolic incident, her mother's offering of a cup of tea. The mother's obsession with domesticity is highlighted from the beginning in the description of the detailed preparations she and her servant embark upon to mark Sophy's return after a three-month absence. Tensions between Sophy's parents are clear: right from the start, Sophy's mother tries to deny that Sophy bears any physical resemblance to her father, insisting that she takes after herself and her sisters. Despite her best efforts, she cannot help revealing her contempt for her husband to Sophy and resents her daughter's eagerness to run upstairs to laugh and chat with her father. It is apparent that Sophy's relationship with her father is the easy and natural one, whereas she hardly finds anything to say to her mother. Her mother attempts to pull Sophy back into domestic life by suggesting that she stay at home for a while: 'It's very nice to have a degree and feel independent, but there's no need to carry things too far and wear yourself out work-ing.'[107] Sophy, however, has other plans for her life, though she has no intention of revealing them to her mother. This story about a clash of personalities has wider resonance in its observation of the gap that was likely to grow up between university-educated daughters and mothers whose lives had been centred on domesticity. Since by 1925 30 per cent of all university students in Ireland were female, this was a situation that many mothers and daughters must have had to face up to, and it was to become more prevalent in the 1970s and 1980s as Irish women began to attend university in larger numbers.[108]

Sophy's rejection of her mother's way of life is symbolized by her refusal of the cup of tea offered by her mother. When Sophy rejects the tea because it has been made with boiled milk, her mother lifts off the offending skin, declaring: 'There's nothing disgusting about it at all. In fact, it's full of calcium and good for you.'[109] She adds that at home they always boiled the milk. However, Sophy refuses to be reconciled to the tea, as she refuses to be reconciled to her mother's view of life: 'You did a lot of things in your home that sound queer to me, if it comes to that.'[110] In order to retain her individuality and her chosen way of life, Sophy must preserve a barrier between herself and her mother, rejecting her mother's efforts to pull her into the feminine, domestic world she shared with her own mother and sisters. For Sophy, her mother features as the abject. In *Powers of Horror*, Julia Kristeva argues that in a patriarchal society the maternal body becomes the abject, representing fear of loss of individual boundaries and the link with animality, sexuality and mortality which society seeks to cover up and contain. The skin on top of the milk is precisely one of the examples of the abject given by Kristeva in *Powers of Horror*: 'Food loathing is perhaps the most elementary and most archaic form of abjection. When the eyes see or the lips touch that skin on the surface of milk – harmless, thin as a sheet of cigarette paper, pitiful as a nail paring – I experience a gagging sensation and, still farther down, spasms in the stomach, the belly.'[111] Sophy's rejection of the cup of tea demonstrates her repudiation of the mother's world, perhaps even the world of the body and sensual satisfaction, in favour of her father's world of the intellect.

'A Cup of Tea' provides a female angle on a theme characteristic of the Irish short story of this period, namely human loneliness. The ending shows Sophy regretting the rift between herself and her mother and contrasting her isolation with the happy photograph of her mother and her aunts, all dressed the same and with their arms around one another. This domestic-centred world embodies a closeness Sophy yearns to experience but not if it means giving up her intellectual independence. The story ends bleakly, suggesting the emotional cost of a daughter being educated outside her mother's range. In real life, the story had a happier ending. Although her relationship with her mother was always difficult, Lavin had a close relationship with her three daughters, with whom she was able to share not only domestic but also intellectual and artistic interests.

Seán O'Faoláin, 'Lovers of the Lake' (1958)

One of O'Faoláin's most accomplished stories, 'Lovers of the Lake', explores the psychological cost of the conflict between tradition and modernity and highlights the loneliness resulting from loss of faith as Jenny, one of the lovers of the title, is torn between her residual religious belief and sexual desire for her married lover, Bobby. It is a conflict Bobby, a determined agnostic, does not at first share, but becomes drawn into by Jenny's determination to join the pilgrims at Lough Derg. We are back in William Carleton territory ('The Lough Derg Pilgrim') but, in keeping with O'Faoláin's belief that the modern short story is concerned with 'an adventure of the mind', the conflict presented in 'Lovers of the Lake' is not an external one, between the individual and society, but an internal struggle, which each individual must solve in the privacy of his/her own soul, between loss of faith and the continuing desire to believe.

O'Faoláin conjures up a comprehensive picture of the frustration, bore-
dom, materialism and uncertainty of modern middle-class Irish life in
which religious belief has not yet quite dwindled away.

Merging with the mass of pilgrims on the island, Jenny becomes
removed from the modern world where individual identity, based on class
and age and other considerations, is all-important: 'She was among
people who had surrendered all personal identity, all pride.'[112] The island
is a place where worldly distinctions dissolve and all the pilgrims are
equal: 'each recognizes the other only as a form of soul: it is a brief, harsh
Utopia of equality in nakedness'.[113] She feels able to confess to Bobby her
feelings of guilt over their affair, as other pilgrims in turn confess to her
about sexual desire and their failure to love. After they leave the island,
Jenny endeavours to prolong the effect of the pilgrimage. She and Bobby
continue fasting until midnight and agree to sleep that night in separate
rooms. Nevertheless, these lovers belong to the world, quickly entering
into the comforts of the hotel bar: 'Within two minutes they were at
home with the crowd.'[114] Once off the island, bodily desires, whether
Jenny's for Bobby or the young married woman's for her Tommy, cannot
be denied. The lovers may sleep apart for one more night but it is unlikely
that they will continue to resist their desire for much longer. The thrust of
the story returns us to the world and the body.

Yet O'Faoláin maintains a careful balance between tradition and
modernity. The inevitable dwindling of religious belief in the modern
world is suggested, but without denying the residual power of religion or
the nobility of those persevering with the age-old tradition of pilgrimage.
For, with the loss of religious belief, comes the disappearance of one form
of communion. After she has left the island and returned to the modern
world, Jenny recognizes that: 'it is only in places like the lake-island that
the barriers of self break down . . . Everybody who ever entered the island
left the world of self behind for a few hours.'[115] Lough Derg becomes a
place where, freed from the social constructs of her middle-class milieu,
Jenny acknowledges the essential fluidity of human identity. In the
modern world, however, individuality is what counts and intimate confessions such as occurred on the island are discouraged. After undergoing
an unselfing on the island, the lovers experience a return to 'that
impenetrable wall of identity that segregates every human being in a
private world of self'.[116] Bobby will not tell her what he confessed to the
priest, and Jenny knows that, incapable of renouncing the material
comforts her marriage brings, she will never live up to the ideal of love as
total self-surrender.

Modernity wins out in the end and this is reflected even in the form of the story. O'Faoláin's lengthy psychological probing of Jenny's state of mind and detailed depiction of the changing moods of the two lovers clearly distinguish 'Lovers of the Lake' from the oral storytelling tradition and define it as a modern short story. 'Unless a story makes this subtle comment on human nature, on the permanent relationships between people, their variety, their expectedness, and their unexpectedness, it is not a short story in any modern sense,' he insisted in his study of the form.[117] Like Lavin's story, 'Lovers of the Lake' challenges Frank O'Connor's view that the form is ill suited to conveying the state of mind of its protagonists. At the same time, both 'A Cup of Tea' and 'Lovers of the Lake', with their portrayals of solitariness arising out of the material conditions of contemporary Irish life, exemplify O'Connor's statement that the characteristic theme of the modern short story is human loneliness. In 'Lovers of the Lake', loss of communal religious belief not only points to the isolation and individualism of modern life but also signals yet another rift in those shared values on which the oral storyteller traditionally relied.

CHAPTER SEVEN

1960–1979: time, memory and imagination

'If it weren't for the *New Yorker* I couldn't live,' said Brian Friel in an interview in 1965, acknowledging that magazine's crucial role in enabling him to pursue a full-time career as a writer.[1] Given the limited markets available in Ireland, the *New Yorker* continued to be an important outlet for Irish writers, publishing work by, among others, Maeve Brennan, Benedict Kiely, William Trevor and Edna O'Brien. At the same time, more favourable economic circumstances in Ireland gave a boost to indigenous publishing. Seán Lemass's election as Taoiseach in 1959 and his implementation of the programme for economic development drafted by T. K. Whitaker to give priority to export industries and open up Ireland to foreign investors, fostered a general air of renewal and self-confidence in the country and turned the tide of emigration. New presses started up, among them Poolbeg, founded in 1976. The growth of bookshops, summer schools and a number of often short-lived literary magazines provided Irish writers with an opportunity to showcase their work. A particular impetus for young and emergent short story writers in Ireland came with the decision of the *Irish Press* in 1968 to devote a weekly page to new Irish writing. The literary editor at the time was David Marcus, and from this date onwards the promotion of new and high quality short story writing in Ireland owes much to his encouragement. Starting with *New Irish Writing* in 1970, Marcus began issuing an annual series of anthologies featuring the best stories and poems published in *The Irish Press* during the year. His 1970 collection mixed established writers, like Edna O'Brien, John B. Keane and Janet McNeill, with newer writers such as Julia O'Faolain, John Banville and John McGahern. The 1970s saw the emergence of a more cosmopolitan Irish generation open to influences outside Ireland: American jazz, for example, made its presence felt in stories by Banville, Desmond Hogan, Neil Jordan and Dermot Healy. Nationalist and Catholic discourses began to lose some of their power as the process of revisionism got under way.

These changes are reflected in Seán O'Faoláin's two collections published in the 1960s, *I Remember! I Remember!* and *The Heat of the Sun*. Though O'Faoláin's principal place of residence remained Dublin, his teaching spells in various American universities had given him a more international outlook. His short stories from these years often feature foreigners in Ireland or the Irish abroad in the USA and Europe: in 'One Night in Turin', Walter thinks nothing of flying to Paris for the weekend. The experience of emigration in these stories also differs from that of previous generations: 'The Planets of the Years' juxtaposes the life of an elderly Irish woman who came to the United States in 1904 to be a hardworking domestic servant with a bored and idle professor's wife who accompanies her husband to America in 1967.

Nevertheless, despite the fact that the country was going through a period of relative, though not always consistent, economic revival, themes of time, memory and the imagination are prominent in the Irish short story of these years. Remarkably, in a country that was making a leap into a new era of economic vitality and modernity, the Irish short story often registers clock time as the enemy, to be resisted or evaded through dreams and imagination. Characters might fantasize about escaping into a more liberated way of life, but all too often memory pulls them back into the past and they remain paralysed to act, or at least to act in Ireland. Emigration for psychological and social reasons, rather than purely economic, continues to be an attractive solution. *I Remember! I Remember!*, examining the tensions between past and present in Irish society and probing the workings of memory, is paradigmatic. The title story reminds us that memory is not constructed from brute facts but out of a mixture of remembrance and desire. As our emotional states change, so do our memories. Recalling every unaltered detail of the past, as the paralysed Sarah Cotter does, becomes unbearable for her sister Mary, for whom, as for everyone else, memory alters as her feelings change. Sarah's infallible memory, likened to a 'Recording Angel's Dictaphone', symbolizes the Ireland in which she lives where nothing changes and where even the clouds seem to Mary to resemble 'one solid, frozen mass, tomblike, so that if they moved they moved massively, and she could not tell if they moved at all'.[2] Mary is a cosmopolitan; living outside Ireland leaves her freer than Sarah to re-imagine the past. 'We are not one person. We pass through several lives of faith, ambition, sometimes love, often friendship', reflects the narrator in 'Dividends'. 'We change, die and live again.'[3] As the nomadic self makes and unmakes itself, so our memories alter to accommodate our shifting view of ourselves. Sarah's insistence on the factual inaccuracy of Mary's memories threatens the latter's more fluid sense of self and necessitates her exile from Ireland for psychological reasons rather than the economic ones of the previous decades. The subliminal message to Ireland in 'I Remember! I Remember!' is that it is time to discard old ideas of fixed national identity and political and economic self-sufficiency, and embrace different traditions more in keeping with the modern Ireland that was straining to come into being.

However, if 'I Remember! I Remember!' marks a plea for moving forward, other stories in this collection reveal an uneasiness about the cost of progress characteristic of the Irish short story of this period and reflecting contemporary debates in the country at large over whether Ireland's distinctive culture, traditions and language were being too quickly sacrificed to the desire to modernize.[4] 'A Shadow, Silent as a Cloud' exposes the tension between those who, like Lily, remember the untouched countryside around Dublin and those like Jerry, who pays lip-service to the past but cannot restrain himself from pressing forward into the future, which in his case means covering the countryside with new housing, a mark of Ireland's rapid urbanization during the period. There are echoes of 'The Dead' in the meeting between the middle-aged Jerry and his childhood sweetheart, Lily, and in Jerry's pompous after-dinner speech evoking Dublin's past glories. The tension between past and present is encapsulated in Jerry's question: 'is it not true that to create is in some sense to change, and to change is in some sense to destroy? All creative work is a form of destruction.'[5] Behind these lines the reader senses O'Faoláin's uneasy awareness that the progress he and other writers and intellectuals desired in order to create a more liberal Ireland might involve destruction of valuable traditions. A similar momentary discomfort affects the self-made business man, Daniel, in 'A Touch of Autumn in the Air'.

O'Faoláin's stories are typical of the period in exploring the psychological strains caused by living through a time of rapid modernization and in focusing on the private world of the individual in order to depict those strains. The old theme of the shift from country to urban life continues to feature in his work but, befitting the short story's increasing psychological focus, the theme becomes interiorized in a story such as the autobiographical 'The Kitchen', published in the first issue of the *Irish University Review* (1970), with a commentary by the author. O'Faoláin's narrator remembers how his parents' acquired urban sophistication vanished at a stroke when the boot-maker downstairs became their landlord and they became overwhelmed by a fear of eviction that had its roots in their past lives as peasants. Recalling how his mother refused to relinquish her kitchen because, like any peasant woman, the kitchen was the room in her house most closely tied up with her identity, the narrator recognizes that we all have our kitchens, our private psychic spaces, which we have to preserve at all costs. For him, ironically, this means banishing the memory of his mother, for he knows that he must free himself from the peasant mentality if he is to go forward in life.

When the constraints of a stifling petty bourgeois society become impossible to escape, too often in this period, rather than envisaging a different way of living, characters take refuge in dreams. In 'One Night in Turin', the egocentric dreams of Walter and Molly run parallel so that the reader anticipates that both Walter's idealization of Molly and Molly's fantasy of marriage with Lord Boyne are doomed. Walter realizes that his mistake was in trying to make his dream a reality: Molly is simply an image of everything unattainable in his life and by trying to make his dream come true he has simply destroyed its consolatory power. 'There is nothing outside ourselves apart from our imaginings,' asserts the narrator of 'Love's Young Dream'.[6] The emphasis on flashbacks and compensatory dreams, whilst demonstrating the Irish short story's lingering attachment to modernism, is remarkable at a time when the country was beginning to move forward in the sort of way O'Faoláin had always worked for. His later collection, *The Heat of the Sun*, is full of characters who live on illusions about themselves, like Anna in 'In the Bosom of the Country', who believes, erroneously, that she is a committed Catholic, or the Don Juan forever chasing the elusive spectre of romantic love in 'Charlie's Greek'. *The Heat of the Sun* marks the beginning of a decline in O'Faoláin's work; the baton of the Irish short story was being handed on in these years to a younger generation of male writers, like John McGahern and William Trevor, as well as to female writers such as Mary Lavin, whom O'Faoláin had published in *The Bell*, Edna O'Brien, whose writing he 'could not bear',[7] and to his own daughter, Julia.

Some of these writers extended O'Faoláin's themes into the next generation. Before moving on to the theatre, Brian Friel published two collections of short stories: *The Saucer of Larks* (1962) and *The Gold in the Sea* (1966), local, intimate stories set against the background of small-town life in the north-west of Ireland. If the influence of O'Connor's 'First Confession' is apparent in Friel's story, 'The First of My Sins', published in *Critic* in 1963, 'The Death of a Scientific Humanist', published in the *New Yorker* in 1964, satirizes the narrowness of Irish Catholicism in the manner of O'Faoláin, and the latter's influence is apparent in Friel's characteristic themes of memory, nostalgia and the necessity of illusions. Indeed, almost all of Friel's stories illustrate the importance of fantasy in sustaining everyday life in these impoverished rural communities, from the schoolmasters in 'The Illusionists' and 'My Father and the Sergeant', whose delusions of grandeur are threatened by outsiders, to Joe in 'The Foundry House', who discovers the need to preserve his self-deceiving memories of the past, to Friel's numerous pigeon fanciers, cock breeders and greyhound owners who live in hopes of winning a fortune. As in O'Faoláin, imagination and fantasy provide moments of liberation for Friel's characters: for Granny in 'Mr Sing My Heart's Delight' and for the fishermen in 'The Gold in the Sea'. For Friel's protagonists, as for O'Faoláin's, the need to fictionalize an often bleak reality is urgent.

In these years also, John McGahern was beginning a career that would rival, and eventually surpass, O'Faoláin's achievements in the short story. Like O'Faoláin's 'The Kitchen', 'A Slip-Up' (*Getting Through*, 1978) illustrates the tenuous hold of city life on the first generation of incomers from the countryside. The reader, allowed directly into the thoughts of Michael, the elderly farmer transplanted to the town, realizes that Michael's farm remains more real to him than what is going on around him in the city. The theme of the transfer from rural to urban life becomes connected with another O'Faoláin theme, namely the power of the imagination to defeat reality. Typical of this period, rather than being forward-looking, imagination pulls Michael back into the past as he relives his farming days.

William Trevor, acclaimed by Kevin Casey in 1978 as 'a scrupulous stylist and one of the very best short story writers now working',[8] is another writer of the period concerned with the theme of the imagination as consolation for everyday life. In 'The Raising of Elvira Tremlett' (*Lovers of Their Time*, 1978), the narrator is a lonely, sensitive boy who, to escape the careless rowdiness of his large Irish Catholic family, fashions a parallel life around his vision of a nineteenth-century English Protestant girl, Elvira Tremlett. This compensatory version of reality helps him to cope with his everyday life and establish a sense of self in opposition to his family. In every way Elvira is other to his family, being feminine, quiet, Protestant and English. Trevor extends O'Faoláin's theme of dreams by turning his narrator's refashioning of a parallel life into a mirror of the writer's effort to transform everyday life through an effort of the imagination. 'The Raising of Elvira Tremlett' exhibits many features characteristic of a Trevor short story, namely a careful construction involving complex time shifts, a delicate balance between lyricism and irony, and a flexible narrative voice capable of moving in a sentence from objective-sounding narration to the subjective. Joyce's influence was starting to become central to the Irish short story.

Imagination in Trevor's stories, however, is as likely to be entrapping and narcissistic as consoling. 'An Evening with John Joe Dempsey' (*The Ballroom of Romance*, 1972) is one of a series of Trevor stories portraying small-town Ireland as a place where sexuality goes wrong in early child-hood and can never be put right because of the silence of Irish society surrounding the subject. All the adult males in the neighbourhood fail John Joe Dempsey by their inability to help him towards a mature understanding of sexuality. Mr Lynch's relationship with his possessive, castrating mother has created in him a puritanism mixed with prurience which is mirrored in young Dempsey's relationship with his mother. In Dempsey's case, though, keeping company with Quigley has corrupted and inflamed his imagination from an early age. The pattern has become fixed so that when his mother forbids him to see Quigley, it is already too late: Dempsey retreats to his bed and to the masturbatory fantasies that are the only outlet left to him in this repressive society. The ending of the story is a parody of the artist's attempt to remake his life through imagination: 'In his iron bed, staring into the darkness, he made of the town what he wished to make of it.'[9] In reality, Dempsey's fantasies are sterile: he is trapped by religion, society and family, and his life will replicate Lynch's. In 'The Death of Peggy Meehan' (*Angels at the Ritz*, 1975), the narrator, like Dempsey, attempts to escape the drabness of his everyday Irish life by sustaining a parallel life of the imagination which then becomes entangled, like Dempsey's, with early, confused notions of sexuality from which as an adult he never escapes. His self-punishing visions of Peggy Meehan spring from a religion preoccupied with evil and a culture that equates sexuality with sin. His visions represent what cannot be spoken of in this society: as an adult the narrator continues hypocritically to attend mass and confession. Joyce's influence is evident thematically, as well as stylistically.

The imagination could not always, therefore, provide escape from the drabness of everyday life in Ireland and, in this era of change, the Irish short story paradoxically invokes the Joycean theme of paralysis. For all the cosmopolitanism of their settings and their European references, a distinct air of stasis hangs over the characters in Aidan Higgins' *Felo de Se*, published in 1960: 'Sooner or later, said Mr Boucher, we all come to rest in the ruins of ourselves . . . Do what we can our progress in the end will be just another bit of time pushed to the side.'[10] Two short stories of this period, William Trevor's 'The Ballroom of Romance' (*The Ballroom of Romance*, 1972) and Edna O'Brien's 'Irish Revel' (*The Love Object*, 1968), though set in rural Ireland, recall 'The Dead' in their descriptions of evening entertainments that end in anti-climax and entrapment.

In 'The Ballroom of Romance', the entertainment provided by Mr Justin Dwyer's rural dance hall, to which not only young people, but all the middle-aged bachelors and spinsters left at home to care for their elderly parents come every Saturday night, provides the only chance of romance. The gender constraints that governed women's lives in this society are conveyed to the reader through the dialogue, while narrative irony is used, as in Joyce, to undermine the central character's romantic illusions. Thirty-six-year-old Bridie, a spinster left to work the small farm and care for her infirm father, has absorbed her society's view of women as passive, domestic and self-sacrificing. Her romantic attitude to love is conditioned by societal and religious expectations that a woman's destiny is to marry, but her illusions are steadily undercut through the voice of the sympathetic but detached narrator, who makes it plain that domestic burdens render the married women and mothers whose lives Bridie is so eager to emulate just as trapped and unhappy as herself. *The Ballroom of Romance* was the collection that established Trevor's reputation as a short story writer, one Irish reviewer commenting: 'The stories in *The Ballroom of Romance* are both original and, technically, highly accomplished . . . On the strength of this book Mr Trevor must be recognized as one of the finest contemporary practitioners in the genre.'[11]

Like 'The Ballroom of Romance', Edna O'Brien's 'Irish Revel', originally published in the *New Yorker* in 1962, transposes Joyce's 'The Dead' to a rural setting. Like 'The Ballroom of Romance', 'Irish Revel' operates through Joycean anti-climax and in addition adopts Joyce's technique of undercutting his central character's illusions through imagery. Seventeen-year-old Mary, whose life has been confined to helping her mother run their 'mountainy farm', sets off for her first party in town with more optimism than the older and more disabused Bridie. During the course of the evening Mary's romantic hopes, like the rotted front tyre of her bicycle, are slowly deflated as the invited male guests exhibit behaviour as sordid as any of Joyce's Dubliners. O'Brien explores her central character's consciousness in greater depth than Trevor and creates a sense of female solidarity when, despite some bitchy competition over men, the girls rescue Mary from an assault by the predatory O'Toole. Like 'The Ballroom of Romance', 'Irish Revel' ends on a note of stasis and despair as Mary realizes that there is no future for her but to return to 'her own house, like a little white box at the end of the world, waiting to receive her', an image that captures both the purity of her country way of life, as compared with the town, but also suggests the entombment of her life henceforth.[12] O'Brien transforms Joyce's snow imagery into a description of frost which, like Joyce's snow, is a many-sided symbol representing not only purity and grace after a sordid night's eating and drinking, but also the lack of warmth in Mary's life.[13]

The credentials of William Trevor and Edna O'Brien to portray Ireland as a cramped, backward place are periodically questioned, since both writers have lived for the greater part of their lives outside Ireland and their view of Ireland may not, it has been argued, have kept up with the changing times. However, a similar paralysis infects the lives of John McGahern's time-serving teachers trapped in an educational system that, until the 1960s, had remained largely unchanged from colonial times.[14] The clock-watching teacher in 'The Recruiting Officer' (*Nightlines*, 1970) falls prey to: 'a total paralysis of the will, and a feeling that any one thing in this life is almost as worthwhile doing as any other'.[15] In an interview, McGahern made it plain that he regarded this kind of negativity as peculiarly Irish: 'He falls into that disease, which is a very Irish malaise, that since all things are meaningless it makes no difference what you do, and best of all is to do nothing. In this way he causes as much trouble to himself and to others as if he had set out deliberately to do evil.'[16] In McGahern's stories, teachers manifest more of this Irish disease than any other group of people. Despite the fact that this was a period when improvements were beginning to take place in the Irish educational system (free secondary schooling from 1967, the introduction of a new primary school curriculum in 1971), McGahern's teacher-centred stories, drawing on autobiographical experience, dwell on inertia rather than change.

Time in McGahern's stories is often seen as repetitive, monotonous and entrapping. 'Wheels', a story from the 1960s republished in 1970 as the first story in the collection, *Nightlines*, set the tone of that volume by portraying the narrator's failure to find meaning in his life, the imagery suggesting, in the words of Antoinette Quinn, 'life's predictable circularities, the pointlessness of onward motion'.[17] Paralysis is shown to affect Ireland's artistic life in 'The Beginning of an Idea', the story McGahern selected to open and thus colour his second collection, *Getting Through*, published in 1978. Another story in that collection, 'Swallows', picks up Mary Lavin's theme from the 1950s, of Ireland as a society based on materialism and philistinism. Even a talented musician like the State Surveyor chooses security over art, unlike Paganini, whose dedication to his vocation took him from the slums of Genoa to world-wide fame. As for the Sergeant, any lingering appreciation of music has been knocked out of him long ago by the narrowly utilitarian society in which he lives, symbolized here by his deaf old servant Biddy and her sock-machine. The picture of Ireland as a society deaf to art is a theme McGahern would develop in the 1980s in stories such as 'Oldfashioned' and 'Eddie Mac'.

Just as McGahern's stories about teachers fail to mention contemporary efforts to improve the Irish education system, so his art-centred stories do not reflect the fact that the improved economic climate of the 1960s and 1970s was revitalizing Ireland's artistic life, allowing writers for the first time to receive bursaries from the Arts Council and freeing artists in general from having to pay tax on their creative work. Whilst McGahern's commitment to exposing flaws in Irish society has been much admired, the lack of interest his writing displays in putting forward some alternative form of society has recently been criticized.[18] Perhaps, as Chekhov argued, it is futile to expect authors to solve problems when their job is to do no more than state a problem correctly.[19] In any case, the central focus of McGahern's stories is never social analysis but the consciousness of the private, disillusioned, more or less stoical, individual. Whilst his stories may be thematically conservative, stylistically they are innovative, extending Joyce's use of symbolism, epiphany and formal patterning in a way that obliges the reader to work to achieve the meaning that eludes McGahern's narrators. For most commentators, however, the aesthetics of the short story form continued to play a minor role in comparison with the mirror it might hold up to Irish life. A review of *Nightlines* observed: 'the author . . . seems determined to show us to ourselves both as individuals and as a nation . . . his Irish are with us and amongst us: the boy-beating priest, the teacher who has long ago given up, the country sergeant turned hypochondriac out of sheer desperation'.[20]

Despite the renewed optimism in Irish society in general, the trend of the Irish short story in this period, even among the younger generation of writers, remained predominantly backward-looking and critical. Nevertheless, some stories did reflect the changes that were taking place in the country, particularly involving the Catholic church. Seán O'Faoláin's 'The Younger Generation' marks a shift in attitudes to the church, portraying educated young parishioners like Anne as quite capable of challenging the clergy. Despite her bishop's prohibition against mixed marriages, Anne is able to escape his influence and establish herself in an independent life in Dublin. Faced with his dwindling influence, the bishop retreats into rules and regulations and can offer no practical help to Anne or her family in their various emotional crises. His pastoral reads like 'a letter not to the living but to the dying and the dead'.[21] O'Faoláin's stories of this period portray the decline of religion into social conformity. Anna in 'In the Bosom of the Country' believes that she is a committed Catholic but Frank's enthusiasm of the newly converted, reminiscent of Rex Mottram in Evelyn Waugh's *Brideshead Revisited*, points up the extent to which Anna's belief is bound up with superstitious adherence to the external forms of religion. The tone of 'In the Bosom of the Country' is light and satirical with none of the genuine angst displayed by the characters in O'Faoláin's earlier story, 'The Lovers of the Lake': the eventual waning of Frank's enthusiasm sees the lovers thankfully fleeing constricting Ireland. Human love survives in this story, the spiritual does not.

John McGahern's pursuit of an objective, non-judgmental style in his stories, in the manner of Flaubert and Chekhov, results in a more sympathetic view of priests. In *Memoir*, McGahern spoke of his gratitude for the intellectual and aesthetic influence of Catholic services on his early life: 'In an impoverished time they were my first introduction to an indoor beauty, of luxury and ornament, ceremony and sacrament and mystery.'[22] Commentators on his writing have remarked that McGahern's early upbringing left him with a post-Christian feeling for the sacramental nature of life, together with a sense of void left by the passing of religious faith.[23] In an interview McGahern explained: 'I don't think it's possible for a writer of my generation born in Ireland to avoid religion, even if it has to be by the path of opposition. It was the dominant force in that society, and, in any sense of the spirit, it was mostly all that was there, even if some of it was unattractive.'[24]

McGahern's 'The Wine Breath' (*Getting Through*, 1978), one of the great Irish short stories of this period, is a lyrical meditation on time and death that could only have been written out of a culture which once understood the sacred. The story, almost a prose poem, links the theme of the religious life with that of memory. This is not, as in O'Faoláin and Trevor, memory based on illusion or compensation, but represents an effort on the part of the priest to penetrate to the heart of his life. The image of the white chips of beech wood prompts the old priest's memory of Michael Bruen's funeral, a day when he gained a fleeting glimpse of the sacred, and this memory leads him to reflect on his life in the light of his approaching death. He is someone who has tried to step out of the Irish attitude of indifference that weighs all things equally and has endeavoured to make his life matter from the perspective of what is timeless. There have been elements of failure: he turned to the church out of a fear of death and a concomitant fear of sex; he allowed his life to be subsumed by his mother's wish that he become a priest and in that sense it has been a lost life, dictated by someone else's wishes, a fate McGahern himself narrowly escaped. The priest endeavours to overcome this sense of failure by imagining a new identity for himself in the form of a young man embarking on a love affair and feeling he has all the time in the world. There are two approaches to time in this story: chronological time, in which the priest is nearing the end of his life, and imaginative time, in which he envisages life starting over again, much as James Sharkey in 'All Sorts of Impossible Things' (*Getting Through*) has a wild longing to begin his life again after the death of his friend. By the priest's act of transcending time through an effort of the imagination, 'The Wine Breath' moves away from the presentation of time as repetitive and entrapping in a story like 'Wheels'. Indeed, McGahern, indicating his debt to Proust both here and elsewhere, remarked: 'One of my favourite definitions of art is that it abolishes time and establishes memory.'[25] The priest's search for the truth about his life is rooted in a Proustian exercise to recapture the lost image that will sum it up.

In McGahern's short stories, the themes of time, memory and imagination so characteristic of this period receive their most sophisticated articulation. *Getting Through* was widely acclaimed as an advance on *Nightlines* and played a major part in establishing McGahern's literary reputation: Tom Paulin called it 'a fine and interesting development from *Nightlines*'[26] and Neil Jordan saw progress from the earlier volume in its longer sentences and more reflective style: 'the insistence on a raw, intensely personal vision which made *Nightlines* such a highly charged collection is absent here, replaced by a newer, more reflective mood'.[27]

One of the greatest changes of the 1960s was the prominence of women writers on the Irish publishing scene, opening up the Irish short story to renewed emphasis on such topics as female sexuality, the mother–daughter relationship and women's quest for liberation. Such themes might be expected to lead the Irish short story away from its preoccupation with the past and into the future. However, this period was not an easy time for women. Asked in an interview to sum up the 1960s, Mary Dorcey made no mention of the economic revival or renewed national self-confidence: 'Silence. Repression. Censorship. Long dark winters. Poor food. Nuns and priests everywhere. Drab clothes. Censorship of books and films. Fear and suspicion surrounding anything to do with the body or the personal life. The near total repression of ideas and information. A Catholic state for a Catholic people.'[28] Because Irish women's short story writing in this period was concerned with analysing and highlighting Irish women's predicament, it remained tied to the realist mode, and its preoccupation with describing the life of a previous generation of women through the eyes of their daughters kept the focus on the past rather than the future.

One of the most widely noticed of these new voices, Edna O'Brien, began publishing in the 1960s, and many of her stories featured the theme of women routinely crushed and defeated, not only by their men folk, but also by the constraints of the patriarchal society in which they lived. 'The Rug', published in *The Love Object* in 1968, portrays a rural woman whose hard life has many traits in common with that of Caithleen Brady's mother in *The Country Girls*. The wistfulness with which the daughter figure speaks of her mother bears resemblances to the tone of that novel, with none of the ambivalence or even hatred towards the mother figure that was to creep into O'Brien's later writing. Married to a feckless husband, the thrifty and hard-working mother nurses a desire for luxury that is revealed in small things like the china ornaments and holy pictures with which she decorates her house. So it is all the more heartbreaking when she allows herself to fancy that the black sheepskin hearthrug that has been sent from America is intended for her. Like 'Irish Revel', 'The Rug' works through Joycean anti-climax as the gift turns out to have been wrongly directed. The mother's final, physical gesture sums up her constricted life and that of many Irish women in this period: 'she undid her apron strings, out of habit, and then retied them slowly and methodically, making a tighter knot'.[29] Rather than her earlier work in the novel form, it was *The Love Object* that established O'Brien's reputation as a serious literary author in the eyes of her contemporaries, one reviewer commenting: 'There is no need any longer to have reservations about Edna O'Brien: this book reveals her unmistakably as a mature craftsman, an unblinking observer, and an unflinching moralist.'[30]

In the same decade, Maeve Brennan tackled the theme of the crushing of a woman's spirit in her series of *New Yorker* stories centred on Rose Derdon, first introduced to the reader in the 1952 story, 'The Poor Men and Women'. Brennan's 1960s stories like 'A Free Choice' go back into the past to explore the roots of Rose's unhappiness. Psychologically scarred by her mother's persistent denigration of her abilities, Rose allows herself to be bullied by her husband, who becomes enraged by Rose's

'lifelong denial of herself, bolstered and fed as it was by fear'.[31] Hubert's
rage against his wife's timidity is, it has been suggested, an expression of
Maeve Brennan's own anger against a mother who failed to provide an
empowering role model.[32] This lack of a positive role model must have
been all the more galling for Brennan, whose mother started out as a rebel
and a feminist, active in the 1916 Rising and in the Anglo-Irish war and
the civil war: 'but then in motherhood and middle age [she] becomes
reduced to silences and domesticities, her individuality occluded by her
relationships and her roles'.[33] Una Brennan's life mirrored the fate of
many Irish women in the middle decades of the century in Ireland and
Brennan underlines these emotional themes by her use of geographical
space. The dark, cramped Ranelagh house in which Rose Derdon lives,
with its 'narrow hall' and its small garden 'bounded by gray cement
walls', suggests oppression and entrapment. 'She kept close to the house,'
the narrator comments in 'Family Walls', adding in an echo of Joyce,
'She might as well have been in a net, for all the freedom she felt.'[34]

In 1970, the Irish Women's Movement was founded to press for,
among other things, equal pay, equal educational and employment
opportunities, access to contraception, and justice for single mothers,
deserted wives and widows, and though it was not until the early 1990s
that real progress was made on some of these issues, nevertheless the
feminist note in the Irish short story became stronger in this decade.
Throughout the 1970s, Maeve Kelly produced a series of well-crafted and
deeply felt short stories, many of which were published for the first time
in David Marcus' 'New Irish Writing' page of *The Irish Press*. Her collection, *A Life of Her Own*, with its obvious echo of Woolf, came out in
1976 and reflected the struggles of the Irish feminist movement in the
1970s to highlight women's issues. 'The Vain Woman' features a protagonist whose artistic talents are crushed first by her husband and then by
her children, but most of all by a religion which has condemned her to
constant childbearing so that in the end she has lost her identity: 'I often
find it hard to remember *who* I am. Not just my name. But my self. I look
in the mirror and I say "Who are you?" '[35] The title story highlights the
invisibility of a woman like Brigid whose life is very far from her own,
being controlled first by her brother then by her husband (she dies in
childbirth). She makes her niece, the narrator of the story, promise that
she will safeguard her independence by training for a profession. Brigid is
a rural woman and many of the stories in Kelly's collection, such as 'The
Last Campaign', 'Amnesty', 'Journey Home' and 'The False God', depict
the hard lives of countrywomen. The realities of their daily battle against

'a litany of disasters, storm damage, pests, disease, accidents' are accurately reflected in 'The Last Campaign', where Joe comments 'It's no life for a woman', as the herd he and his wife have so painstakingly built up is revealed to be diseased and has to be taken away to be slaughtered.[36] 'Journey Home' recounts one woman's attempts to hang on to the farm she has worked all her life against the casual assumption of both her mother and her brother that he will inherit. Though the feminist note may have become stronger in short stories by Irish women in this decade, there was not much optimism about the future.

Edna O'Brien's stories from the 1970s are also bleak and forceful, their presentation of women's lives highlighting the vulnerability of battered wives, single mothers and widows. A contemporary review by Mary Maher described O'Brien's stories in *A Scandalous Woman* (1974) as 'savage and incisive'.[37] O'Brien's heroines, not all of them Irish, often lose touch with a reality that is too painful for them to contemplate. In 'A Scandalous Woman', such is society's hatred for the female body that it is internalized by children: in the childhood game the narrator plays with Eily and Nuala, Nuala pretends to be a doctor cutting away all the female organs in the narrator's body. It is not surprising then that when the beautiful Eily, previously an object of lust among the neighbourhood men, becomes pregnant outside marriage, she turns into the abject and is sacrificed to her community's sense of respectability by being married off hastily. A once lively girl, Eily goes through a period of insanity before settling down to such mindless conformity that when the narrator meets her again she wonders whether her friend has been drugged. The story opens out to a wider social critique as the narrator remarks: 'ours indeed was a land of shame, a land of murder, and a land of strange, throttled, sacrificial women'.[38]

The 1970s was a period when Irish women's history began to be seriously researched. A story by Maeve Kelly, 'The Sentimentalist', reflects this in its attempt to convey the trajectory of Irish women's experience in the twentieth century. The cynical, disillusioned tone of the narrator stands in stark contrast with her cousin, Liza, who has based her life's struggle on a romantic notion of rural, Gaelic-speaking Ireland. Liza participated in the Gaelic League and the struggle for independence but, like many Irish women previously prominent in public life, found herself relegated to the sidelines in the new state, regarded as an embarrassment and an obstacle to progress. She concludes that the romanticized nationalism on which she has based her life has no future and decides that she should instead have fought for political power. The narrator, by contrast, employs Joycean weapons of silence, exile and cunning in order to achieve her aim, that of rivalling and even surpassing male philosophers. Her cousin's predicament inspires the narrator to abandon her stance of non-involvement and take up the campaign for Liza to keep her home. Liza suddenly becomes a heroine, a symbol of 'the integrity of the past standing against the hollow men of the present'.[39] Nevertheless, after her death, her home is demolished. The entire thrust of 'The Sentimentalist' bears out the significance of Hanna Sheehy Skeffington's warning in *Bean na hÉireann* in 1909 that Irish women should put the gender struggle before the nationalist one in order to avoid being sidelined in the new Irish state.[40]

Though less overtly polemical than Kelly's work, Mary Lavin's stories of the lives of widows in this period are no less powerful in highlighting society's often unjust and insensitive attitudes to this marginal group. Lavin's widow stories drew on her own experiences but also reflected the political attention widows were beginning to attract in the 1960s with The Succession Act of 1965 and the founding of the National Association of Widows in 1967. 'In the Middle of the Fields' portrays the vulnerability of the widow in 1960s Ireland, forced to earn a living in a society where the world of business was still largely male-dominated. When the unnamed widow who single-handedly runs a farm in Meath, as Lavin herself did after the death of her first husband, negotiates the topping of her fields with a neighbouring farmer, Bartley Crossen, he tries to take advantage of her supposed ignorance. The physical dangers of a woman living alone with her children in the Irish countryside are plain, but it is her mental vulnerability that is emphasized. Tormented by 'anxieties by day, and cares, and at night vague, nameless fears', the widow longs to escape memories of her husband and the sexual passion they shared.[41] When Bartley clumsily attempts to kiss her, the widow forgives him, for she understands that it was the power of his memories of an old love that reawakened his sexual feelings. Though never regarded as a radical writer, Lavin presents in 'In the Middle of the Fields' a frank account, for the time, of a widow pulled reluctantly back into the past by her memory of sexual passion. By portraying the way in which the onward march of time is defeated by memory Lavin, like McGahern, attempts to free the realist short story from the linear grip of plot.

Another Lavin story from this period, 'In a Café', also deals with the twin themes of memory and widowhood. The marginalized social status of the widow is emphasized in Mary's realization that she fits right into the bohemian café she would never have dreamed of entering if Richard had still been alive. A meeting with a younger widow, Maudie, makes her aware that she is marginalized also by age: Maudie takes it for granted that she will remarry, but that the older Mary will not. 'In a Café' portrays both society's obtuseness when confronted with a grieving widow, and Mary's emotional vulnerability as memories of Richard are liable to ambush her at any moment and pull her back into the past. 'In a Café' is a beautifully controlled story of a turning-point in Mary's life as she struggles to regain the identity 'she lost willingly in marriage, but lost doubly, and unwillingly, in widowhood'.[42] Unlike many Irish short stories of this period, 'In a Café' portrays a protagonist who is able to overcome her entrapment by the past: Mary's liberation comes when she is finally able to imagine Richard as a complete individual and therefore separate from herself. Claiming back 'her rights', she steps without hesitation into the driver's seat of her car.

During these decades, the father–son relationship continued to feature prominently in the work of Irish male authors such as John McGahern, John Banville and Desmond Hogan. In stories like Banville's 'Lovers', fathers, shaped by a repressive Ireland, hinder their sons' embrace of a freer, more cosmopolitan future. They even, as in 'Korea', McGahern's story of a murderous Oedipal struggle between father and son, threaten their sons' lives. The recurring topic of sons' memories of their fathers reinforces the backward-looking trend of the Irish short story in this period. Belonging to the generation that fought for Ireland's independence, the fathers in stories such as 'Korea' or Banville's 'A Death' represent the sort of heroism that is outmoded and unnecessary in modern Ireland, but from whose shadow the sons find it hard to escape. 'Korea' depicts the son's initiation into his father's view of life as a war of survival and, in this respect, these father–son stories prolong into the next generation the critique of violent nationalism found in earlier stories by Frank O'Connor and Seán O'Faoláin. In McGahern's 'Wheels', the relationship is tied to the theme of time as the son finds himself caught in the repetitive cycle of generations. The failed father–son relationship is set in the context of the Irish nation: just as the educated, urban son hopes for a rapprochement with his rural father that will never take place, so life in Ireland after independence has been a matter of waiting for 'the rich whole that never came but that all the preparations promised'.[43] However, in the context of familial relationships, it was the mother–daughter relationship that struck a new note in the period and from this date onwards challenged the centrality of the father–son relationship in the Irish canon. Women's short stories about the mother–daughter relationship link up with Irish male writers' exploration of the themes of memory and time as, despite themselves, Irish daughters' memories of their mothers pull them back into the past.

In Edna O'Brien's stories, Irish mothers are portrayed as joyless, self-denying victims of male violence. Lacking a secure identity of their own, they fail to empower their daughters with a sense of confidence, and this has a catastrophic impact on the daughters' ability to mother. In her pioneering study of the mother–daughter relationship, Adrienne Rich famously stated that: 'The nurture of daughters in the patriarchy calls for a strong sense of *self*-nurture in the mother.'[44] Where this is lacking, Rich argued, the daughter will grow up without pride in her femaleness, ambivalent about her mother and needing to reject her in order to avoid duplicating her subjugated life. In much Irish women's writing of the period the mother–daughter relationship was portrayed as a negative one, with the daughters fleeing their mother and often their mother country in order to avoid repeating their mothers' thwarted lives. The perennial Irish theme of the conflict between tradition and modernity took on a different perspective as removal to a new environment exacerbated the disjunction between mothers and daughters, the daughters embracing the culture of their new country, whilst their mothers remained locked in old ways of thinking. O'Brien's short story, 'Cords', is paradigmatic. The narrator, Claire, who has lived in London for several years and mixed with people holding very different views from the people back home in Ireland, receives a visit from her mother. Faced with her mother's disapproval of her friends, Claire begins to feel the pull of old values and starts to doubt whether her present life is satisfactory: 'her present life, her work, the friends she had, seemed insubstantial compared with all that had happened before'.[45] In England, Claire has found no positive new identity to set against the Irish one she has only partly outgrown. Mothers' values weigh down their daughters in O'Brien's fiction as much as fathers represent entrapment for their sons in the stories of McGahern and Banville.

Whilst Edna O'Brien's stories generally portray the mother–daughter relationship from the point of view of the daughter, in her stories from this period, Maeve Brennan endeavoured to give the mother a voice. If her portraits of the Derdon family revealed Brennan's anger against her mother, after Una's death in 1958 Brennan, in some confusion as to her own identity, sought to understand her mother's life.[46] To this end, she embarked on a series of stories about the Bagot family, published between 1964 and 1968 in the *New Yorker*. Like Rose Derdon, Delia Bagot annoys her husband with her anxiety and passivity, but her relationship with her two small daughters is more positive. In 'The Sofa', Delia, waiting in her empty front room for the arrival of a new sofa, experiences a moment outside time: 'the clock, which had been so domineering all these years, had no power over her today'.[47] In the light of Kristeva's association of clock time with the father in 'About Chinese Women',[48] it is arguable that what Delia is experiencing here in her moment out of time is women's time. Ceasing to be bullied by the clock, Delia recovers some of the confidence that had been hers before marriage: 'She was in touch then with a spirit she did not know she possessed, and when she smiled, her face was lighted by the faint and faraway glimmer of an assurance that was truly hers, but truly buried, buried deep down under the sound, useful earth of her thirty-five years of unquestioning, obedient life.'[49] What Brennan seems to be trying to do in this story is to peel away the layers of years of socialization and marriage in an effort to reclaim the authentic voice of her mother and affirm the strength of the mother–daughter bond. In another short story in this series, 'A Shadow of Kindness', Delia is rescued from loneliness over her daughters' absence by retrieving a moment of kinship with her own mother, whose shadow she sees reflected on the wall.

Despite Brennan's attempts to retrieve the mother's voice, however, her mother figures remain trapped in domesticity. After the freedom of a moment outside time, 'The Sofa' ends with mother and daughters eating dinner in the kitchen as usual. In 'The Carpet with the Big Pink Roses on It', Delia is too conscious of what the neighbours will say to be able to yield to the temptation to lie down on the carpet laid out on the lawn during spring cleaning. It is her daughter, Lily, who defies the neighbours' opinions, climbs on to the carpet and imagines flying away to foreign cities, as Brennan herself escaped her mother's life of domesticity in Dublin to live a cosmopolitan life as a writer. Brennan's Bagot stories are an early example of a daughter trying, and perhaps in the end failing, to present the mother's world in a way that might be empowering for a daughter's sense of identity.

Some of Mary Lavin's stories from this period portray the mother–daughter relationship in a more positive light. 'Happiness', published in 1969, is one of Lavin's great short stories and one with clear autobiographical resonances, portraying a widow, Vera, with three growing daughters, a difficult elderly mother and a family friend, Father Hugh (based on Lavin's second husband, Michael Scott). As Vera lies dying, her eldest daughter, Bea, pushes aside Father Hugh's attempts to console her mother, recognizing that what her mother dreads is not death but having to relive the early days of her widowhood when onslaughts were constantly made on her happiness by well-meaning but ghoulish relatives. Understanding the painfulness of this memory, Bea is able to comfort her mother in the way Father Hugh cannot, by reassuring her that she will not be forced to relive that time. For Vera, as for all Lavin's widows, the future, even when it means moving forward into death, is more comforting than being pulled back into the past. In this respect, Lavin's widow stories, like McGahern's 'The Wine Breath', resist the backward glance so characteristic of the Irish short story in this period.

Affirmation of the mother–daughter bond is linked to themes of memory and time in a different way in Maeve Kelly's story, 'Ruth', where the bond stretches across four generations of women. Kelly perceptively records Eithne's ambivalence about motherhood and her efforts to prevent her sense of self from being swallowed up by the mothering task. The close, almost symbiotic, bond between Eithne and her elderly mother helps to strengthen the former's sense of identity. When Eithne remarks to her mother, 'You are funny', the latter recalls her own mother using the same phrase to her. Later, Eithne's daughter, Maureen, will repeat the phrase back to her. These echoes between the generations recall Jung's description of the continuity of identity between mothers and daughters: 'Every mother contains her daughter within herself, and every daughter her mother . . . This participation and intermingling gives rise to that peculiar uncertainty as regards *time*: a woman lives earlier as a mother, later as a daughter. The conscious experience of these ties produces the feeling that her life is spread out over generations.'[50] Time functions positively in Kelly's mother–daughter story, where awareness of family traits repeated down through the generations reinforces the women's sense of identity, in contrast to McGahern's father–son stories where the son experiences time as entrapping and longs to escape from the repetitive cycle of generations.

In this period, the perennial Irish theme of repressed sexuality was treated with a new frankness. In stories like 'An Evening with John Joe Dempsey', 'The Death of Peggy Meehan' and 'Death in Jerusalem', William Trevor explores sexuality gone wrong in childhood, often as the result of a possessive, castrating mother. Many of John McGahern's stories in his 1970s collections, *Nightlines* and *Getting Through*, feature failed relationships and sexuality gone awry. 'Coming into his Kingdom' depicts a boy's sexual awakening in a story that contains more than a hint of sexual abuse as father and son share a bed. 'Lavin', on one level a rewriting of Joyce's 'An Encounter', describes sexual perversion resulting from prolonged sexual repression. Many McGahern stories, such as 'Doorways', 'Along the Edges' and 'My Love, My Umbrella', portray casual affairs in the city and men's difficulties in relating to women. In 'My Love, My Umbrella', both the narrator and his girlfriend use sex in an exploitative and mechanical way. In 'Along the Edges', an affair ends because the narrator and his girlfriend fail to turn it into anything more than a sexual habit. 'Peaches' tells of married love gone wrong, in which the stink of the dead shark becomes a metaphor, not only for the narrator's failure as a writer, but also for the state of his marriage. Many of McGahern's narrators are sexually irresponsible or fail in other ways: in 'Peaches', the husband is unable to protect his wife from the sexual attentions of the magistrate. Not until the 1980s does the McGahern narrator achieve the serenity in love of a story like 'Bank Holiday'.

In 'A Ball of Malt and Madame Butterfly', from his collection of the same name published in 1973, Benedict Kiely adopts a humorous, at times bawdy, tone in dealing with sexuality. Pike Hunter's repressed sexuality is treated with sympathy and understanding by the more worldly denizens of the Dark Cow pub, though in the end Hunter's sub-Yeatsian sensibility bores his loved one. The story turns to black comedy as Hunter develops a drinking habit and is incarcerated in St Patrick's Hospital. 'A Ball of Malt and Madame Butterfly' is recounted in Kiely's characteristic voice of the Irish storyteller, drawing on Irish sayings, references and turns of phrase. Its many digressions and verbal playfulness nevertheless also owe much to Joyce (the Joyce of *Ulysses* rather than *Dubliners*) and the popular tone adroitly conceals its careful structure and an erudite range of reference that takes in, among others, Spenser, Tennyson, Yeats, Joyce, Synge and Maupassant. A darker tone is adopted for 'Bluebell Meadow' (*A Cow in the House*, 1978), a Romeo and Juliet story of love thwarted by the growing sectarianism in Northern Ireland. In comparison with McGahern and Trevor, Kiely's stories have often been sidelined in accounts of the Irish short story, the copiousness of the storyteller not fitting well with modern preference for understatement and psychological subtlety. Yet his stories tap into central concerns in the Irish canon: the use of the Romeo and Juliet theme in the context of Irish violence, for example, goes back to the early nineteenth century, featuring, as Kiely would have known, in Carleton's 'The Battle of the Factions'.

What was new in these decades was the frankness with which Irish women writers spoke of female sexuality and the female body. Edna O'Brien's work has long been associated with sexual themes, and her story, 'The Love Object', first published in the *New Yorker*, details the progress of a love affair with unusual frankness. We are in familiar O'Brien territory: the narrator, Martha, is divorced from a husband who bears a family resemblance to Eugene Gaillard of *The Country Girls* trilogy, her two boys are in boarding school and, like Nell in *Time and Tide*, she consoles herself for their absence with a lover. Since she and her married lover cannot meet in public Martha becomes, like Simone de Beauvoir's woman in love in *The Second Sex*, a woman whose life is centred on waiting for her lover. The dream motif allows for frank descriptions of sexuality, possibly franker than had yet appeared in the Irish short story. At the same time, Martha's subconscious warns her that she risks losing her identity and becoming a love object herself. When her lover breaks off the relationship Martha contemplates suicide, an all too likely danger, de Beauvoir warns, when a woman turns herself into a victim of love.[51] In O'Brien's story, more pragmatically, Martha's attention is diverted from thoughts of suicide by the practicalities of having to care for her sick son.

'The Love Object' is a convincing portrayal of the illusions and self-deceptions of a woman in love. The new sexual frankness is reinforced by O'Brien's extension of Joyce's method, breaking with the realist mode through the technique of recounting everything from within Martha's head, without authorial commentary. In the 1970s she would experiment with stream-of-consciousness techniques in her novel *Night*, written in the second person, and her short story, 'Over', a stream-of-consciousness about a love affair gone wrong directly addressed by the woman to her ex-lover. In 'The Love Object', the leisurely tracking of the various stages of the affair reinforces the authenticity of the account. There is no temptation to cut the story short or to end with a melodramatic parting between the lovers (Martha and her lover lamely continue to meet from time to time). Instead, O'Brien does something more interesting: she shows how the man gradually turns into a mental image, a love object, which sustains his lover even after he has left her. The theme of sexuality thus becomes linked with this period's characteristic themes of memory and imagination as the love affair turns into a memory fictionalized by Martha to satisfy her own narcissistic needs.[52]

Also innovatory was O'Brien's 'The Mouth of the Cave', one of the few examples before the 1980s of an Irish short story dealing with lesbian sexuality. The two roads available to the narrator symbolize her sexual options. Her choice of 'a dusty ill-defined stretch of road littered with rocks' indicates both the narrator's fear of lesbianism and the hidden nature of lesbian sexuality in this period.[53] It is on this road that the narrator sees a young girl of twenty dressing behind a clump of trees. She is both attracted and afraid, and the lesbian love affair is thwarted as the narrator waits in vain for the girl to turn up for a meal. It is significant that O'Brien's brief exploration of lesbian sexuality is set outside Ireland in some unspecified foreign country: lesbianism would have to wait till the 1980s to find its expression in stories set in Ireland.

The theme of sexuality highlights the complicated social issues surrounding Irish women's bodies during this period. O'Brien's 'A Scandalous Woman' portrays a pregnant young girl hastily married off to preserve the respectability of her family and her community, and in 'The House of My Dreams', from the same collection, the narrator's unmarried sister is sent away to a Magdalene laundry to have her baby. Julia O'Faolain's first volume of short stories, *We Might See Sights!* (1968), was notable for its exploration of youthful sexuality in stories such as 'We Might See Sights!', 'First Conjugation' and 'A Pot of Soothing Herbs'; indeed the 'sights' referred to in the title explicitly refer to lifting the lid on Irish sexuality. 'A Pot of Soothing Herbs' takes the form of a letter written by twenty-one-year-old virgin, not unusual in Ireland at that time, lamenting the sexual repressions of the narrator's generation. Like Maeve Kelly's 'The Sentimentalist', 'A Pot of Soothing Herbs' casts a retrospective eye over Irish women's history, as the narrator reflects that life has become more constricting for women since the founding of the Irish state. She looks back nostalgically to the sexual freedoms of her mother's college days and her dances in mountain farmhouses with soldiers who were likely to be fighting a few hours later. Now her mother has so far retreated into conformity as to forbid her daughter to go on an excursion with a woman of doubtful reputation. Reviewing this collection for *The Irish Times*, John Broderick characterized it as 'a savage and sometimes tender picture of the growing pains of a modern young Irish girl'.[54] The repetition of the word 'savage' in contemporary reviews of O'Faolain and O'Brien testifies to the impact of these strong female voices on their first readers.

If O'Faolain's story is representative of many Irish stories published during these decades in depicting Irish sexuality as repressed and constricted, Desmond Hogan's collection, *The Diamonds at the Bottom of the Sea*, published in 1979 (though withdrawn for a period because of a libel writ), points forward to the following decades in its celebration of the loosening of sexual mores in Ireland. In 'Embassy', Sheila reflects on the time when the priest had preached against her from the pulpit for pursuing her affairs with men: 'That was in the bad old days. Now Ireland had changed and her nieces courted men on the pavement outside and priests talked about sex and the papers wrote about it.'[55] In contrast to O'Faolain's 'A Pot of Soothing Herbs', 'The Bombs' portrays the older generation's envy of the sexual freedom experienced by those growing up in Ireland during the 1970s. Dermot Healy, like Hogan a representative of an emerging generation of young Irish writers, began to publish short stories in the 1970s that reflected a new sense of risk taking in speaking of sexual matters. Stories like 'Reprieve' deal with abortion, whilst 'A Family and a Future' centres on a prostitute in rural Ireland. Healy's stories were later collected and published in 1982 by Brandon under the title *Banished Misfortune*.

From George Moore onwards, the theme of emigration in the Irish short story has been linked to themes of memory and ambivalence about the lost homeland, and the short story of this period is no different. However repressive life in Ireland still was, there was no guarantee that emigration would result in happiness. Maeve Kelly's 'Morning at my Window', published in *New Irish Writing* in 1972, presents the wry stream-of-consciousness of an Irish nurse as she goes about the unrelenting routine of hospital work in England. Edna O'Brien and Julia O'Faolain set many of their stories outside Ireland in these decades but what their stories highlight is that even when their heroines escape abroad, they remain psychologically trapped by myths and stereotypes about Irish women. This led one contemporary reviewer to remark: 'Miss O'Brien is still a thoroughly Irish writer, in spite of her locations in sun-dried Europe...The emotional and spiritual roots of her heroines are clearly identifiable and their eyes, looking out on an exotic scene, make the kind of unspoken comparisons which any Irish reader will understand.'[56] O'Brien's exiled Irish young women often find themselves in an in-between state, having found no positive new identity abroad to set against the old Irish one they have only partly outgrown: in 'Paradise', the Irish heroine's search for a new identity abroad ends in failure and attempted suicide. In 'Mrs Rossi', O'Faolain extends the theme to an Italian immigrant woman in America whose identity has been so completely absorbed in the struggle for survival for herself and her six children that, like Lavin's Bedelia, her heart has shrivelled and she lacks the compassion to lend her estranged husband money to save his dying child.

The corresponding male version of emigration, the tough life of the Irish labourer in England, features in John McGahern's early stories, 'Hearts of Oak' and 'Faith, Hope and Charity', as well as in Dermot

Healy's 'Kelly'. In Neil Jordan's hands, the theme develops in 'Last Rites' into a detailed analysis of a mind on the edge of despair. The success of the story lies in Jordan's precise evocation of the labourer's state of mind as he is about to take his own life in a London bathhouse. It is an Irish story stripped of its Irishness: the labourer's memories of Ireland become transformed into universal descriptions of home, and the mention of African immigrants anticipates the opening up of the Irish short story in the 1990s to other cultures. *Night in Tunisia*, in which this story appears, was published in 1976 by the Irish Writers' Co-operative that Jordan had helped found. The collection immediately attracted international attention, winning the Guardian Fiction Prize in 1979 and marking out Jordan as the leading representative of a younger generation of Irish writers who were bringing renewed energy to Irish writing.

In Ireland, however, the past is never far away and these decades were witness to the reawakening of conflicts thought buried in Irish history. In 1972, against the background of the emerging violence in Northern Ireland, David Marcus published *Tears of the Shamrock*, subtitled *An Anthology of Contemporary Short Stories on the Theme of Ireland's Struggle for Nationhood*, with the aim of explaining the Irish Question to 'the non-Irish man-in-the-street'. The very structure of Marcus' anthology illustrates the way in which the Troubles were drawing Ireland back into its past: before moving into the contemporary period, Marcus felt it necessary to include an initial section dealing with the struggle for Irish independence, portrayed in stories by Corkery, Lavin and O'Connor, and the civil war, depicted in stories by O'Flaherty, Seán O'Faoláin and Denis Johnston.

Stories by O'Faoláin ('No Country for Old Men'), Brendan Behan ('The Execution') and Patrick Boyle ('The Lake') deal with the IRA at mid-century but John Montague's 'The Cry', published in *Kilkenny Magazine* in 1961, stands out in this period as remarkably prescient about the growing problems of sectarianism and the reluctance of the people of Northern Ireland to confront them. By contrast, Robert Harbinson's two collections, *Tattoo Lily* (1961) and *The Far World* (1962), are wry evocations of pre-Troubles life in Northern Ireland, filled with details about rural customs and beliefs, though even these stories record the bigotry of the two communities in Northern Ireland prior to the Troubles. 'The Hot-Bed', portraying Mrs Wilfoe as a domestic tyrant and castrating mother responsible for her son's stunted sexuality, captures the puritanical attitudes of a middle-class Protestant household in a way that evokes comparisons with the novels of Janet McNeill. 'Tattoo Lily', a tragi-comic tale of Lily, so staunchly Protestant that she is rumoured to have Orange symbols tattooed on her body, operates largely through farce but there is a bleakness to the ending as both sides of the religious divide claim to know with certainty what has happened to Lily in the afterlife.

Stories from Northern Ireland in this period continued to have parallels with writing from the Republic. Bernard MacLaverty's volume, *Secrets and Other Stories*, published by the Belfast-based Blackstaff Press in 1977, includes stories dealing with emigration and sexual repression. In 'Between Two Shores', an exhausted Irish labourer returns to his family in Belfast knowing that he has caught venereal disease in England. In 'The Bull With the Hard Hat', Dick has eight children under twelve because his Catholic wife believes it is a sin to take the Pill. Nonetheless, the beginnings of the violence can be glimpsed beneath these descriptions of domestic life: 'A Happy Birthday' is set against the background of the student civil rights marches and the rise of the IRA. The Troubles were to become a prominent theme in MacLaverty's 1980s stories.

The effect of the Troubles on the Irish short story was paradoxical in that they both drew Ireland back into the past but also opened up the genre to modernity, as the escalating violence attracted international attention and writers were presented with new and urgent themes. The Troubles weave their way through many of the stories in Desmond Hogan's collection, *The Diamonds at the Bottom of the Sea*. In 'The Bombs', Sandra may have gone abroad to study but she remains haunted by her memory of the day bombs exploded in Dublin. In 'Afternoon', the memories of the sick traveller woman, Eileen, range over the whole of the twentieth century, demonstrating how the Troubles have impacted on her life, causing increased violence and discontent among the travelling community with her own great-grandson rumoured to be in the IRA.

William Trevor's dual focus, as an Irishman of Protestant extraction living in England, came to the fore in his short stories exploring the impact of the Northern Irish situation on the Irish in England and on the Anglo-Irish in the Republic. They reveal the way in which, as ancient tribal loyalties resurfaced, both these groups, marginalized in their respective communities, came to be perceived as a threat. 'Another Christmas' (*Lovers of Their Time*), set in England in the mid-1970s, shows how a chance remark could bring out lurking bigotry in both English and Irish. Mr Joyce's condemnation of the Irish bombers is shared by his Irish tenants, Norah and Dermot, but the latter feels the need to point out the injustice suffered by Northern Irish Catholics and in doing so ruins a friendship of years. Trevor makes the point that the violence in Northern

Ireland was not only wreaking obvious death and destruction but also perpetrating many smaller personal tragedies in people's daily lives. 'The Distant Past' (*Angels at the Ritz*) exposes a similar sectarianism lurking beneath daily life in the Republic. The elderly Middletons have been tolerated in the neighbourhood for years, despite their obstinate loyalty to pre-independence Ireland. The Troubles shatter their peaceful co-existence with their neighbours by aligning them, at least in others' eyes, with the British army. Trevor's style of short story, in which he juxtaposes incidents in order to make simple but effective moral points, works particularly well in his writing on Northern Ireland, which often goes back into the past to find an explanation for present actions. His emphasis is always on the personal and the individual as a way of under-standing the conflict. As he explained in an interview: 'What interests me is people, and if one is interested in people one cannot be uninterested in the mentality that can, on a pretext, wipe them out.'[57] He would continue to explore the mentality behind the bombings and the historical legacy of the Troubles in his stories from the 1980s.

John Morrow expanded the realist mode into black comedy in order to capture the tragic absurdity of everyday life in Northern Ireland during the Troubles. In 'The Humours of Ballyturdeen', published in 1979 in *Northern Myths*, Jeffers, a representative for Sinduo washing machines, is obliged to leave the familiar dangers of Belfast to go to the infamous Ballyturdeen area. Warned off by a Reservist, Jeffers, hoping for triple overtime, nevertheless decides to enter both the Catholic Kilbraddock's Braes and the Protestant enclave of Turberry's Meadows. Though these areas are separated by no man's land, Jeffers finds that 'In every respect save wall graffiti Kilbraddock's Braes was a mirror of Turberry's Meadows.'[58] Ironically he escapes unscathed from the violent Catholic working-class estate but is lynched by a crowd of Reservists in the middle-class Protestant estate and ends up in hospital, forfeiting his triple pay. Morrow's use of a Tom Sharpe style black farce effectively underlines his point that, under these conditions, daily life can never be normal.

Eugene McCabe's trilogy of stories published in 1976 – 'Cancer', 'Heritage' and 'Victims'– portrays the effect of the Troubles on Irish people living close to the borders. The aim of these stories was somewhat similar to that in the later John McGahern, namely to explore the net-work of relations in one small community and let this stand as a microcosm for life in the wider society, here Northern Ireland. McCabe's stories reveal the extent of the bigotry in this border region so that his use of the cancer analogy by no means seems extreme in the context of

Northern Ireland's diseased body politic. 'Victims', a much extended
short story, brings together characters from the previous two and demonstrates McCabe's dramatic skills in the build-up of tension as five IRA
members hold an Anglo-Irish family to ransom.

Benedict Kiely's remarkable *tour de force*, 'Proxopera' (1977), likewise
exploits the tension of a situation where a grandfather is forced into
carrying a bomb while his family is held to ransom. Like 'Victims',
'Proxopera' registers a forceful condemnation of violence and uses the
Troubles to stimulate general reflections on life and death. In common
with many of Kiely's stories, 'Proxopera' incorporates the copiousness of
the oral storytelling tradition and here, the chaotic stream-of-consciousness
of the elderly Mr Binchey as he drives to deliver the bomb reinforces
Kiely's point that this is a dysfunctional society where order is breaking
down. Though dealing with contemporary violence, 'Proxopera' offers no
solutions and its tone is predominantly elegiac as Mr Binchey reflects on a
rapidly disappearing rural world where, rather than being desecrated by
violence, the landscape used to be honoured in myth and legend. As if
seeking the protection of some mythical Mother Ireland, he drives his
death-dealing load into the bog. 'Proxopera' presents an Ireland brought to
the brink of dissolution through forces of anarchy and violence. The fact
that both 'Proxopera' and 'Victims' should properly be classed as novellas
on account of their length indicates the difficulty writers faced in
attempting to confine exploration of the moral and psychological effects of
acts of terrorism to the limits of a short story. At a later date, Colum
McCann would also rely on the greater discursive resources of the novella
to portray the violence in Northern Ireland, in 'Hunger Strike', published
in *Everything in This Country Must* (2000).

Viewed in the context of the changes taking place in Irish society, the
Irish short story of this period was, then, still remarkably backward-
looking. 'It would be a shallow present that didn't contain the past,' John
McGahern remarked in an interview.[59] The sentiment is incontrovertible,
yet the reader may feel that the Irish short story of the 1960s and 1970s,
rather than envisaging what shape the future might take, dwells too much
on what has gone before, as if only now, when changes were beginning to
take place, could a critical eye be cast on the nation's past. The rise of
revisionist history is reflected in stories by Flann O'Brien ('The Martyr's
Crown') and Tom MacIntyre ('An Aspect of the Rising'), where revisionism descends into farce.[60] Whether in father–son or mother–daughter
stories, memory constantly pulls characters back into the past. There is an
emphasis, especially in the 1960s, on dreams and the consolatory life of the

imagination at the expense of a determined effort to move forward into the future. Even women writers, who might have been expected to look towards a bright new future, remain tied to an oppositional politics that dwells on the past, a tendency reinforced by the centrality of the mother–daughter relationship in their work. In Northern Ireland, the eruption of the Troubles renewed the tendency to retrospection. Viewed from one perspective, the period ended as it had begun with characters in Desmond Hogan's stories as ambivalent about the future as any of Seán O'Faoláin's protagonists: 'Sculptures' evokes contemporary anxieties over the encroachment of urban sprawl in the Irish countryside, while in 'Two Women Waiting', Nora fears that progress will simply mean the increased materialism and vulgarization of Irish life.

Echoes of Joycean paralysis, not only in William Trevor's 'The Ballroom of Romance' and Edna O'Brien's 'Irish Revel', but also in several of Maeve Brennan's short stories from this period, reinforce the feeling of stasis. By contrast, the aesthetic advantages of Joyce's influence are evident, notably in John McGahern's work, with its emphasis on recurring symbols and formal patterning.[61] Even thematically, Joyce's influence was not always backward-looking but opened up new themes, as in Neil Jordan's 'Skin', a reworking of the Gertie episode in *Ulysses* from the point of view of a middle-aged woman exploring her sensuality. In Michael McLaverty's case, Joyce's influence enabled him to overcome a prolonged period of writer's block and publish, in the 'New Irish Writing' page of *The Irish Press* (1976), 'After Forty Years', a poignant elegy for a vanished love that contains echoes of 'The Dead'. Apart from Joyce, Chekhov and Flaubert continued to be claimed as influences by Irish writers such as Edna O'Brien and John McGahern, and in the latter's case Proust must also be added. As the period drew to a close, the range of European references present in the work of writers such as Aidan Higgins and Desmond Hogan anticipated the intertextuality of the Irish short story of the 1990s. Hogan's characters read Hesse and Kerouac, and the lyrical, poetical style of his stories reflects the fluidity of his characters' lives as they move between Ireland, Europe and the United States.

Some changes were noticeable, then, particularly towards the end of the 1970s. By 1978, the increased prominence of Irish women writers led Benedict Kiely to muse that 'some eager young man' should make 'a study of contemporary Irish writers who happened to be women'.[62] And, in an article titled 'The Rise and Rise of the Lady Short Story Writer', *The Irish Times* posed the question: 'Do you have to be a lady to write a fine story?'[63] Janet Madden-Simpson's anthology, *Women's Part* (1979), underlined the association of women writers with the form.

Youth as a theme began to come into its own, not the innocent children traditional in the Irish short story, but the troubled teenagers and students who feature in the stories of Julia O'Faolain, Neil Jordan and Desmond Hogan, as well as in Kate Cruise O'Brien's wry, perceptive stories of student and young married life in *A Gift Horse*, published by Poolbeg in 1978. Though many writers continued to rely on the realist mode, others were more willing to innovate. The experiments of Edna O'Brien and Maeve Kelly with stream-of-consciousness reflected modernism's belated influence on the mainstream Irish short story. Benedict Kiely's stories may be linked to tradition through their incorporation of the musicality, humour and digressions of the oral tradition, but their complex structures and wide-ranging intertextual references pointed forward to the Irish short story of the 1990s.

By 1974, one Irish commentator felt able to assert that: 'As a form the short story has, more than most, had its ambitions settled.'[64] Yet, as if to demonstrate that the history of the Irish short story in every period escapes both rigid categorization and national boundaries, during these years Samuel Beckett was producing a series of short fictions in French that defy classification to the extent that if Joyce may be said to have stretched the novel form to its limits in *Finnegans Wake* by dint of copiousness, so Beckett, employing the opposite technique of minimalism, pushed the short story form to the point of dissolution. The fluidity of his short fictions is demonstrated by the fact that, until Beckett's intervention, a story like 'neither' (1976) was categorized as poetry by his publisher.[65] Hovering on the borders between short story, poetry and drama, many of these short works incorporate an oral speaking voice that facilitated their subsequent adaptation for the stage. Beckett's short fictions extend the dissolution of self to the point where only the disembodied voice exists, 'an expiring consciousness', in David Lodge's words.[66] This move 'from impenetrable self to impenetrable unself'[67] results in a curious conjunction of postmodernist formal experimentation with the speaking voice of the Irish oral tradition.

John Banville called Beckett's 'First Love' (1946), 'the most nearly perfect short story ever written', drawn as much to the father–son theme, perhaps, as to Beckett's formal experimentation.[68] Banville's own collection, *Long Lankin*, explores themes of atonement and violence that were to become prominent in Banville's later work as a novelist, but the collection is notable in its own right for Banville's interest in developing a hybrid form, somewhere between novel and story. When *Long Lankin* was first published in 1970, it was described as 'a work of fiction' and included a novella as well as nine stories. The stories are based around the notion of relationships ruined or disturbed by a third party, the Long Lankin interloper, making it a thematically coherent collection along the lines of those by Joyce, Moore and Beckett. When the collection was revised for publication in 1984, Banville strengthened this unity by reverting to the label of short story collection and omitting the concluding novella. The addition of 'De Rerum Natura' rounded off the volume on a less bleak note than the original. By setting his stories in the framework of the ballad of Long Lankin, who kills his master's baby and wife out of revenge, anxiety and tension are added to what are essentially psychological studies of fractured relationships. Banville's protagonists encounter difficulties establishing the identity they crave: Julie as wife and mother in 'Sanctuary', Morris as artist in 'Nightwind'. In 'A Death', Stephen finds his intention to write a book about his love for Alice confounded by the fluidity of life when he discovers that love has evolved into estrangement. In Banville, as in Beckett, postmodern fragmentation of identity becomes explicit, anticipating a theme that will become prominent in the Irish short story of the 1990s.

By the end of the seventies, then, the thrust of the future was becoming stronger than the pull of the past. The short story of the closing years of the 1970s caught up with changes in Irish society and finally reflected the fact that Ireland was moving out of the paralysis of earlier decades and recovering its energy. This new mood was summed up in Desmond Hogan's 'Sculptures', in which Angela encourages Teresa to break free of the past, saying: 'There's a future, always a future that escapes the past if you're strong enough and determined enough. That's all in life that's important, not visions, not children, but this energy that deflates and can conquer again.'[69]

READINGS: WILLIAM TREVOR AND EDNA O'BRIEN

William Trevor, 'Attracta' (1978)

'Time is the most interesting thing to write about besides people,' William Trevor once claimed in an interview.[70] Time and imagination are central themes in 'Attracta', Trevor's story of two episodes of brutal violence in Northern Ireland: imagination because the story focuses, not so much on the violence itself, as on the characters' exercise of imaginative sympathy in response to it; time because the two episodes are fifty-eight years apart. From 1977 onwards Trevor, like Frank O'Connor before him, had a first reading agreement with the *New Yorker*, and 'Attracta' appeared initially in that magazine. The fact that the story was written with an international audience in mind may have influenced its shape: the juxtaposition of the Black and Tan period, during which Attracta's parents were murdered, with the sectarian violence of the 1970s highlights very clearly for a reader unfamiliar with Ireland the reawakening of the nightmare of Irish history in Northern Ireland.

The earlier story emphasizes the possibility of redemption. The Protestant Mr Devereux and his Catholic companion and lover, Geraldine Carey, jointly responsible for murdering Attracta's parents in a case of mistaken identity during an ambush intended for the Black and Tans, have renounced violence and, in an act of imaginative sympathy, have endeavoured to make amends to the orphaned Attracta. The fact that they are of different faiths suggests that both sides accept responsibility for the murders, and Attracta, three years old at the time of her parents' death, comes to regard Mr Devereux and Geraldine as a second family. Only when she is eleven does the fanatical Orangeman, Mr Purce, enlighten her about their role in her parents' death, ironically in front of the town's statue of the Maid of Erin, the abstraction in whose name so much of the violence, past and present, has been perpetrated. At first, Attracta has difficulty reconciling the two images in her mind – her parents' murder with the kindly Mr Devereux and his devout, mass-going housekeeper. She certainly rejects Mr Purce's more bigoted embellishments of the story, a rejection endorsed by her aunt in her retelling of the story and by the Archdeacon, who advises Attracta to put it all in the past, reminding her that people may be changed by events and come to acknowledge their guilt. Resisting Mr Purce's attempt to turn her into a bigot, Attracta grows up to become the teacher in the town's Protestant school.

Attracta is sixty-one when she reads the story of Penelope Vade in newspaper accounts. On the surface, this second story of violence offers no hope of redemption. Penelope Vade's British Army husband was brutally murdered in Belfast, his body decapitated and the head sent to Penelope through the post. As a way of expressing her grief and anger, twenty-three-year-old Penelope moves from England to Belfast and in a gesture of reconciliation and defiance to the gunmen joins the Women's Peace Movement. Penelope's attempt to overcome sectarian divisions recalls Kathleen's border crossing actions in Jennifer Johnston's novel, *Shadows on Our Skin* (1977), in which Kathleen, born in the Republic and fiancée of a British soldier, moves to Northern Ireland in an attempt to understand the violence. As Kathleen has her head shaved by republicans when they discover the identity of her fiancé, so Penelope's actions enrage the men who killed her husband. All seven rape her and in despair she commits suicide, her body being found four days later covered in mouse droppings.

In the light of such atrocity, Attracta feels that she has been teaching the children the wrong lessons all her life. Remarks Trevor made in an interview about the themes of time and memory that play such an important role in his work serve to illuminate Attracta's state of mind here: 'Memory also forms character – the way you remember things makes you who you are. People struggle to share a very private side of themselves with other people.'[71] Attracta believes she should have told the children that hope is possible; that her own experience shows that men and women may not stay violent for ever; Penelope's rapists may repent and understand her gesture of reconciliation, however unlikely that may seem now. Attracta has perhaps underestimated the effectiveness of her teaching since the walls of her schoolroom underline boundary crossing, decorated as they are with portraits of England's kings and queens and Irish republican heroes such as Lord Edward Fitzgerald and Wolfe Tone. The legends she has taught them cross several national boundaries: Ariadne, Finn MacCool, King Arthur. Moreover, in telling Penelope's story to the schoolchildren, Attracta exerts the kind of imaginative sympathy Trevor regarded as necessary if the situation in Northern Ireland was to be resolved: in the following decades, this would be a recurring theme in his stories such as 'Beyond the Pale' and 'Against the Odds'. Attracta reaches out to the other, her voice merging with that of Penelope as she slips from the third person into the first, telling the story as if she herself was suffering Penelope's fate:

'My story is one with hers,' she said. 'Horror stories, with different endings only. I think of her now and I can see quite clearly the flat she lived in in Belfast. I can see the details, correctly or not I've no idea. Wallpaper with a pattern of brownish-purple flowers on it, gaunt furniture casting shadows, a tea-caddy on the hired television set. I drag my body across the floors of two rooms, over a carpet that smells of dust and cigarette ash, over rugs and cool linoleum. I reach up in the kitchen, a hand on the edge of the sink: one by one I eat the aspirins until the bottle's empty.'[72]

Attracta's story of Penelope Vade has little effect on the children she teaches since they have become desensitized to images of violence and she pays for her moral courage with her job. Yet her attempt at boundary crossing remains, and the reintegration of former gunmen and women like Mr Devereux and Geraldine into society offers a ray of hope in the bleak present, if not for her schoolchildren with a grim future ahead of them, at least for the reader, who sees further than they into Attracta's mind and her memories of a childhood that was happy, despite tragedy. Trevor allies himself with other writers on Northern Ireland, discussed by Patrick Grant in *Literature, Rhetoric and Violence in Northern Ireland*, who indicate a way forward into a different sort of future through imaginative acts of forgiveness and reconciliation which may free those who perpetrate violence, as much as those who are its victims.[73]

Edna O'Brien, 'A Rose in the Heart of New York' (1978)

Like Trevor's story, 'A Rose in the Heart of New York' first appeared in the *New Yorker* before its subsequent publication in O'Brien's collection, *Mrs Reinhardt*. The story depicts the material and psychological oppressions weighing on the life of a rural Irish woman and the way these oppressions become transferred to her daughter so that a relationship begun in love eventually turns to hatred. 'A Rose in the Heart of New York' is set against a rural Irish background similar to that in *The Country Girls*, with additional material that will later be used to sketch in Nell's childhood and upbringing in O'Brien's 1992 novel, *Time and Tide*. The difference between the novels and the short story is that the shortened form requires O'Brien to edit out material about the heroine's husband and lovers, putting the focus entirely on the mother–daughter story. Both mother and daughter remain unnamed, lending the story an archetypal quality that belies its many autobiographical resonances. The title, for example, referring to the mother's pivotal period of independence in New York, may seem tailor-made to arouse an American reader's interest, but in fact it draws on an episode in the life of O'Brien's own mother, described in more detail in O'Brien's later novel, *The Light of Evening* (2006).

The mother–daughter relationship portrayed in 'A Rose in the Heart of New York' is characteristic of O'Brien's writing: the early, almost symbiotic closeness between mother and daughter as they form a bond against an often drunk and violent father; the use of food as a symbol of maternal love; the separation from the mother that begins when the daughter is sent away to convent school; the transfer of the daughter's affections to a favourite nun and the lesbian overtones of that relationship (which will feature again in 'Sister Imelda' and *Down by the River*); finally, the inability of the daughter to separate herself entirely from her mother and the consequent transformation of love into hate. The mother in this story is a Catholic martyr mother who, on hearing of her daughter's divorce, requests her never to touch alcohol or have anything more to do with men. She is a suffocating mother who, like Nell's mother in *Time and Tide*, talks of her wish for her daughter and herself to be buried together. As in many short stories by Irish women in this period, the mother–daughter bond is portrayed as a regressive one, pulling the daughter back into the past and hindering her move forward into a wider, more liberating future.

In 'A Rose in the Heart of New York' the adult daughter, now living in London, endeavours to prompt a reconciliation with her mother, but when she pays for them both to go away on holiday, the treat comes too late; the mother has become too accustomed to her sacrificial way of life to take pleasure in it. The daughter tries to cross 'the chasm' that stretches between them by encouraging her mother to talk about the days before she married and learned to suppress her desires. Here and there, she catches a glimpse of her mother's former independence: when her mother tells stories about her first lover or the time she climbed a ladder into chapel in order to jump the queue for confession or the period she spent as a young single woman earning her living in New York. This episode of independence in her mother's life is the moment the narrator yearns to return to in order to create a bond between them, hence the significance of the title. However, the mother rejects any similarity between her life in the United States and her daughter's London life, filled as it is with lovers, and asserts that the only worthwhile love is that of a mother for her child. The narrator finally realizes that it will be impossible for her mother and herself to meet as adult women: 'The reconciliation that she had hoped for, and indeed intended to instigate, never came.'[74] 'A Rose in the Heart of New York' is an elegy for a failed mother–daughter relationship.

'A Rose in the Heart of New York' is also the story of a silenced mother. The daughter has tried to urge the mother to speak but the mother has resisted and retreated to the silence of the womb, lying 'curled up on the bed, knotted as a foetus, with a clump of paper handkerchiefs in front of her mouth'.[75] Later, seeing her mother lying in her coffin, the daughter feels that 'The mouth was trying to speak.'[76] This silenced mother will recur in *Down by the River* and she must be resisted by the daughter, for whom she is no help in entering the symbolic order.[77] We have already noted Adrienne Rich's stress on the importance of an empowering mother figure for the daughter. In O'Brien's story, the daughter has tried to find the mother's voice, but failed:

A new wall had arisen, stronger and sturdier than before. Their life together and all those exchanges were like so many spilt feelings, and she looked to see some sign or hear some murmur. Instead, a silence filled the room, and there was a vaster silence beyond, as if the house itself had died or had been carefully put down to sleep.[78]

'A Rose in the Heart of New York' is characteristic of the Irish short story of this period in portraying the tension between past and present, between memory and imagination, using the relationship between the generations. The daughter's effort to heal the breach with her mother through an act of sympathetic imagination is unsuccessful. The final sentence suggests that she must 'put to sleep' the memories of her mother that suffuse this narrative if she is to move forward into the future.

CHAPTER EIGHT

1980 to the present: changing identities

Writing in *The Irish Times* in 1990, Fintan O'Toole was somewhat dismissive of the short story form: 'short stories, if they are written at all, are there to keep things ticking over in the spaces between novels', and he commented on 'the marginalisation of the Irish short story since the days of O'Connor, O'Flaherty and O'Faolain'.[1] Such a view, understandable in the context of O'Toole's argument about recent developments in the Irish novel, ignored the fact that the closing decades of the twentieth century saw an upsurge in short story writing in Ireland with a variety of outlets and opportunities for new authors to get their work published or aired on the radio.

Short stories are not generally regarded as profitable by publishers but their length makes them suitable for newspapers, magazines and radio, and more satisfactory for the reader or listener than extracts from novels. In 1988, the *Sunday Tribune* took over David Marcus' New Irish Writing Page and under Ciaran Carty's editorship it continued to support emerging Irish writers. Writers who were published in its pages became eligible for a Hennessy Award and anthologies arising out of this, *The Hennessy Book of Irish Fiction* (1995) and *The New Hennessy Book of Irish Fiction* (2005), edited by Ciaran Carty and Dermot Bolger, featured high quality writing by Joseph O'Connor, Hugo Hamilton, Colum McCann, Neil Jordan, Philip Ó Ceallaigh, Anne Enright, Deirdre Madden, Angela Bourke and Claire Keegan, among others. In 1996, David Marcus began producing his annual anthology of Irish short stories, published in London by Phoenix. The first volume featured established names such as William Trevor and Julia O'Faolain alongside younger writers like Frank Ronan and Clairr O'Connor. In later years, the Phoenix anthology became a showcase for emergent writers and it must rank as one of his many services to the Irish short story that Marcus' annual editions not only promoted the genre but also provided the reader with glimpses into changing Irish social mores almost as they occurred. The connection between the short story and modernity was never so evident as in these closing decades of the twentieth century and the opening decade of the twenty-first. For the reader who likes to keep abreast of current social trends, the short story, on account of its brevity, is able to anticipate themes that take five years or more to make their appearance in other genres.

Following on from the 1970s, Irish women short story writers featured in reasonable numbers. Benedict Kiely's anthology *The Penguin Book of Irish Short Stories*, published in 1981, presaged women's future dominance of the form by his inclusion of, alongside Somerville and Ross, Bowen and Lavin, contemporary female writers like Val Mulkerns, Edna O'Brien, Julia O'Faolain, Ita Daly and Eithne Strong. Attic Press was founded in 1984 to promote women's writing and in 1993 it published *Virgins and Hyacinths*, a collection of stories previously serialized in *The Irish Times*. The volume was edited by Mary Lavin's daughter, Caroline Walsh, and demonstrated the quality and range of Irish women's short stories. Many other anthologies published in these decades highlighted women's contribution to the genre.[2] They ranged from those with popular appeal, such as *If Only: Irish Women's Short Stories of Love and Divorce*, edited by Kate Cruise O'Brien and Mary Maher and published by Poolbeg in 1997, to those like *Cutting the Night in Two*, edited by Evelyn Conlon and Hans-Christian Oeser and published by New Island Books in 2001, presenting examples of Irish women's literary short stories spanning the entire century. There were also anthologies with a particular angle such as *The Female Line: Northern Irish Women Writers*, published in 1985 to celebrate ten years of the Northern Ireland Women's Rights Movement.

The advent of the Troubles brought anthologies devoted to that theme, such as Michael Parker's *The Hurt World* (1995). Issues of sexuality and different lifestyles came to the fore in collections like *Alternative Loves: Irish Gay and Lesbian Stories* (1994), edited by Marcus with a foreword by Ailbhe Smythe. During the 1990s, with unflagging commitment to the genre, Marcus edited a series of anthologies for particular popular markets bearing titles such as *Irish Christmas Stories*, *Irish Ghost Stories*, *Irish 'Eros'*, *Irish Sporting Stories* and *Irish Love Stories*. In that decade also, the opportunities for new writers to get published greatly expanded. The rise in self-publishing allowed local writers' groups to produce short story compilations, among them, the North Clare Writers' Workshop, the Fingal Writers' Group and the Bennettsbridge Creative Writers. From 1998 onwards, under the guidance of Brendan Kennelly and Gerald Dawe, there have been annual anthologies arising out of the MPhil creative writing programme at Trinity College, Dublin. Recent years have also seen a proliferation of short story competitions both at home and abroad. The Frank O'Connor International Short Story Award for a collection of short stories published in English anywhere in the world was inaugurated in 2005. Organized under the auspices of Cork City Council and the Munster Literature Festival, it is the largest award in the world for short story writing. Other opportunities for the nascent Irish short story writer include the Bryan MacMahon short story award administered by Listowel Writers' Week, the Francis MacManus short story competition for broadcasting on radio and the annual Fish international short fiction prize, administered out of Bantry by a publishing company committed to the fostering of new talent by offering numerous other story competitions, on-line critiques and editorial services. These decades have seen a real sense of vibrancy about the short story writing scene in Ireland that can only encourage the genre to grow and expand.

Both gender identity and Irish identity have been increasingly interrogated, deconstructed and diversified in the short stories of this period, so that the key to these decades is transformation, of society, of the family and finally of the Irish short story itself. In *The Irish Writer and the World*, Declan Kiberd noted that few Irish novels of the 1990s risked portraying the seismic changes in Irish society following the advent of the Celtic Tiger.[3] Short story writers are in a different situation, for the short story, requiring less of a panoramic view than the novel, is arguably better suited to provide rapid insights into these changes. Short story writers can be risk takers. Where life is changing fast, the form allows the freedom of a glance: 'the short story does not present a world to enter, as does the novel, but a vignette to contemplate'.[4] Definitions of the short story given by Nadine Gordimer ('the light of the flash') and Mary Lavin ('an arrow in flight') lay stress on the genre as ignoring causality in favour of conveying a moment of insight.[5] This, as Clare Hanson has pointed out, makes the short story ideally suited to portray the fragmentation of modern life, where there is uncertainty about society as a cohesive whole and the grand narratives underpinning it.[6] Hanson's remarks are particularly appropriate to the huge changes brought about in Irish society by the Celtic Tiger, such as the breakdown of the family unit, the questioning of traditional forms of Irish nationalism and the declining influence of the Catholic church. In an unstable and often confusing society, the short story is ideally framed to present momentary insights, its characteristic features of economy, tension and irony making it particularly suited to the modern age.

At first, transformation did not seem likely. Reviewing Edna O'Brien's volume, *Returning* (1982), Maev Kennedy commented:

We are back in very familiar O'Brien country, back in her peculiarly desolate Irish Midland countryside. Really Bord Failte should have sent a hit squad to deal with Miss O'Brien years ago – how could anyone read this book and want to set foot on the sodden, dung-spattered soil of Ireland? The worst of it is that some wincing corner of the brain admits that it's true, all true.[7]

Evelyn Conlon's short story, 'The Park', recalls the occasion of Pope John Paul II's visit in 1979, exploring what it felt like to be a dissenter on the day of his celebration of mass in the Phoenix Park: 'Those who thought otherwise were, simply, invisible for the day.'[8] The narrator and her liberal-minded friends fear the regressive effect his visit will have on Irish society, and indeed the Pope's challenge to the Irish people to uphold Catholic traditions did provide an opportunity for right-wing Catholic groups during the 1980s to seek to strengthen Catholic values in the areas of divorce, homosexuality and abortion. Economic recession and high unemployment reinforced conservative attitudes: in 1985, *The Irish Times* described John McGahern as one 'of the generation of Irish writers pulling away, often desperately, from crippling artistic censorship'.[9] Nowhere is the restrictive effect of Catholic values felt more strongly than in short stories written by Irish women during the 1980s, focusing on women's domestic lives as wives, mothers and daughters.

Mary Lavin's collection, *A Family Likeness and Other Stories* (1985), portrays mothers and daughters who fail to disentangle themselves from social and religious pressures to conform to notions of self-sacrificing femininity, and these constraints have an invidious effect on their relationship. In 'A Family Likeness', past misunderstandings between Ada and her mother are replicated in the entangled relationship Ada has with her own daughter, Laura, and the portrayal of three generations of mother–daughter relationships gone awry underlines the sense of entrapment. Women's willingness to allow themselves to be constrained by Catholic values is sharply scrutinized by Clare Boylan in her short story, 'You Don't Know You're Alive' (*Concerning Virgins*, 1989), where Annie's life is dominated by her Catholic faith and by her wish for a baby; indeed, the one is predicated on the other: Annie's deep Catholic beliefs lead her to feel that she is failing in her gender role by not becoming a mother. Despite the warning example of Maevie, driven to insanity by trying to fulfil the Catholic ideal of wife and mother, Annie is delighted when she learns, in a scene that points up her ignorance of how her body works, that her barrenness can easily be rectified. She walks home rejoicing and so deeply imbued with the Catholic notion of motherhood that even the 'dull domestic chatter' of the mothers in front of her fails to warn her of what her life will become.[10] Boylan's story, like Lavin's, raises doubts whether, in a culture where women are forced to shoulder the whole burden of domestic responsibility, any healthy female identity is possible.

Several of Ita Daly's short stories in *The Lady with the Red Shoes* (1980), highlight what Betty Friedan as early as 1965 in *The Feminine Mystique* branded 'the problem with no name', that is, that relegating women to childbearing and domestic work infantilizes them. In 'A Family Picnic', Mary's mother (significantly she is never given her own name) survives the dwindling of her life after marriage by escaping into a world of dreams, so that to Mary, a professional woman working alongside men, her mother seems naïve. In 'The Birthday Girl', marriage and mother-hood have a similar infantilizing effect on Mrs Browning, an apparently happily married mother of four, who has taken on the roles her society expects of her and in the process lost her identity. Like many of the women in Daly's collection, Mrs Browning attempts to break out from the constraints of her life, relinquishing her household chores to buy a new dress and drink in a bar with a stranger. For a brief moment, she finds herself again, but the episode ends in defeat as her behaviour becomes sordid and embarrassing and she is driven home drunk in a taxi. *The Lady with the Red Shoes* was in many ways a groundbreaking col-lection in its portrayal of Irish women deeply entangled in the masculinist values of their society and their often fruitless attempts to break free. 'Aimez-vous Colette?' underlines the fact that conservative attitudes remained entrenched in other areas of Irish life: Ireland's attitude towards racial minorities is reflected in Daly's picture of African and Indian students huddled together in run-down bedsits in Rathmines, where their Irish girlfriends visit them furtively on Saturday afternoons. Nevertheless, the fact that Mary in 'A Family Picnic' has left her mother's life behind suggests that change was on the way for Irish women.

In Evelyn Conlon's first collection, *My Head is Opening*, published by Attic Press in 1987, Conlon, like Daly, uses the short story to highlight women's issues, particularly around motherhood. 'As Good a Reason As Any' looks at the pressure on women to become mothers; 'Park-going Days' presents the unrelenting drudgery of mothers' lives; 'Transition' and 'The Day She Lost the Last of Her Friends' examine the social unacceptability of unmarried mothers and separated mothers, respect-ively, in 1980s Ireland. However, in Conlon's stories, published seven years on from Daly's collection, there is more of a sense of women beginning to find their voice. In 'My Head is Opening' Louise who, like Mrs Browning, has become engulfed by marriage and motherhood, manages to return to her books and recover her identity. In 'In Reply to Florence', Mona attacks Michelangelo's statue of David in protest against male domination of the world of art whilst in 'Once Upon a Time', when God begins a story about Moira, a woman who would not stay with her husband, the story is taken out of God's hands as Moira insists on telling her story herself: 'Someone else took over the story. He couldn't control the pen.'[11] Summing up what was happening to the Irish short story in this decade as more and more Irish women were taking up their pens and telling their stories in their own way, Moira enlightens God about a thing or two concerning women's lives, until eventually he comes to understand why she cannot stay in her marriage. Conlon's witty, often angry stories register a strong protest against women's secondary status in Irish society, and the fact that the problems of, for example, single mothers could now be aired suggests that change was on the way. Indeed, during these years of right-wing backlash, there developed, as Ailbhe Smyth has argued, a feminist counter-culture with a focus on education and the arts.[12] Women writers and artists became more visible, feminist publishing houses started up, and in the universities women's studies programmes developed. As Smyth puts it: 'the tide was on the turn and Irish women were once again signalling their desire for change and their determination to bring it about'.[13] In this move to transform Irish society, short stories by Irish women played a crucial part.

If Daly's collection named women's problems and Conlon's expressed women's anger, Clare Boylan's two volumes published during this decade, *A Nail on the Head* (1983) and *Concerning Virgins* (1989), marked a progression by using humour to present, in some of her stories, a more optimistic picture than Daly and Conlon about women's chances of achieving a balance between the competing claims on their lives. Unlike Edna O'Brien's reworking of *Rebecca* in *Girl with the Green Eyes*, where Cait is defeated by the shadow of Eugene's sophisticated American wife, Boylan's 'The Wronged Wife' transforms the *Rebecca* plot of rivalry between first and second wives into a tale of two women uniting to resist a controlling husband. In 'A Model Daughter', a woman invents an imaginary daughter in order to solve her financial problems and, crucially, she is not punished for her behaviour.

In the 1980s, Irish women writers also began their foray into popular writing, a genre they were later to make their own with the spectacular success of the Irish 'chick lit' novel, for which several short story collections in this decade prepared the way. In *An Idle Woman*, a series of satirical stories on Irish life published by Poolbeg in 1980, Val Mulkerns maintains a lightness of touch, but there is some pointed commentary on the Catholic church's ban on contraception which in 'Humanae Vitae' drives husband and wife apart as the wife insists on obedience to the Pope's teaching. Even a light-hearted collection like Maeve Binchy's *Dublin 4* (1982) reveals that beneath the supposed liberalism of Dublin's professional classes ran a deep vein of traditional thinking and hypocrisy in sexual matters. In story after story, Binchy exposes what lay hidden in Irish life: unwanted pregnancy, homosexuality, infidelity and alcoholism. In a different register, in 1985 Attic Press brought out a collection of reworkings of fairy tales by Irish women writers: *Rapunzel's Revenge: Fairy Tales for Feminists*. These have no specific Irish dimension but the old tales are rewritten in a way that is usually empowering for women: in Maeve Binchy's retelling of the Cinderella story, Cinderella rejects marriage in favour of a career.

There was therefore an increased willingness even in the popular short story of this period to challenge the Irish Catholic construct of female identity and expose the limitations of the family unit on which the Irish Constitution had been founded. A more searing indictment of family life can be found in Leland Bardwell's collection, *Different Kinds of Love*, published by Attic Press in 1987. In this courageous collection, Bardwell paints a disturbing picture of familial relationships by focusing on several topics not previously much represented in the Irish short story. Domestic violence features in 'Euston' and 'Out-patients', in which Nina's self-confidence is shattered by her constant battering. Since she lacks the economic independence to leave her husband, Nina remains silent about her experiences, a silence in which the society around her colludes. The sexual repressions and hypocrisy of this society are underlined in 'The Dove of Peace', in which Columbine, sexually abused by her father, dies alone in the fields struggling to give birth to her baby, a fate reminiscent of the teenage Ann Lovett's tragic death in 1984. Bardwell's stories challenge the automatic association of women with the maternal instinct, implicit in article 41 of the Irish Constitution: in 'The Quest', Nan never regrets giving up her son for adoption since by this action she has preserved the freedom to focus on her musical career. Reviewing this collection, Mary Leland, while noting Bardwell's already distinguished reputation as a writer in other forms, saw these short stories as a breakthrough: 'the publication of her first book of short stories does seem to mark the unqualified emergence of something very tough, durable, and unflinching'.[14]

Male writers, too, often turned family relations into a metaphor for the changes that were going on beneath the surface of Irish society. In 'Gold Watch', published in the US edition of *Getting Through*, 1980, John McGahern uses the uneasy relationship between an urban-dwelling, university-educated son and his farmer father to measure the seismic shift in Irish society during this period, that often left older and younger generations in a state of mutual incomprehension. His son's refusal to take over the family farm is at the root of this corrosive relationship and the father's anguish at his loss of power in a changing world is expressed in his unwillingness to validate his son's present life by passing on to him the gold watch inherited from his own father. When the son buys his father a replacement watch, his father rejects all bonds between them by endeavouring to smash what has become a reminder of his frailty and mortality. By contrast, the son comes to accept change as an inevitable part of life and this is reflected in the open-endedness of 'Gold Watch', compared to the cyclical and repetitive view of time present in McGahern's stories from the previous decades.

In Desmond Hogan's story, 'The Mourning Thief', published in his 1981 collection, *Children of Lir*, the father–son relationship is likewise set in the context of social change. The dying father represents an older generation who fought in the General Post Office in 1916 and believes it right to shed blood in the cause of an independent Ireland. Liam, his son, seeing the link between a state founded on violence and the current Troubles in the North, rejects his father's romantic nationalism, taking as icons for modern Ireland the figures of the pacifist Francis Sheehy-Skeffington and his feminist wife, Hannah. Like the son in McGahern's story, Liam turns his back on his father's profession, opting for an artistic career over the police force. Time, which was such a threat to the father in 'Gold Watch', is presented as 'a thief' in Hogan's story, stealing away the older generation's beliefs and putting new ones in their stead. Both McGahern and Hogan use the father–son relationship and its entanglement in the theme of time to portray the dying off of the generation that fought for Ireland's independence and the very different values and expectations of the new generation. Liam has rejected his father's Catholic and heterosexual lifestyle in favour of an open marriage that includes his wife, his male lover and her lovers. 'Ireland is dying,' says Liam, referring to 'the ghosts of Irish Republicans, of policemen, military men, priests' who haunt his father's house.'[15] By contrast, in his own life, he feels that 'experiment was only beginning'.[16] Liam's optimism here contrasts with many of the daughter figures in stories by Hogan's female contemporaries, in which the bid for freedom is often hindered by domestic responsibility.

In other contexts, too, the Irish short story of the 1980s marked changes going on beneath the surface of what was outwardly a regressive period. In the title story of McGahern's collection, *High Ground* (1985), the alcoholic schoolmaster, Leddy, whose out-of-date methods have held back generations of schoolchildren, seems likely to be ousted in a more disciplined and competitive era by the machinations of Senator Reegan. Senator Reegan is a forerunner of the new breed of corrupt, unscrupulous Irish politicians whose dealings were to be unmasked in the tribunals of the 1990s, as Master Kennedy's entirely materialistic view of his profession in 'Crossing the Line' foreshadows the materialism of the Celtic Tiger years. In both stories, McGahern's youthful narrator observes the older generation's failings and knows he must carve out a path different from theirs. Generally in McGahern's stories of this period, the theme of paralysis gives way to that of social change. The sense of society's structures shifting is apparent in 'Oldfashioned', discussed in the interchapter, and two other stories from *High Ground*, 'Eddie Mac' and 'The Conversion of William Kirkwood', provide a similar overview of the transformation of Irish rural society where, as in William Trevor's stories, the decline of an Anglo-Irish family becomes a symbol for the perceived loss of moral and cultural values in late twentieth-century Ireland.

McGahern's treatment of religion in *High Ground* also reflects changes in Irish society. In dealing with loss of faith, 'Like All Other Men' moves one step closer to the secular than 'The Wine Breath' from the previous decade. Again the theme of time is involved: Michael Duggan's loss of belief and his departure from the seminary have made all the days equal and indifferent to him. Haunted by the absence of teleological certainties, he is attracted to a woman in a dance hall precisely because of her air of calm detachment. Later he learns the reason for this when she informs him that she is about to enter a religious order. Michael's loss of belief has shackled him to linear time – 'He knew that no matter how eagerly he found himself walking in any direction it could only take him to the next day and the next' – whereas Susan has had the faith to step out of time into a life lived in the context of eternity.[17] 'Like All Other Men' is a story that could only have been written by someone brought up in a society still possessing a sense of the sacred and thus able to measure the cost of its absence. It confirms Eamon Grennan's accuracy in situating McGahern in a line of post-Catholic Irish writers stretching back to Joyce, who portray characters living among the spiritual remnants of a lost faith.[18]

In the 1980s, William Trevor began to write more often about Ireland, his long years of exile having made that country as strange to him as England had been earlier in his life. In an interview, he explained how important this sense of alienation is for him as a writer: 'To me, England was an amazing and strange place. I'd never been outside of Ireland until I was twenty-two. When I *now* write about Ireland I'm doing a faintly similar thing, because I'm going back to a country which has become strange to me. Personally, I think that kind of thing is essential.'[19] The pursuit of artistic detachment is as evident in Trevor's skilfully wrought, technically accomplished stories as it is in John McGahern's search for inspiration in Flaubert and Joyce. In contrast to the leaning of many Irish short story writers in this period towards socio-cultural commentary, Trevor employs the form to explore universal moral problems centred around tolerance, forgiveness and reconciliation, whilst McGahern's focus, particularly in his later writing, is on language, the aesthetic and the metaphysical. Both are skilled (which not all short story writers are) in the art of brief, telling dialogue. Both use indirection, understatement and irony to achieve their aims, and in both writers, concrete objects bear considerable weight. Though there is a greater sense of urgency and personal engagement in McGahern's stories than in Trevor's, a deeper commitment to Irish life and Irish themes and more use of symbolism, both authors' avoidance of authorial self-assertion and their commitment to artistic patterning put them at odds with the subjective, often impassioned and angry style of writing in many Irish short stories of the 1980s, notably by women. The difference is evident when Trevor's treatment of Ireland's changing attitudes to sexuality is compared with women's stories on the same topic.

In 'The Paradise Lounge' (*Beyond the Pale and Other Stories*, 1981), Trevor employs Joycean irony to counterpoint the resentment of an earlier generation of Irish at the sexual freedoms enjoyed by the young with the disillusionment of the younger generation. The elderly Miss Doheny mistakenly believes Beatrice and her lover are in the throes of a passionate affair, whereas in fact their adulterous love is ending in a manner as tawdry as the ironically named Paradise Lounge in which they drink. Miss Doheny might marvel at the change in attitudes to sexuality in Ireland but, as Trevor's use of parallel stories shows, liberation brings only a different form of unhappiness to adulterous lovers. Beatrice similarly misreads the unrequited love between Miss Doheny and the married Mr Meldrum as untarnished by the lies and deceptions that have accompanied her own affair. The final paragraph of the story is closer to *Dubliners* than *Brief Encounter* as Miss Doheny dwells on 'the agony of her stifled love',[20] her curiously immobile features, noted by Beatrice, summing up the unending paralysis of her life. The story makes its point about changing sexual mores in Ireland through patterning and Joycean irony, and the tone is one of sympathetic detachment: 'the less your fingerprints blur your novels and stories the better,' Trevor has commented.[21]

Trevor's artistic detachment stands in stark contrast to Mary Dorcey's impassioned and subjective tone in her collection, *A Noise from the Woodshed* (1989), which gives a voice to those defined as marginal in the life of the Irish nation: battered wives, the elderly and above all in this collection, lesbians. Lesbianism, previously such a muted theme in the Irish short story, became more prominent in the 1980s. Ita Daly's short story, 'Such Good Friends', skilfully manipulates the device of the unreliable narrator in order to illustrate the self-deceptions of a lesbian unwilling to acknowledge her sexual identity, even to herself. Lesbianism is also the subject of Leland Bardwell's 'The Launching', where a brief lesbian encounter inspires Emily to carry on with her investigations into early Irish women's history. However, it is Mary Dorcey's short stories that gave a powerful voice to the Irish lesbian, so long excluded from Ireland's definition of itself and from visibility in the life of the nation. The pulsing, hypnotic rhythms of Dorcey's prose in the title story, together with her use of the second person, break down boundaries between the self and the other, compelling the reader to become involved in this account of lesbian love. Rejecting objectivity, Dorcey's language aims to bring about a revolution in Irish attitudes. The noise from the woodshed turns out to be the sound of lovemaking between two women and Dorcey's story suggests that this 'startling and disturbing noise' is spreading out from the woodshed to be heard across the whole nation.[22] Mary Dorcey's lesbians come in from the boundaries to which they have been relegated for so long and demand inclusion in the nation's definitions of Irish identity.

Maeve Kelly's 'Orange Horses', originally appearing in Ailbhe Smyth's anthology, *Wildish Things*, published by Attic Press in 1989, likewise breaks the bounds of realism. Kelly follows Bardwell and Dorcey in using the short story to feature domestic violence, this time within the travelling community, a group, with the exception of Juanita Casey's *Hath the Rain a Father?* (1966), under-represented in the Irish short story. The community is presented as unremittingly patriarchal: Elsie's beatings by Fonsie, her husband, so severe as to cause her to miscarry, gain her little sympathy from the other travelling women. Surrounded by patriarchal women and violent men, Elsie struggles to preserve a life, or even a space, of her own: despite the very different setting and period, Virginia Woolf's admonitions about a room of one's own and £500 a year hang over this story. Having no safe domestic space, Elsie buries money in the ground as a way of preserving her independence. Elsie's eldest child, eleven-year-old Brigid, with her transgressive yearning to defy her brothers by riding ponies, expresses all the rebellion her mother is too beaten and weary to express. Yet there are signs that this rebellion will soon be quashed: approaching puberty, Brigid seems likely to repeat her mother's life, falling in love at fifteen with some boy with 'bad blood' and becoming resigned to a life of beatings and childbearing. Brigid, however, is significantly named. In both of her manifestations as pagan goddess and fifth-century Christian saint, Brigit is associated with imagery of fire and sun,[23] and the imagery of fire recurring through Kelly's story points to a submerged woman's world under Brigit's protection, which will offer Elsie a way to survive. The ending of the story is ambivalent. Fire engulfs the caravan but no trace of mother and daughter is found. Have Elsie and Brigid managed to escape with her money? Or, more in keeping with the move of the story towards the visionary, does the story break the bounds of realism by suggesting that mother and daughter have somehow been transported by the flames into Brigit's kingdom, a world outside the patriarchy where they can be free?

Other short stories reveal sympathy for those left behind by the changes in Ireland. In Bryan MacMahon's 'My Love Has a Long Tail', published in *The Sound of Hooves* (1985), generations of Mike's family have survived famines, wars and evictions only to be brought down by European Community directives from Brussels which have left a smallholder like himself in debt to a strong farmer, Mr Hogan, whose business in turn is threatened by the local supermarket. The economic recession of the 1980s not only affected traditional ways of earning an income but also led to high emigration, a topic that is reflected in the short fiction of the period. The stories in both Dermot Healy's *Banished Misfortune* (1982) and Desmond Hogan's *Children of Lir* are as likely to feature the Irish in London as the Irish in Dublin. Hogan presents male and female experiences of emigration in, respectively, 'The Sojourner', a story of an Irish labourer in London, and 'Soho Square Gardens', a story of an Irish prostitute. In 'Memories of Swinging London', an Irish nun uses drama as a means to give young Irish labourers a sense of trust in their Irish identity. Under her guidance, Liam learns to see his country, not as cramped and defeated, but as a place that has produced great writers like Yeats, Synge, Lady Gregory and O'Casey. A central theme of Hogan's collection, pointing forward to the Ireland of the 1990s, is that there are now many different Irelands.

The extent of the transformation Irish society was undergoing is underlined in several stories from this period dealing with returned emigrants who fail to grasp the recent shifts in power. Ita Daly's 'The Lady with the Red Shoes' is narrated through the voice of a middle-aged Anglo-Irishman, Mr Montgomery, whose fondness for the rituals and comfort of the old-fashioned McAndrews hotel in Mayo provokes, he is well aware, mirth among the younger generation. Whereas memories of her past as a barefoot village girl render the lady with the red shoes, who has achieved her dream of returning to Mayo a wealthy woman, ill at ease in the snobbish atmosphere of McAndrews hotel, the narrator knows that both McAndrews and himself belong to the past:

I wanted to go to her, to tell her, to explain to her that it didn't matter any more – the world itself was disintegrating. She should realize that places like McAndrews weren't important any longer, people only laughed at them now . . . She had no need to be saddened, for she, and all those other little Irish girls who had spent their days washing other people's floors and cooking other people's meals, they would inherit the earth. The wheel had come round full circle.[24]

Borrowing McGahern's image of the wheel, Daly uses it to suggest, not entrapment by time, but a shift in the class structures of Irish society.

Edna O'Brien's *Returning* (1982) is literally a return to the setting and even some of the characters of *The Country Girls*, written from the perspective of someone who has long lived outside Ireland. In 'The Connor Girls', the narrator returns to her home as an adult and, a sign that social mores are changing, finally receives the promise of a longed-for invitation to tea with the local Anglo-Irish family, the Connors. Her husband's dismissal of the import of such an invitation shows the narrator how far she has travelled: 'I realized that by choosing his world I had said goodbye to my own and to those in it. By such choices we gradually become exiles, until at last we are quite alone.'[25] Like many of O'Brien's characters, in exile the narrator has found no new identity to set against the Irish one she has only partly outgrown: in 'The Doll' the narrator describes her present uncomfortable in-between situation: 'I live in the city. I am a cosmopolitan . . . I too play a part . . . So I am far from those I am with, and far from those I have left.'[26] In a sense what O'Brien's stories are saying is that though the old Ireland may no longer exist the narrator, like Daly's lady with the red shoes, still carries it with her: 'that far-off region called childhood, where nothing ever dies, not even oneself'.[27] The bewilderment of returning emigrants was to become a prominent theme in the Irish short story of the 1990s.

In the 1980s, under pressure from political events, many short stories focused on Northern Ireland, though not all of them dealt specifically with the Troubles. Mary Beckett's stories in *A Belfast Woman* (1980) are simply told tales, in the realist tradition, but significant in supplying the inner lives of ordinary Northern Irish women struggling to make meaningful lives for themselves in a sectarian society. The sense of paralysis in these stories parallels a corresponding feeling of paralysis found in much short fiction from the Republic in the early 1980s. Beckett's protagonists often fail to fit into stereotypes of womanhood and as a consequence live on the margins of society: in 'The Excursion', the wife's loneliness due to the isolation of her farm and her husband's inability to communicate is exacerbated by her childlessness. Beckett's stories portray rural Northern Ireland as a harsh, repressed society where the only person capable of showing love is a young girl who is 'wanting' ('Ruth'). Her stories probe the psychological attitudes of the region: 'Saints and Scholars' depicts Irish mothers using their sons to compensate for their husbands' deficiencies, while in 'Theresa', Northern Ireland's racist attitudes are confronted. Other stories, such as 'A Belfast Woman', 'The Balancing of the Clouds', 'Flags and Emblems' and 'The Master and the Bombs', deal more directly with political divisions and bigotry in Northern Ireland: 'A Belfast Woman' shows Beckett experimenting with an unreliable narrator similar to that used in her novel, *Give Them Stones*, while in 'The Master and the Bombs', a husband and wife escape an unhappy marriage through relying on traditional Northern Irish gender roles, the woman devoting herself to motherhood whilst her husband masquerades as a revolutionary hero.

The harshness of life in rural Northern Ireland is also a feature of Patrick Boyle's stories in *The Port Wine Stain* (1983). The stories display a variety of tones. Some are tragic, portraying the sexual frustration of an old farmer whose young wife refuses to sleep with him ('Go Away, Old Man, Go Away'), the loneliness of a man shunned on account of a disfiguring birth mark ('The Port Wine Stain'), or the marginalization of an elderly couple gossiped about in the community because of their seemingly odd behaviour caused, it turns out, by caring for their retarded son ('A Quiet Respectable Couple'). Others are comic: in 'Interlude' two lodgers, found in bed together, are forced to pretend they are engaged. 'The Betrayers' begins in comic mode, drawing a parallel between Sheba, the mare Willie is trying to school, and Cassie, the girl he would like to ask out, but the story turns to tragedy as both pony and girl escape Willie. Boyle uses comparisons between animal and human behaviour in several of his stories, lending them an elemental quality that recalls the work of Liam O'Flaherty: 'Meles Vulgaris' is a powerful presentation of a middle-aged husband's meditation on his life, interspersed with memories of a badger hunt of long ago and his admiration for the badger's courage.

Sectarian violence, however, was the focus of most short fiction set in Northern Ireland during the 1980s, leading one commentator to claim that: 'No issue has been treated so extensively and so probingly in the modern Irish story as the Troubles.'[28] Given the equal prominence in this period of such themes as the shift in social mores, the father–son relationship and the changing role of women, this statement could be challenged. Nevertheless the Troubles was an urgent theme for Irish writers in this decade and one that was likely to appeal to an international readership. Several of William Trevor's stories of the 1980s deal directly or indirectly with the impact of the violence, probing both the roots of the conflict and the psychology of those caught up in it. His stories not only portray the impact of the Troubles on the lives of individuals, but also stress the individual's responsibility to the wider world. 'Beyond the Pale' (*Beyond the Pale*, 1981) illustrates this by employing the characteristic Trevor device of juxtaposing two stories. The first concerns a group of English people who have been coming to Ireland for years for their holidays and do not intend to let the conflict in the North deter them. The narrator, the self-deluding Milly, reduces the Troubles to 'unpleasantness' and a 'nasty carry-on'.[29] Her companions' willed ignorance and complacency are shattered, however, by the intrusion of a stranger who commits suicide. This parallel story exploring historical themes urges the importance of holding a balance between being overwhelmed by history, like the suicidal stranger, and ignoring it, like Cynthia's companions, who dismiss her reconstruction of the stranger's story as a mad fantasy. In this respect, 'Beyond the Pale' recalls Elizabeth Bowen's statement that she wished the Irish would remember history a little less and the English a little more: Cynthia is the only one of the English visitors who makes an effort to read up on Irish history and is thus able to reach across national barriers to understand the stranger's state of mind. Empathy and a moral responsibility to understand the world beyond the private self are the keynotes of this story as they are in much of Trevor's writing about Northern Ireland.

'Autumn Sunshine', from the same collection, also underlines English lack of understanding of Irish history. The Englishman, Harold, latches on to Irish republicanism out of hatred of his own country, his empty rhetoric simplifying the complexities of the relationship between the two countries. For Harold, and by extension all the other English who have espoused the cause of Irish violence, history is an excuse to take revenge on his own country, recycling past acts of violence under the pretext of making amends for England's actions, whereas for Canon Moran, as for Cynthia in the previous story, history is a motive for understanding and forgiveness. In his short stories on Northern Ireland, Trevor uses the form didactically to urge a particular message on his readers, namely a plea for the exercise of moral imagination. Addressed more often to English or American readers than to Irish (both 'Beyond the Pale' and 'Autumn Sunshine' first appeared in the *New Yorker*), they exemplify Patrick Grant's argument that literature in Northern Ireland can act as a moral agent, challenging the depersonalizing strategies employed by someone like Harold to feed the cycle of violence.[30]

Desmond Hogan's 'Protestant Boy', from *Children of Lir*, deals with themes of masculinity, nationalism and identity in the context of the Troubles in Northern Ireland and, like William Trevor's story, emphasizes the necessity of crossing boundaries, both political and psychological, if the violence is to be resolved. The opening paragraph signals the theme of national and ideological boundaries as the Catholic narrator from the Republic and thirteen-year-old Danny, a Protestant from Belfast, become friends in the no-man's-land of Butlin's Holiday Camp in Meath by the sea. When the boys next meet the Troubles have started up and the divisions between them have intensified, as the narrator sympathizes with the aims of the Provisional IRA whilst Danny has become a pacifist interested in eastern mysticism. Yet identity is never fixed in this story. A few years later, with an abruptness characteristic of Hogan's dislocated city dwellers, Danny has dropped his pacifism and joined the IRA as an active member while the narrator now regards republicanism as a disease, finding his heroes instead in the community workers who cross the Catholic and Protestant dividing lines. Danny's metamorphosis into IRA member is not his last: horrified by the violence, he quits the IRA and moves to London. His last meeting with the narrator suggests yet another change of heart as Danny moves towards a greater understanding of the integrity of the Ulster Protestant ethos in which he was raised.

Danny's death, falling under a train at Paddington station, is left deliberately ambivalent. 'I knew he had been pushed by a para-military, by the
ghost of the old croney Mother Ireland,' the narrator says.[31] Whether an
act of revenge by the IRA or suicide prompted by remorse for his
involvement in violence, it is evident that Danny's death is a punishment,
or self-punishment, for transgressing too many boundaries. His changing
identities suggest a postmodern fluidity at odds with the fixed ideological
positions asserted by the paramilitaries of both sides. The narrator, more
successful than Danny in maintaining a fluid identity, illustrates the value
of uncertainty. Realizing that he can no longer acquiesce in the IRA's
demonization of England, he reaches out to the other to such an extent
that the other (Ulster Protestant) becomes internalized: 'somewhere
inside myself I knew that they existed, Danny's peoples, they weren't a
figment of anyone's political imagination. They were real.'[32]

Bernard MacLaverty's 'Some Surrender' (*The Great Profundo*, 1987),
like the stories of John McGahern and Desmond Hogan discussed above,
portrays a father–son relationship in a precise socio-political context, this
time that of an Ulster Protestant family living through the Troubles. The
notion of partial surrender applies not only to the political situation but
also to the relationship between a father and a son coming together after a
breach of many years caused by the son's marriage to a Roman Catholic.
When Roy suggests that the slogan 'Some Surrender' should be substi-
tuted for the blunt 'No Surrender' of Ulster's Protestants, his father
expresses the Ulster Protestant viewpoint: just as his own life's work, in
the form of flats he designed, is in the process of being demolished, so
Ulster's Protestants feel that their identity is being compromised by a
British government that seems to favour the other side. The changes leave
Roy's father feeling, like the fathers in the stories of McGahern and
Hogan, a stranger in his own country, with his work dismantled and his
political identity in danger of dissolution: 'The constructive thing to get
into these days is demolition,' he declares bitterly.[33] 'Some Surrender' is
an elegantly constructed story that articulates with sympathy a viewpoint
rarely depicted except through caricature.

'The Daily Woman', from the earlier MacLaverty collection, *A Time to
Dance* (1982), presents a female angle on the Troubles, painting a bleak
picture of a young working-class woman's struggle to survive everyday life
in Belfast and demonstrating MacLaverty's uncanny ability to get inside
the head of his female protagonists. 'The Daily Woman' is reminiscent of
women's writing about everyday life in Northern Ireland where, in novels
such as *To Stay Alive* by Linda Anderson and plays like Anne Devlin's

Ourselves Alone, the violence in the streets is shown as spilling into the home. Liz's husband, Eamonn, drinks in Provo clubs, beats her when drunk and once hid something in their attic for two days. Brenda Murphy's story, 'A Social Call', set in Ballymurphy, a Catholic area of Belfast, similarly links male violence in the home with male paramilitary activities out of doors. Both stories illustrate Catherine Shannon's point that in Northern Ireland during the Troubles there was no safe domestic space: 'Oral material as well as official studies have shown that women in heavily-armed areas of the north were more vulnerable to sexual harassment, exploitation and domestic violence, owing to the easy availability of guns.'[34] This is precisely the situation in which MacLaverty's protagonist, Liz, finds herself: abused at home and at work and liable to be stopped and searched on the streets. Under these circumstances any pretence at normal life becomes impossible.

A more youthful, contemporary voice than Mary Beckett, Anne Devlin looks at the impact of the Troubles specifically on young women in her collection, *The Way-Paver* (1986). 'Five Notes After a Visit' has autobiographical overtones as a young Northern Irish Catholic woman from Andersonstown now living in England, as Devlin herself was at the time, returns to Belfast on a visit. Like Edna O'Brien's returning emigrant, though more traumatically, Devlin's narrator finds herself in an uneasy in-between position, blamed in England for the bombs her fellow countrymen are setting off, threatened in Belfast for staying in a Protestant area. At home neither in Belfast nor London, interrogated in both cities about her Irish Catholic identity, Devlin's unnamed protagonist remains traumatized. Like the father in 'Some Surrender', she anticipates the loss of her political identity, feeling that next time, she will write 'don't know' under the space for nationality.[35]

Trauma is also evident in Devlin's 'Naming the Names', one of the few stories of this period that attempts to explore the mind of a female IRA activist. Both Irish history (her grandmother's stories of meetings with de Valera on the run and the Countess Markievicz in jail) and the current political situation (in August 1969, her grandmother was burned out of her home during the violence in West Belfast following the Derry riots) conspire to turn Finn into someone capable of luring her English lover into a death trap. But at the same time as she asserts her political identity through this act of violence, she loses her sense of self. 'Where are you, Finn?' asks Jack, her former lover.[36] The fact that both Jack and her current lover are English and both in different ways betray her emotionally complicates Finn's motives. Failure in her emotional life has propelled her to locate her identity in political action. The story suggests that Finn's actions are futile. However much she tries to cling on to the names of the West Belfast streets by reciting them like a litany, change is inevitable: very soon the Falls Road, the area that symbolizes her political identity, will be torn down by developers. Like the Ulster Protestant father in 'Some Surrender', Finn's ideological identity is in danger of unravelling as a result of the alteration of the physical landscape of Belfast.

Writing out of a situation where violence was underpinned by rigid sectarian identities, many short stories from Northern Ireland in this period depict political and personal identity under threat of dissolution from the impact of the violence. In a parallel movement, writing from the Republic in the 1980s reveals Irish identity beginning to expand and alter, whether in the context of women's lives, the changing sexual mores, or the relationship between fathers and sons and mothers and daughters. As the decade wore on, the Irish short story began increasingly to record formerly fixed definitions of Irish identity shifting under the pressure of change. The narrator in Aidan Higgins' 'Sodden Fields', an autobiographer looking back over Irish history, gives voice to one of the clearest expressions of this sense of dissolution: 'Who am I? Am I or am I not the same person I have always taken myself to be? In that case, who am I?'[37] For this narrator, even the past alters when looked at from the viewpoint of the present: 'I spend much of the time looking back into the past. It is no longer there. It has moved. Where to?'[38] If personal identity seemed evanescent, there remained national identity, but nationalism is given short shrift by Higgins' narrator, as it is in many Irish stories from the 1980s. The feeling that traditional certainties about Irish identity were dissolving was to increase in the 1990s as Ireland went through a period of accelerated transformation.

The election in 1990 of Mary Robinson, a feminist and civil rights lawyer, as Ireland's first female President was regarded as a triumph for those supporting a modernizing liberal agenda over those associated with traditional nationalist and Catholic values: in the years following her election, divorce, contraception and homosexuality would all be legalized. The economic phenomenon named the Celtic Tiger, 'two words that had slipped off the tongue of some wiggling economist',[39] ushered in a period of rapid change. Urbanization and secularization continued apace and, as Ireland entered the global economy, the country displayed a growing national confidence, economic optimism and cultural sophistication. Detta, formerly Bernadette, narrator of Éilís Ní Dhuibhne's story 'Holiday in the Land of Murdered Dreams', returns to Ireland, where she worked as a chambermaid in the 1970s, and reflects on: 'The new mood of Ireland, the Ireland where it's OK to be Irish, where it's the cool thing to be'.[40] Whereas hotel rooms once had notices about mass times on the back of their doors, now she observes that they publicize the opening times of gyms.

Many of the stories in *Arrows in Flight: Short Stories from a New Ireland* (2002), edited by Caroline Walsh, comment on the increasing commercialization of Irish life, and the hedonism ushered in by Ireland's new-found prosperity is portrayed in Colm Tóibín's account of a drug-fuelled rave in 'Three Friends', published in his 2006 collection, *Mothers and Sons*. Several stories in *New Dubliners*, a volume edited by Oona Frawley to mark the centenary of the composition of Joyce's collection, reflect the street-wise vocabulary and the rising affluence of the inhabitants of the new cool, brash Dublin. So cosmopolitan had Dublin become that in 'Two Little Clouds', Joseph O'Connor, picking up themes and characters from his collection, *True Believers* (1991), is able to reverse Joyce's story so that Dublin rather than London or Paris is the home of Eddie Virago, his up-dated Ignatius Gallaher, who brandishes his Irish sophistication in front of his friend from dull old London. Beneath the cool image, however, O'Connor's story reveals a darker side to Dublin life, namely traffic gridlock, drunkenness, vulgarity, racism and a philistinism that turned Temple Bar into a giant drinking den, rather than the cultural quarter originally projected. Many short stories from the 1990s and the first years of the new century reveal that, beneath their new affluence, the inhabitants of Dublin continued to endure the same problems as Joyce's Dubliners, namely entrapment, loneliness and family breakdown. For Ireland's economic boom also led to an increase in materialism, individualism and selfishness in regard to people excluded from the general rise in standards of living, such as the elderly, the disabled and immigrants. Such attitudes were not confined to Dublin: Tom Humphries' 'Australia Day', published in *Arrows in Flight*, provides a sardonic look at the modernization of a rural Irish town during the years of the Celtic Tiger and the narrator's consequent dislocation.

In many ways Ireland's rapid globalization created a more divided society, as illustrated by Éilís Ní Dhuibhne's portrait of two working-class sisters from Crumlin in 'Wuff Wuff Wuff for de Valera!' (2001). Ní Dhuibhne contrasts Bernie's marriage to Conor from Palmerston Park and their increasingly luxurious lifestyle, thanks to the Celtic Tiger, with Pauline's entrapment in working-class Kimmage as a single mother with a special needs son for whom the Celtic Tiger brings no benefits. As Anne

Marie McGurran, narrator of Evelyn Conlon's 'Escaping the Celtic Tiger, World Music and the Millennium', remarks, the Celtic Tiger was 'a smokescreen, behind which to hide the poor mean lives that were still being lived on the terraces, despite the New Financial Centre, coloured mobile phones and exploding property prices'.[41] Ireland's new-found wealth, making some Irish very rich whilst marginalizing others, resulted in a new kind of exile in which a proportion of the population did not have to leave their country to feel they were no longer at home. Anne Marie returns to Ireland in the late 1990s to find that even the language has changed, phrases like Celtic Tiger, World Music and the Millenium replacing 'the old sod' deemed 'too rural, too muddy' for Ireland's sophisticated new image.[42] Realizing that she has become an outsider in her own country, she decides to resume her nomadic life. The narrator of Hugo Hamilton's short story, 'The Homesick Industry', expresses a similar feeling of alienation. A successful element in the Celtic Tiger phenomenon was the marketing of Irishness abroad, and Hamilton's narrator works for a firm that exports traditional music CDs, Irish language lessons and Aran sweaters to remote parts of the world in an attempt to give those homesick for Ireland a sense of belonging. The narrator, who feels little empathy with this Irish identity fabricated for export, rejects the suffocating birthday gift of an Aran sweater and defines himself instead through the nomadic identity of 'not belonging'.[43] 'The Homesick Industry' neatly encapsulates the way a national identity may be fabricated and marketed abroad in a way that bears little connection to the lives of the people back home.

In the 1990s, too, a darker side of the nation's life came to the fore with investigations into financial impropriety among politicians. Disenchantment with those in positions of authority increased following the flood of revelations about the cruelty and abuse of children in church-run orphanages and children's homes, as well as the sexual abuse of children by individual Catholic priests. 'This was the sound of Ireland,' thinks Detta in 'Holiday in the Land of Murdered Dreams', 'Keening and weeping, children wailing'.[44] Several significant short stories from this period portray the trauma and confusion consequent on the unravelling of the Catholic church's central influence on Irish life. In Colm Tóibín's ironically titled 'A Priest in the Family' (*Mothers and Sons*), the priest who in the past would have conferred respectability on his family has become a source of disgrace. In Conlon's 'Escaping the Celtic Tiger, World Music and the Millennium', the Catholic Anne Marie consults is at a loss to know what to think, whilst 'The Last Confession', Conlon's satire of clerical hypocrisy surrounding the sex lives of priests, recalls the 1992 furore over revelations that Bishop Eamonn Casey had fathered a son.

A story by William Trevor, 'Of the Cloth' (*The Hill Bachelors*, 2000), delicately marks the waning of the Catholic church's influence in contemporary Ireland. The story is constructed to reveal layers of Irish history, opening with a rural Church of Ireland rector, the significantly named Reverend Grattan Fitzmaurice, feeling out of touch with modern Ireland. The theme of the Protestant remnant is given a new twist, however, when the rector is visited by the local Catholic curate, Father Leahy. The rector believes Father Leahy has come on an errand of mercy, to cheer up an elderly clergyman whose flock is dwindling, but he slowly realizes that, far from pitying Grattan, Father Leahy, shocked by recent newspaper revelations concerning the paedophile Catholic priest, Brendan Smyth, has turned to his Church of Ireland counterpart for a clue as to how to survive as a minority in Irish life. In Trevor's use of the short story form to illustrate the constant shifts and reversals in Irish history, one might compare the way Sheridan Le Fanu, fearing the imminent demise of his own class, looked back obsessively to the moment when the fortunes of the Catholic gentry began to fade in the aftermath of William's victory over James II at the Battle of the Boyne. Trevor's story skilfully encapsulates the decline of the Catholic church from triumphant inheritor of an independent Ireland to a fast-decreasing remnant, endeavouring to keep the faith alive in a time of darkness.

A later Trevor story, 'Justina's Priest' (*A Bit on the Side*, 2004), underlines the poignancy of a priestly order in decline as Father Clohessy finds his congregation dwindling until his chief priestly role is reduced to hearing the confessions of the simple-minded Justina, for whom alone he still embodies God. Eugene McCabe's collection, *Heaven Lies About Us* (2005), contains powerful and haunting stories of a society whose myths are dying, clung to only by simpletons like Mickey ('Roma') or bigots like Mary in the title story. The ending of 'Heaven Lies About Us' is particularly bleak as Mary's faith goes unrewarded: first her husband, then her daughter dies, the latter having been abused by her own brother. The story illustrates how easily abuse can remain invisible in a society where a certain type of religious faith has a strong purchase.

Less bleak is John McGahern's masterpiece, 'The Country Funeral', contrasting the loss of a sense of the sacred in city life with its preservation in country communities in ceremonies surrounding the burial of the dead. 'The Country Funeral' contains striking parallels in theme and tone with McGahern's final novel, *That They May Face the Rising Sun*. There is the same elegiac and leisurely tone ('The Country Funeral' almost qualifies as a novella), and a similar emphasis on the local and on the small rituals and hospitality of a community where lives are lived in harmony with their natural environment. Like the novel, the story evokes a sense of the sacredness of life in the face of death: the stories the mourners tell about the dead man celebrate what was essentially a humane way of life, and the dignity and calm generosity of this community, contrasting with the restlessness and emptiness of urban life, attract Philly. In their presence, he finds a sense of the value of life and a neighbourliness that all his wild acts of generosity in the city have failed to arouse. Tomás Ó Criomhthain's *The Islandman* is an acknowledged influence, and by writing out of and to a community, McGahern's story thematically, though not stylistically, preserves continuity with the oral tradition whilst also conveying, despite his characters' loss of faith, a sense of warmth and humanity: Joycean stasis has become transmuted into a timelessness that is cause for celebration. There is a residual echo, also, of Frank O'Connor's 'The Mass Island' where, in defiance of his city-dwelling brother's impatience, Father Fogarty's fellow priests take the time to respect his last wishes and the rural community turns out to honour him at his funeral mass. The significance of 'The Country Funeral' in McGahern's oeuvre was confirmed when he retained its position as the final story in what he knew would be his last collection, *Creatures of the Earth* (2006).

A fresh theme entered the Irish short story as growing prosperity transformed Ireland in the late 1990s from a country of emigrants into one that attracted increasing numbers of immigrants. In Ní Dhuibhne's 'Holiday in the Land of Murdered Dreams', Detta observes that where once the woman begging at the side of the road would have belonged to the travelling community now she is a Romanian refugee. Immigrants themselves have yet to find their voice in the Irish short story to any significant degree. When they do, we might hope for a renewal of Irish writing similar to that given to British writing by writers like Salman Rushdie, Zadie Smith and Monica Ali. In the meantime, Roddy Doyle's initiative in reaching out to the immigrant community by writing a monthly short story about immigrants' lives in *Metro Éireann*, together with his inauguration of the *Metro Éireann* writing award open to all immigrants resident in Ireland for at least two years, will surely do much to prepare the ground for the emergence of immigrant writers in Ireland. Doyle's stories were subsequently published under the title, *Desperadoes* (2007); though these are pioneering in confronting Irish racism, even, in three of them, adopting the immigrant's voice, they inevitably lack the hinterland of Irish immigrants' own cultural, political and psychological experiences.

One result of the unprecedented wave of immigration during the 1990s was to encourage Irish writers to turn back to the past to examine the immigration experience in earlier decades. Several of the stories in Hugo Hamilton's collection, *Dublin Where the Palm Trees Grow* (1996), are recounted through the eyes of a German-Irish boy growing up in Ireland during the 1960s. In Colum McCann's 'A Basket Full of Wallpaper' (*Fishing the Sloe-Black River*, 1994), Osobe, a Japanese man who has relocated to Ireland after the Second World War, comes up against Irish racist attitudes that do not dissolve until after his death, when the community finally recognizes all he has done for them over the years by employing their young men in his painting and decorating business. Present-day exploitation of immigrants is the theme of George O'Brien's 'A Good Turn', published in *The Faber Book of Best New Irish Short Stories* (2005). O'Brien portrays Irish people latching on to immigrants for cheap labour (Mr Devanny), to fill the churches (the Professor) or even for sex (Sally), while in Colum McCann's fine story, 'As If There Were Trees', published in *New Dubliners*, simmering resentment of Irish workers at their replacement by cheap immigrant labour boils over into violence.

In the 1990s, drawing strength from developments in the previous decade, Irish women's short stories gathered pace and became more outspoken. Motherhood and women's ambivalence towards it continued to be a theme but, unlike previous generations of Irish women, protagonists are no longer prepared to endure passively, forging instead new identities for themselves. In Clare Boylan's 'That Bad Woman' (title story of her collection published in 1995), Jude, unlike the heroines of Daly and even Conlon in the previous decade, displays increasing confidence in her assertion of independence, retaining her sense of responsibility towards her family without allowing herself to be swamped by their demands. Boylan's 'The Stolen Child', from the same collection, provides a satirical view of the burdens contemporary society places upon mothers. The narrator, a single woman, craves a baby and harshly criticizes the mothers she observes around her as inadequate. Her attitude changes when she steals a baby and discovers the realities of motherhood. She tries to get rid of the baby but, unlike Yeats' child, Clint is all too human and will not be taken away by the fairies. The ending of the story is ambivalent, the narrator's conclusion that 'Some women don't deserve to have children' suggesting that some women are unworthy of motherhood, but also that women do not deserve the heavy burden of motherhood.

Various stories in this decade record the effect of women's changing role not only on women themselves but also on the entire family unit. Stories like 'Men and Women' from Claire Keegan's collection, *Antarctica* (1999), record the shifting of the balance of power between husband and wife, even in a conservative rural family. Mothers emerge from their traditional role of self-sacrificing domestic martyrs in Colm Tóibín's collection, *Mothers and Sons*, which presents a variety of new twists on the old Irish theme of the bond between mother and son. Far from idealizing their sons these mothers are often sceptical about them: in 'The Name of a Game', Nancy refuses to sacrifice her future to that of her son, in whom she sees many traits of his authoritarian father. In 'Song', echoing Leland Bardwell's 'The Quest', a mother chooses her musical career over her son.[45]

In the 1990s, Irish women, later than their counterparts in other countries, took to writing the body with a vengeance. Menstruation features in Éilís Ní Dhuibhne's stories, 'Some Hours in the Life of a Witch' and 'Eating Women is Not Recommended' (*Eating Women is Not Recommended*, 1991); menstruation ('A Lazy Eye') and venereal disease ('Possibilities') in Mary Morrissy's *A Lazy Eye*. Nevertheless the female body remained problematic: Grace in 'Possibilities' is ignorant about the inner workings of her body, whilst menstruation turns both Bella in 'A Lazy Eye' and Lennie in 'Eating Women is Not Recommended' into the abject: Bella is thrown out of the train for bloodying the sheets, whilst Lennie becomes a pariah in a supermarket because of her blood-stained trousers.

In *The Portable Virgin* (1991), a collection in which Anne Enright deconstructs myths of femininity and marriage, 'Fatgirl Terrestrial' is a convincing and witty exploration of why educated and successful women nevertheless feel pressurized to conform to society's expectations of femininity. In the title story of this collection, the narrator endeavours to fit into the feminine ideal by dying her hair blonde and applying make-up; conforming to the female stereotype familiar from the media, she finds ironically that 'the new fake me looks twice as real as the old'.[46] This idea of gender as a performance was explored by other women writers: Mary Morrissy's short story, 'Drag' (*The Faber Book of Best New Irish Short Stories*, 2005) evokes Judith Butler's theories in its use of parodic repetition to expose the masquerade of femininity. In contrast with the previous decades, in the 1990s and beyond, Irish short stories by women became less preoccupied with using the realist mode to register an angry feminist protest against the conditions of marriage and motherhood than

with exploring the changing nature of femininity and the instability of
female identity in a playful, postmodernist style. *The Portable Virgin*, in
particular, was widely acclaimed by Irish commentators as heralding 'a
new voice in Irish fiction'[47] and marking 'a real departure in women's
fiction in this country'.[48] In *Taking Pictures* (2008), Enright continued
her edgy exploration of contemporary life, stories like 'Honey' and 'Little
Sister' showing an advance on her earlier collection by combining stylistic
subtlety with emotional depth.

Éilís Ní Dhuibhne, one of the most significant contemporary Irish
short story writers, is unusual among Irish women writers in employing
the voice of a detached, omniscient storyteller, allowing her to give an
overview of changes in Irish society and making her one of the most
penetrating observers of the Irish scene. Her stories concern social change
in Ireland ('The Truth about Married Love'), cultural differences between
Irish and Americans ('The Day Elvis Presley Died'), or draw parallels
between the colonization of nature and the colonization of women ('The
Pale Gold of Alaska'). The quality of Ní Dhuibhne's spare, ironic prose,
precisely probing her characters' fractured states of mind, lifts her stories
above any tendency to reportage, however, and her constant experiments
with the short story form, with unreliable narrators, non-linear plots,
complex ironies and lack of closure, align her closely with postmodernism. Though written in a deceptively transparent style, her stories often
require a range of intertextual knowledge on the part of her readers.

Ní Dhuibhne's metafictional 'The Wife of Bath' (1991) moves away
from the symbolic realism of John McGahern into a postmodern,
intertextual world, inhabiting the borders between fantasy and reality, as
the Wife of Bath takes it upon herself to liberate the narrator from the
constraints of contemporary Irish womanhood. The story is constructed
around a central irony: the Wife of Bath, fictional creation of a male
author, is freer and more in control of her life than the modern-day Irish
narrator, whose identity has become so submerged in the roles of wife and
mother that she is confused as to her own name. The meeting between
the Wife of Bath and the narrator in a pub leads to a lengthy discussion of
the war between the sexes, with the Wife getting in a few sideswipes at
Jane Austen's husband-obsessed fiction along the way. Their conversation
provides an opportunity for the narrator to assess some of the narratives
controlling her life, and it soon becomes apparent that the Wife of Bath,
an illiterate woman with no other way of gaining power and status except
through marriage, is managing her life better than the narrator. Free from
contemporary anxiety about body image, the Wife is 'pleasantly plump,

as people used to say, in the old days before health and anorexia came in', at ease with her body in a way that the narrator, who worries about bananas making her fat, is not.[49] Exempt from modern expectations on mothers and from the demands of child-centred childcare, the Wife has been less hampered by her fifteen children than is the narrator by her only child, Johnny. In an act of rebellion, the Wife and the narrator ignore the warning signs and dive into the hot baths. Noticing that they are both beginning to dissolve, the narrator opts to stay in the liberating waters: disencumbered of her roles as wife and mother, she floats lightly in the water, watching 'as I melted, laughing, into the sacred spring'.[50] Post-modern fluidity of identity joins the shape-shifting of Irish folklore as the mention of the 'sacred spring', together with echoes of Woolf and the emphasis on the narrator's search for a new identity, suggest that, released from her duties as wife and mother, the narrator may have a future as a writer.

Ní Dhuibhne's 'Oleander' (*The Pale Gold of Alaska*, 2000) records how one woman's love affair with literature turns out to be more lasting and profound than her relationship with Robert, her married lover. The surprises in this story are chiefly aesthetic – Brenda's discovery of the beauty of Siena's architecture and her preference for the stories of Henry James over those of Richard Ford. By interrogating the act of reading and writing, 'Oleander' recalls Mary Lavin's 'A Story with a Pattern'. Like 'A Story with a Pattern', 'Oleander' resists the notion that short stories require a strong plot. Though Brenda admires the leisurely stories of Richard Ford, she comes to realize that his stories are marred for her because they always conclude with a dramatic act: 'This is the E. M. Forster touch, the false sparkle that screams "FICTION!"'[51] On the train to Rome, Brenda replaces Ford with Henry James, a writer whose stories are even more diffuse and turn, like the relationship in this story between Brenda and Robert's wife, on subtle reversals of power.

'Oleander' may be compared with Angela Bourke's story, 'Dreams of Sailing' (*By Salt Water*, 1996) where the heroine's first sexual experience is eclipsed by her love affair with literature: 'I got a lot of reading done in those six days [of making love with Kevin]. I finished *The French Lieutenant's Woman* and went on to three or four Jane Austens.'[52] There are other parallels between the two authors. Both Ní Dhuibhne and Bourke have used their scholarly expertise in folklore to rework folk tales into contemporary settings in a way that emphasizes the continuing relevance of the oral tradition (Ní Dhuibhne's 'The Mermaid' and 'Midwife to the Fairies', Bourke's 'Deep Down'). In 'Midwife to the

Fairies', for instance, folk tale is used to comment indirectly on the 1984 Kerry Babies case.[53] Ní Dhuibhne's collection, *The Inland Ice and Other Stories* (1997), marries new and old, interspersing the rituals and repetitions of a folk tale, 'The Search for the Lost Husband', with contemporary stories of love and loss in a collection marked by the wish to write beyond the romantic ending. A similar probing of Irish folklore for purposes of subverting social myths that are disempowering for women, particularly those aligning women with the body and with the Irish landscape, is present in Bourke's *By Salt Water*.[54]

Mirroring feminist historians' work in the late 1980s and 1990s in retrieving Irish women's history, Irish women's short stories of this period explore women's lives in the past. In 'Men and Angels' (*The Portable Virgin*), Anne Enright makes the point that past ideals of femininity still prevail, by contrasting angels of the past, like the wives of Brewster and Huygens, whose lives were completely subordinated to their husbands' work, with Ruth, a modern woman who has found her vocation as a composer, treats men the way these inventors treated their wives and is called selfish for it. Recovering women's history is the focus of Emma Donoghue's 2002 collection, *The Woman Who Gave Birth to Rabbits*, portraying women from various historical periods struggling against patriarchal society to secure their independence and find their voice. Often they are women like Mary Toft in the title story or Miss F. in 'Cured', who find their stories taken out of their hands by more powerful and better-educated males. Some of Donoghue's stories have a specifically Irish dimension: in 'Acts of Union', an Irish woman summarily married off to an English soldier acts to ensure her independent economic future. 'Night Vision' is a recreation of the early life of the blind Donegal poet, Frances Brown, depicting her struggle to get an education in a society that denies her worth. 'Words for Things' presents Mary Wollstonecraft's brief period as a governess in Ireland, when her observation of the idle lives led by Anglo-Irish women provided a catalyst for her views on the educative role of mothers in her *Vindication of the Rights of Woman*. The historical notes at the end of each story underpin the authenticity of these tales and anchor them in the feminist project of recovering women's history.

All of the stories in Donoghue's collection depict strong bonds between women, and some of them ('The Fox on the Line', 'Salvage', 'How a Lady Dies') attempt to uncover a lost lesbian history, recalling Donoghue's earlier volume, *Kissing the Witch* (1997), a series of interlocking stories containing feminist and sometimes lesbian rewritings of fairy tales (in 'The Tale of the Shoe', Cinderella goes off with the Fairy

Godmother). As part of this renewed emphasis on the bonds between women, there is in this period evidence of an attempt by Irish women writers to write themselves into a female literary tradition. 'The Flowering', the opening story of Éilís Ní Dhuibhne's collection, *Eating Women is Not Recommended*, records Lennie's attempt to construct a female artistic inheritance for herself in the manner of Virginia Woolf and Alice Walker, whilst 'The Banana Boat' from *The Pale Gold of Alaska* specifically refers to Mary Lavin as a forerunner in the short story form. Several short stories by Irish women during this decade rewrite female canonical texts in a more empowering way. In 'The Secret Diary of Mrs Rochester' (1995), Clare Boylan wittily reworks the ending of Charlotte Brontë's novel in a manner that eschews romance and emphasizes instead issues of power and dominance in the relationship between Jane and Rochester, with Jane eventually gaining power over Rochester by virtue of her independent fortune.

If this section has dwelt so far on female rather than male writers that is because the extraordinary range and quality of Irish women's short story writing in the 1990s demands attention. 'Women's writing in Ireland is in a healthy state,' commented Éilís Ní Dhuibhne in 1991.[55] Setting Irish women's short stories alongside those of their male counterparts does not necessarily reveal a different approach to the form, but it does emphasize women writers' determination to put women's lives (the mother–daughter relationship, female emigration, female sexuality) at the centre of their work. The success of Irish women in claiming the Irish short story for women's themes is evidenced in what might be termed the increasing feminization of the Irish short story, notably in the number of male writers who began to place women at the centre of their stories where previously they had not done so (as opposed to writers like William Trevor and Bernard MacLaverty whose stories from the outset featured female protagonists). The dialogue between male and female writers echoes down the history of the Irish short story, from Maria Edgeworth's influence on Gerald Griffin and William Carleton, to Joyce's influence on Edna O'Brien and Elizabeth Bowen's on Seán O'Faoláin. A reading of Irish short fiction from this period continues to reveal topics moving back and forth between female and male authors. One clear example of this is John McGahern's reworking of an episode of domestic violence recorded in the title story of Evelyn Conlon's 2000 collection, *Telling*.

In 'Telling', a satire on creative writing classes, a male writer, 'one of the best', recounts to his female students the story of a woman subjected to years of domestic violence around which her neighbours preserve a veil of silence. The unnamed woman is eventually shot by her husband as she is baking bread and she dies with raisins in her hand. The writer passes on this story to his horrified class, telling them that the story is in the raisins. Conlon ends in good postmodernist fashion by challenging the reader to decide what s/he makes of the story, the male writer and his students' reaction, a challenge McGahern apparently took up in 'Love of the World', one of two new stories included in his final collection, *Creatures of the Earth*. 'Love of the World' returns to the lake setting of *That They May Face the Rising Sun* in order to retell Conlon's story of domestic violence. Many of the details are similar. Harkin, the husband, works as a guide for tourists, who find him good company, while his wife, Kate, endures years of abuse at his hands before recovering some of her self-esteem by taking work outside the home. Resenting her new-found independence, Harkin locks her out of the house and, in an echo of Kate Gaillard's predicament in *Girls in their Married Bliss*, Kate forfeits custody of their children because she is deemed to have left voluntarily. Like Conlon's unnamed woman, Kate returns every day to spend time with her children after school till eventually she is shot in the back of the head and dies holding currants in her hand. McGahern's story is an extended exploration of Kate's abuse at the hands of her husband and provides psychological motivation for Harkin's violence in his failed career as a Guard. In the end, though, McGahern's focus is not on Kate but, as in *That They May Face the Rising Sun*, on the life of the wider rural community and its relationship with the natural environment which, as in the novel, takes on a presence of its own and becomes a yardstick against which the community's behaviour is measured. The story's concluding focus is on Kate's mother, Maggie, a woman who lives according to the quiet rituals and moral values of her community.

The echoes of both Evelyn Conlon and Edna O'Brien in 'Love of the World' shed an interesting light on McGahern's final years. Was he aiming to express something about the troubled relations between men and women in Ireland? In rising to Conlon's challenge to the reader, was McGahern attempting to wrest the form away from Conlon's emphasis on gender divisions by proving that men can write equally sympathetically about domestic violence? Was he making the point that such topics do not need to be treated subjectively but can be successfully conveyed in his characteristic late style, working through an impersonal voice of a narrator speaking out of a community? Was he even the original of Conlon's 'great writer'? Whatever the case, in 'Love of the World', McGahern took up the challenge explicit in Conlon's story and made it his own.

McGahern's influence continued to be felt on a younger generation of Irish short story writers. Colum McCann's collection of two short stories and a novella set against the background of the Troubles, *Everything in this Country Must* (2000), employs concrete objects as symbols in a manner reminiscent of McGahern. Like McGahern, McCann uses implication, indirection and understatement to require the reader to supply the missing information, particularly appropriate in these stories where the fragmentary, uncertain central consciousnesses belong to children and teenagers observing the adult world around them. McGahern's influence is also felt in Claire Keegan's second collection, *Walk the Blue Fields* (2007), with its spare, quiet evocations of life in an Irish countryside almost untouched by the Celtic Tiger. The title story places the same emphasis on the ritualistic life of the community, though it makes more use of interior monologue than McGahern. The penultimate story in the volume, 'Surrender', explicitly acknowledges McGahern's influence by imaginatively expanding on an episode from his *Memoir*. In contrast to many of her female predecessors of the 1970s and 1980s, Keegan eschews the short story as a vehicle for socio-cultural messages, concentrating instead, like McGahern, on the quality of seeing.

Study of the Irish short story in this period queries Joe Cleary's argument in *Outrageous Fortune* that contemporary Irish writing is largely regressive and reactionary, retreating into history and failing to take account of the changing times.[56] In the 1990s and beyond, the Irish short story showed its readiness to tackle current ideas and topics (gender as performance, retrieving women's history, immigration), as well as a willingness to experiment with language and form and embrace complex, non-linear narratives. The contemporary Irish short story is often a far cry from tales told round a fireside. Anne Enright's quirky, linguistically inventive stories, revealing influences ranging from Joyce to Flann O'Brien, are a direct challenge to the reader to tease out their meanings. These fast-moving stories deliberately distance themselves from what the narrator of 'What are Cicadas?' describes as 'one of those country stories that I never want to hear, stories that take their time'.[57] In Mary Morrissy's collection, *A Lazy Eye*, women's resistance to motherhood is a theme running through such stories as 'Rosa' and 'Agony Aunt', but the tone of these stories, comic with an edge of Gothic horror, is as important as the theme. The contemporary Irish short story has also gained much energy from the wit and word play of a writer like Clare Boylan.

Joyce remained an influence, as the appearance of *New Dubliners* in 2005 attested, though he was not always revered. Anne Enright's 'The

Brat', a cheeky feminist rereading of Joyce, imitates the Joycean mock heroic tone, but the Joycean protagonist, the alcoholic patriarch Mr O'Donnel, is no longer taken seriously. Intertextual references range far wider than Joyce, however, and the contemporary Irish short story often demands a sophisticated and knowledgeable readership: William Wall's 2006 collection, *No Paradiso*, includes references to Coleridge, Kant, Freud, Dante, John Tradescant, Shakespeare, Thucydides, Heraclitus and Horace, among others. As we have seen, openness to foreign literary influences has always been characteristic of the Irish short story but in this decade intertextuality became such a feature that one is tempted to draw a glib parallel between the opening up of Ireland's borders to welcome immigrants in the 1990s and a willingness to expand the borders of the Irish short story.

The question of whether postcolonialism has given way to globalization in terms of literary themes affects the short story no less than other branches of Irish writing. The Irish short story these days is as likely to be set in Bucharest as Dublin or Boston. *Notes from a Turkish Whorehouse* by Philip Ó Ceallaigh (2006) is a series of Jean Rhys-type tales of marginals and down and outs set in Turkey, Romania and the USA, with echoes of Beckett, Dostoevsky and Hemingway. Notwithstanding one reviewer's description of the collection as lying somewhere between Ireland and Eastern Europe, the only Irish trace, apart from the author's name on the cover, is a brief reference to the Irish language in 'Reporting the Facts'. Once again we see economic circumstances shaping the Irish short story: over and above current Irish interest in Eastern Europe, Ó Ceallaigh has explained that his decision to live in Bucharest was determined, ironically, by the fact that twenty-first century Ireland is too expensive to provide an easy environment for writers struggling to establish themselves: 'I couldn't afford to be poor in Ireland and write,' he stated in an interview.[58] If Ireland's dire economic situation caused Frank O'Connor to spend much of the 1950s in the United States, Ireland's prosperity has had a similar impact on aspiring contemporary Irish writers.

In contrast with the transformation of social mores in the Republic, stories set in Northern Ireland continued to record the polarization of national and religious identity. In 1992, the Sinn Féin President, Gerry Adams, was prompted to publish his own collection of stories, *The Street*. Never straying far from Adams' home territory of Catholic West Belfast and endorsing an outmoded militant romantic nationalism, these sentimental stories address themselves firmly to one section of the community. In Briege Duffaud's story, 'Innocent Bystanders' (*Nothing Like Beirut*,

1994), the narrator returns home to Northern Ireland to find that despite superficial changes (*Dallas* on the TV, Mills and Boon on her mother's bookshelves), people's attitudes have not altered. Stories from Northern Ireland attest that there was no easy escape from the psychological effects of living through conflict: even Duffaud's seemingly cosmopolitan exiles bear the scars of their upbringing.

William Trevor's 'Lost Ground', published in the *New Yorker* in 1992 and set in an Ulster Loyalist farming family, employs the ghost motif used in earlier stories such as 'The Raising of Elvira Tremlett' and 'Death of Peggy Meehan' to reveal the suppressed and demonized Catholic other, returning in fifteen-year-old Milton's visions of St Rosa. Milton's visions disturb the fiercely proprietorial attitudes of both sides in the conflict and his family attempts to suppress them by locking up Milton and then acquiescing in his murder by his Protestant paramilitary brother, ensuring 'lost ground had been regained'.[59] What is not mentioned is that Milton's death means there is no one left to carry on the family farm: the Leesons' territorial ambitions turn out to be self-defeating. Like 'Lost Ground', William Wall's 'Surrender' also plays on the idea of lost territory, seeing it as a natural metaphor for a narrator from Northern Ireland: 'the stubborn Northern cold surfacing in me at last, the no surrender'.[60]

Michael Parker's anthology, *The Hurt World* (1995), is a wide-ranging collection displaying the confusion, anger and fear caused by the violence in Northern Ireland. Following David Marcus' example in the earlier anthology, *Tears of the Shamrock*, in order to illustrate the historical roots of the present-day violence Parker selects four pre-Troubles stories (Frank O'Connor's 'Guests of the Nation, Michael McLaverty's 'Pigeons', John Montague's 'The Cry' and Mary Beckett's 'The Master and the Bombs'), as well as William Trevor's incursion into the past in 'The Distant Past' and Maurice Leitch's beautifully constructed 'Green Roads', where the presence of a British Army patrol awakens an old man's memory of a past incident of violence in the Irish countryside. Concentrating on the lives of private individuals, the stories in this anthology cut across ideological rigidities to expose bigotry and prejudice on both sides: Shane Connaughton's story, 'Beatrice', written out of a Catholic community, reveals the father's anti-Protestant bigotry and class prejudice against the Anglo-Irish, whilst John Montague's 'The Cry' portrays the brutality of the B Specials but also criticizes the passivity of the pre-civil rights Catholic community who opted to suffer in silence rather than to speak out about atrocities. Stories by women writers – Anne-Marie Reilly's 'Leaving' and

Fiona Barr's 'The Wall-Reader' – highlight female entrapment. Almost all the stories convey the feeling that living through the Troubles in Northern Ireland was to have your life determined by others. In Una Woods' novella, 'The Dark Hole Days', two teenagers attempt to write themselves out of their entrapment. This works for Colette, who gains a sense of new possibilities through her writing, but Joe experiences an increasing loss of self as he gets drawn into paramilitary activities. Even leaving Northern Ireland was no guarantee of escape: in David Park's trauma narrative, 'Oranges from Spain', the random sectarian murder of his employer witnessed by a sixteen-year-old boy continues to haunt him years later.

The Northern Irish short story of the 1990s recorded some tentative steps towards change. The title story of Bernard MacLaverty's 1995 collection, *Walking the Dog*, features a protagonist who saves his life by refusing to reveal to his abductors his religious and political affiliation. His repudiation of any sectarian identity points forward to one possible way of resolving the Northern Irish situation. Colum McCann's 'Cathal's Lake' (*Fishing in the Sloe-Black River*, 1994) portrays a character who exercises his moral imagination to sympathize with both victims and perpetrators of sectarian violence: for each act of violence, Cathal frees a swan from the mud. If McCann's story of empathy and reconciliation operates on the level of fantasy, William Trevor's stories from this period use the realist mode to portray progress towards forgiveness and reconciliation. 'The Mourning', published in the *New Yorker* in 1997, illustrates the way in which compassion can rise above grand narratives of history. Liam, an Irish labourer in London, is of limited intelligence and easily manipulated into agreeing to plant a bomb on a London bus. His mission gives him a sense of purpose but he is brought back from the edge by a moment of imaginative sympathy with his intended victims. In another Trevor story, 'Against the Odds' (*The Hill Bachelors*, 2000), the background of the Good Friday Agreement gives a wider resonance to the beginnings of the fragile trust between Mrs Kincaid, who abandons her project of revenge against the male sex, and Blakely, whose faint 'flicker of optimism' helps bring about the tentative reconciliation between them.[61] Trevor's story suggests the sort of attitudes needed in Northern Ireland if the warring parties are to find a way forward out of history's nightmare. With weapons decommissioning and the restoration of devolution to the Northern Ireland Assembly as of May 2007, it might be expected that the energies of Northern Irish writers, for so long held in thrall to the political situation, will be renewed. It may be that Northern Irish writing in the future will register in the short story, as writing from the Republic has done, the breakdown of the grand narratives of the past and a more international focus.

The stories in David Marcus' impressive *Book of Best New Irish Short Stories 2006–7*, showcasing the outstanding array of short story writers that Ireland possesses in the twenty-first century, are as good a place as any to end our exploration of the Irish short story. The anthology contains exactly half the proportion of female writers to male, but Marcus goes to considerable pains in his brief introduction to highlight the contribution of women writers to the genre. The stories range from Victor Banville's lyrical evocation of an Ireland already past to Breda Wall Ryan's trans-formation of the traditional mother–son story of the Irish bachelor growing old on his farm into a mother–daughter story where the farmer is a lesbian. They include stories as Irish in reference as Éilís Ní Dhuibhne's sharp, insider satire on Dublin's literati in 'A Literary Lunch', Harry Clifton's equally knowing satire on management structures in an Irish university ('A Visitor from the Future') and Carlo Gébler's depiction of the long shadow still cast by the violence in Northern Ireland on people's private lives ('Room'), and stories like Eoin McNamee's 'North of Riga' which make no mention of Ireland and yet share the current Irish interest in Eastern European countries struggling to establish their national identities after decades of oppression.

This study has attempted to track the emergence of the modern short story in Ireland and to underline the seriousness with which the form has been regarded. Irish publishers continue to find new and inventive ways of keeping the short story published while new avenues of research are currently opening up, notably in the domain of popular writing, the Irish children's story and the Irish detective story. Irish writers, past and pre-sent, have demonstrated their commitment to the genre by experimenting with different stylistic techniques, often in the face of public indifference or incomprehension, and by revising their stories even after publication: Frank O'Connor, John McGahern, William Trevor (and in earlier times, William Carleton, W. B. Yeats, George Moore).[62] In Ireland it is not always the case that a short story collection is merely preparation for a career as a novelist. William Trevor, for instance, insists that his short stories take precedence over his novels: 'I really feel it is the most demanding art form. It is so exciting, so intense... I'm a short story writer who writes a novel occasionally.'[63] Two contemporary Irish writers, Colm Tóibín and Anne Enright, after establishing their reputations as novelists have recently turned back to the short story in *Mothers and Sons* and *Taking Pictures*, respectively. Both collections reveal a decided break with the incident-packed story, opting instead for static, mood pieces in which the influence of Hemingway is evident. The vibrancy of the genre in Ireland was attested when for two years running the Rooney Prize for Irish Literature, awarded to Irish writers under forty, went to authors of short story collections. The two collections aptly illustrate the see-sawing between Ireland and the rest of the world characteristic of the form in this period: in 2006 Philip Ó Ceallaigh won with stories where Ireland scarcely features, whereas in 2007 Kevin Barry won with a collection that, apart from an up-dating of language and behaviour, sits so squarely within the Irish short story tradition that it could have been written at any point during the past fifty years.

One benefit of a broad historical survey is the opportunity to show certain themes recurring through different historical periods: exile, dislocation, dreams, memory, time, spirituality, death, fathers and sons, mothers and daughters, childhood, the family. In every period the Irish short story seems to perceive the inadequacy of quotidian reality. This postmodern awareness of the fragility of identity, present in the nineteenth century in writers as diverse as Sheridan Le Fanu and William Carleton, was submerged by the rush post-independence to fix national identity but kept alive by writers like Elizabeth Bowen, Samuel Beckett and Liam O'Flaherty, to re-emerge in the latter part of the twentieth century. It is a trajectory that challenges previous associations of the paradigmatic Irish short story with mid twentieth-century realism and suggests that what might seem normative is in fact a historically determined set of conventions. Irish short fiction frequently portrays individuals on the cusp of change and Irish identity at the moment of dissolution, nomadic, restless, open to the future but containing traces of past identities: in some of the best Irish short stories (Joyce, McGahern, arguably Colum McCann) there is an almost sacramental quality to the writing, as if the authors' abandoned Catholicism has yet found its way into the authors' quality of seeing: 'I don't think there is any serious work that is not religious,' McGahern commented.[64]

Paul Muldoon's observation that 'the ideas of liminality and narthe-cality are central to the Irish experience,'[65] suits the nomadic, fragmented identity of the Irish short story that, at its best, indicates an awareness of other worlds, other possibilities, shadowing this one. This awareness of other worlds is a feature of any colonized society, but was especially strong in Ireland with its parallel worlds of Gaelic and Anglo-Irish culture. It may be seen, for instance, in the shadowy 'Otherworld' present in medieval Irish tales[66] and in the way in which, for many Irish writers, the oral tradition shadows the written short story. An awareness of submerged other worlds is evident in Le Fanu's fear that the ancient Catholic nation was about to arise and destroy his class, in Yeats' attempt to revive the world of the *sidhe* (fairy folk), even in Joyce's incomplete parallelogram, as well as in later Irish writers' exploration of the themes of time and memory, of a lost Gaelic culture and of the experience of living among the shards of vanished belief. All reflect 'some deep-seated sense of liminality that was, and is, central to the Irish psyche'.[67] Irish short fiction is a restless genre, constantly alert to other worlds and the possibility of other identities.

The liminal quality of Irish experience may also partly account for the flourishing of the short story in Ireland. As far back as Poe in 1842 the short story has been characterized, not only by the unity of its effects, but also by its element of suggestion, requiring from the reader an attentiveness to what is going on beneath the surface equal to that of the writer, in what Poe termed 'a kindred art'.[68] A liminal form, hovering on the border between known and unknown worlds, withholding as much as it tells, the modern short story may have found in the Irish, a people accustomed to looking beneath the surface for lost worlds, its ideal readers.

READINGS: JOHN MCGAHERN AND ÉILÍS NÍ DHUIBHNE

John McGahern, 'Oldfashioned' (1985)

In 'Oldfashioned', McGahern uses the short story form to portray the shifting nature of Irish society in a style that refuses to remain confined within the realist mode. 'Oldfashioned' presents characteristic McGahern themes: the guards barracks, the difficult sergeant father who fought during the war of independence and now fears his country is being taken away from him, the sensitive, intelligent son at odds with him. A reading of McGahern's *Memoir* reveals how much of the material in 'Oldfashioned' is autobiographical: the local Anglo-Irish Big House owned by the King-Harmons, Rockingham House, later burned down; the Christian Brothers school that McGahern attended; the father's memories of fighting with the IRA; his antipathy to his son's reading. However, the main thrust of this story is not the father–son relationship but a broader historical and social charting of shifts in Irish society. The opening sentence places the focus on social change: 'The Protestants had so dwindled that there was no longer a living in Ardcarne.'[69] McGahern himself commented: ' "Oldfashioned" is an unusual story in that it takes society as a character in very much the same way as Hardy uses the heath or nature.'[70] In this context, 'Oldfashioned' points forward to McGahern's portrayal of a vanishing culture in his final novel, *That They May Face the Rising Sun*. What is remarkable about 'Oldfashioned' is that in the narrow compass of the modern short story McGahern conveys a sense of overlapping historical periods succeeding, where William Carleton failed in 'Tubber Derg', in portraying a series of social transformations. To achieve this, McGahern employs several shifts in narrative focus.

The story opens with a wide-angled view of Ardcarne during the Second World War and afterwards. The portrait of Ardcarne incorporates both past and future into the present through emphasizing the transfer of power: the British military barracks has given way to the Christian Brothers school; the modern Catholic church has replaced the Protestant in prestige and influence. McGahern suggests that the move from colonial era to independence has not been without loss: the 'stark ugliness' of the Catholic church compares badly to the Protestant church with its Purser windows. The sense that independent Ireland has fallen short of the dreams of those who, like Johnny's father, fought for it, is suggested in the juxtaposition of this lost beauty with a present-day society based on utility, materialism and philistinism. Moreover, the state's independence is threatened: the economy cannot provide jobs for all, and those Irish who go to work in Britain become infected by foreign manners. Present anxieties are proleptic: though the Catholic church is 'crowded' and the influence of Canon Glynn paramount in people's lives, yet the church fears the effects of mass emigration and the dying of the Irish language.

McGahern's narrative angle then shifts from a panoramic view of society to focus on three individuals whose values cause them to stand out in this narrow, pragmatic, community. Like the Purser windows and the local Nash Big House, the Sinclairs represent a beauty and luxury that is missing from people's lives. The beauty and the privacy of their lives draw sixteen-year-old Johnny to the Sinclairs and he in turn attracts their attention by taking time to admire the aesthetics of Mrs Sinclair's arrangement of apples. McGahern's flexible narrative voice moves smoothly from objective narration, to portrayal of the Sinclairs and other members of the community through dialogue, to recording the inner world of Johnny's consciousness. Time spent working in the Sinclairs' garden introduces Johnny to a world of 'order and luxury', but his father's rage at the Colonel's offer to help him get into the British Army shuts the door for Johnny on the Sinclairs' Garden of Eden.

The story returns to a wider focus, recording the changing life of Ardcarne as Rockingham House is burned, the Sergeant resigns in a fit of pique and returns to farming, and Colonel Sinclair becomes involved in the life of the town when he takes over management of the saw mills. Stephen Dedalus' tactics of 'silence, exile and cunning' propel Johnny through university and a lectureship, to work in television as a documentary maker producing films about the bleaker aspects of Irish rural life which attract criticism similar to that dealt out in the early years to McGahern's own stories. The account of Johnny's intervening years before he returns to make a film about Ardcarne is eclipsed by the changing story of Ireland as an upturn in the economy stems the tide of emigration and improves education prospects. The changes bring material prosperity but also shallowness and vulgarity: instead of the lamps before the Sacred Heart, the glow from houses now comes from television sets. The last remnants of the aesthetic way of living Johnny admired have gone to be replaced by the ugly and the utilitarian: graffiti is scrawled in the chapel on the Rockingham estate; Nash's ruined house is replaced by a concrete look-out tower.

Johnny returns to try to capture the lost Eden of his childhood represented by the Georgian parsonage, the Protestant church and the remains of the Rockingham estate. His Proustian desire to recover lost time in an effort to understand what he has become is characteristic of many of McGahern's protagonists but film, unlike the short story, can capture only what is in front of it and what there is in Johnny's eyes is simply wilderness. 'Oldfashioned' does not end, however, with Johnny but with the objective narrator, someone who understands his community thoroughly – hence the comment that if the producer had really understood how rural Ireland had changed he would have curried favour with the politician rather than the priest – and whose medium (the short story) allows him to portray changes in society in a way that Johnny's film cannot. The camera arrives too late and registers only absence, whereas McGahern's story has been able to capture the shifts and changes in Irish rural society. 'Oldfashioned' not only marks the transitions in Irish society but also proclaims the superiority of the short story over film in this regard as McGahern moves from depicting Irish society into problems of representation. Whilst Johnny's comment, 'all is wilderness again', may be his final word on his particular lost Eden and on the barbarity of modern Ireland, it is not the end of the story.[71] Through sensual detail the story suggests that, whatever changes Irish society will go through, the beauty of the Irish landscape will endure, only the troubling reference to Northern Ireland indicating another kind of barbarity in contemporary Ireland.

The narrator therefore provides a counterpoint to Johnny's point of view. Johnny fails to find his lost Eden, the story suggests, because he is looking in the wrong place. The whole thrust of 'Oldfashioned' has been to emphasize that human institutions (the Protestant Big House, the Catholic church) rise and fall; the ending of the story indicates that nature's beauty survives these incidental changes. Wilderness there may be in the manners of modern Ireland but beauty can still be found in the untamed landscape of rural Ireland to which Johnny seems oblivious. In *That They May Face the Rising Sun* McGahern will go on to portray characters who achieve that unity of style and purpose, of beauty and utility which Johnny desires, by living in harmony with the landscape to form the aesthetic pattern Johnny admired in the lives of the Sinclairs. The ending of 'Oldfashioned' suggests that the sacramental, lost to Irish society, survives in the Irish landscape. Despite Joe Cleary's criticism that McGahern's fiction critiques the old order but is unable to suggest what might replace it,[72] the story's gesture back to the Celtic tradition of honouring the sacred in nature is also, paradoxically, a pointer towards the future and the necessity of healing the current ecological crisis.

McGahern writes from within the realist tradition but it is a realism that, as Antoinette Quinn has remarked, is 'laced with lyricism'.[73] In the end the anthropological details are less important than the overall patterning of the story. Concrete objects take on symbolic force: as Mrs Sinclair's apples are arranged in a beautiful circular pattern, so the circular movement of the story brings Johnny back to Ardcarne, Colonel Sinclair back to the parsonage, and the Sergeant to farming. As the power of the Catholic priest is transferred to the politician so, reflecting an older Celtic tradition, a sense of the sacramental is transferred from the church to the landscape. In an interview McGahern remarked: 'I don't think anything really ends, but takes different forms, and almost everything comes round again if we can wait.'[74] 'Oldfashioned' depicts the shift towards an urban, secular Irish identity, while retaining traces of older identities. References to the Garden of Eden and the Fall underline McGahern's rejection of straightforward realism in favour of a Chekhovian symbolism that, as Denis Sampson has commented, calls on the reader 'to respond to a type of fiction which is increasingly experimental and conscious of its own patterns as poetic fiction'.[75]

Éilís Ní Dhuibhne, 'Nomads Seek the Pavilions of Bliss
on the Slopes of Middle Age' (2000)

Éilís Ní Dhuibhne's story, 'Nomads Seek the Pavilions of Bliss on the Slopes of Middle Age' (hereafter 'Nomads'), published in *The Pale Gold of Alaska*, picks up the characteristic 1990s theme of the instability of personal identity and reinforces it through the intertextuality that is also characteristic of the 1990s Irish short story. Both themes announce themselves in the first paragraph, where Mary, walking in the rain with an umbrella, sees herself as a motif in a work of art: 'What she sees is not herself but Leech's portrait of his wife.'[76] There is an irony here that will unfold as the story progresses: Mary is Michael's mistress, not his wife, and her umbrella is borrowed from her respectably married woman friend, Monica. Mary has no right to compare herself to William Leech's wife (who in any case holds a sunshade not an umbrella in Leech's portrait) for her respectability is borrowed. Mary's real affinity, under-lined by her name, is with Leech's mistress, May, who met Leech in 1919 and became his lover but only married him in 1953, after the deaths of their respective spouses. This moment of identification with Leech's wife represents a fleeting desire for respectability that Mary will disown by the end of the story.

Ní Dhuibhne's story may be read through the lens of Rosi Braidotti's *Nomadic Subjects*, in which Braidotti uses the image of the nomad to challenge the notion of a unified identity, nomadism standing for resistance to boundaries and the avoidance of closure. In particular, the nomad is a performative image, allowing Braidotti, among other things, to challenge the phallocentric vision of the subject. In Ní Dhuibhne's story, Mary has grown up in a society that endorsed rigid boundaries, both of gender and class, a society in which boys never demeaned themselves by dancing and girls' ambitions were modest. Mary used to adhere to some of these boundaries: as a young girl, believing that the class division between herself and Michael was too great, she allowed him to be pushed into the more suitable arms of her friend, Monica. Now, however, Mary is prepared to transgress social codes, notably the rules of sexual behaviour adhered to by her friends that require that you do not steal another woman's husband. She is beginning to glimpse the fragility behind even the most solid of gender performances, observing the vul-nerability beneath Michael's social performance as a solid middle-class banker with a wife and two children.

Mary is presented as a female *flâneur*, a nomad, her self-identification with Elizabeth Leech only one of several identities through which she passes during the course of the story. The instability of her identity is underlined in the first sentence by the blurred outlines of her reflection in the puddle, 'a shirred impression of smudged red, blurred green'.[77] She is fully aware of her identity as nomadic: her 'tinker's heart', as she calls it, does not, even when offered the opportunity, desire public acknowledgment as

Michael's lover.[78] She slides away rather than let Penelope see Michael and herself together: 'Mary's natural habitat is the forest of ambiguity, where you don't see the wood for the trees.'[79] Images of tents and other impermanent shelters are woven through the story to indicate Mary's nomadic state: 'Mary gets the billowing tents, the sheets on the wind, the umbrellas.'[80] In the end, she recognizes that she prefers the rootless ambiguity of her life as Michael's lover to 'solid structures'.[81]

In 'Nomads', we see Mary moving back and forth through different identities: schoolgirl, daughter, mother of Sonia, English teacher, sexual outsider, motif in art. Resisting what Braidotti names 'the perversely monological mental habits of phallocentrism',[82] Mary rejoices in the multiple identities being in love brings: 'For her lover she is wondrous, heroic, an angel on tiptoe through the treacherous streets, an amazon hacking her way through jungles of stomach-deadening threats, of shattering deceits, of glittering risk and gleaming promises. A lady with an umbrella, alone in the rainwashed wildernesses of the heart.'[83] At the end of the story, she renounces her momentary identification with Leech's wife by lending Monica's umbrella, symbol of her borrowed respectability, to Michael. Mary will remain outside the respectable world, a perpetual nomad: 'even her certainty contains the possibility of uncertainty'.[84]

Ní Dhuibhne portrays identity as multiple, complex and infinitely variable, a self always in process in a way that chimes in with Braidotti's description of nomadism: 'Nomadic shifts designate therefore a creative sort of becoming; a performative metaphor that allows for otherwise unlikely encounters and unsuspected sources of interaction of experience and knowledge.'[85] Unusually alert to the social performances of her contemporaries, Mary chooses to live outside the ruling narratives of her society. The end of the story suggests the encounter with Michael is not the last affair Mary will have in her life as she continues to experiment with different identities. 'The dangerous instability of female identity in a male-dominated society', which Anne Fogarty pinpoints as a key Ní Dhuibhne theme, is seen in a positive light in this story as Mary embraces her nomadic freedom.[86]

Notes

1 INTRODUCTION

1 Nadine Gordimer, 'The Flash of Fireflies', in *The New Short Story Theories*, ed. Charles May (Athens: Ohio University Press, 1994), pp. 264–5.

2 Elizabeth Bowen, preface to the *Faber Book of Modern Short Stories* (1937), reprinted in May, *The New Short Story Theories*, pp. 256–62.

3 Terence Brown, 'Two Post-Modern Novelists: Samuel Beckett and Flann O'Brien', in *The Cambridge Companion to the Irish Novel*, ed. John Wilson Foster (Cambridge: Cambridge University Press, 2006), p. 205.

4 Declan Kiberd, 'Story-Telling: the Gaelic Tradition', in *The Irish Short Story*, ed. Patrick Rafroidi and Terence Brown (Gerrards Cross: Colin Smythe, 1979), p. 19.

5 Walter Benjamin, 'Observations on the Works of Nikolai Leskov' (1936), in *Selected Writings: Volume Three 1935–1938*, trans. Edmund Jephcott *et al.*, ed. Howard Eiland and Michael Jennings (Cambridge, MA and London: Harvard University Press, 2002), pp. 143–66.

6 Walter Ong, *Orality and Literacy: the Technologizing of the Word* (London and New York: Routledge, 2002).

7 Eamon Maher, *John McGahern: From the Local to the Universal* (Dublin: The Liffey Press, 2003), p.159.

8 These arguments have recently come under scrutiny in the studies on the Irish novel by Belanger and Foster, referred to above.

9 Graham Good, 'Notes on the Novella', in May, *The New Short Story Theories*.

10 Valerie Shaw, *The Short Story: A Critical Introduction* (London and New York: Longman, 1983), p. 16.

11 Suzanne Ferguson, 'Defining the Short Story: Impressionism and Form', in May, *The New Short Story Theories*, pp. 218–30.

12 Edgar Allan Poe, 'Review of *Twice-Told Tales*', in May, *The New Short Story Theories*, p. 61.

13 See Anton Chekhov, *Letters on the Short Story, the Drama and Other Topics*, ed. Louis S. Friedland (New York: Dover Publications, 1966) and Susan Lohafer and Jo Ellen Clarey (eds.), *Short Story Theory at a Crossroads* (Baton Rouge: Louisiana State University Press, 1989).

14 See Leah Levenson, *The Four Seasons of Mary Lavin* (Dublin: Marino Books, 1998), pp. 208–9.

15 Frank O'Connor, *The Lonely Voice: a Study of the Short Story* (Cork: Cork City Council, 2003), p. 12.

16 Poe, 'Review of *Twice-Told Tales*', p. 61.

17 Clare Hanson, ' "Things out of Words": Towards a Poetics of Short Fiction', in *Rereading the Short Story*, ed. Clare Hanson (Basingstoke: Macmillan, 1989), pp. 22–33.

18 Introduction, in May, *The New Short Story Theories*, p. xxiii.

19 Brander Matthews, *The Philosophy of the Short-Story*, quoted in May, *The New Short Story Theories*, p. 77.

20 Good, 'Notes on the Novella', pp. 147–64.

21 O'Connor, *The Lonely Voice*, pp. 1–2.

22 See R.C. Feddersen, 'Introduction: a Glance at the History of the Short Story in English', in *A Reader's Companion to the Short Story in English*, eds. E. Fallon *et al.* (Chicago: Fitzroy Dearborn, 2001), p. 4.

23 Patrick Rafroidi and Terence Brown (eds.), *The Irish Short Story* (Gerrards Cross: Colin Smythe, 1979).

24 Seamus Deane, *A Short History of Irish Literature* (London: Hutchinson, 1986), p. 110.

25 O'Connor, *The Lonely Voice*, p. 141.

26 Quoted in Raymond Carver, 'On Writing', in May, *The New Short Story Theories*, p. 277.

27 See Joe Cleary, *Outrageous Fortune: Capital and Culture in Modern Ireland* (Dublin: Field Day Publications, 2007) for a sustained argument about contemporary Irish writing's failure to respond to the new world order.

28 Declan Kiberd, *Inventing Ireland: the Literature of the Modern Nation* (London: Vintage, 1996); Richard Kearney, *Transitions: Narratives in Modern Irish Culture* (Manchester: Manchester University Press, 1988); Derek Hand, *John Banville: Exploring Fictions* (Dublin: The Liffey Press, 2002), p. 10.

29 Eavan Boland, 'The Women', *New Collected Poems* (Manchester: Carcanet, 2005), p. 141.

30 Kiberd, *Inventing Ireland*, p. 646.

31 Aidan Higgins, *Helsingør Station and Other Departures: Fictions and Autobiographies 1956–1989* (London: Secker and Warburg, 1989), p. 49.

32 *Ibid.*, p. 87.

33 Paul Muldoon, *To Ireland, I* (Oxford: Oxford University Press, 2000), p. 8.

34 S.T.D. in *The Bell* 5 (October 1942), 72–3.

2 THE NINETEENTH CENTURY: NATION AND SHORT STORY IN THE MAKING

1 Angela Bourke, 'The Baby and the Bathwater: Cultural Loss in Nineteenth-Century Ireland', in *Ideology and Ireland in the Nineteenth Century*, ed. Tadhg Foley and Seán Ryder (Dublin: Four Courts Press, 1998), pp. 79–92. One must remember, however, that as late as 1841 almost half the population remained illiterate and many (2 million in 1800) spoke Irish as their sole

language. By the 1851 census, famine and emigration had diminished the number of Irish speakers to 25 per cent of the population.

2 The impulse to use storytelling to explain Ireland to the English is found in as early a text as *Acallam na Senórach* (*c.* 1200); see Georges Zimmermann, *The Irish Storyteller* (Dublin: Four Courts Press, 2001), pp. 16–17.

3 *Dublin University Magazine* 24 (November 1844), 504.

4 For some readers they were apparently not didactic enough: 'Great was the outcry against Maria Edgeworth's children's tales, because they did not inculcate religious dogmas', *Blackwood's Edinburgh Magazine* 64 (396), (October 1848), 462.

5 Brian Hollingworth, *Maria Edgeworth's Irish Writing: Language, History, Politics* (Basingstoke: Macmillan, 1997), p. 20.

6 *Dublin University Magazine* 1 (January 1833), 32.

7 Sharon Murphy, *Maria Edgeworth and Romance* (Dublin: Four Courts Press, 2004), p. 44.

8 Edgeworth played a crucial role in encouraging Hall's literary ambitions; see Maureen Keane, *Mrs S.C. Hall: A Literary Biography* (Gerrards Cross: Colin Smythe, 1997), pp. 121–2.

9 Zimmermann, *The Irish Storyteller*, p. 173.

10 W.B. Yeats, *Representative Irish Tales* [1891] (Gerrards Cross: Colin Smythe, 1979), p. 249.

11 Zimmermann, *The Irish Storyteller*, p. 179.

12 *The Illustrated Dublin Journal* (23 November 1861), 179.

13 *Dublin University Magazine* 1 (January 1833), 87–8.

14 *Dublin University Magazine* 23 (January 1844), 72–101.

15 A letter from Griffin to his brother, dated 1826, quoted in the *Dublin University Magazine* 23 (February 1844), 164.

16 John Cronin, *Gerald Griffin (1803–40): A Critical Biography* (Cambridge: Cambridge University Press, 1978), p. 35.

17 *Ibid.*, p. 49.

18 Gerald Griffin, *'Holland-Tide'; or, Munster Popular Tales* (New York and London: Garland Publishing, 1979), p. 79.

19 *Dublin University Magazine* 23 (February 1844), 168.

20 Gerald Griffin, *Tales of the Munster Festivals* (New York and London: Garland Publishing, 1979), vol. 11, p. 12.

21 *Ibid.*, vol. 1, p. 354.

22 *Dublin University Magazine* 23 (February 1844), 170.

23 *The Illustrated Dublin Journal* (5 October 1861), 69.

24 Barbara Hayley, 'A Reading and Thinking Nation: Periodicals as the Voice of Nineteenth-Century Ireland', in *Three Hundred Years of Irish Periodicals*, eds. Barbara Hayley and Enda McKay (Mullingar: Lilliput Press, 1987), pp. 29–46.

25 *Dublin University Magazine* 100 (April 1841), 528.

26 *Ibid.*, 531.

27 William Carleton, *Traits and Stories of the Irish Peasantry*, with a Foreword by Barbara Hayley (Gerrards Cross: Colin Smythe, 1990), vol. 1, p. vi.

28 Samuel Lover and Thomas Croker, *Myths and Legends of Ireland* (Middlesex: Senate, 1998), p. 15.

29 *Ibid.*

30 *Ibid.*, p. 99.

31 W. B. Yeats, *The Collected Letters: Volume 1, 1865–1895*, ed. John Kelly (Oxford: Clarendon Press, 1986), pp. 440–5.

32 *Dublin University Magazine* 4 (September 1834), 302.

33 See Eve Patten's study, *Samuel Ferguson and the Culture of Nineteenth-Century Ireland* (Dublin: Four Courts Press, 2004).

34 Samuel Ferguson, *Hibernian Nights' Entertainment* (Dublin: Sealy, Bryers and Walker, 1887), pp. 45–6.

35 Later in the century Yeats was to publish a critical appreciation of Ferguson, in *Dublin University Review* (November 1886), 923–41.

36 *Dublin University Magazine* 12 (August 1838), 219.

37 *Dublin University Magazine* 4 (September 1834), 302.

38 See *The Life and Letters of Maria Edgeworth*, ed. Augustus Hare (London: Edward Arnold, 1894), vol. 11, p. 202. However, she continued to portray the effects of the successive famines through her correspondence and in 1848 published a children's tale, 'Orlandino', to earn money for famine relief; see Margaret Kelleher, ' "Philosophick Views"? Maria Edgeworth and the Great Famine', in *Hungry Words: Images of Famine in the Irish Canon*, eds. George Cusack and Sarah Goss (Dublin: Irish Academic Press, 2006), pp. 47–65.

39 *Dublin University Magazine* 26 (December 1845), 752.

40 Yeats, *Representative Irish Tales*, p. 98.

41 *Ibid.*, p. 98.

42 Keane, *Mrs S. C. Hall*, p. 82.

43 Wayne Hall, *Dialogues in the Margin: a Study of the* Dublin University Magazine (Gerrards Cross: Colin Smythe, 2000), p. 113.

44 Barbara Hayley, *Carleton's 'Traits and Stories' and the Nineteenth-Century Anglo-Irish Tradition* (Gerrards Cross: Colin Smythe, 1983), p. 394.

45 *Dublin University Magazine* 17 (January 1841), 66.

46 *Ibid.*, 71.

47 William Carleton, *The Life of William Carleton, Completed by David O'Donoghue* (New York and London: Garland Publishing, 1979), vol. 11, p. 305.

48 *Dublin University Magazine* 17 (January 1841), 66.

49 *Dublin University Magazine* 4 (September 1834), 303.

50 Declan Kiberd, *Irish Classics* (London: Granta, 2001), p. 273.

51 See, for example, Terry Eagleton, *Heathcliff and the Great Hunger: Studies in Irish Culture* (London and New York: Verso, 1995) and David Lloyd, *Anomalous States: Irish Writing and the Post-Colonial Moment* (Dublin: Lilliput Press, 1993).

52 *Dublin University Magazine* 26 (December 1845), 751.

53 *Dublin University Magazine* 17 (January 1841), 70.

54 Franco Moretti, 'Conjectures on World Literature', *The New Left Review* 1 (2000), 54–68. Joe Cleary highlights the applicability of Moretti's argument to nineteenth-century Irish fiction in his illuminating discussion, 'The Nineteenth-Century Irish Novel: Notes and Speculations on Literary Historiography', in *The Irish Novel in the Nineteenth Century: Facts and Fictions*, ed. Jacqueline Belanger (Dublin: Four Courts Press, 2005), pp. 202–21.

55 Hayley, *Carleton's 'Traits and Stories'*, p. 394.

56 *Dublin University Magazine* 17 (January 1841), 67.

57 An earlier version of this story, 'Confessions of a Reformed Ribbonman', was published anonymously in the *Dublin Literary Gazette* in 1830; see Hayley, *Carleton's 'Traits and Stories'*, p. 123. Carleton was in the area shortly after the events described and heard first-hand accounts of the murders.

58 The only discrepancy is that the narrator speaks in dialect but addresses the reader in standard English, in the urbane tones Carleton had learned from eighteenth-century English essayists; see Hayley, *Carleton's 'Traits and Stories'*, p. 131, for the remark made by the editor of the *Dublin Literary Gazette* to the effect that the Ribbonman must have gone to school after these events.

59 For fuller discussion, see Terence Brown, 'Carleton and Violence', in *William Carleton: The Authentic Voice*, ed. Gordon Brand (Gerrards Cross: Colin Smythe, 2006), pp. 184–97.

60 For Carleton's political agenda and his mingling of fact and fiction, as well as the socio-economic background to this story, see Terence Dooley, *The Murders at Wildgoose Lodge: Agrarian Crime and Punishment in Pre-Famine Ireland* (Dublin: Four Courts Press, 2007).

61 Carleton, *Traits and Stories of the Irish Peasantry*, vol. II, p. 361.

62 There were three minor famines in the 1890s alone; see Margaret Kelleher, *The Feminization of Famine: Expressions of the Inexpressible?* (Cork: Cork University Press, 1997), p. 114.

63 D. J. O'Donoghue, *The Life of William Carleton* (London: Downey and Co., 1896), vol. II, p. 293. In 1861, *The Dublin Illustrated Journal* picked out these same three names to feature in the first three biographical portraits in its series 'National Tintings' (5 October, 2 November, 23 November).

64 There is a literature of the Famine; see Kelleher, *The Feminization of Famine*; Cusack and Goss, *Hungry Words: Images of Famine in the Irish Canon*; and Christopher Morash, ed., *The Hungry Voice: The Poetry of the Irish Famine* (Blackrock: Irish Academic Press, 1989); but the calamity seems often to have traumatized writers into silence. See Eagleton, *Heathcliff and the Great Hunger*, pp. 1–26.

65 *Dublin University Magazine* 100 (April 1841), 531.

66 Kelleher, *The Feminization of Famine*, p. 115.

67 Rosa Mulholland's 'The Hungry Death' is most accessible in *The Penguin Book of Irish Fiction*, ed. Colm Tóibín (Harmondsworth: Penguin, 1999), p. 268.

68 *Dublin University Review* (March 1886), 279.

69 Sarah Orne Jewett, *The Irish Stories*, ed. Jack Morgan and Louis A. Renza (Carbondale and Edwardsville: Southern Illinois University Press, 1996), p. xix.

70 Roy Foster, 'Ascendancy and Union', in *The Oxford History of Ireland*, ed. Roy Foster (Oxford: Oxford University Press, 1989), p. 173.

71 See particularly, W. J. McCormack, *Dissolute Characters: Irish Literary History through Balzac, Sheridan Le Fanu, Yeats and Bowen* (Manchester: Manchester University Press, 1993), pp. 45–7.

72 Sheridan Le Fanu, *In A Glass Darkly*, ed. Robert Tracy (Oxford: Oxford University Press, 1993), p. xiv.

73 *Ibid.*, pp. 27–8.

74 Not surprisingly, James Joyce was an admirer of Le Fanu's writings and 'The Familiar' may have had some influence on the portrait of Dublin in *Finnegans Wake*; see *In A Glass Darkly*, pp. xv–xvi.

75 Eagleton, *Heathcliff and the Great Hunger*, pp. 187–99.

76 Charlotte Riddell, *Handsome Phil and Other Stories* (London: F.V. White and Co., 1899), p. 139. For more on this theme of obstacles to publication for women, see Riddell's autobiographical *A Struggle for Fame* (London: Sampson, Low, Marston and Co., 1900). John Wilson Foster discusses reasons for the neglect of Riddell and other popular Irish writers in *Irish Novels 1890–1940: New Bearings in Culture and Fiction* (Oxford: Oxford University Press, 2008), pp. 1–24.

77 *Ibid.*, p. 39.

78 W. B. Yeats, *Uncollected Prose Vol. 1: First Reviews and Articles 1886–1896*, ed. John Frayne (London: Macmillan, 1970), pp. 382–7.

79 Gregory Schirmer, 'Tales from Big House and Cabin: the Nineteenth Century', in *The Irish Short Story: A Critical History*, ed. James Kilroy (Boston: Twayne, 1984), p. 41.

80 Julie Anne Stevens, *The Irish Scene in Somerville and Ross* (Dublin: Irish Academic Press, 2007).

81 Gifford Lewis, *Somerville and Ross: The World of the Irish R.M.* (Harmondsworth: Penguin, 1987), p. 9.

82 Bi-Ling Chen, 'From Britishness to Irishness: Fox Hunting as a Metaphor for Irish Cultural Identity in the Writing of Somerville and Ross', *The Canadian Journal of Irish Studies* 23 (2), 1997, 39–54.

83 E. Somerville and Martin Ross, *The Irish R.M.* (London: Abacus, 1989), p. 575.

84 *Ibid.*, p. 572.

85 Peter Denham, 'William Carleton and Samuel Ferguson: Lives and Contacts', in Brand, *William Carleton: the Authentic Voice*, pp. 360–77.

86 *Dublin University Magazine* 24 (September 1844), 269.

87 *Ibid.*

88 See Heidi Hansson, *Emily Lawless 1845–1913: Writing the Interspace* (Cork: Cork University Press, 2007), p. 13.

89 For more on Lawless' use of the male narrator, see *ibid.*, pp. 39–53.

90 Emily Lawless, *Traits and Confidences* (New York: Garland Publishing, 1979), p. 165.
91 *Ibid.*, p. 180.
92 *Ibid.*, p. 181.
93 *Ibid.*, p. 184.
94 *Ibid.*, p. 217.
95 Lawless may have known that tapping on the window was interpreted as an omen of death in the west of Ireland. For this belief, see John Wilson Foster, *Fictions of the Irish Literary Revival: A Changeling Art* (Dublin: Gill and Macmillan, 1987), p. 168.

3 *FIN DE SIÈCLE* VISIONS: IRISH SHORT FICTION AT THE TURN OF THE CENTURY

1 *The Dublin University Review* (November 1886), 924–5.
2 *The Irish Times*, 15 October 1892, 1.
3 For this correspondence see *Dana* 8 (December 1904) and 9 (January 1905).
4 For these figures, see F. S. Lyons, *Ireland since the Famine* (London: Fontana, 1985), pp. 87–8.
5 T. Coulson, 'The Revival in Letters', *The Irish Review* (June 1911), 173.
6 For recent critical work on the links between the Revival and modernism, see Adrian Frazier, 'Irish Modernisms, 1880–1930', in *The Cambridge Companion to the Irish Novel*, ed. John Wilson Foster (Cambridge: Cambridge University Press, 2006), pp. 113–32. See also John Wilson Foster's earlier essay on 'Irish Modernism', in his *Colonial Consequences: Essays in Irish Literature and Culture* (Dublin: The Lilliput Press, 1991), pp. 44–59.
7 Nadine Gordimer, 'The Flash of Fireflies', in *The New Short Story Theories*, ed. Charles May (Athens: Ohio University Press, 1994), p. 265.
8 See Georges Zimmermann, *The Irish Storyteller* (Dublin: Four Courts Press, 2001), pp. 273–427.
9 John Wilson Foster, *Fictions of the Irish Literary Revival: A Changeling Art* (Dublin: Gill and Macmillan, 1987), p. 225; see also pp. 211–18. Elizabeth Fine explores this problem of moving from performance to text in *The Folklore Text: from Performance to Print* (Bloomington and Indianapolis: Indiana University Press, 1994).
10 Walter J. Ong, *Orality and Literacy: The Technologising of the Word* (London and New York: Routledge, 1991), p. 67. On this point, see also Walter Benjamin, 'Observations on the Works of Nikolai Leskov', in *Selected Writings: Volume Three 1935–1938*, trans. Edmund Jephcott *et al.*, ed. Howard Eiland and Michael Jennings (Cambridge, MA and London: Harvard University Press, 2002).
11 W. B. Yeats, *Writings on Irish Folklore, Legend and Myth*, ed. Robert Welch (Harmondsworth: Penguin, 1993), p. 108.
12 Zimmermann, *The Irish Storyteller*, p. 346.
13 Yeats, *Writings on Irish Folklore, Legend and Myth*, p. 86.

14 *Ibid.*, p 329.
15 See Terence Brown, *The Life of W. B. Yeats* (Dublin: Gill and Macmillan, 2001), pp. 71–2.
16 W. B. Yeats, *Representative Irish Tales* (Gerrards Cross: Colin Smythe, 1979), p. 32.
17 *The Irish Monthly* 19 (July 1891), 378–9.
18 For this period in Yeats' life, see Brown, *The Life of W. B. Yeats*, pp. 47–70.
19 William O'Donnell, *A Guide to the Prose Fiction of W. B. Yeats* (Epping: Bowker Publishing Company, 1983), p. 7.
20 For details of these turn of the century discussions on the short story in an international context, see Valerie Shaw, *The Short Story: a Critical Introduction* (London and New York: Longman, 1983), pp. 1–28.
21 For details of the availability of English translations of Chekhov, see Charles May, *The Short Story: the Reality of Artifice* (New York: Simon and Schuster, 1995), pp. 51–2.
22 Henry James, 'Preface to "The Lesson of the Master"', in *The Art of the Novel: Critical Prefaces*, introduction by Richard Blackmur (New York: Charles Scribner's Sons, 1934), pp. 217–20.
23 *The Irish Times*, 28 April 1894, 4.
24 Deirdre Toomey, 'The Story Teller at Fault: Oscar Wilde and Irish Orality', in *Wilde the Irishman*, ed. Jerusha McCormack (New Haven, CT and London: Yale University Press, 1998), pp. 24–35.
25 Richard Pine, *The Thief of Reason: Oscar Wilde and Modern Ireland* (Dublin: Gill and Macmillan, 1995), p. 165.
26 *Ibid.*, p. 180.
27 Oscar Wilde, *The Complete Letters*, ed. Merlin Holland and Rupert Hart-Davis (New York: Henry Holt and Co., 2000), p. 388.
28 Neil Sammells, *Wilde Style: The Plays and Prose of Oscar Wilde* (Harlow: Pearson, 2000); Jarlath Killeen, *The Fairy Tales of Oscar Wilde* (Burlington, VT: Ashgate Press, 2007). For folk-Catholic themes in Wilde's other works, see *The Faiths of Oscar Wilde: Catholicism, Folklore and Ireland* (Basingstoke and New York: Palgrave, 2005) by the same author.
29 Sammells, *Wilde Style*, p. 11.
30 Brown, *The Life of W. B. Yeats*, p. 31.
31 Declan Kiberd, *Inventing Ireland: The Literature of the Modern Nation* (London: Vintage, 1996), p. 35.
32 Jerusha McCormack, 'Wilde's Fiction(s)' in *The Cambridge Companion to Oscar Wilde*, ed. P. Raby (Cambridge: Cambridge University Press, 1998), p. 102.
33 By contrast those Irish writers who were working on popular detective fiction contemporary to Wilde apparently followed English conventions; see John Wilson Foster, *Irish Novels 1890–1940: New Bearings in Culture and Fiction* (Oxford: Oxford University Press, 2008), pp. 374–9.
34 Yeats' review of *Lord Arthur Savile's Crime* appeared in *United Ireland* (26 September 1891). William Sharp also wrote a critical review in the *Academy* (5 September 1891).

35 Jarlath Killeen, 'Diaspora, Empire, and the Religious Geography of Victorian Social relations in Wilde's Fairy Tales', in *New Voices in Irish Criticism*, ed. P. J. Mathews (Dublin: Four Courts Press, 2000), pp. 183–9.

36 Declan Kiberd, *Irish Classics* (Cambridge, MA: Harvard University Press, 2001), p. 330.

37 Wilde, *The Complete Letters*, p. 354.

38 W. B. Yeats, *The Collected Letters of W. B. Yeats: Volume 1, 1865–95*, ed. J. Kelly, (Oxford: Clarendon Press, 1986), p. 459.

39 Richard Finneran, *The Prose Fiction of W. B. Yeats: The Search for 'Those Simple Forms'* (Dublin: Dolmen Press, 1973), p. 9.

40 W. B. Yeats, *Short Fiction*, ed. G. J. Watson (Harmondsworth, Penguin, 1995), p. xiv.

41 *Ibid.*, p. 41.

42 The *Irish Monthly* (December 1891), 662–3.

43 W. B. Yeats, *The Collected Letters of W. B. Yeats: Volume 11, 1896–1900*, ed. W. Gould, J. Kelly and D. Toomey (Oxford: Clarendon Press, 1997), p. 104.

44 Brown, *The Life of W. B. Yeats*, p. 96.

45 W. B. Yeats, *Autobiographies* (London: Macmillan, 1955), p. 287.

46 O'Donnell, *A Guide to the Prose Fiction of W. B. Yeats*, p. 49.

47 *Ibid.*, pp. 38–9.

48 Yeats, *Short Fiction*, p. 147.

49 W. B. Yeats, *Mythologies*, ed. W. Gould and D. Toomey (New York: Macmillan, 2005), p. xxv.

50 R. F. Foster, *W. B. Yeats: A Life. Vol. 1, The Apprentice Mage 1896–1914* (Oxford: Oxford University Press, 1997), pp. 176–8.

51 Yeats, *Short Fiction*, p. 202.

52 Richard Ellmann, *Yeats: the Man and the Masks* (Harmondsworth: Penguin, 1987), pp. 121–30.

53 Yeats, *Short Fiction*, p. 213.

54 *The Speaker*, 8 May 1897, 524–5.

55 Finneran, *The Prose Fiction of W. B. Yeats*, pp. 30–1.

56 Elaine Showalter (ed.), *Daughters of Decadence: Women Writers of the Fin de Siècle* (London: Virago, 1993), pp. viii–ix.

57 Lyn Pykett, *The 'Improper' Feminine: The Women's Sensation Novel and the New Woman Writing* (London: Routledge, 1992), pp. 165–74.

58 Sally Ledger, *The New Woman: Fiction and Feminism at the Fin de Siècle* (Manchester: Manchester University Press, 1997), p. 192.

59 George Egerton, *Keynotes and Discords*, ed. Sally Ledger (London: Continuum, 2006), p. 16.

60 Reprinted in Showalter (ed.), *Daughters of Decadence*, pp. 69–73.

61 Hugh Stutfield, 'Tommyrotics', *Blackwood's Magazine* 157 (June 1895), 836.

62 On spiritualism's empowerment of women, see Brown, *The Life of W. B. Yeats*, p. 39.

63 Terence de Vere White (ed.), *A Leaf from The Yellow Book* (London: Richards Press, 1958), p. 14.

64 See Mary O'Donoghue, 'An Intensity of Irishness: George Egerton's Representations of Irish Femininity', in Mathews, *New Voices in Irish Criticism*, pp. 83–91.
65 Letter dated May 1939 in de Vere White, *A Leaf from The Yellow Book*, p. 166.
66 *The Irish Times*, 13 December 1905, 8.
67 George Egerton, *Flies in Amber* (London: Hutchinson and Co., 1905), p. 41.
68 Egerton, *Keynotes and Discords*, p.xviii.
69 Showalter, *Daughters of Decadence*, p. 287.
70 For a discussion of Grand that sets her in her Irish context, see Foster, *Irish Novels 1890–1940*, pp. 283–91.
71 See Joseph Campbell's translations of these stories in Pádraic Pearse, *Collected Works* (Dublin and London: Maunsel and Co., 1917) and Desmond Maguire's translations in Pádraic Pearse, *Short Stories* (Cork: Mercier Press, 1968).
72 Foster, *Irish Novels 1890–1940*, p. 32.
73 Patricia McFate, *The Writing of James Stephens: Variations on a Theme of Love* (London: Macmillan, 1979), p. 123.
74 Quoted in *ibid.*, p. 120.
75 *Ibid.*, p. 140.
76 Augustine Martin, *James Stephens: A Critical Study* (Dublin: Gill and Macmillan, 1977), p. 63.
77 James Stephens, *Here Are Ladies* (London: Macmillan, 1928), pp. 41–2.
78 James Stephens, *Etched in Moonlight* (London: Macmillan, 1928), p. 80.
79 *The Irish Times*, 9 March 1928, 3.
80 *The Irish Times*, 14 April 1928, 3.
81 May, *The New Short Story Theories*, p. 133.
82 This idea was the focus of a symposium on Irish modernism held at Trinity College, Dublin, 19–21 October 2007.
83 W. B. Yeats, *Collected Letters, vol. 1*, p. 36.
84 Eve Patten, 'Afterword', in W. B. Yeats, *John Sherman and Dhoya* (Dublin: Lilliput Press, 1990), p. 96.
85 Quoted in W. B. Yeats, *John Sherman and Dhoya*, ed. R. J. Finneran (New York: Macmillan, 1991), p.xxii.
86 Deirdre Toomey, 'Away', in *Yeats and Women,* ed. Deirdre Toomey (Basingstoke: Macmillan, 1997), pp. 135–67.
87 Yeats, *Collected Letters*, vol. 1, pp. 274–5.
88 Janet Sayers, *Mothering Psychoanalysis* (London: Hamish Hamilton, 1991), p. 226.
89 Yeats, *Collected Letters*, vol. 1, pp. 245–6.
90 See Egerton, *Keynotes and Discords*, pp. xxi–xxii.
91 *Ibid.*
92 See Mary Daly, *Gyn/Ecology: the Metaethics of Radical Feminism* (London: The Women's Press, 1979).
93 See, for example, Showalter, *Daughters of Decadence* (1993), p. xiv.
94 Egerton, *Keynotes and Discords*, p. 108.
95 George Egerton, 'A Keynote to *Keynotes*' (1932), quoted in Showalter, *Daughters of Decadence*, p. xiii.

96 Egerton, *Keynotes and Discords*, p. 8.
97 *Ibid.*
98 See Angela Leighton, ' "Because men made the laws": the Fallen Woman and the Woman Poet', *Victorian Poetry* 27 (1989), 109–27.

4 THE MODERN IRISH SHORT STORY: MOORE AND JOYCE

1 James Joyce, *Stephen Hero*, ed. Theodore Spencer (London: Jonathan Cape, 1944), pp. 182–4.
2 Richard Ellmann, *James Joyce* (Oxford: Oxford University Press, 1959), p. 170.
3 George Moore, *Hail and Farewell: Ave* (London: William Heinemann, 1937), p. 41.
4 R. F. Foster, 'The Gift of Adaptability: Yeats, Joyce and Modern Ireland', in *That Island Never Found: Essays and Poems for Terence Brown*, ed. Nicholas Allen and Eve Patten (Dublin: Four Courts Press, 2007), p. 58.
5 Edith Wharton, *The Writing of Fiction* (New York: Touchstone, 1997), p. 29.
6 Anton Chekhov, *Letters on the Short Story, the Drama, and Other Literary Topics*, ed. Louis Friedland (New York: Dover Publications, 1966), p. 64; see also pp. 17, 69, 292.
7 Valerie Shaw, *The Short Story: A Critical Introduction* (London and New York: Longman, 1983), p. 137.
8 Charles May, 'Chekhov and the Modern Short Story', in *Anton Chekhov*, ed. Harold Bloom (New York: Chelsea House, 1999), p. 151.
9 See Charles May, *The Short Story: The Reality of Artifice* (New York: Simon and Schuster, 1995), pp. 51–2.
10 See Ellmann, *James Joyce*, p. 171. For the influence of the American writer, Bret Harte, on Joyce, see *Dubliners*, ed. Terence Brown (London: Penguin, 1992), p. xlviii, note 27.
11 George Moore, *The Untilled Field*, ed. Richard Cave (Gerrards Cross: Colin Smythe, 2000), p. ix.
12 Ben Forkner and Philippe Séjourné, 'Interview with V. S. Pritchett', *Journal of the Short Story in English* 6 (1986), 12.
13 Suzanne Ferguson, 'Defining the Short Story', in *The New Short Story Theories*, ed. Charles May (Athens: Ohio University Press, 1994), pp. 218–30.
14 See George Moore, *Hail and Farewell: Salve* (London: William Heinemann, 1947), pp. 107–31.
15 For the genesis of 'The Wedding Gown', see *ibid.*, p. 121.
16 *Ibid.*, pp. 122–3.
17 For an assessment of these Irish translations, see Pádraigín Riggs, '*An-t-Úr-Ghort* and *The Untilled Field*', in *George Moore: Artistic Visions and Literary Worlds*, ed. Mary Pierse (Newcastle: Cambridge Scholars Press, 2006), pp. 130–41.
18 Moore, *Hail and Farewell: Salve*, p. 125.
19 Moore, *The Untilled Field*, p. 97.
20 *Ibid.*, p. 105.

21 *Ibid.*, p. 120.
22 In a letter to Stanislaus of 1905, quoted in James Carens, 'In Quest of a New Impulse: George Moore's *The Untilled Field* and James Joyce's *Dubliners*', in *The Irish Short Story: a Critical History*, ed. James Kilroy (Boston: Twayne, 1984), p. 66.
23 For Joyce's sense of rivalry with Moore the short story writer, see *ibid.*, pp. 66–9.
24 Thomas Staley, 'A Beginning: Signification, Story, and Discourse in Joyce's "Sisters"', *Genre* 12 (1979), 533–49.
25 Jean-Michel Rabaté, *James Joyce: Authorized Reader* (Baltimore: Johns Hopkins University Press, 1991).
26 Suzette Henke, *James Joyce and the Politics of Desire* (New York and London: Routledge, 1990).
27 Robert Spoo, 'Uncanny Returns in "The Dead"', in *Joyce: The Return of the Repressed*, ed. Susan Stanford Friedman (Ithaca, NY: Cornell University Press, 1993).
28 Kevin Dettmar, *The Illicit Joyce of Postmodernism: Reading against the Grain* (Madison: University of Wisconsin Press, 1996).
29 Bonnie Kime Scott, *Joyce and Feminism* (Bloomington: Indiana University Press, 1984).
30 Cheryl Herr, *Joyce's Anatomy of Culture* (Urbana: University of Illinois Press, 1986); R. B. Kershner, *Joyce, Bakhtin and Popular Culture: Chronicles of Disorder* (Chapel Hill: University of North Carolina Press, 1989).
31 Vincent J. Cheng, *Joyce, Race and Empire* (Cambridge: Cambridge University Press, 1995); Seamus Deane, David Lloyd and Luke Gibbons, in *Semicolonial Joyce*, ed. Derek Attridge and Marjorie Howes (Cambridge: Cambridge University Press, 2000).
32 See Patrick Kavanagh's comment: 'There is nothing wrong with Joyce, who, as Chesterton said about someone else, is sane enough; it is his commentators who are mad', *Envoy* 17 (April 1951), 70.
33 Ellmann, *James Joyce*, pp. 259–60.
34 See Carens, 'In Quest of a New Impulse', pp. 68–9. For parallels between Moore and Joyce, see also Deborah Averill, *The Irish Short Story from George Moore to Frank O'Connor* (Lanham, MD: University Press of America, 1982), pp. 45–65. Averill, however, has a tendency to overstate the resemblances, which often arose out of their common admiration for Russian and French writers.
35 Frank O'Connor, *The Lonely Voice: a Study of the Short Story* (Cork: Cork City Council, 2003), pp. 74–84. For more on O'Connor's resistance to Joyce, see Carol Taaffe, 'Coloured Balloons: Frank O'Connor on Irish Modernism', in *Frank O'Connor: Critical Essays*, ed. Hilary Lennon (Dublin: Four Courts Press, 2007), pp. 205–17.
36 O'Connor, *The Lonely Voice*, p. 106.
37 Ellmann, *James Joyce*, p. 216.
38 For details of the tortuous publication history of *Dubliners*, see Ellmann, *James Joyce*, pp. 239–40, 250, 276–7, 324–6, 360, 364.

39 *Envoy* 17 (April 1951), 44.

40 Declan Kiberd, *Inventing Ireland: The Literature of the Modern Nation* (London: Vintage, 1996), p. 330.

41 Though Poe to some extent anticipated the modernist short story in his characterization of the genre as a form that requires from its readers attentiveness to what is going on beneath the surface equal to that of the writer, in what he termed 'a kindred art'; see Edgar Allan Poe, 'Review of *Twice-Told Tales*', in *The New Short Story Theories*, ed. Charles May (Athens: Ohio University Press, 1994), p. 61.

42 See Margot Norris, 'Narration under a Blindfold: reading Joyce's "Clay"', *PMLA* 102 (2) (1987), 206–15.

43 L. J. Morrissey, 'Joyce's Revision of "The Sisters": from Epicleti to Modern Fiction', *James Joyce Quarterly* 24 (1986), 33–54.

44 For criticism of these kinds of readings, see C. H. Peake, *James Joyce: The Citizen and the Artist* (London: Edward Arnold, 1977), p. 8.

45 Shawn St Jean has pointed to the dangers of 'solving' Joyce's stories in a way that does violence to their complexity; see 'Readerly Paranoia and Joyce's Adolescent Stories', *James Joyce Quarterly* 35 (4) (1998), 665–82.

46 O'Connor, *The Lonely Voice*, p. 75.

47 Marion Eide, *Ethical Joyce* (Cambridge: Cambridge University Press, 2002), pp. 35–6.

48 Florence L. Walzl, '*Dubliners*: Women in Irish society', in *Women in Joyce*, ed. Suzette Henke and Elaine Unkeless (Chicago: University of Illinois Press, 1982), pp. 31–56.

49 Cheng, *Joyce, Race, and Empire*, p. 81.

50 Julia Kristeva, 'Women's Time', in *The Portable Kristeva*, ed. Kelly Oliver (New York: Columbia University Press, 1997), p. 351.

51 For a discussion of Joyce's attitudes to women, to feminism and to the feminism of writers like Moore, Shaw and Ibsen, see Scott, *Joyce and Feminism*.

52 Julia Kristeva, *Powers of Horror* (New York: Columbia University Press, 1982), p. 208.

53 Joyce, *Dubliners*, p. 22.

54 Cheng, *Joyce, Race, and Empire*, p. 100.

55 Letter to Grant Richards in 1906, quoted in Ellmann, *James Joyce*, p. 230.

56 Joyce, *Dubliners*, p. 29.

57 Garry Leonard, 'Wondering Where All the Dust Comes From: *jouissance* in "Eveline"', *James Joyce Quarterly* 29 (1) (1991), 23–42.

58 We may suspect that Frank's intentions are not honourable, given that the phrase 'going to Buenos Ayres' was apparently current slang for taking up the life of a prostitute; see Joyce, *Dubliners*, p. 255.

59 See, for example, Hélène Cixous, 'The Laugh of the Medusa', in *New French Feminisms*, ed. Elaine Marks and Isabelle de Courtivron (Hemel Hempstead: Harvester, 1981), pp. 245–64, and Luce Irigaray, 'Women-Mothers, the Silent Substratum of the Social Order', in *The Irigaray Reader*, ed. Margaret Whitford (Oxford: Basil Blackwell, 1991), pp. 47–52.

60 Donald Torchiana, 'Joyce's "Two Gallants": A Walk through the Ascendancy', *James Joyce Quarterly* 6 (2) (1968), 115–27.

61 Joyce, *Dubliners*, pp. 57–8.

62 On the gender politics of this story, see Eugene O'Brien, '"You can never know women": Framing Female Identity in *Dubliners*', in *A New and Complex Sensation: Essays on Joyce's Dubliners*, ed. Oona Frawley (Dublin: Lilliput Press, 2004), pp. 212–22.

63 Joyce, *Stephen Hero*, p. 207.

64 Joyce, *Dubliners*, pp. 58, 57.

65 Trevor Williams, 'No Cheer for the Gratefully Oppressed: Ideology in Joyce's *Dubliners*', *Style* 25 (3) (1991), 416–35.

66 Norris, 'Narration under a Blindfold', pp. 206–15.

67 Joyce, *Dubliners*, p. 282.

68 *Ibid.*, p. 113.

69 Jane Miller, ' "O, she's a nice lady!": A Rereading of "A Mother" ', *James Joyce Quarterly* 28 (2) (1991), 407–26.

70 Letter dated 25 September 1907, quoted in Ellmann, *James Joyce*, p. 239.

71 *Ibid.*, p. 403.

72 *Ibid.*, p. 412.

73 Reprinted in *Envoy* 17 (April 1951), 48.

74 Joyce, *Dubliners*, p. 216.

75 *Ibid.*, p. 175.

76 O'Connor, *The Lonely Voice*, p. 83.

77 Joyce, *Dubliners*, p. 191.

78 *Ibid.*, p. 211

79 *Ibid.*, p. 218.

80 *Ibid.*, pp. 224–5.

81 Ellmann, *James Joyce*, pp. 262–3. On the theme of death in 'The Dead', see also J. W. Foster, *Fictions of the Irish Literary Revival: A Changeling Art* (Dublin: Gill and Macmillan, 1987), pp. 145–7.

82 Joyce, *Dubliners*, p. 180.

83 *Ibid.*, p. 225.

84 'It was Yeats's imagination which always dazzled him ... Joyce often recited Yeats's poems from memory, and seemed to wonder if his own work was imaginative enough' (Ellmann, *James Joyce*, p. 673, fn). For a reassessment of the relationship between Yeats and Joyce that argues for their mutual influence being greater than hitherto believed, see Foster, 'The Gift of Adaptability: Yeats, Joyce and Modern Ireland', in Allen and Patten, *That Island Never Found*, pp. 53–69.

85 Joyce, *Dubliners*, p. 224.

5 1920–1939: YEARS OF TRANSITION

1 Liam O'Flaherty, *The Letters*, ed. A. A. Kelly (Dublin: Wolfhound Press, 1996), p. 76.

2 *The Irish Statesman* 1 (1) (1923), 16.

3 *The Irish Times*, 21 January 1932, 99.
4 *The Dublin Magazine*, 1, (January–March 1926), 1.
5 O'Flaherty, *Letters*, p. 90.
6 In a review of *Mr Gilhooley*, *The Dublin Magazine* 2 (1) (January–March 1927), 66.
7 See Maurice Harmon, *Sean O'Faolain* (London: Constable, 1994), pp. 97–9.
8 See Robert C. Evans, 'Frank O'Connor's American Reception: the First Decade (1931–41)', in *Frank O'Connor: Essays*, ed. Hilary Lennon (Dublin: Four Courts Press, 2007), pp. 71–86.
9 *The Irish Times*, 4 December 1935, 12. Strong published several short story collections during this period: *Doyle's Rock* (1925), *The English Captain* (1929), *Tuesday Afternoon* (1935). The fairly undistinguished 'tales and sketches' that make up *Doyle's Rock* are mainly set in England but contain some reminiscences of childhood summers spent in Ireland.
10 *The Irish Times*, 4 December 1935, 12.
11 John Wilson Foster, *Irish Novels 1890–1940: New Bearings in Culture and Fiction* (Oxford: Oxford University Press, 2008), p. 495, note 4.
12 Hugh MacCartan, *Silhouettes: Some Character Studies from North and South* (Dublin: Thomas Kiersey, 1918), p. 125.
13 Seumas O'Kelly, *The Weaver's Grave*, Introduction by Benedict Kiely (Dublin: O'Brien Press, 1984), pp. 33, 18.
14 *Ibid.*, p. 68.
15 'Haunting' was the word used by both the *Manchester Guardian* and *The Times Literary Supplement*; see the *Manchester Guardian*, 12 December 1919, 7.
16 *The Irish Times*, 21 January 1932, 99.
17 In 1948 McLaverty wrote to Corkery saying that it was to him that he owed his beginnings as a writer; see Michael McLaverty, *In Quiet Places: The Uncollected Stories, Letters and Critical Prose of Michael McLaverty*, ed. Sophia Hillan King (Dublin: Poolbeg, 1989), p. 127. McLaverty's correspondence also reveals McGahern's early admiration for Corkery.
18 ' "The Leaca for prayer!" he said. "The Leaca for wheat," said the master, a third time.' Daniel Corkery, *The Stones and Other Stories*, ed. Paul Delaney (Cork: Mercier Press, 2003), p. 21.
19 *Ibid.*, p. 9.
20 After the civil war, however, Corkery turned against foreign models, see Harmon, *Sean O'Faolain*, p. 66.
21 Daniel Corkery, *The Stormy Hills* (London: Jonathan Cape, 1929), p. 208.
22 *Ibid.*, p. 203.
23 Alexander Gonzalez, 'A Re-Evaluation of Daniel Corkery's Fiction', *Irish University Review* 14 (2), (1984), 191.
24 Terence Brown, *Ireland: a Social and Cultural History, 1922–2002* (London: HarperCollins, 2004), p. 10.
25 *Tales of the R.I.C.* (London and Edinburgh: William Blackwood and Sons, 1922), pp. 284–5.

26 Dorothy Macardle, *Earth-bound: Nine Stories of Ireland* (Dublin: The Emton Press and Worcester, MA: The Harrigan Press, 1924), p. 91.

27 *Ibid.*, p. 72.

28 For Macardle's interest in the occult, see Nadia Clare Smith, *Dorothy Macardle: a Life* (Dublin: The Woodfield Press, 2007), pp. 56–8.

29 Macardle, *Earth-bound*, p. 7.

30 Liam O'Flaherty, *Shame the Devil* (London: Grayson and Grayson, 1934), p. 18.

31 On O'Flaherty's bilingualism, see J. M. Calahan, *Liam O'Flaherty: A Study of the Short Fiction* (Boston: Twayne Publishers, 1991), pp. 12–29.

32 *The Spectator*, 4 October 1924, 468.

33 Liam O'Flaherty, *The Short Stories* (London: Jonathan Cape, 1937), p. 28.

34 *Ibid.*, p. 114.

35 Brinsley MacNamara, *The Smiling Faces and Other Stories* (London: The Mandrake Press, 1929), pp. 45–6.

36 O'Flaherty, *The Short Stories*, p. 204.

37 *Ibid.*, p. 92.

38 *The Irish Statesman*, 2 (13) (June 1924), 404.

39 O'Flaherty, *The Letters*, p. 10.

40 *Ibid.*, p. 187. O'Flaherty's comparison between the short story and poetry finds a later echo in Walter Allen's judgment that the form is akin to lyric poetry; see *The Short Story in English* (Oxford: The Clarendon Press, 1981), p. 8.

41 See Deborah Averill, *The Irish Short Story from George Moore to Frank O'Connor* (Lanham, MD: University Press of America, 1982), p. 125 and Calahan, *Liam O'Flaherty*, pp. 41–52.

42 *The Irish Times*, 28 November 1924, 3.

43 O'Flaherty, *The Letters*, p. 126.

44 O'Flaherty, *The Short Stories*, p. 131.

45 Frank O'Connor, *My Father's Son* (Dublin: Gill and Macmillan, 1968), pp. 28–35.

46 James Matthews, *Voices: A Life of Frank O'Connor* (Dublin: Gill and Macmillan, 1983), p. 65.

47 Quoted in Harmon, *Sean O'Faolain*, p. 97.

48 Frank O'Connor, *An Only Child* (London: Macmillan, 1961), p. 197.

49 'Interview with V. S. Pritchett', *Journal of the Short Story in English* 6 (1986), 12. For Isaac Babel's influence on O'Connor's war stories, see Elmer Andrews, 'Frank O'Connor's "War Book": *Guests of the Nation*', in *Modern Irish Writers and the Wars*, ed. Kathleen Devine (Gerrards Cross: Colin Smythe, 1999), pp. 107–10.

50 See, for example, *The Irish Review* (March 1911), 23 and *ibid.* (April 1913), 104.

51 R. T. Gill, quoted in Maurice Sheehy (ed.), *Michael/Frank: Studies on Frank O'Connor* (Dublin: Gill and Macmillan, 1969), p. 43.

52 Frank O'Connor, *Collected Stories* (New York: Vintage, 1982), p. 13.

53 *Ibid.*, p. 14.

54 O'Connor, *My Father's Son*, p. 49.
55 O'Connor, *An Only Child*, p. 210.
56 Averill, *The Irish Short Story*, p. 247.
57 Seán O'Faoláin, *The Collected Stories of Sean O'Faolain*, vol. 1 (London: Constable, 1980), p. 64.
58 Averill, *The Irish Short Story*, pp. 170–2.
59 Donal McCartney, 'Seán O'Faoláin: a Nationalist Right Enough', *Irish University Review* 6 (1) (Spring 1976), 75.
60 Seán O'Faoláin, 'The Craft of the Short Story', *The Bell* 7 (6) (March 1944), 534.
61 Quoted in Harmon, *Sean O'Faolain*, p. 103.
62 'The Journey' was published in *The Dublin Magazine* 1 (4) (October–December 1926), 39–44. See also Hugh MacCartan's use of the train device to assemble characters of differing political views in 'The World on Wheels' in *Silhouettes*.
63 O'Faoláin, *The Collected Stories*, vol. 1, p. 171.
64 *Ibid.*, vol. 1, p. 173.
65 Seán O'Faoláin, *The Finest Stories of Seán O'Faoláin* (Boston: Little, Brown and Co., 1957), p. vii.
66 O'Faoláin, *The Collected Stories*, vol. 1, p. 319.
67 Norah Hoult, 'Obituary', *John O'London's Weekly*, 27 July 1935, p. 582.
68 Olivia Manning, *A Romantic Hero* (London: Random House, 2001), p. 76.
69 Michael McLaverty, *Collected Short Stories* (Belfast: The Blackstaff Press, 2002), p. xi.
70 Seán O'Faoláin, *The Short Story* (Cork: Mercier Press, 1972), p. 213.
71 *The Irish Times*, 4 December 1935, 12.
72 Elizabeth Bowen, *The Collected Stories* (Harmondsworth: Penguin, 1983), p. 203.
73 Elizabeth Bowen, *Bowen's Court and Seven Winters* (London: Virago, 1984), p. 451.
74 Bowen, *The Collected Stories*, p. 424.
75 Belacqua had made an earlier appearance, in 'Sedendo et Quiescendo', published in Eugene Jolas' *transition*, where Beckett's first published story, 'Assumption' (1929), also appeared; see S. E. Gontarski, ed., *Samuel Beckett: the Complete Short Prose, 1929–1989* (New York: Grove Press, 1995).
76 Samuel Beckett, *More Pricks Than Kicks* (1934) (London: John Calder, 1993), p. 39.
77 *Dublin Magazine* 9 (July–September 1934), 85.
78 Declan Kiberd, *Inventing Ireland: the Literature of Modern Ireland* (London: Vintage, 1996), p. 456.
79 Beckett, *More Pricks Than Kicks*, p. 16.
80 Alec Reid, 'Test Flight: Beckett's "More Pricks than Kicks"', in *The Irish Short Story*, ed. Patrick Rafroidi and Terence Brown (Gerrards Cross: Colin Smythe, 1979), p. 233.

81 John Harrington, 'Beckett, Joyce, and Irish Writing: The Example of Beck-ett's "Dubliners" Story', in *Re: Joyce 'N Beckett*, ed. Phyllis Carey and Ed Jewinski (New York: Fordham University Press, 1992), pp. 31–42.
82 Letter dated 1948, quoted in Samuel Beckett, Georges Duthuit, Jacques Pitman, *Bram Van Velde* (Paris: G. Fall, 1958), preface.
83 Brown, *Ireland: A Social and Cultural History*, p. 105.
84 Beckett, *More Pricks Than Kicks*, p. 146.
85 Samuel Beckett, *All That Fall* (London: Calder, 1965), pp. 10–11.
86 Declan Kiberd, 'John McGahern's *Amongst Women*', in *Language and Tradition in Ireland: Continuities and Displacements*, ed. Maria Tymoczko and Colin Ireland (Amherst and Boston: University of Massachusetts Press, 2003), p. 212.
87 *The Irish Times*, 4 February 1935, 12.
88 Frank O'Connor, *Collected Stories* (New York: Vintage, 1982), p. 4.
89 Frank O'Connor, *The Lonely Voice: A Study of the Short Story* (Cork: Cork City Council, 2003), p. 3.
90 Frank O'Connor, *The Cornet-Player Who Betrayed Ireland* (Dublin: Poolbeg, 1981), p. 8.
91 O'Connor, *Collected Stories*, p. 12.
92 O'Connor, *An Only Child*, p. 244.
93 *Ibid.*, p. 275.
94 O'Connor, *The Lonely Voice*, p. 4.
95 Norah Hoult, *Poor Women!* (London: William Heinemann, 1930), p. 284.
96 *Ibid.*, p. 270.
97 Edith Somerville and Martin Ross, *Sarah's Youth* (London: Longmans Green and Co., 1938), p. 264.
98 Hoult, *Poor Women!*, p. 284.

6 1940–1959: ISOLATION

1 Olivia Manning, 'Twilight of the Gods', in *A Romantic Hero* (London: Random House, 1967), p. 149.
2 Clair Wills, *That Neutral Island: A Cultural History of Ireland during the Second World War* (London: Faber and Faber, 2007), pp. 281–8, 305–8.
3 *The Irish Times*, 5 January 1946, 4.
4 *Ibid.*
5 Elizabeth Bowen, *The Mulberry Tree: Writings of Elizabeth Bowen*, ed. Hermione Lee (London: Vintage, 1999), p. 98.
6 *Ibid.*, p. 95.
7 *Ibid.*, p. 33.
8 Elizabeth Bowen, *The Collected Stories* (Harmondsworth: Penguin, 1983), p. 585.
9 Bowen, *The Mulberry Tree*, p. 33.
10 Bowen, *The Collected Stories*, p. 591.
11 *The Irish Times*, 5 January 1946, 4.

12 Maurice Harmon, *Sean O'Faolain* (London: Constable, 1994), p. 123.
13 Bowen, *The Collected Stories*, p. 497.
14 *Ibid.*, p. 616.
15 Gerardine Meaney, 'Identity and Opposition: Women and Writing, 1700–1960', in *The Field Day Anthology of Irish Literature. Volume 5*, ed. Angela Bourke *et al.* (Cork: Cork University Press, 2002), p. 979.
16 Eve Patten, 'Olivia Manning, Imperial Refugee', in *That Island Never Found: Essays and Poems for Terence Brown*, ed. Nicholas Allen and Eve Patten (Dublin: Four Courts Press, 2007), pp. 91–104.
17 James Matthews, *Voices: A Life of Frank O'Connor* (Dublin: Gill and Macmillan, 1983), pp. 188–90.
18 Frank O'Connor, *The Lonely Voice: a Study of the Short Story* (Cork: Cork City Council, 2003), p. 5.
19 *Ibid.*
20 *Ibid.*, p. 6.
21 Frank O'Connor, *Collected Stories* (New York: Vintage, 1982), p. 458.
22 Bryan MacMahon, *The Lion-Tamer and Other Stories* (London: Souvenir Press, 1995), p. 138.
23 O'Connor, *The Lonely Voice*, p. 1.
24 *Ibid.*
25 *The Irish Times*, 30 October 1946, 11.
26 James Alexander, 'Frank O'Connor in *The New Yorker*, 1945–1967', *Éire-Ireland* 30 (1) (1995), 130–44.
27 Ben Yagoda, *About Town: The* New Yorker *and the World it Made* (London: Duckworth, 2000), p. 153.
28 *Envoy* 2 (January 1950), 10.
29 *Envoy* 3 (February 1950), 11.
30 *The Irish Times*, 7 December 1946, 5.
31 *The Irish Times*, 1 March 1941, 5.
32 Seán O'Faoláin, 'The Gaelic and the Good', *The Bell* 3 (2) (1941), 102.
33 O'Faoláin, 'Silent Ireland', *The Bell* 6 (6) (1943), 457–66.
34 O'Faoláin, 'The State and Its Writers', *The Bell* 7 (2) (1943), 97.
35 O'Faoláin, 'The Gaelic Cult', *The Bell* 9 (3) (1944), 193.
36 O'Faoláin, 'Past Tense', *The Bell* 7 (3) (1943), 191.
37 Eilís Dillon, 'Seán O'Faoláin and the Young Writer', *The Irish University Review* 6 (1) (Spring 1976), 37–44.
38 Seán O'Faoláin, *The Short Story* (Cork: The Mercier Press, 1948), p. 200.
39 See Roy Foster's comments in *The Irish Times*, 16 April 1976, 10.
40 O'Faoláin, *The Short Story*, p. 185.
41 *Ibid.*, p. 213.
42 'A Lowbrow', *The Bell* 7 (6) (1944), 536.
43 Michael McLaverty, *In Quiet Places: The Uncollected Stories, Letters and Critical Prose of Michael McLaverty*, ed. Sophia Hillan King (Dublin: Poolbeg, 1989), p. 112.
44 *Ibid.*

45 *Ibid.*, p. 165.
46 *Envoy* 20 (July 1951), 8.
47 *Envoy* 7 (June 1950), 10.
48 *Envoy* 6 (May 1950), 85–6.
49 *Envoy* 14 (January 1951), 92–5.
50 Frank O'Connor, *The Backward Look: A Survey of Irish Literature* (London: Macmillan, 1967), p. 227.
51 Seán O'Faoláin, *The Collected Stories* (London: Constable, 1980), vol. 1, p. 429.
52 *Ibid.*, vol. 1, p. 431.
53 Terence Brown, *The Field Day Anthology of Irish Writing*, ed. Seamus Deane (Derry: Field Day Publications, 1991), vol. III, p. 92.
54 O'Connor, *Collected Stories*, p. 55.
55 Liam O'Flaherty, *The Collected Stories*, ed. A. A. Kelly (New York: St Martin's Press, 1999) vol. II, p. 234.
56 *Ibid.*, p. 235.
57 This story appears in the only modern edition of Margaret Barrington's stories, *David's Daughter, Tamar*, Introduction by William Trevor (Dublin: Wolfhound, 1982).
58 Michael McLaverty, *Collected Short Stories* (Belfast: The Blackstaff Press, 2002), p. 195.
59 O'Faoláin, *The Collected Stories*, p. 348. Possibly it was this line that caused McLaverty to pick out the story as an example of O'Faoláin's silliness in a letter to Cecil Scott in 1966; McLaverty, *In Quiet Places*, p. 219.
60 Liam O'Flaherty, *Two Lovely Beasts and Other Stories* (London: The Camelot Press, 1948), p. 31.
61 *The Irish Times*, 1 July 1944, 2.
62 O'Connor, *The Lonely Voice*, p. 140.
63 *Ibid.*, p. 144.
64 *Ibid.*, p. 141.
65 'This is an important book, the critic assumes, because it deals with war. This is an insignificant book because it deals with the feelings of women in a drawing room'; Virginia Woolf, *A Room of One's Own and Three Guineas*, ed. Morag Shiach (Oxford: Oxford University Press, 1992), p. 96.
66 O'Connor, *The Lonely Voice*, p. 147.
67 Mary Lavin, *In a Café: Selected Stories* (Harmondsworth: Penguin, 1999), p. 225.
68 Leah Levenson, *The Four Seasons of Mary Lavin* (Dublin: Marino Books, 1998), p. 54.
69 Examination of her manuscript revisions reveals detailed and painstaking efforts towards concision and clarity: Mary Lavin, 'The Great Wave', Trinity College, Dublin MS. 10985. For Lavin's methods, see also Janet Egleson Dunleavy, 'The Making of Mary Lavin's "Happiness"', *Irish University Review* 9 (2) (1979), 225–31.
70 Mary Lavin, *Selected Stories* (New York: Macmillan, 1959), preface.

71 McLaverty, *In Quiet Places*, p. 129.
72 Levenson, *The Four Seasons of Mary Lavin*, p. 225.
73 Evelyn Conlon, in Mary Lavin, *Tales from Bective Bridge* (Dublin: Town and Country House, 1996), p. vii.
74 V. S. Pritchett, quoted in Levenson, *The Four Seasons of Mary Lavin*, p. 57.
75 James Heaney, ' "No Sanctuary from Hatred": a Re-appraisal of Mary Lavin's Outsiders', *Irish University Review* 28 (2) (1998), 307.
76 Anton Chekhov, *Letters on the Short Story, the Drama, and Other Literary Topics*, ed. Louis Friedland (New York: Dover Publications, 1966), pp. 275–6.
77 O'Flaherty, *The Collected Stories*, p. 329.
78 *Ibid.*, p. 338.
79 'I was living in County Wicklow at the time and became aware that all round me there were farmed-out illegitimate children, many of whom were cruelly ill-treated...Out of that experience I must have written a dozen stories'; O'Connor, *The Backward Look*, p. 227.
80 Angela Bourke, *Maeve Brennan: Homesick at the 'New Yorker'* (London: Jonathan Cape, 2004), p. 78.
81 Maeve Brennan, *The Springs of Affection* (London: Flamingo, 2000), p. 48.
82 Bourke, *Maeve Brennan*, p. 154.
83 Maeve Brennan, *The Visitor* (London: Atlantic Books, 2001), p. 80.
84 Maeve Brennan, *The Rose Garden* (Washington: Counterpoint, 2000), p. 188.
85 For an opposite view, see Bourke, *Maeve Brennan*, pp. 210–14.
86 Mary Lavin, *The Stories of Mary Lavin*, vol. II (London: Constable, 1974), p. 54.
87 For an insightful commentary on 'Ghosts', see Robert C. Evans, 'Frank O'Connor and the Irish Holocaust', in *Hungry Words: Images of Famine in the Irish Canon*, ed. George Cusack and Sarah Goss (Dublin: Irish Academic Press, 2006), pp. 225–44.
88 Bourke, *Maeve Brennan*, p. 176.
89 Mary Corey, *The World Through a Monocle: the 'New Yorker' at Mid-century* (Cambridge, MA: Harvard University Press, 1999), pp. 125–6.
90 Brennan, *The Rose Garden*, p. 112.
91 G. W. F. Hegel, *The Phenomenology of Mind*, trans. J. B. Baillie (New York: Macmillan, 1931), pp. 229–40.
92 Breman, *The Rose Garden*, p. 61.
93 Corey, *The World Through a Monocle*, pp. 1–17.
94 Brennan, *The Rose Garden*, p. 52.
95 Bourke, *Maeve Brennan*, p. 266.
96 *The Bell* 4 (4) (1942), 303.
97 *The Bell* 7 (5) (1944), 449.
98 *The Bell* 4 (5) (1942), 320.
99 Seán O'Faoláin, quoted in *The World of Bryan MacMahon*, ed. Gabriel Fitzmaurice (Cork: Mercier Press, 2005), p. 25.

100 MacMahon, *The Lion-Tamer*, p. 185.

101 *Ibid.*, p. 103.

102 For commentary on this story, see John Brannigan, 'Race, Cosmopolitanism, and Modernity: Irish Writing and Culture in the Late Nineteen Fifties', *Irish University Review* 34 (2) (2004), 332–50.

103 *The Irish Times* 7 December 1946, 5.

104 *The Bell* 3 (6) (1942), 419.

105 Seán O'Faoláin, *The Irish* (Harmondsworth: Penguin, 1980), pp. 140–1.

106 For details of Lavin's life, see Levenson, *The Four Seasons of Mary Lavin*.

107 Lavin, *In a Café*, p. 90.

108 For the figures on Irish female university attendance, see Anne Macdona (ed.), *From Newman to New Woman: UCD Women Remember* (Dublin: New Island, 2001), p. x.

109 Lavin, *In a Café*, p. 95.

110 *Ibid.*, p. 96.

111 Julia Kristeva, *Powers of Horror: An Essay on Abjection* (New York: Columbia University Press, 1982), pp. 2–3.

112 Seán O'Faoláin, *The Heat of the Sun: Collected Short Stories*, vol. 11 (Harmondsworth: Penguin, 1983), p. 25.

113 *Ibid.*, p. 35.

114 *Ibid.*, p. 42.

115 *Ibid.*, pp. 37–8.

116 *Ibid.*, p. 37.

117 O'Faoláin, *The Short Story*, p. 200.

7 1960–1979: TIME, MEMORY AND IMAGINATION

1 Graham Morison, 'An Ulster Writer: Brian Friel', in *Brian Friel in Conversation*, ed. Paul Delaney (Ann Arbor: University of Michigan Press, 2000), pp. 33. The interview provides an interesting insight into editorial processes at the *New Yorker*.

2 Seán O'Faoláin, *The Heat of the Sun* (Harmondsworth: Penguin, 1983), p. 114.

3 *Ibid.*, p. 307.

4 See Terence Brown, *Ireland: A Social and Cultural History 1922–2002* (London: Harper Perennial, 2004), pp. 254–96.

5 O'Faoláin, *The Heat of the Sun*, p. 124.

6 *Ibid.*, p. 177.

7 Maurice Harmon, *Sean O'Faolain* (London: Constable, 1994), p. 255.

8 *The Irish Times*, 21 January 1978, 11.

9 William Trevor, *The Collected Stories* (Harmondsworth: Penguin, 1992), p. 273.

10 Aidan Higgins, *Felo de Se* (London: John Calder, 1960), pp. 114–15.

11 *The Irish Times*, 6 May 1972, 10. In 1982, 'The Ballroom of Romance' was made into a highly successful film by Pat O'Connor. The influence of cinema on the Irish short story has yet to be explored but it would certainly merit study: both Trevor and O'Brien have commented on the importance of the cinema in the Ireland of their youth.

12 Edna O'Brien, *A Fanatic Heart: Selected Stories* (London: Phoenix, 2003), p. 198.
13 For O'Brien's reworking of Joyce and her later revisions to this story, originally titled 'Come Into the Drawing-Room, Doris', see Rachel Jane Lynch, '"A Land of Strange, Throttled, Sacrificial Women": Domestic Violence in the Short Fiction of Edna O'Brien', *The Canadian Journal of Irish Studies*, 22 (2) (1996), 45–6; and Rebecca Pelan, 'Reflections on a Connemara Dietrich', in *Edna O'Brien: New Critical Perspectives*, ed. K. Laing, S. Mooney and M. O'Connor (Dublin: Carysfort Press, 2006), pp. 12–37.
14 See Brown, *Ireland: a Social and Cultural History*, pp. 236–8.
15 John McGahern, *Collected Stories* (London: Faber and Faber, 1992), p. 100.
16 Eamon Maher, *John McGahern: from the Local to the Universal* (Dublin: The Liffey Press, 2003), p. 149. McGahern is referring specifically to the protagonist of *The Pornographer* (London: Faber and Faber, 1979).
17 Antoinette Quinn, 'Varieties of Disenchantment: Narrative Technique in John McGahern's Short Stories', *Journal of the Short Story in English* 13 (1989), 84.
18 Joe Cleary, *Outrageous Fortune: Capital and Culture in Modern Ireland* (Dublin: Field Day Publications, 2007), pp. 164–5.
19 Anton Chekhov, *Letters on the Short Story, the Drama, and Other Topics*, ed. Louis Friedland (New York: Dover Publications, 1966), p. 60.
20 *The Irish Times*, 1 January 1971, 33.
21 O'Faoláin, *The Heat of the Sun*, p. 153.
22 John McGahern, *Memoir* (London: Faber and Faber, 2005), p. 201.
23 See Eamon Grennan, ' "Only What Happens": Mulling over McGahern', *Irish University Review* 35 (1) (2005), 16–19.
24 Maher, *John McGahern*, p. 155.
25 *Ibid.*, p. 146.
26 *Encounter* 50 (6) (June 1978), 64–71.
27 *The Irish Times*, 17 June 1978, 13.
28 Quoted in I. O'Carroll and E. Collins (eds.), *Lesbian and Gay Visions of Ireland* (London and New York: Cassell, 1995), p. 25.
29 O'Brien, *A Fanatic Heart*, p. 206.
30 *The Irish Times*, 29 June 1968, 10.
31 Maeve Brennan, *The Springs of Affection* (London: Flamingo, 2000), p. 155.
32 Angela Bourke, *Maeve Brennan: Homesick at the 'New Yorker'* (London: Jonathan Cape, 2004), pp. 144–5.
33 *Ibid.*, p. 4.
34 Brennan, *The Springs of Affection*, p. 171.
35 Maeve Kelly, *Orange Horses* (Belfast: The Blackstaff Press, 1991), p. 96.
36 *Ibid.*, pp. 81, 86.
37 *The Irish Times*, 7 September 1974, 12.
38 O'Brien, *A Fanatic Heart*, p. 265.
39 Kelly, *Orange Horses*, p. 49.
40 Margaret Ward (ed.), *In Their Own Voice: Women and Irish Nationalism* (Dublin: Attic Press, 1995), p. 36.

41 Mary Lavin, *In a Café: Selected Stories* (Harmondsworth: Penguin, 1999), p. 1.

42 *Ibid.*, p. 185.

43 McGahern, *Collected Stories*, p. 11.

44 Adrienne Rich, *Of Woman Born: Motherhood as Experience and Institution* (London: Virago, 1977) p. 245.

45 O'Brien, *A Fanatic Heart*, p. 144.

46 Bourke, *Maeve Brennan*, p. 220.

47 Brennan, *The Springs of Affection*, p. 248.

48 Julia Kristeva, 'About Chinese Women', in *The Kristeva Reader*, ed. Toril Moi (Oxford: Basil Blackwell, 1986), p. 153.

49 Brennan, *The Springs of Affection*, p. 249.

50 Carl Jung and C. Kerenyi, *Essays on a Science of Mythology* (New York: Harper and Row, 1963), p. 162.

51 Simone de Beauvoir, *The Second Sex* (Harmondsworth: Penguin, 1972), p. 672.

52 For an extended analysis of this story, see Bernice Schrank and Danine Farquharson, 'Object of Love, Subject to Despair: Edna O'Brien's *The Love Object* and the Emotional Logic of Late Romanticism', *The Canadian Journal of Irish Studies* 22 (2), (1996), 33.

53 O'Brien, *A Fanatic Heart*, p. 173.

54 *The Irish Times*, 22 June 1968, 8.

55 Desmond Hogan, *Stories* (London: Picador, 1982), p. 72.

56 *The Irish Times*, 29 June 1968, 10.

57 *The Sunday Press*, 24 April, 1983, 14.

58 John Morrow, *Northern Myths* (Belfast: Blackstaff Press, 1979), p. 101.

59 Quoted in Maher, *John McGahern*, p. 144.

60 Flann O'Brien, *Stories and Plays* (London: Hart-Davis, MacGibbon, 1973); Tom MacIntyre, *Dance the Dance* (London: Faber and Faber, 1970).

61 Denis Sampson, *Outstaring Nature's Eye: the Fiction of John McGahern* (Dublin: Lilliput Press, 1993).

62 *The Irish Times*, 3 June 1978, 13.

63 *The Irish Times*, 23 September 1980, 8.

64 Seamus Deane in his review of Mary Lavin's *Stories*, *Irish University Review* 4 (2) (1974), 284.

65 S. E. Gontarski, *Samuel Beckett: The Complete Short Prose, 1929–1989* (New York: Grove Press, 1995), p. xii.

66 David Lodge quoted in Gontarski, *Samuel Beckett*, p. xxviii.

67 Samuel Beckett, 'neither', in Gontarski, *Samuel Beckett*, p. 258.

68 *The Irish Times*, 11 March 1995.

69 Hogan, *Stories*, p. 96.

70 Suzanne Poulson, *William Trevor: A Study of the Short Fiction* (New York: Twayne, 1993), p. 125.

71 *Ibid.*

72 William Trevor, *Collected Stories* (Harmondsworth: Penguin, 1992), p. 688.

73 Patrick Grant, *Literature, Rhetoric and Violence in Northern Ireland, 1968–98* (New York: Palgrave, 2001), pp. 150–1.

74 O'Brien, *A Fanatic Heart*, p. 400.
75 *Ibid.*
76 *Ibid.*, p. 403.
77 Heather Ingman, *Twentieth-Century Fiction by Irish Women: Nation and Gender* (Aldershot and Burlington, VT: Ashgate, 2007), pp. 84–7.
78 O'Brien, *A Fanatic Heart*, p. 404.

8 1980 TO THE PRESENT: CHANGING IDENTITIES

1 *The Irish Times*, 12 May 1990, 25.
2 Though not all women were pleased at being included in the category of women writers; see Val Mulkerns' remarks in *The Irish Times*, 25 September 1980, 8.
3 Declan Kiberd, *The Irish Writer and the World* (Cambridge: Cambridge University Press, 2005), pp. 276–8. The Celtic Tiger was the name given to Ireland's unprecedented economic growth during the 1990s.
4 Charles May, *The Short Story: the Reality of Artifice* (New York: Simon and Schuster, 1995), p. 13.
5 Nadine Gordimer, 'The Flash of Fireflies', in *The New Short Story Theories*, ed. Charles May (Athens: Ohio University Press, 1994), pp. 264–5; Mary Lavin, quoted in Leah Levenson, *The Four Seasons of Mary Lavin* (Dublin: Marino Books, 1998), p. 54.
6 Clare Hanson (ed.), *Re-Reading the Short Story* (Basingstoke: Macmillan, 1989), p. 53.
7 *The Irish Times*, 8 May 1982, 13.
8 Evelyn Conlon, *Taking Scarlet as a Real Colour* (Belfast: Blackstaff Press, 1993), p. 67.
9 *The Irish Times*, 13 August 1985, 10.
10 Clare Boylan, *The Collected Stories* (London: Abacus, 2000), p. 105.
11 Evelyn Conlon, *My Head is Opening* (Dublin: Attic Press, 1987), p. 107.
12 Ailbhe Smyth, *Irish Women's Studies Reader* (Dublin: Attic Press, 1993), p. 265.
13 *Ibid.*, p. 266.
14 *The Irish Times*, 13 June 1987, 24.
15 Desmond Hogan, *Stories* (London: Pan, 1982), p. 154.
16 *Ibid.*, p. 159. See also Julia O'Faolain's 'Why Should Not Old Men Be Mad?', in *Daughters of Passion* (Harmondsworth: Penguin, 1982), which takes a tragi-comic view of the plight of the older generation in its portrait of two elderly men, Edward, an ex-Senator, and Michael, a former bishop, who are out of step with the modern age.
17 John McGahern, *The Collected Stories* (London: Faber and Faber, 1993), p. 280. Julia Kristeva's association in 'Women's Time' (1977) of men with linear time and women with cyclical or 'monumental' time (by which she means eternal) provides another route into this story: see Kristeva, 'Women's Time', in *The Portable Kristeva*, ed. Kelly Oliver (New York: Columbia University Press, 1997), pp. 349–69.

18 Eamon Grennan, ' "Only What Happens": Mulling Over McGahern', *Irish University Review* 35 (1) (2005), 17.

19 Peter Finchow (ed.), *The Writer's Place: Interviews on the Literary Situation in Contemporary Britain* (Minneapolis: University of Minnesota Press, 1974), p. 306.

20 William Trevor, *The Collected Stories* (Harmondsworth: Penguin, 1992), p. 869.

21 William Trevor, *Excursions in the Real World: Memoirs* (New York: Alfred A. Knopf, 1994), pp. xi–xii.

22 Mary Dorcey, *A Noise from the Woodshed* (London: Onlywomen Press, 1989), p. 15.

23 Mary Condren, *The Serpent and the Goddess: Women, Religion and Power in Celtic Ireland* (Dublin: New Island Books, 2002), p. 66.

24 Ita Daly, *The Lady with the Red Shoes* (Dublin: Poolbeg Press, 1980), pp. 18–19.

25 Edna O'Brien, *A Fanatic Heart: Selected Stories* (London: Phoenix, 2003), p. 16.

26 *Ibid.*, p. 52.

27 *Ibid.*, p. 123.

28 Michael Storey, *Representing the Troubles in Irish Short Fiction* (Washington, DC: The Catholic University of America Press, 2004), p. 1.

29 Trevor, *The Collected Stories*, p. 751.

30 Patrick Grant, *Literature, Rhetoric and Violence in Northern Ireland, 1968–98* (Basingstoke and New York: Palgrave, 2001).

31 Hogan, *Stories*, p. 237.

32 *Ibid.*, p. 238.

33 Bernard MacLaverty, *The Great Profundo* (London: Vintage, 1997), p. 129.

34 Catherine Shannon, 'The Woman Writer as Historical Witness: Northern Ireland, 1968–1994. An Interdisciplinary Perspective', in *Women and Irish History*, ed. M. Valiulis and M. O'Dowd (Dublin: Wolfhound Press, 1997), p. 249.

35 Anne Devlin, *The Way-Paver* (London: Faber and Faber, 1986), p. 124.

36 *Ibid.*, p. 118.

37 Aidan Higgins, *Helsingør Station and Other Departures, Fictions and Auto-biographies 1956–1989* (London: Secker and Warburg, 1989), p. 49.

38 *Ibid.*

39 Evelyn Conlon, *Telling* (Belfast: The Blackstaff Press, 2000), p. 212.

40 Éilís Ní Dhuibhne's 'Holiday in the Land of Murdered Dreams' was first published as 'The Master Key' in *Ladies' Night at Finbar's Hotel*, ed. Dermot Bolger (Dublin: New Island Books, 1999). It was later published in *Midwife to the Fairies* (Dublin: Attic Press, 2003), p.118.

41 Conlon, *Telling*, p. 212.

42 *Ibid.*, p. 213.

43 Hugo Hamilton, 'The Homesick Industry', in *The Faber Book of Best New Irish Short Stories 2004–5*, ed. David Marcus (London: Faber and Faber, 2005), p. 222.

44 Ní Dhuibhne, *Midwife to the Fairies*, p. 97.

45 For an analysis of the mother–son relationship in Tóibín's collection, see the essays by John McCourt and Anne Fogarty in *Reading Colm Tóibín*, ed. Paul Delaney (Dublin: The Liffey Press, 2008).

46 Anne Enright, *The Portable Virgin* (London: Vintage, 2002), p. 87.

47 *The Irish Times*, 25 February 1991, 8.

48 *The Irish Times*, 2 March 1991, 37.

49 Éilís Ní Dhuibhne, *Eating Women is Not Recommended* (Dublin: Attic Press, 1991), p. 91.

50 *Ibid.*, p. 104.

51 Éilís Ní Dhuibhne, *The Pale Gold of Alaska* (London: Review, 2001), p. 175.

52 Angela Bourke, *By Salt Water* (Dublin: New Island Books, 1996), p. 38.

53 For a detailed analysis of the interweaving of legend and contemporary Ireland in 'Midwife to the Fairies', see Jacqueline Fulmer, *Folk Women and Indirection in Morrison, Ní Dhuibhne, Hurston, and Lavin* (New York: Ashgate, 2007), pp. 149–57. For details of the Kerry Babies case, see *The Field Day Anthology of Irish Literature*, vol. v, ed. Angela Bourke *et al.* (Cork: Cork University Press, 2002), pp. 1439–44.

54 See Donna Wong, 'Literature and the Oral Tradition', in *The Cambridge History of Irish Literature, Volume I: To 1890*, ed. Margaret Kelleher and Philip O'Leary (Cambridge: Cambridge University Press, 2006), pp. 668–9. For an analysis of Bourke's use of folklore to subvert stereotypes about women, see Tudor Balinisteanu, 'Otherworldly Women and Neurotic Fairies: The Cultural Construction of Women in Angela Bourke's Writing', *Irish University Review* 37 (2) (2007), 492–516.

55 *The Irish Times*, 21 October 1991, 9.

56 Joe Cleary, *Outrageous Fortune: Capital and Culture in Modern Ireland* (Dublin: Field Day Publications, 2007), pp. 174–9.

57 Enright, *The Portable Virgin*, p. 155.

58 *Sunday Business Post*, 2 April 2006.

59 William Trevor, *After Rain* (London: Viking, 1996), p. 183.

60 William Wall, *No Paradiso* (Dingle: Brandon, 2006), p. 110.

61 William Trevor, *The Hill Bachelors* (Harmondsworth: Penguin, 2001), p. 206.

62 For Carleton's revisions, see Barbara Hayley, *Carleton's 'Traits and Stories' and the Nineteenth-century Anglo-Irish Tradition* (Gerrards Cross: Colin Smythe, 1983); for O'Connor, see Michael Steinman, *Frank O'Connor at Work* (New York: Syracuse Press, 1990); for Trevor, see Jonathan Bloom, *The Art of Revision in the Short Stories of V. S. Pritchett and William Trevor* (New York and Hampshire: Palgrave, 2006).

63 *The Irish Times*, 26 April 2008, 7.

64 *The Irish Times*, 30 December 1977, 8.

65 Paul Muldoon, *To Ireland, I* (Oxford: Oxford University Press, 2000), p. 5.

66 Proinsias MacCana, 'Early and Middle Irish Literature', in *The Field Day Anthology of Irish Writing*, ed. Seamus Deane, vol. I (Derry: Field Day Publications, 1991), p. 4. See also Seán O'Faoláin *The Irish* (Harmondsworth: Penguin, rev. edn 1980), p. 23.

67 Muldoon, *To Ireland, I*, p. 8.
68 Edgar Allan Poe, 'Review of *Twice-Told Tales*', in May, *The New Short Story Theories*, p. 61.
69 McGahern, *The Collected Stories*, p. 249.
70 Eamon Maher, *John McGahern: from the Local to the Universal* (Dublin: The Liffey Press, 2003), p. 158.
71 McGahern, *The Collected Stories*, p. 271.
72 Cleary, *Outrageous Fortune*, p. 165.
73 Antoinette Quinn, 'Varieties of Disenchantment: Narrative Technique in John McGahern's Short Stories,' *Journal of the Short Story in English* 13 (1989), 79.
74 Maher, *John McGahern*, p. 160.
75 Denis Sampson, 'The "Rich Whole": John McGahern's *Collected Stories* as Autobiography', *Journal of the Short Story in English* 34 (2000), 27.
76 Ní Dhuibhne, *The Pale Gold of Alaska*, p. 75. For a more detailed discussion of intertextual echoes in this story, see Antoinette Larkin's paper, 'Éilís Ní Dhuibhne Re-Presents Ireland: William Leech, Edith Somerville and "Nomads Seek the Pavilions of Bliss on the Slopes of Middle Age"', presented to the International Association for the Study of Irish Literatures conference in 2004.
77 Ní Dhuibhne, *The Pale Gold of Alaska*, p. 75.
78 *Ibid.*, p. 85.
79 *Ibid.*, p. 84.
80 *Ibid.*, p. 89.
81 *Ibid.*
82 Rosi Braidotti, *Nomadic Subjects: Embodiment and Sexual Difference in Contemporary Feminist Theory* (New York: Columbia University Press, 1994), p. 2.
83 Ní Dhuibhne, *The Pale Gold of Alaska*, p. 76.
84 *Ibid.*, p. 92.
85 Braidotti, *Nomadic Subjects*, p. 6.
86 Anne Fogarty, Introduction, Éilís Ní Dhuibhne, *Midwife to the Fairies*, p. xiv.

Biographic glossary

DCU Dublin City University
DUM Dublin University Magazine
QUB Queen's University, Belfast
TCD Trinity College, Dublin
UCC University College, Cork
UCD University College, Dublin

Banim, John (1798–1842); b. Kilkenny; father prosperous Catholic farmer and trader; ed. Kilkenny College; 1813–1815 studied art in Dublin; taught art in Kilkenny; early unhappy love affair affected his health; thereafter abandoned art for literature and lived in Dublin, London (where he assisted Gerald Griffin), Paris and Kilkenny; novelist, playwright, poet; first success with *Damon and Pythias* performed in Covent Garden 1821; wrote twenty-four tales with his brother Michael (1796–1874) under the pseudonym 'The O'Hara family'; died of spinal tuberculosis.

Banville, John (1945–); b. Wexford; ed. St Peter's College, Wexford; literary editor of *The Irish Times* from 1988; first publication short story collection, *Long Lankin* (1970, revised 1984); subsequently turned to novels, plays and screenplays; novels include his scientific trilogy, *Doctor Copernicus* (1976), *Kepler* (1981), *The Newton Letter* (1982) as well as *The Book of Evidence* (1989), *The Untouchable* (1997); *The Sea* won the Booker Prize in 2005.

Bardwell, Leland (1928–); b. India of Irish parents; returned to Ireland in 1932 and grew up in Co. Kildare; has lived most of her life in Ireland and London; from 1970 published novels, poetry, plays and short stories; novels include *Girl on a Bicycle* (1977), *The House* (1984) and *Mother to a Stranger* (2002); poetry includes *Dostoevsky's Grave* (1993) and *The White Beach* (1998); short stories, *Different Kinds of Love* (1987).

Barlow, Jane (1857–1917); b. Clontarf, Co. Dublin; daughter of TCD vice-provost; poet, short story writer and novelist; nationalist, friend of Yeats and Tynan; poetry includes *Bogland Studies* (1892); nineteen fiction titles include *Irish Idylls* (1892), sketches of peasant life in Connemara, followed by *Strangers at Lisconnel: a Second Series of Irish Idylls* (1895); other collections include *Maureen's Fairing and Other Stories* (1896), *Mrs Martin's Company* (1896), *From the East unto the West* (1898), *From the Land of the Shamrock* (1900), *By Beach and*

Bogland (1905), *Irish Neighbours* (1907), *Irish Ways* (1909), *Doings and Dealings* (1913).

Beckett, Mary (1926–); b. Belfast; worked as a primary school teacher in Ardoyne before moving to Dublin in 1956; in the 1950s her stories were published in *The Bell*; two collections of stories, *A Belfast Woman* (1980) and *A Literary Woman* (1990); novel, *Give Them Stones* (1987); several children's books.

Beckett, Samuel (1906–89); b. Dublin into a Protestant, professional family; ed. Portora Royal School, Enniskillen and TCD; lived in Paris most of his life; became close friend of Joyce; worked for the French Resistance; wrote prose and poetry during the 1930s and 1940s; his first published piece was an essay on *Finnegans Wake*; his short story collection, *More Pricks than Kicks* (1934), banned in Ireland, was heavily influenced by Joyce; other writing from this period includes poetry collection, *Whoroscope* (1930), a study of Proust (1931) and novels *Murphy* (1938), *Watt* (1944); subsequent novels include his trilogy *Molloy, Malone Dies* and *The Unnameable* (1959); found fame with his play, *Waiting for Godot* (1953); from the mid-fifties wrote for stage, radio, film and television; equally at ease in French and English; subsequent plays include *End Game* (1957), *Krapp's Last Tape* (1959), *Breath* (1969), *Not I* (1972); Nobel Prize for Literature, 1969.

Bell, Sam Hanna (1909–90); b. Glasgow of Irish parents; raised in Co. Down; studied at the Belfast College of Art; 1945–64 worked as a radio producer for the BBC; novelist, short story writer and playwright; short story collection, *Summer Loanen and Other Stories* (1943); novels include *December Bride* (1951) later filmed; non-fiction includes *Erin's Orange Lily: Ulster Customs and Folklore* (1956).

Bolger, Dermot (1959–); b. Finglas, Co. Dublin; ed. St Canice's and Beneavin College; poet, playwright, novelist and publisher; co-founded the Irish Writers' Co-operative with Neil Jordan and others; founder of Raven Arts Press (1979) and co-founded New Island in 1992; plays include *The Lament for Arthur Cleary* (1989); novels include *Father's Music* (1997), *Night Shift* (1985), *The Journey Home* (1990); edited short story collections, *Finbar's Hotel* (1997) and *Ladies' Night at Finbar's Hotel* (1999) and, with Ciaran Carty, *The Hennessy Book of Irish Fiction* (1995).

Bourke, Angela (1952–); b. Dublin; senior lecturer in Irish at UCD; lectured widely in Europe and the USA on the Irish oral tradition and literature; *By Salt Water* (1996) was her first short story collection; non-fiction, *The Burning of Bridget Cleary: a True Story* (1999); co-editor of *The Field Day Anthology of Irish Writing*, vols. iv and v; biography of Maeve Brennan (2004).

Bowen, Elizabeth (1899–1973); b. Dublin; ed. in England after mother's death; 1923 married Alan Cameron and thereafter divided her time between Oxford, London and her family home, Bowen's Court (Co. Cork) which she inherited in 1930; equally distinguished in novels and short stories; between 1927 and 1969 published ten novels, including *The Last September* (1929), on the Anglo-Irish; her first story collection was *Encounters* (1923); subsequently published numerous collections including *Anne Lee's and Other Stories* (1926), *Joining*

Charles (1929), *The Cat Jumps* (1934), *Look at All Those Roses* (1941), *The Demon Lover* (1945), *A Day in the Dark* (1965); non-fiction includes a history of Bowen's Court (1942), a memoir of her Dublin childhood (1942) and a history of the Shelbourne hotel (1951); during the 1950s she taught in the USA; 1959 left Ireland after selling Bowen's Court; honorary doctorates from TCD and Oxford; made Companion of Literature, 1965.

Boylan, Clare (1948–2006); lived most of her life in Dublin; journalist with *The Irish Press*, editor of *Image* magazine, short story writer and novelist; novels include *Holy Pictures* (1983), *Black Baby* (1988), *Room for a Single Lady* (1997) and *Emma Brown* (2003); three short story collections, *A Nail on the Head* (1983), *Concerning Virgins* (1989), *That Bad Woman* (1995); her *Collected Short Stories* appeared in 2000.

Boyle, Patrick (1905–82); b. Ballymoney, Co. Antrim; worked for Ulster Bank in Derry, Tyrone and Donegal for forty-five years, eventually becoming bank manager in Wexford; he was sixty when most of his work appeared; one novel, *Like Any Other Man* (1966), and three short story collections, *At Night All Cats are Grey* (1966), *All Looks Yellow to the Jaundiced Eye* (1969), *A View from Calvary* (1976).

Brennan, Maeve (1917–1993); b. Dublin to parents involved in the republican movement; brought up in Ranelagh, which provides the setting for many of her stories; ed. Scoil Bríghide; moved to Washington in 1934 when her father appointed Secretary of the Irish Legation; ed. the Immaculata Seminary, the American University and the Catholic University of America; worked as a fashion writer for *Harper's Bazaar* and from 1949 as a staff writer with the *New Yorker* for thirty years, contributing short stories, fashion notes, book reviews, sketches of New York life under the persona 'The Long-Winded Lady'; 1954 married fellow *New Yorker* writer, St Clair Kelway and moved to Snedens Landing, but the marriage foundered amidst debt and alcoholism; from 1959, Brennan lived alone in rented rooms in Manhattan; in the 1970s she suffered a mental breakdown and from then on was in and out of hospitals; her short stories appeared in the *New Yorker* between 1953 and 1972, were collected in *In and Out of Never-Never Land* (1969) and *Christmas Eve* (1974), and more recently in *The Springs of Affection* (1997) and *The Rose Garden* (2000); her novella, 'The Visitor', written in the 1940s, was rediscovered and published posthumously in 2001.

Carleton, William (1794–1869); b. Co. Tyrone, youngest of fourteen children of a Catholic tenant farmer; grew up bilingual; ed. various hedge schools; pilgrimage to Lough Derg in 1817 a life-changing experience that diverted him from the priesthood into literature; changed political and religious allegiances, moving from Ribbonman to Protestant convert; in Dublin began writing sketches for the anti-Catholic *Christian Examiner*; contributed to the *DUM*, *The Nation*, *The Irish Penny Journal* and many others; *Traits and Stories of the Irish Peasantry* (1830–3) established him as the first major Irish Catholic writer in English; novels include *Fardarougha the Miser*, serialized in the *DUM* (1837–8), *Valentine M'Clutchy* (1841), *The Black Prophet* (1847); began an autobiography before his death, completed by David O'Donoghue and published in two volumes, *The Life of William Carleton* (1896).

Conlon, Evelyn (1952–); b. Co. Monaghan; lived for a number of years in Australia; travelled widely in New Zealand, Asia and the Soviet Union before studying at St Patrick's College, Maynooth; founder member of the Dublin Rape Crisis Centre; short stories, novels, scripts; novels include *Stars in the Daytime* (1989), *A Glassful of Letters* (1998); short story collections, *My Head is Opening* (1987), *Taking Scarlet as a Real Colour* (1993), *Telling* (2000).

Corkery, Daniel (1878–1964); b. Cork; ed. St Patrick's Teacher Training College, Dublin; taught in elementary schools in Cork until 1931; actively involved in the Gaelic League and the Irish Ireland movement; 1908 co-founded the Cork Dramatic Society, for which he wrote his first plays; also wrote short stories, journalism and a novel, *The Threshold of Quiet* (1917); short story collections, *A Munster Twilight* (1916), *The Hounds of Banba* (1919), *The Stormy Hills* (1929), *Earth out of Earth* (1939); non-fiction includes *The Hidden Ireland* (1925), a study of the Gaelic poets of eighteenth-century Munster, and the contentious and nationalistic *Synge and Anglo-Irish Literature* (1931); Professor of English, UCC, 1931–47; Senator, 1951–4.

Croker, Thomas Crofton (1798–1854); b. Cork; held a position in the Admiralty 1818–50; antiquarian, collected Irish poetry, songs and folklore; publications include *Researches into the South of Ireland* (1824) based on walking tours he took between 1812 and 1822 in the south of Ireland; it went into six editions and was translated by the Brothers Grimm; *Fairy Legends and Traditions of the South of Ireland* (1825) was edited by Croker but written by many different people; *Popular Songs of Ireland* (1837); d. London.

Daly, Ita (1945–); b. Co. Leitrim; ed. UCD; worked as a teacher; lives in Dublin; won two Hennessy Awards – in 1972 for 'Virginibus Pueresque' and in 1975 for 'The Lady with the Red Shoes', later published in her collection of the same name in 1980; novels include *A Singular Attraction* (1987), *Dangerous Fictions* (1989), *All Fall Down* (1992), *Unholy Ghosts* (1996); has also published children's books.

Devlin, Anne (1951–); raised in Andersonstown; studied English in Coleraine; taught in Antrim before moving to Germany in 1976; 1984 moved to Birmingham, UK; 1982, won a Hennessy Award for her short story, 'Passages', later published in *The Way-Paver* (1986); plays include *The Long March* (1982), *Ourselves Alone* (1985), first produced at the Royal Court Theatre, London and won several awards, *After Easter* (1994), produced in Stratford-upon-Avon and Belfast; both stories and plays deal with the lives of Catholic women during the Troubles in Northern Ireland; several radio and TV screenplays, including *Naming the Names* (1987).

Donoghue, Emma (1969–); b. Dublin; ed. Mount Anvill, Muckross Park Convent, UCD and Cambridge; now lives in Canada; short story writer, novelist, playwright and literary historian; lesbian coming-of-age novel, *Stir-Fry* (1994); *Hood* (1995); historical novels, *Slammerkin* (2000) and *Life Mask* (2004), and contemporary novel about emigration, *Landing* (2007); fairy tales,

Kissing the Witch (1997); collection of historical stories, *The Woman Who Gave Birth to Rabbits* (2002), followed by *Touchy Subjects* (2006); historical studies include *Passions Between Women: British Lesbian Culture 1668–1801* (1993) and *We Are Michael Field* (1998).

Dorcey, Mary (1950–); b. Dublin; ed. Open University, UK and the University of Paris; founder member of Women for Radical Change; lived and worked in England, France, Spain, the USA and Japan; poet, novelist and short story writer; poetry collections include *Kindling* (1982), *Moving into the Space Cleared by Our Mothers* (1991), *The River That Carries Me* (1995), *Like Joy in Season, Like Sorrow* (2001); novel, *Biography of Desire* (1997); her short story collection, A *Noise from the Woodshed* (1989), was awarded the Rooney Prize for Irish Literature.

Doyle, Roddy (1958–); b. and lives in Dublin; novels, plays, children's books; found fame with *The Barrytown Trilogy* (*The Commitments* (1987), *The Snapper* (1989), *The Van* (1991)), all successfully filmed; *Paddy Clarke Ha Ha Ha* won the Booker Prize in 1993; other novels include *The Woman Who Walked into Doors* (1996), *A Star Called Henry* (1999), *Oh, Play That Thing* (2004), *Paula Spencer* (2006); published short stories in *Metro Eireann,* Ireland's first multicultural paper, collected as *The Deportees and Other Stories* (2007).

Duffaud, Briege; b. to a Catholic family in Co. Armagh; lived in England and Holland, now lives in Brittany; freelance journalist, novelist and short story writer; novels, *A Wreath Upon the Dead* (1993), set in Northern Ireland; *A Long Stem Rose* (1995), set in France; short stories, set in Ireland and France, *Nothing Like Beirut* (1994).

Edgeworth, Maria (1767/8–1849); b. Oxfordshire to a Protestant Ascendancy family; ed. in England; returned to Edgesworthstown (Co. Longford) in 1782 to help her father run the estate and rear her numerous siblings; first book, *Letters for Literary Ladies* (1795), published anonymously, is a defence of female education; collaborated with her father on educational treatise, *Practical Education* (1798); children's stories, *The Parent's Assistant* (1796) and *Moral Tales* (1801); English society novels, *Belinda* (1801) and *Helen* (1834), emphasize women's domestic and educational responsibilities; Irish novels, *Castle Rackrent* (1800), *Ennui* (1809), *The Absentee* (1812), *Ormond* (1817), criticize absentee landlords; came into contact with leading literary figures of the period, including Sir Walter Scott, on whose writing she had a strong influence.

Egerton, George (1859–1945); b. Mary Chavelita Dunne, Melbourne, Australia to an Irish father and Welsh mother; lived in, among other places, New Zealand, Chile, Dublin, Germany, New York, Norway and Co. Cork; after her mother's death in 1875, cared for her siblings in Dublin; 1887 eloped to Norway with Henry Higginson and came under the influence of the Scandinavian modernists; 1892 settled in Millstreet, County Cork with her first husband, Canadian novelist, George Egerton Clairmonte; first short story collection, *Keynotes* (1893), marked her as a New Woman writer; after her second collection, *Discords* (1894), moved to London and frequented decadent and aesthetic circles; autobiographical novel, *The Wheel of God*, published 1898; after the disappointing reception of her subsequent story collections, *Symphonies* (1896), *Fantasias* (1898) and *Flies in Amber* (1905), and her marriage to theatrical agent, Reginald Bright, turned to writing plays; *His Wife's Family* was accepted by Shaw and performed in London in 1907, but she had little success thereafter; the death of her son in World War I effectively ended her literary career.

Enright, Anne (1962–); b. Dublin; ed. Vancouver and TCD; MA Creative Writing University of East Anglia; worked as television producer and broadcaster with RTE; short story collection, *The Portable Virgin* (1991), won the Rooney Prize for Literature; second collection, *Taking Pictures* (2008); novels, *The Wig My Father Wore* (1995), *What Are You Like?* (2000), *The Pleasure of Eliza Lynch* (2002); *The Gathering* won the Booker Prize, 2007; non-fiction, *Making Babies: Stumbling into Motherhood* (2004).

Ferguson, Samuel (1810–86); b. Belfast; ed. TCD; called to the Irish bar 1838; lived in Dublin for most of his life; knighted 1878; 1881 President of the Royal Irish Academy; antiquarian, with interests in poetry, Gaelic culture, archaeology, science and public administration; contributed to *Blackwood's Magazine* and the *DUM*; publications include *Lays of the Western Gael* (1867), *Hibernian Nights' Entertainment* (1887), *Congal: an Epic Poem* (1872), *Poems* (1880), *The Remains of St Patrick* (1888).

Friel, Brian (1929–); b. Omagh, Co. Tyrone; ed. St Columb's College, Derry, St Patrick's College, Maynooth and St Mary's Training College, Belfast; taught in Derry 1950–60; wrote short stories (his first was published in *The Bell* in 1952, others in the *New Yorker*) before finding fame as a playwright with such plays as *Philadelphia, Here I Come!* (1964), *Faith Healer* (1979), *Translations* (1980) and *Dancing at Lughnasa* (1990); two volumes of short stories, *The Saucer of Larks* (1962) and *The Gold in the Sea* (1966). *The Diviner: Brian Friel's Best Short Stories* edited by Seamus Deane in 1983.

Grand, Sarah (1854–1943); b. Frances Clarke, Donaghadee, Co. Down; English parents, father a naval lieutenant; 1856 moved to Mayo, 1861 to London; at sixteen married a thirty-nine-year-old naval surgeon; lived with him in Hong Kong and Far East, Norwich and Warrington; separated 1890 and moved to London to write; short story collections include *Our Manifold Nature* (1894) and *Emotional Moments* (1908); novels include the highly successful *The Heavenly Twins* (1893), featuring syphilis, and *The Beth Book: A Study in the Life of a Woman of Genius* (1897); moved to Bath in 1920, where she was several times mayoress.

Griffin, Gerald (1803–40); b. Limerick into Catholic merchant class family; 1823 moved to London to write, encouraged by John Banim; worked as a journalist in London and wrote for the stage; poverty and the failure of his play, *Aguire*, in 1824, made him turn to short fiction; returned to Ireland in 1827, the same year that *'Holland-Tide'* and *Tales of the Munster Festivals* appeared; found fame with his novel *The Collegians* (1829); other publications include the

Gothic novel, *The Rivals and Tracey's Ambition* (1830), *Tales of My Neighbourhood* (1835), a historical novel, *The Duke of Monmouth* (1836) and the posthumous *Talis Qualis, or, Tales of the Jury Room* (1842); growth of religious scruples marred his later work; after an unhappy love affair, he burned his manuscripts and joined the Christian Brothers in 1838; died in the North Monastery, Cork.

Hall, Anna Maria (1800–81); b. Anna Maria Fielding in Dublin of Huguenot descent, but spent much of her childhood in Co. Wexford; moved to London at the age of fifteen; married Samuel Carter Hall, an editor and publisher; together they travelled widely and published numerous travel books; a popular regional writer; *Sketches of the Irish Character* (1829); *Lights and Shadows of Irish Life* (1838); *Stories of the Irish Peasantry* (1850).

Hamilton, Hugo (1953–); b. Dublin to a German mother and an Irish father who insisted he speak only Irish or German; recounts his upbringing in the widely praised memoir, *The Speckled People* (2003) and its sequel, *The Sailor in the Wardrobe* (2006); novels include three set in Central Europe, two crime novels set in Dublin, *Headbanger* (1996) and *Sad Bastard* (1998); short story collection, *Dublin Where the Palm Trees Grow* (1996).

Harbinson, Robert (1928–); b. Robert Harbinson Bryans to a working-class Protestant household in Belfast; his father, a window cleaner, died when he was five; his mother took in lodgers and worked as a cleaner; became an apprentice in Harland and Wolff, then attended the Barry School of Evangelism in South Wales; went to Canada intending to convert Native Americans, but got diverted into writing travel books during the 1960s and early 1970s; between 1960 and 1963 published four volumes of autobiography and two collections of short stories, *Tattoo Lily* (1961) and *The Far World* (1962).

Healy, Dermot (1947–); b. Finea, Co. Westmeath and brought up in Cavan; editor, director and actor; has published stories, novels, four collections of poetry and nine plays; story collection, *Banished Misfortune* (1982); novels, *Fighting with Shadows* (1984), *A Goat's Song* (1994), *Sudden Times* (1999); memoir, *The Bend for Home* (1996).

Higgins, Aidan (1927–); b. Celbridge, Co. Kildare to a landed Catholic family; ed. Clongowes Wood College; lived in Spain, Germany, South Africa and the UK; now lives in Kinsale, Co. Cork; published short stories, novels and travel books; novels include *Langrishe, Go Down* (1966), awarded the James Tait Black Memorial Prize for Fiction and later adapted for television by Harold Pinter; *Balcony of Europe* (1972), *Bornholm Night-Ferry* (1983); short story collections, *Felo de Se* (1961; reprinted as *Killachter Meadow*, 1961); *Helsingør Station and Other Departures* (1989); three volumes of memoirs.

Hogan, Desmond (1951–); b. Ballinasloe, Galway; studied at UCD; novels, plays, short stories; novels include *The Ikon Maker* (1976), *Leaves on Grey* (1980), *A Curious Street* (1984), *A New Shirt* (1986), and *Farewell to Prague* (1995); short story collections, *The Diamonds at the Bottom of the Sea* (the John Llewellyn Rhys memorial prize, 1980), *The Children of Lir* (1981), *The Mourning Thief* (1987), *Larks Eggs: New and Selected Stories* (2005); in 1997, he received the

Rooney Award for Irish Literature; new story, 'Red Tide' published in *The Faber Book of Best New Irish Stories 2006–7*.

Hoult, Norah (1898–1984); b. Dublin of an Irish Catholic mother and English Protestant father; after the death of her parents attended English schools; journalist for the *Sheffield Daily Telegraph*; after the success of *Poor Women!* became a full-time writer and returned to Ireland in 1931; lived in the USA 1937–9, in London 1939–57, in Ireland 1957–84; between 1928 and 1972 published twenty-five books; short story collections, *Poor Women!* (1928), *Nine Years Is a Long Time* (1938), *Selected Stories* (1946) and *Cocktail Bar* (1950); novels, psychological and sociological studies of women's lives, include *Holy Ireland* (1935), *Coming from the Fair* (1937), *Father and Daughter* (1957), *Husband and Wife* (1959), all set in Ireland.

Jordan, Neil (1951–); b. Sligo and raised in Dublin; set up the Irish Writers' Co-operative in 1974; first attracted attention with his short story collection, *Night in Tunisia* (1976), which won the Guardian Fiction Prize; novels, *The Past* (1980), *The Dream of a Beast* (1983), *Sunrise with Sea Monster* (1994), *Shade* (2004); since writing and directing his first feature film, *Angel*, in 1982, has become an acclaimed director whose films include *Mona Lisa*, *The Crying Game*, for which he won an Oscar, *Michael Collins* and *The Butcher Boy*.

Joyce, James (1882–1941); b. Rathgar, Dublin; ed. Clongowes Wood College, Belvedere and UCD; after graduation in 1902 moved to Paris but was summoned home when his mother was dying; lived in a Martello Tower with Oliver St John Gogarty and taught in a school in Dalkey; began publishing poems and short stories in magazines; left Ireland in 1904 with Nora Barnacle to live in Trieste, Rome, Paris and Zurich; returned to Ireland twice in 1909 and for the last time in 1912; after a frustrating wait, his short stories were eventually published as *Dubliners* in 1914, followed by *A Portrait of the Artist as a Young Man* (1916), *Ulysses* (1922), *Collected Poems* (1936) and *Finnegans Wake* (1939); d. Zurich.

Keegan, Claire (1968–); b. Co. Wicklow; grew up on a farm; ed. Loyola University, New Orleans; first short story collection, *Antarctica* (1999), won numerous awards including the 2000 Rooney Prize for Irish Literature; writer in residence at DCU; second collection, *Walk the Blue Fields*, published in 2007.

Kelly, Maeve (1930–); b. Co. Clare; grew up in Dundalk, Co. Louth; trained as a nurse in London and Oxford; farmed for many years in Co. Clare; founder member of the Limerick Federation of Women's Organizations and of Adapt, centre for abused women and their children; published novels, short stories and poetry; poetry, *Resolution* (1986); novels, *Necessary Treasons* (1985), *Florrie's Girls* (1989), *Alice in Thunderland* (1993); short story collections, *A Life of Her Own* (1976) (the title story won a Hennessy Award) and *Orange Horses* (1990).

Kiely, Benedict (1919–2007); b. Dromore, Co. Tyrone, ed. Christian Brothers in Omagh; 1937 entered the Jesuit novitiate in Co. Laois; left to study at UCD; lectured widely in Ireland and the USA; short story writer, journalist, playwright, novelist, radio and TV broadcaster; leader writer and literary critic for the *Irish Independent*; novels include *Nothing Happens in Carmincross* (1985), novella, 'Proxopera' (1977); non-fiction, *Poor Scholar* (1947), a study of William Carleton; first collection of short stories, *A Journey to the Seven Streams* (1963) followed by *A Ball of Malt and Madame Butterfly* (1973), *A Cow in the House* (1978), *A Letter to Peachtree* (1987), culminating in his *Collected Stories* (2001); autobiography, *Drink to the Bird: an Omagh Boyhood* (1992) and *The Waves Behind Us* (1999).

Laffan (Hartley), May (c. 1850–1916); b. Blackrock, Dublin; Catholic but in 1882 married Walter Hartley, a Protestant lecturer at King's College, London and later at the Royal College of Science in Dublin; published anonymously four Irish novels, *Hogan, M.P.* (1876), a satire on newly rich middle-class Catholics, *The Hon. Miss Ferrard* (1877), *Christy Carew* (1880), *Ismay's Children* (1887); pioneer in Irish urban realism; her tales set in Dublin's slums appeared in *Flitters, Tatters and the Counsellor and Other Sketches* (London, 1879), featured on Yeats' list of best Irish books (1895) and were praised by John Ruskin; her interest in children's welfare led her to work for the NSPCC (1889–93); spent 1910–16 in Bloomfield Asylum, Dublin, where she died.

Lavin, Mary (1912–96); b. in the USA to Irish parents; returned to Ireland in 1921; ed. Loreto College, Dublin and UCD; 1942 married William Walsh (d. 1954) and ran Abbey Farm in Co. Meath; three daughters; her Dublin home, the Mews, became a magnet for young writers in the 1950s and 1960s; 1969 married ex-priest Michael Scott, a friend since UCD days; two novels, *The House in Clewe Street* (1945) and *Mary O'Grady* (1950) and a novella, 'The Becker Wives' (1946); but best known as short story writer; published in, among others, *Harper's Bazaar*, the *New Yorker*, the *Atlantic Monthly* and *The Bell*; nineteen collections starting with *Tales from Bective Bridge* (1942) and including *The Great Wave* (1961), *In the Middle of the Fields* (1967), *Happiness* (1969), *A Memory and Other Stories* (1972); awarded a Guggenheim fellowship in 1959 and 1961; 1964–5, President of Irish PEN; 1972–4, President of the Irish Academy of Letters.

Lawless, Emily (1845–1913); b. Co. Kildare into a family recently recruited to the Ascendancy; poet, novelist, biographer, botanist, marine zoologist; best-known novels are set in Ireland, *Hurrish* (1886), *Grania* (1892), *Plain Frances Mowbray and Other Tales* (1889); essays and short fiction in *Traits and Confidences* (1897); historical novels, *With Essex in Ireland* (1890) and *Maelcho* (1894); biography, *Maria Edgeworth* (1904); first collection of poems, *With the Wild Geese* (1902); unsympathetic to Home Rule but critical of British government in Ireland; awarded honorary DLitt by TCD in 1905; 1910, founder member of United Irishwomen (Irish Countrywomen's Association since 1935); from mid-1890s lived in England but continued to visit Ireland.

Le Fanu, Joseph Sheridan (1814–73); Huguenot ancestry; father Church of Ireland clergyman, first in Dublin, then in Limerick; ed. TCD and King's Inns, Dublin; called to the bar 1839; married Susanna 1844 (d. 1858); first short fiction published in 1838 in the *DUM*, of which he later became editor and proprietor; novels include *The House by the Churchyard* (1861–3) and *Uncle*

Silas (1864); short fiction collected in *Ghost Stories and Tales of Mystery* (1851), *Chronicles of Golden Friars* (1871), *In a Glass Darkly* (1872); *The Purcell Papers* was published posthumously in 1880.

Leitch, Maurice (1933–); b. Co. Antrim; worked initially as a schoolteacher and then as a producer for the BBC in London and Belfast; novels include *The Liberty Lad* (1965), *Poor Lazarus* (1969), *Silver's City* (1981), for which he won a Whitbread Award, and *Gilcrist* (1994); short story collection, *The Hands of Cheryl Boyd and Other Stories* (1987).

Lover, Samuel (1797–1868); b. Dublin; ed. privately; painter, song writer, playwright, novelist; 1831, first series of his very successful *Legends and Stories of Ireland*, based on oral tales collected in the west of Ireland (second series, 1834); *Songs and Ballads* (1839); 1833, co-founded the *DUM*; 1837, moved to London and became a successful society painter; founded *Bentley's Miscellany* with Dickens; novel, *Handy Andy* (1842), was serialized there; wrote several dramas and musicals, including the stage version of his novel, *Rory O'More* and a burlesque opera, *Il Paddy Whack in Italia* (1841), produced at the English Opera House; 1846–8 toured USA and Canada with his one-man show of songs and stories; in the latter part of his life devoted himself to song writing.

Macardle, Dorothy (1889–1958); b. Dundalk into a wealthy brewing family; ed. Alexandra College and UCD; taught at Alexandra College; member of Cumann na mBan and Sinn Féin; republican activist during the war of independence and the civil war; friend of de Valera but also worked for the feminist cause; arrested in 1922, imprisoned in Mountjoy and Kilmainham jails, where she wrote many of the stories in *Earth-bound* (1924); became involved with the League of Nations; helped refugee children during and after World War II and wrote *Children of Europe* (1949); novels, plays, short stories, journalism; film and drama critic for *The Irish Press*; her best-known work is *The Irish Republic* (1937), a history of the war of independence from a republican perspective.

MacCartan, Hugh (1885–?); b. Co. Down; civil servant, lived in Belfast and Dublin; *Little White Roads and Other Poems* (1916); *Silhouettes: Some Character Studies of the North and South* (1918); *The Glamour of Belfast* (1921); *O'Neill's Folly* (1929).

McCabe, Eugene (1930–); b. Glasgow; moved to Ireland 1939; ed. UCC; farmed on the Monaghan–Fermanagh border from 1964; playwright, including *King of the Castle* (1964; filmed 1977); screenplays, children's literature; novels include *Death and Nightingales* (1992); in 1976 wrote *Cancer*, a trilogy of plays for TV; out of this published a novella, 'Victims' (1976) and short stories, 'Cancer' and 'Heritage' in *Heritage* (1978); his short stories from 1970s, 1980s and 1990s collected in *Heaven Lies About Us* (2005).

McCann, Colum (1965–); b. Dublin, lived in Japan, now lives in New York; his first story collection, *Fishing the Sloe-Black River* (1993), won the Rooney Prize for Irish Literature; novels, *Songdogs* (1995), *This Side of Brightness* (1998), *A Dancer* (2003), *Zoli* (2007); short story collection and novella, *Everything in this Country Must* (2000).

McGahern, John (1934–2006); b. Dublin, one of seven children; father a Garda sergeant and mother a national school teacher; lived with his mother in different parts of Leitrim while his father worked in Co. Roscommon; after mother's death in 1944 he and his siblings moved to the Guards' barracks at Cootehall; ed. the Presentation Brothers' Secondary School in Carrick-on-Shannon and St Patrick's College, Drumcondra; 1954 taught in Drogheda; moved to Dublin in 1955 to teach in Clontarf; started to frequent Dublin literary circles; 1957 BA from UCD; 1963 *The Barracks* was published to critical acclaim; won the Macaulay Fellowship and took a year's sabbatical; 1965 *The Dark* was banned in Ireland, McGahern fired from his teaching job, moved to London and worked on building sites; 1968 Research Fellow at the University of Reading; 1970 published his first collection of short stories, *Nightlines*, and began farming in Co. Leitrim; 1972 Visiting Professor in USA; during this period short stories were important for keeping his creativity alive; *Getting Through* (1978), *High Ground* (1985); in 1990, published *Amongst Women*, his first novel since 1979, shortlisted for the Booker Prize; first *Collected Stories* appeared in 1992; subsequently revised and arguably weakened in *Creatures of the Earth* (2006); widely praised elegiac novel, *That They May Face the Rising Sun* (2002); autobiographical *Memoir* (2005).

Macken, Walter (1915–67); b. Galway; joined the Taibhdhearc, Irish language theatre, where in 1939 he became manager; began writing in Irish and English; 1946 his first play in English, *Mungo's Mansion*, staged at the Abbey Theatre; 1948 joined the Abbey Theatre; after a successful USA tour became a full-time writer; popular novelist; eleven novels, a historical trilogy, children's books, plays and three books of short stories.

MacLaverty, Bernard (1942–); b. Belfast; worked for ten years as a medical lab technician before studying English at QUB; moved to Scotland to teach; lives in Glasgow and writes full time; novels, short stories, radio, TV and screenplays; novels include *Lamb* (1980), *Cal* (1983), both successfully made into films, *Grace Notes* (1997), shortlisted for the Booker Prize, and *The Anatomy School* (2001); short story collections, *Secrets* (1977), *A Time to Dance* (1982), *The Great Profundo* (1987), *Walking the Dog* (1994), *Matters of Life and Death* (2006).

McLaverty, Michael (1904–92); b. Co. Monaghan but lived in Belfast most of his life; spent childhood holidays on Rathlin Island, which features in many of his stories; ed. St Malachy's College, Belfast and QUB; trained as a teacher in London and worked as a teacher and later headmaster in Belfast; published eight novels between 1939 and 1965, including *Call My Brother Back* (1939) and *Lost Fields* (1941); but especially known for short stories, *The White Mare* (1943) and *The Game Cock* (1947); 1964 retired from teaching hoping to become a full-time writer but suffered writer's block, from which he recovered, encouraged by David Marcus' publication of a short story in his 'New Irish Writing' page in *The Irish Press* in 1968; new collection of stories *The Road to the Shore* (1976); *Collected Short Stories* (1978).

MacMahon, Bryan (1909–98); b. Listowel, Co. Kerry, where he taught for forty-four years, eventually becoming principal of Listowel National School;

storyteller and pioneer of national education in the new Irish state; novels, short stories, plays, TV scripts and children's books; contributed to *The Bell*; first collection of stories, *The Lion-Tamer* (1948), followed by many more, including *The Red Petticoat* (1955), *The End of the World* (1976), *The Sound of Hooves* (1985); autobiographical memoir, *The Master* (1992); *Peig* (1973), translation of Peig Sayers's autobiography.

MacNamara, Brinsley (1890–1963); b. John Weldon, near Delvin, Co. Westmeath; 1909–12 acted with the Abbey Players and toured in the USA, 1911–13; later succeeded James Stephens as registrar of the National Gallery, Dublin; between 1919 and 1945 had nine plays produced at the Abbey Theatre, Dublin; his novel, *The Valley of the Squinting Windows* (1918), was his best-known and most controversial work; other novels include *The Clanking of the Chains* (1920), *The Various Lives of Marcus Igoe* (1929); one short story collection, *The Smiling Faces* (1929).

Maginn, William (1793–1842); b. Cork; ed. TCD; taught at his father's old school; in 1823 moved to London to pursue a literary career; contributed articles, stories, reviews and verse to *Blackwood's Magazine* and *Fraser's Magazine*, which he founded; in 1842 appeared before the bankruptcy court and died later that year of consumption contracted in prison; *Ten Tales by Dr William Maginn* was published in London in 1933.

Manning, Olivia (1908–80); b. Portsmouth, daughter of English naval officer and Northern Irish mother; spent much of her childhood in Ireland; trained as an artist; moved to London, where Stevie Smith helped find a publisher for *The Wind Changes* (1937), a novel set in Ireland; married R. D. Smith in 1939 and travelled with him to Bucharest, where he was a British Council lecturer; during the war fled to Greece, Egypt and Palestine; worked for the British Council in Jerusalem 1941–5; returned to England in 1946; best known for her trilogies of autobiographical novels based on her wartime experiences, *The Balkan Trilogy* and *The Levant Trilogy*; short stories published in *Growing Up* (1948) and *A Romantic Hero* (1967).

Mathews, Aidan (1956–); b. Dublin; ed. UCD, TCD and Stanford University, California; RTE drama producer; poet, playwright and fiction writer; two short story collections, *Adventures in a Bathyscope* (1988) and *Lipstick on the Host* (1992); a novel, *Muesli at Midnight* (1990).

Moore, George (1852–1933); b. Moore Hall, Co. Mayo, son of a Catholic landlord; lived in Paris, Dublin and London; 1873–80 studied art in Paris, where he became acquainted with many leading literary and artistic figures; French influence apparent in his early novels including *A Drama in Muslin* (1886) and the highly successful *Esther Waters* (1894); in 1901 returned to Dublin and became involved in the Irish Revival and the founding of the Abbey Theatre; out of his involvement with the Gaelic League came *The Untilled Field* (1903), hailed as first Irish modern short story collection; converted to Protestantism; 1911 returned to London disillusioned with Irish life; 1923 Moore Hall burned by republicans; reinvented himself several times over the course of his life, as may be seen in his three-volume autobiography, *Hail and Farewell* (1911–14); other experiments with short fiction include *Celibates* (1895), revised as *Celibate Lives* (1927), and *A Storyteller's Holiday* (1918).

Morrissy, Mary (1957–); b. Dublin; journalist with *The Irish Times*; collection of stories, *A Lazy Eye* (1993); novels, *Mother of Pearl* (1996), *The Pretender* (2000); won a Hennessy Award for her short stories in 1984; shortlisted for the Whitbread Prize in 1996.

Morrow, John (1930–); b. Belfast; left school at fourteen to work in a shipyard and various other jobs, as navvy, salesman, and in insurance; short stories began to appear in literary magazines in the late 1960s; novels, *The Confessions of Proinsias O'Toole* (1977), *The Essex Factor* (1982); short story collections, *Northern Myths* (1979), *Sects and Other Stories* (1987).

Mulholland, Rosa (1841–1921); b. Belfast into an upper-middle-class Catholic family; studied art in London; published novels, short stories and three collections of poetry; from 1891 lived in Blackrock, Dublin; encouraged by Dickens, who published her early stories in *Household Words* and *All the Year Round*, and by W. B. Yeats, who published her in *Representative Irish Tales*; first novel, *Dunmara* (1864); short story collection, *The Walking Trees* (1884); Mulholland often wrote stories in the Gothic mode, such as the title story of *The Haunted Organist of Hurly Burly* (1891) and 'Not to be Taken at Bed-Time', a wild Irish tale of revenge that reveals influences of Le Fanu and Carleton and was published by Charles Dickens in *All the Year Round*.

Mulkerns, Val (1925–); b. Dublin; ed. Dominican College, Dublin; civil servant 1945–9; associate editor of *The Bell* under Peadar O'Donnell, 1952–4; weekly columnist in the *Evening Press*, 1968–83; four novels, *A Time Outworn* (1951), *A Peacock Cry* (1954), *The Summerhouse* (1984), *Very Like a Whale* (1986); short story collections include *Antiquities* (1978), *An Idle Woman* (1980), *A Friend of Don Juan* (1988).

Ní Dhuibhne, Éilís (1954–); b. Dublin; ed. UCD and the University of Denmark, Copenhagen; 1982, doctorate in Folklore and Medieval Literature from UCD; works as a keeper at the National Library of Ireland and lectures on folklore; first short stories, *Blood and Water,* published by Attic in 1988, followed by *Eating Women Is Not Recommended* (1991), *The Inland Ice* (1997), *The Pale Gold of Alaska* (2000); novels include futuristic dystopia, *The Bray House* (1990), an Irish *Bildungsroman*, *The Dancers Dancing* (1999) and a portrait of Celtic Tiger Ireland, *Fox, Swallow, Scarecrow* (2007); also scholarly works, plays in Irish and English, and children's fiction under the pseudonym Elizabeth O'Hara.

O'Brien, Edna (1930–); b. Co. Clare; ed. the Sisters of Mercy Convent, Loughrea and the Pharmaceutical College, Dublin; left Ireland in 1959 and has lived most of her life in London; found fame with her Country Girls trilogy, *The Country Girls* (1960), *The Lonely Girl* (1962) and *Girls in Their Married Bliss* (1964); prolific output, ranging from the experimental fiction of *Night* (1972) to the political engagement of her 1990s trilogy, *House of Splendid Isolation* (1995), *Down by the River* (1996), *Wild Decembers* (1999); continued to cause scandal with the publication of *In the Forest* (2002), based on a real murder case; short story collections include *The Love Object* (1968), *A Scandalous Woman* (1974), *Mrs Reinhardt* (1978), *Returning* (1982), *A Fanatic Heart* (1984), *Lantern Slides* (1990); plays, film scripts, children's books and travel books; non-fiction works include *Mother Ireland* (1976) and *James Joyce* (1999).

Ó Ceallaigh, Philip; b. Co. Waterford; has lived in Spain, Russia, USA, Kosovo and Georgia; since 2000 has lived mainly in Bucharest; first short story collection, *Notes from a Turkish Whorehouse* (2006), won the Rooney Prize for Irish Literature.

O'Connor, Frank (1903–66); b. Michael O'Donovan, Cork, only child of an alcoholic, violent father and a mother who went out charring; left school at fourteen, thereafter self-taught; influenced by Daniel Corkery, he joined the republicans and was interned during the civil war; worked as a librarian first in Cork and then in Dublin, where he came into contact with literary circles and became involved with the Abbey Theatre, of which he was director 1935–9; first volume of stories, *Guests of the Nation*, appeared in 1931, followed by *Bones of Contention* (1936), *Crab Apple Jelly* (1944) and *The Common Chord* (1947), both banned in Ireland; novels, *The Saint and Mary Kate* (1932) and *Dutch Interior* (1940), which was banned; disillusioned by Irish life, lived in England in the 1940s and 1952–62 in the USA; frequent contributor to the *New Yorker*; further short story collections include *Traveller's Samples* (1951), *Domestic Relations* (1957), *My Oedipus Complex and Other Stories* (1963) and the posthumous *The Cornet-Player who Betrayed Ireland* (1981); returned to Ireland to find greater acceptance; 1962 received DLitt from TCD and published his study of the short story, *The Lonely Voice*; the first volume of his autobiography, *An Only Child* (1961), has become a classic, followed by the unfinished *My Father's Son*, published posthumously in 1968.

O'Connor, Joseph (1963–); b. Co. Dublin; ed. UCD; novels, short stories, non-fiction, stage and screen plays; novels include *Cowboys and Indians* (1991), *Desperadoes* (1993), *The Salesman* (1998), *Inishowen* (2000), *Star of the Sea* (2002), *Redemption Falls* (2007); short story collection, *True Believers* (1991).

O'Faolain, Julia (1932–); b. London, raised in Dublin; ed. UCD and studied in Rome and Paris; worked as a language teacher and translator in Italy; lived outside Ireland for most of her life; novels include the underrated *No Country for Young Men* (1980), *The Obedient Wife* (1982), *The Irish Signorina* (1984) and *The Judas Cloth* (1992); short story collections, *We Might See Sights!* (1968), *Man in the Cellar* (1974), *Melancholy Baby* (1978), *Daughters of Passion* (1982); non-fiction works include *Not in God's Image: Women in History from the Greeks to the Victorians* (1973).

O'Faoláin, Seán (1900–91); b. John Whelan, Cork; ed. Presentation Brothers College and UCC; 1916 transferred his allegiance to Irish nationalism and learned Irish; fought on the anti-treaty side during the civil war; 1926–9 scholarship at Havard; 1929–33 lectured at teacher training college in London; in 1933 on Edward Garnett's advice devoted himself full-time to writing and moved to Co. Wicklow; first story collection, *Midsummer Night Madness* (1932) banned in Ireland; in 1940 founded *The Bell*, which he edited until 1945;

subsequently spent long periods outside Ireland in Italy and lecturing at various US universities, including Princeton; 1956–9 Director of the Irish Arts Council; published ten volumes of short stories, four novels, plays, criticism, five biographies, autobiography, *Vive Moi!* (1963); short story collections include *A Purse of Coppers* (1937), *Teresa* (1947), *The Man Who Invented Sin* (1948), *The Heat of the Sun* (1966), *The Talking Trees* (1971), *Foreign Affairs* (1976), *The Collected Stories* (3 vols., 1980–2); also published a study of the form, *The Short Story* (1948).

O'Flaherty, Liam (1896–1984); b. Inis Mór in the Aran Islands; raised in bilingual peasant community; ed. Rockwell College, Tipperary, Blackrock College, Dublin, and UCD; left UCD in 1915 to fight in the Irish Guards in France; 1917 discharged shell-shocked and wounded; wandered around Europe and the USA working in various jobs as recounted in his autobiography, *Two Years* (1930); participated in the civil war on republican side; left for England in 1922 to begin writing; became a protégé of Edward Garnett; returned to Ireland and founded the short-lived literary magazine *To-morrow* in 1924; disillusioned with Irish literary life, left in 1927; thereafter lived in USA, France and England and only for brief periods in Ireland, where he finally settled for the last years of his life; published two volumes of autobiography, novels (including *Famine*, 1937) and short stories; most of his best stories were written in 1920s and early 1930s and by the early 1950s he had largely given up writing for publication; short story collections, *Spring Sowing* (1924), *The Tent* (1926), *The Mountain Tavern* (1929), *Two Lovely Beasts* (1948), *Dúil* (1953).

O'Kelly, Seumas (1878/80–1918); b. Loughrea, Co. Galway; father a prosperous corn-factor; edited *The Southern Star* in Skibbereen; 1906 joined Sinn Féin and moved to Naas to edit *The Leinster Leader*; 1912–15 edited the *Saturday Evening Post* in Dublin until ill-health forced him to retire; stood in for Arthur Griffiths as editor of *Nationality* when Griffiths arrested in 1918; offices of *Nationality* wrecked three days after armistice by soldiers and their wives, angry at Sinn Féin's war policy; O'Kelly left unconscious and did not recover; given a hero's funeral by Sinn Féin; novels, short stories, plays and poetry; novels, *The Lady of Deerpark* (1917), *Wet Clay* (1922); his play *The Shuiler's Child* was performed at the Abbey Theatre, Dublin, 1909; collections of tales include *By the Stream of Kilmeen* (1906), *Waysiders* (1917), *The Golden Barque* (1919), *Hillsiders* (1921); the novella, 'The Weaver's Grave' (1919), is his acknowledged masterpiece.

Park, David (1954–); b. Belfast; now lives in Co. Down; novels, *The Healing* (1992), *The Rye Man* (1994), *Stone Kingdoms* (1996), *The Big Snow* (2002), *Swallowing the Sun* (2004); short stories, *Oranges from Spain* (1990).

Plunkett, James (1920–2003); b. James Plunkett Kelly to Dublin working-class family; ed. Synge Street Christian Brothers School and the College of Music; worked in the drama department at Radio Éireann and later head of features at RTE; trade union official; novels, short stories, radio, TV and film scripts; contributor to *The Bell;* in 1954 his short story collection, *The Eagles and the Trumpets*, was published in place of its regular issue; novels include *Strumpet City*

(1969) about the years leading up to 1913 Lockout, subsequently televised; short story collection, *The Trusting and the Maimed* (1955); *Collected Stories* (1977).

Riddell, Charlotte (1832–1906); b. Charlotte Cowan Carrickfergus, Co. Antrim; moved to London 1855 to establish herself as a writer; her difficulty in finding a publisher is reflected in her short story, 'Out in the Cold' (1899) and in her novels, *The Rich Husband* (1858) and *A Struggle for Fame* (1883); 1857 married Joseph Hadley Riddell (d. 1880); her early novels were published under various pseudonyms but from 1866 used her married name; popular writer of sensational fiction and stories of the supernatural; wrote to support her family; 1883–6 lived with Arthur Hamilton Norway and travelled with him to Ireland in 1885; from 1886 lived in seclusion and poverty in England; short story collections include *The Banshee's Warning and Other Stories* (1894), *Handsome Phil and Other Stories* (1899).

Ross, Martin (1862–1915); b. Violet Martin, Ross House, Co. Galway; moved to Dublin in 1872; ed. Alexandra College, Dublin; journalism; 1886, met her cousin, Edith Somerville, with whom she formed a literary and emotional partnership; *see below.*

Somerville, Edith (1858–1949); b. Corfu, raised in Castletownshend, Co. Cork; ed. by governesses and for one term at Alexandra College, Dublin; trained as an artist in Paris; lived most of her life in Co. Cork running the family estate; collaborated with Violet Martin on, among others, *An Irish Cousin* (1889), *Naboth's Vineyard* (1891), *The Real Charlotte* (1894), as well as the immensely popular *Irish R.M.* volumes; other short story collections, *All on the Irish Shore* (1903) and *Some Irish Yesterdays* (1906); after Martin's death, Somerville wrote other works, including *Mount Music* (1919) and *The Big House of Inver* (1925), which appeared under both their names.

Stephens, James (1882–1950); b. in a north Dublin slum; ed. Meath Industrial School; encouraged to write by AE and became a leading figure in the Irish Literary Revival; poet, novelist and short story writer; novels include *A Charwoman's Daughter* and the fantasy, *The Crock of Gold*, both published in 1912; moved to Paris in 1913; short stories, *Here Are Ladies* (1913) and second prose fantasy, *The Demi-Gods* (1914); returned to Dublin in 1915 and became registrar of the National Gallery, Dublin; poetry, *Songs from the Clay* (1915), novella, 'Hunger' (1918), translations of Gaelic poetry, *Reincarnations* (1918), and retellings of old Irish saga and epic literature, *Irish Fairy Tales* (1920), *Deirdre* (1923), *In the Land of Youth* (1924); 1925 moved to London where he became a popular broadcaster for the BBC; *Etched in Moonlight* appeared in 1928; d. London.

Tóibín, Colm (1955–); b. Enniscorthy, Co. Wexford; son of a schoolmaster; ed. UCD; lived in Spain and South America; journalism, novels, short stories, a play and non-fiction; edited numerous anthologies; editor of *Magill* (1982–5); novels, *The South* (1990), *The Heather Blazing* (1992), *The Story of the Night* (1996), *The Blackwater Lightship* (1999), *The Master* (2004), which was widely acclaimed and won many awards; non-fiction includes *Bad Blood: A Walk along the Irish Border* (1994), *The Sign of the Cross: Travels in Catholic Europe*

(1994), *Love in a Dark Time: Gay Lives from Wilde to Amodóvar* (2002) and *Lady Gregory's Toothbrush* (2002); *Mothers and Sons* (2006) is his first short story collection.

Trevor, William (1928–); b. William Trevor Cox, Mitchelstown, Co. Cork; attended many schools ending with St Columba's in 1944; TCD 1946–51; trained as a sculptor; moved to England in 1953 for economic reasons; taught in prep schools and concentrated on sculpture before turning to writing at the end of the 1950s; 1960–7 worked in London advertising agency; 1967 resigned to write full time; novels, short stories, autobiographical essays, plays for radio, stage and television; novels include *The Old Boys* (1964), winner of the Hawthornden Prize, *Elizabeth Alone* (1973), *Fools of Fortune* (1983) and *Felicia's Journey* (1994), both winners of the Whitbread Award, *The Story of Lucy Gault* (2002), shortlisted for the Booker Prize; novellas include 'Reading Turgenev' (1992); publishes a new collection of stories almost annually, starting with *The Day We Got Drunk on Cake* (1967); his seven volumes of stories published as *Collected Stories* in 1992; since then has published *After Rain* (1996), *The Hill Bachelors* (2000), *A Bit on the Side* (2004) and *Cheating at Canasta* (2007); awarded CBE in 1977.

Trollope, Anthony (1812–82); b. London; lived in Ireland 1841–54; reversing the usual Irish literary experience, moving to Ireland turned Trollope into a writer; forty-seven novels, five volumes of stories, travel books and biographies; on his return to England in 1859 he wrote stories centred around his travels, publishing them under the title *Tales of All Countries*; retired from the civil service in 1867 to devote himself full time to writing, producing highly successful portraits of the professional and landed classes, notably *Chronicles of Barsetshire* (1855–67) and the Palliser novels (1864–80).

Tynan, Katharine (1861–1931); b. Dublin into a prosperous Catholic farming family; ed. Dominican convent school, Drogheda; in the 1880s moved in Irish literary circles and was a friend of Yeats, with whom she published *Poems and Ballads of Young Ireland* (1888); 1893, married Henry Hinkson and moved to England; 1911, returned to Ireland and between 1914 and 1919 lived in Mayo, where her husband was Resident Magistrate; after his death travelled widely and supported herself through writing; published over 160 volumes of prose, fiction and poetry; poetry includes *Louise de Vallière and Other Poems* (1885), *Shamrocks* (1887), *Ballads and Lyrics* (1891), *Collected Poems* (1930); novels include *The House* (1920), *The Rich Man* (1929); memoirs, *Twenty-Five Years* (1913), *The Middle Years* (1916), *The Years of the Shadow* (1919), *The Wandering Years* (1922); edited anthologies of Irish literature, including *The Cabinet of Irish Literature* (1902).

Wall, William (1955–); b. Co. Cork; ed. UCC; taught in the Presentation Brothers College, Cork; novelist, poet, short story writer; novels, *Alice Falling* (2000), *Minding Children* (2001), *The Map of Tenderness* (2002), *This is the Country* (2005); short stories, *No Paradiso* (2006).

Wilde, Oscar (1854–1900); b. Dublin; father eminent eye surgeon, mother the nationalist poet 'Speranza'; ed. Portora Royal School, Enniskillen, TCD and

Magdalen College, Oxford; playwright, poet, essayist and conversationalist, highly influential in the aesthetic movement; his three volumes of short fiction, *The Happy Prince* (1888), *Lord Arthur Savile's Crime* (1891) and *A House of Pomegranates* (1891) and his novel, *The Picture of Dorian Gray* (1891) gained him a literary reputation; highly popular playwright; *Lady Windermere's Fan, A Woman of No Importance, An Ideal Husband* and *The Importance of Being Earnest* were all performed in London between 1892 and 1895; 1895 brought a libel action against the Marquess of Queensberry, father of his lover, Lord Alfred Douglas; lost the case and was subsequently imprisoned for homosexual offences 1895–7; wrote *The Ballad of Reading Gaol* (1898); died in exile in Paris.

Yeats, William Butler (1865–1939); b. Dublin; son and brother of artists John Butler Yeats and Jack Yeats; childhood in Sligo, Dublin and London; published poetry, plays, essays and occult works; between 1881 and 1887 lived in Dublin, studying art and mysticism and working to establish an Irish literary movement; 'Dhoya' and 'John Sherman' published in London in 1891; *The Celtic Twilight* (1893) consolidated his position as leader of the Irish Literary Revival; *The Secret Rose* was published in 1897 and subsequently went through many revisions; 1902, his play, *Cathleen Ni Houlihan*, was staged and in 1904 he co-founded the Abbey Theatre; 1917 purchased a Norman tower in Ballylee, Co. Galway and married Georgie Hyde-Lees, whose automatic writing became the basis of his occult work, *A Vision* (1925); Senator in the Irish Free State 1922; Nobel Prize for Literature, 1923; died in France.

Bibliographic essay

General studies of the short story include *The New Short Story Theories*, ed. Charles May (Ohio, 1994), Charles May, *The Short Story: the Reality of Artifice* (New York, 1995), Valerie Shaw, *The Short Story: a Critical Introduction* (London and New York, 1983) and *Short Story Theory at a Crossroads*, ed. Susan Lohafer and Jo Ellyn Clarey (Baton Rouge, LA, 1989). *Re-Reading the Short Story*, ed. Clare Hanson (Basingstoke, 1989) is particularly useful on general techniques. *The Journal of the Short Story in English* publishes regular articles on Irish writers; in the past these have included James Joyce, Mary Lavin, Elizabeth Bowen, Frank O'Connor, Neil Jordan and John McGahern (special edition, vol. 34, 2000).

Critical surveys of the Irish short story include Frank O'Connor, *The Lonely Voice: a Study of the Short Story* (London, 1963), Seán O'Faoláin, *The Short Story* (Cork, 1948), *The Irish Short Story*, ed. Patrick Rafroidi and Terence Brown (Gerrards Cross, 1979), *The Irish Short Story: a Critical History* ed. James Kilroy (Boston, 1984), Deborah Averill, *The Irish Short Story from George Moore to Frank O'Connor* (Lanham, 1982).

For material on the oral tradition see: Walter J. Ong, *Orality and Literacy: the Technologising of the Word* (London and New York, 1991), Walter Benjamin, 'Observations on the Works of Nikolai Leskov' (1936), in *Selected Writings: Volume Three 1935–1938* trans. Edmund Jephcott *et al.*, ed. Howard Eiland and Michael Jennings (Cambridge and London, 2002), pp. 143–66, Axel Olrik, *Principles for Oral Narrative Research*, trans. Kirsten Wolf and Jody Jensen (Bloomington and Indianapolis, 1992). For the oral storytelling tradition in Ireland, see Georges Zimmermann's magisterial study, *The Irish Storyteller* (Dublin, 2001). Other useful reference points are Angela Bourke, 'The Baby and the Bathwater: Cultural Loss in Nineteenth-Century Ireland', in *Ideology and Ireland in the Nineteenth Century*, ed. Tadhg Foley and Seán Ryder (Dublin, 1998), pp. 79–92, Diarmuid Ó Giolláin, *Locating Irish Folklore: Tradition, Modernity, Identity* (Cork, 2000), Clodagh Harvey, *Contemporary Irish Traditional Narrative: the English Language Tradition* (Berkeley, n.d.) and Donna Wong, 'Literature and the Oral Tradition', in *The Cambridge History of Irish Literature, Volume 1: To 1890*, ed. Margaret Kelleher and Philip O'Leary (Cambridge, 2006), pp. 668–9. Also invaluable is Sean O'Sullivan and R. T. Christiansen, *The Types of Irish Folklore* (Helsinki, 1967) and O'Sullivan's translations, *Folktales of Ireland* (London, 1966) and *The Folklore of Ireland* (London, 1974).

The anthologies mentioned in chapter one of this study are a useful resource for Irish short stories but introductions to anthologies are often too succinct to be very helpful. Exceptions include: W. B. Yeats, *Representative Irish Tales* (Gerrards Cross, 1979), Vivian Mercier's introduction to *Great Irish Short Stories* (New York, 1964) and William Trevor's introduction to *The Oxford Book of Irish Short Stories* (Oxford, 1989).

NINETEENTH CENTURY

The volumes of the *Dublin University Magazine* from 1833 onwards are a vital source, publishing work by William Carleton, Samuel Lover, Maria Edgeworth and Sheridan Le Fanu, among others. *A Guide to Irish Fiction 1650–1900* by Rolf and Magda Loeber (Dublin, 2006) is an invaluable bibliographical tool for this period, as is volume I of *The Cambridge History of Irish Literature*, ed. Margaret Kelleher and Philip O'Leary (Cambridge, 2006). Barbara Hayley provides a guide to nineteenth-century periodicals in 'A Reading and Thinking Nation: Periodicals as the Voice of Nineteenth-Century Ireland', in *Three Hundred Years of Irish Periodicals*, ed. Barbara Hayley and Enda McKay (Mullingar, 1987), pp. 29–46. See also Wayne Hall, *Dialogues in the Margin: A Study of the 'Dublin University Magazine'* (Gerrards Cross, 2000) and Tom Clyde, *Irish Literary Magazines* (Dublin, 2003). *The Irish Novel in the Nineteenth Century: Facts and Fictions*, ed. Jacqueline Belanger (Dublin, 2005), Thomas Flanagan, *The Irish Novelists 1800–1850* (New York, 1959), *The Cambridge Companion to the Irish Novel*, ed. John Wilson Foster (Cambridge, 2006) and John Wilson Foster's *Irish Novels 1890–1940: New Bearings in Culture and Fiction* (Oxford, 2008) contain observations that are pertinent to the Irish short narrative, as do *Irish Literature: the Nineteenth Century*, vols. I, II, III, ed. A. Norman Jeffares and Peter van de Kamp (Dublin: Irish Academic Press, 2006–7) and *The Field Day Anthology of Irish Literature*, vols. II and III, ed. Seamus Deane (Derry, 1991).

Useful works for short fiction by individual authors include: Sharon Murphy, *Maria Edgeworth and Romance* (Dublin, 2004), Brian Hollingworth, *Maria Edgeworth's Irish Writing: Language, History, Politics* (Basingstoke, 1997), Maureen Keane, *Mrs S. C. Hall: A Literary Biography* (Gerrards Cross, 1997), John Cronin, *Gerald Griffin (1803–40): A Critical Biography* (Cambridge, 1978), Heidi Hansson, *Emily Lawless 1845–1913: Writing the Interspace* (Cork, 2007), Eve Patten, *Samuel Ferguson and the Culture of Nineteenth-Century Ireland* (Dublin, 2004), John Sutherland's preface to Anthony Trollope, *Early Short Stories*, ed. John Sutherland (Oxford, 1994), Gifford Lewis, *Somerville and Ross: The World of the Irish R.M.* (Harmondsworth, 1987), Julie Anne Stevens, *The Irish Scene in Somerville and Ross* (Dublin, 2007). There is an informative introduction to Sarah Orne Jewett, *The Irish Stories*, by the editors Jack Morgan and Louis A. Renza (Carbondale and Edwardsville, IL, 1996).

For Carleton, see Barbara Hayley's study of Carleton's revisions, *Carleton's 'Traits and Stories' and the Nineteenth-Century Anglo-Irish Tradition* (Gerrards Cross, 1983). Also useful are *William Carleton: the Authentic Voice*, ed. Gordon

Brand (Gerrards Cross, 2006), William Carleton, *The Life of William Carleton, Completed by David O'Donoghue* (New York and London, 1979), Declan Kiberd's chapter on Carleton in *Irish Classics* (London, 2001), pp. 265–86, Terry Eagleton's comments on Carleton and other nineteenth-century authors in *Heathcliff and the Great Hunger: Studies in Irish Culture* (London and New York 1995), and Julian Moynahan, *Anglo-Irish: the Literary Imagination in a Hyphenated Culture* (Princeton, 1995).

Important studies on Le Fanu include W. J. McCormack: *Dissolute Characters: Irish Literary History through Balzac, Sheridan Le Fanu, Yeats and Bowen* (Manchester, 1993) and *Sheridan Le Fanu and Victorian Ireland* (Oxford, 1980).

FIN DE SIÈCLE

John Wilson Foster's *Fictions of the Irish Literary Revival: a Changeling Art* (Dublin, 1987) remains an essential point of departure for study of the period's fiction and the links back to folklore and saga literature. Criticism on Yeats is vast. For discussions of how the short fiction fits into his overall career, see Terence Brown, *The Life of W. B. Yeats* (Dublin, 2001) and R. F. Foster, *W. B. Yeats: A Life. Vol. 1: The Apprentice Mage 1865–1914* (Oxford, 1997). Specific studies of Yeats' short fiction include William O'Donnell, *A Guide to the Prose Fiction of W. B. Yeats* (Epping, 1983), Steven Putzel, *Reconstructing Yeats: 'The Secret Rose' and 'The Wind Among the Reeds'* (Dublin, 1986), Richard Finneran, *The Prose Fiction of W. B. Yeats: the Search for 'Those Simple Forms'* (Dublin, 1973) and his introduction to *John Sherman and Dhoya*, ed. R. J. Finneran (New York, 1991). On Yeats' revisions, see *The Secret Rose, Stories by W. B. Yeats: a Variorum Edition*, ed. Phillip Marcus, Warwick Gould and Michael Sidnell (Ithaca, NY and London, 1981) and W. B. Yeats, *Mythologies*, ed. Warwick Gould and Deirdre Toomey (New York, 2005).

Criticism on Wilde is wide-ranging. For work specifically on Wilde the storyteller, see Deirdre Toomey, 'The Story Teller at Fault: Oscar Wilde and Irish Orality', in *Wilde the Irishman*, ed. Jerusha McCormack (New Haven and London, 1998), pp. 24–35, Richard Pine, *The Thief of Reason: Oscar Wilde and Modern Ireland* (Dublin, 1995), Neil Sammells, *Wilde Style: The Plays and Prose of Oscar Wilde* (Harlow, 2000), Jerusha McCormack, 'Wilde's Fiction(s)', in *The Cambridge Companion to Oscar Wilde*, ed. P. Raby (Cambridge, 1998), pp. 96–117 and Jarlath Killeen, 'Diaspora, Empire, and the Religious Geography of Victorian Social Relations in Wilde's Fairy Tales', in *New Voices in Irish Criticism*, ed. P. J. Mathews (Dublin, 2000), pp. 183–9. For the relationship between Wilde's fairy tales, Roman Catholicism and Irish nationalism, see Jarlath Killeen, *The Fairy Tales of Oscar Wilde* (Burlington, VT, 2007). For Wilde's own comments on his stories, see *The Complete Letters of Oscar Wilde*, ed. Merlin Holland and Rupert Hart-Davis (New York, 2000).

For general studies of the New Woman writing which include discussion of Egerton and Grand see, among others, Elaine Showalter's introduction to *Daughters of Decadence: Women Writers of the Fin de Siècle* (London, 1993), Lyn

Pykett, *The 'Improper' Feminine: The Women's Sensation Novel and the New Woman Writing* (London, 1992), *The New Woman in Fiction and in Fact: Fin-de-Siècle Feminisms*, ed. Angelique Richardson and Chris Willis (London, 2001) and Sally Ledger, *The New Woman: Fiction and Feminism at the Fin de Siècle* (Manchester, 1997). Specifically on George Egerton, the introduction to *Keynotes and Discords*, ed. Sally Ledger (London, 2006), is useful. For Egerton's correspondence and views on Ireland, see *A Leaf from The Yellow Book*, ed. Terence de Vere White (London, 1958). Mary O'Donoghue discusses Irish themes in Egerton's stories in 'An Intensity of Irishness: George Egerton's Representations of Irish Femininity', in *New Voices in Irish Criticism*, ed. P. J. Mathews (Dublin, 2000), pp. 83–91.

For discussion of Patrick Pearse's short stories, see Ruth Dudley Edwards, *Patrick Pearse: The Triumph of Failure* (London, 1977) and Seán Farrell Moran, *Patrick Pearse and the Politics of Redemption: The Mind of the Easter Rising, 1916* (Washington, DC, 1994). For James Stephens' short fiction, see Augustine Martin, *James Stephens: A Critical Study* (Dublin, 1977) and Patricia McFate, *The Writing of James Stephens: Variations on a Theme of Love* (London, 1979).

JOYCE AND MOORE

Indispensable are the five-volume edition, *The Collected Short Stories of George Moore: Gender and Gender*, ed. A. Heilmann and M. Llewellyn (London, 2007), highlighting the range of Moore's short fiction, Adrian Frazier, *George Moore, 1852–1933* (New Haven and London, 2000) and *George Moore: Artistic Visions and Literary Worlds*, ed. Mary Pierse (Newcastle, 2006). Useful for the publishing background are Richard Cave's introduction in George Moore, *The Untilled Field*, ed. Richard Cave (Gerrards Cross, 2000) and Moore's own three-volume autobiography, *Hail and Farewell* (London and New York, 1911–14).

The scholarship on Joyce is vast. Details of the tortuous publication history of *Dubliners* are given in Richard Ellmann, *James Joyce* (Oxford, 1959). Useful collections of essays on Joyce's stories include *A New and Complex Sensation: Essays on Joyce's Dubliners*, ed. Oona Frawley (Dublin, 2004) and, for undergraduate purposes, *Dubliners: Contemporary Critical Essays*, ed. Andrew Thacker (*Basingstoke and New York, 2006*). For the folktale elements in *Dubliners*, see Robert Tracy, *The Unappeasable Host: Studies in Irish Identities* (Dublin, 1998), pp. 145–64. Articles on individual stories are regularly published in the *James Joyce Quarterly*. Notable are Donald Torchiana, 'Joyce's "Two Gallants": A Walk through the Ascendancy', *James Joyce Quarterly* 6 (2) (1968), 115–27, Florence L. Walzl, 'Joyce's "The Sisters": A Development', *James Joyce Quarterly* 10 (4), (1973), 375–421, L. J. Morrissey, 'Joyce's Revision of "The Sisters": From Epicleti to Modern Fiction', *James Joyce Quarterly* 24 (1986), 33–54, Jane Miller,' "O, she's a nice lady!": a Rereading of "A Mother"', *James Joyce Quarterly* 28 (2), (1991), 407–26, David Weir, 'Gnomon is an Island: Euclid and Bruno in Joyce's Narrative Practice', *James Joyce Quarterly* 28 (2) (1991), 343–60, Garry Leonard, 'Wondering Where All the Dust Comes From: *jouissance* in "Eveline"', *James Joyce Quarterly*

29 (1), (1991), 23–42, Shawn St Jean, 'Readerly Paranoia and Joyce's Adolescent Stories', *James Joyce Quarterly* 35 (4) (1998), 665–82 and David Spurr, 'Colonial Spaces in Joyce's Dublin', *James Joyce Quarterly* 37 (1) (1999), 23–42. Useful feminist approaches to *Dubliners* include Marion Eide, *Ethical Joyce* (Cambridge, 2002), Florence L. Walzl, '*Dubliners*: Women in Irish Society', in *Women in Joyce*, ed. Suzette Henke and Elaine Unkeless (Urbana, IL, 1982), pp. 31–56 and Suzette Henke, *James Joyce and the Politics of Desire* (New York and London, 1990). In the area of postcolonial studies, Vincent J. Cheng, *Joyce, Race, and Empire* (Cambridge, 1995) has a chapter on *Dubliners*, and see also Luke Gibbons, ' "Have you no homes to go to?" James Joyce and the Politics of Paralysis', in *Semicolonial Joyce*, ed. Derek Attridge and Marjorie Howes (Cambridge, 2000), pp. 150–70.

1920S AND 1930S

Irish periodicals such as *The Bell*, *The Irish Statesman* and *The Dublin Magazine* are invaluable starting points for research into the Irish short story during this period. *The Cambridge History of Irish Literature*, ed. Margaret Kelleher and Philip O'Leary (Cambridge, 2006), vol. II, is a useful bibliographical source. Terence Brown provides general cultural and social background as well as some insightful comments on the short story in the section 'The Counter Revival: Provincialism and Censorship 1930–65', in *The Field Day Anthology of Irish Writing*, ed. Seamus Deane (Derry, 1991), vol. III, pp. 89–93; see also Terence Brown, *Ireland: a Social and Cultural History 1922–2002* (London, 2004), pp. 3–158. General studies mentioned above such as *The Irish Short Story*, ed. Rafroidi and Brown, *The Irish Short Story: a Critical History*, ed. Kilroy, Averill, *The Irish Short Story from George Moore to Frank O'Connor*, all carry discussions of Corkery, O'Connor, O'Flaherty and O'Faoláin.

A good up-to-date discussion of Corkery may be found in Paul Delaney's edition of his selected stories, *The Stones and Other Stories* (Cork, 2003); also useful is Alexander Gonzalez, 'A Re-Evaluation of Daniel Corkery's Fiction', *Irish University Review* 14 (2) (1984), 191–201. For Frank O'Connor, the collection edited by Hilary Lennon, *Frank O'Connor: Critical Essays* (Dublin, 2007) supersedes the earlier *Michael/Frank: Studies on Frank O'Connor*, ed. Maurice Sheehy (Dublin, 1969). See also James Matthews' biography, *Voices: a Life of Frank O'Connor* (Dublin, 1983) and *Frank O'Connor: New Perspectives*, ed. Robert C. Evans and Richard Harp (West Cornwall, CT, 1998). Michael Steinman discusses O'Connor's revisions to his stories in *Frank O'Connor at Work* (New York, 1990), while *Twentieth Century Literature* 36 (3) 1990 is devoted to O'Connor.

For Seumas O'Kelly see Averill, *The Irish Short Story*, pp. 69–81, *The Irish Short Story: a Critical History*, ed. Kilroy, pp. 141–3, Foster, *Fictions of the Irish Literary Revival*, pp. 316–22 and George Brandon Saul, *Seumas O'Kelly* (Lewisburg, PA, 1971). For O'Flaherty, see A. A. Kelly, *Liam O'Flaherty the Storyteller* (London, 1976), J. M. Calahan, *Liam O'Flaherty: A Study of the Short Fiction* (Boston, 1991) and George Jefferson, *Liam O'Flaherty: A Descriptive Bibliography of his Works* (Dublin, 1993). For Dorothy Macardle's life and works, see Nadia Clare Smith, *Dorothy Macardle: A Life* (Dublin, 2007).

Most scholars have concentrated on Elizabeth Bowen's novels. For discussion of her short stories, see Phyllis Lassner, *Elizabeth Bowen: a Study of the Short Fiction* (New York, 1991), Hermione Lee, *Elizabeth Bowen*, revised edition (London, 1999), pp. 127–48 and diverse references in Maud Ellmann, *Elizabeth Bowen: The Shadow across the Page* (Edinburgh, 2003). For an introduction to Beckett's short fiction, see *Samuel Beckett: The Complete Short Prose, 1929–1989*, ed. S. E. Gontarski (New York, 1995) and Alec Reid, 'Test Flight: Beckett's "More Pricks than Kicks"', in *The Irish Short Story*, ed. Rafroidi and Brown, pp. 227–35. Seán O'Faoláin and Michael McLaverty are dealt with in the following section.

1940S AND 1950S

Clair Wills, *That Neutral Island: a Cultural History of Ireland during the Second World War* (London, 2007), is illuminating on the general literary and cultural life of this period. For this period in O'Connor's life, see James Alexander, 'Frank O'Connor in *The New Yorker*, 1945–1967', *Éire-Ireland* 30 (1) (1995), 130–44. Useful comments on Seán O'Faoláin's stories can be found in Maurice Harmon, *Sean O'Faolain* (London, 1994), Denis Sampson, 'The Big House in Seán O'Faoláin's Fiction', in *The Big House in Ireland: Reality and Representation*, ed. Jacqueline Genet (Dingle, 1991), pp. 179–90 and Joseph Rippier, *The Short Stories of Sean O'Faolain: A Study in Descriptive Techniques* (Gerrards Cross, 1976). For Michael McLaverty, see J. W. Foster, 'Private Worlds: the Stories of Michael McLaverty', in *The Irish Short Story*, ed. Rafroidi and Brown, pp. 249–61, *In Quiet Places: The Uncollected Stories, Letters and Critical Prose of Michael McLaverty*, ed. Sophia Hillan King (Dublin, 1989) and her edition of McLaverty's *Collected Short Stories* (Belfast, 2002), with an introduction by Seamus Heaney. On Olivia Manning, see Eve Patten, 'Olivia Manning, Imperial Refugee', in *That Island Never Found: Essays and Poems for Terence Brown*, ed. Nicholas Allen and Eve Patten (Dublin, 2007), pp. 91–104.

For brief discussions of individual stories in the context of Mary Lavin's life, see Leah Levenson, *The Four Seasons of Mary Lavin* (Dublin, 1998). For an illuminating discussion of 'The Will', see James Heaney, ' "No Sanctuary from Hatred": a Re-appraisal of Mary Lavin's Outsiders', *Irish University Review* 28 (2) (1998), 294–307. See also Janet Dunleavy, 'Mary Lavin, Elizabeth Bowen, and a New Generation: the Irish Short Story at Mid-century', in *The Irish Short Story: A Critical History*, ed. Kilroy, pp. 145–68 and A. A. Kelly, *Mary Lavin, Quiet Rebel: A Study of her Short Stories* (Dublin, 1980). For a discussion of Brennan's stories in the context of her life, see Angela Bourke, *Maeve Brennan: Homesick at the 'New Yorker'* (London, 2004). *The World of Bryan MacMahon*, a collection of essays edited by Gabriel Fitzmaurice (Cork, 2005), is a useful introduction to MacMahon's stories, and see also Patrick Rafroidi, 'From Listowel with Love: John B. Keane and Bryan MacMahon', in *The Irish Short Story*, ed. Rafroidi and

Brown, pp. 263–73. For mention of James Plunkett, Walter Macken, Aidan Higgins and other writers from this period, see Robert Hogan, 'Old Boys, Young Bucks, and New Women: the Contemporary Irish Short Story', in *The Irish Short Story: a Critical History*, ed. Kilroy, pp. 169–215.

1960S AND 1970S

John McGahern and William Trevor are the writers whose short stories have attracted the most critical attention. Both have written memoirs that illuminate some of the background to their stories: Trevor's *Excursions in the Real World: Memoirs* (New York, 1994) and McGahern's *Memoir* (London, 2005). Two illuminating general studies of McGahern's work are Denis Sampson, *Outstaring Nature's Eye: The Fiction of John McGahern* (Washington, DC, 1993) and Eamon Maher, *John McGahern: From the Local to the Universal* (Dublin, 2003). For McGahern's short stories useful articles include: Antoinette Quinn, 'Varieties of Disenchantment: Narrative Technique in John McGahern's Short Stories', *Journal of the Short Story in English* 13 (1989), 77–89, Eamon Grennan, ' "Only What Happens": Mulling Over McGahern', *Irish University Review* 35 (1) (2005), 16–19, Bertrand Cardin, 'Figures of Silence: Ellipses and Eclipses in John McGahern's *Collected Stories*', *Journal of the Short Story in English* 40 (2003), 57–67, Maguy Pernot-Deschamps, 'Loss and Failure in *High Ground*', *Journal of the Short Story in English* 34 (2000), 31–9 and Denis Sampson, 'The "Rich Whole": John McGahern's *Collected Stories* as Autobiography', *Journal of the Short Story in English* 34 (2000), 21–9. In addition, journals have devoted special issues to McGahern's work, including *The Canadian Journal of Irish Studies* 17 (1) (1991), *Journal of the Short Story in English* 34 (2000), *Irish University Review* 35 (1) (2005). The latter contains a comprehensive bibliography.

The 1990s produced a number of general works on William Trevor, namely Gregory A. Schirmer, *William Trevor: a Study of his Fiction* (London, 1990), Kristin Morrison, *William Trevor* (New York, 1993), Dolores MacKenna, *William Trevor: the Writer and his Work* (Dublin, 1999), followed by Mary Fitzgerald-Hoyt, *William Trevor: Re-imagining Ireland* (Dublin, 2003). Specifically on his short stories, see Suzanne Morrow Paulson, *William Trevor: A Study of the Short Fiction* (New York, 1993) and Jonathan Bloom, *The Art of Revision in the Short Stories of V. S. Pritchett and William Trevor* (New York and Hampshire, 2006).

For general studies on Edna O'Brien that include reference to her short stories, see the special Edna O'Brien issue of *The Canadian Journal of Irish Studies* 22 (2) (1999), 45–6, *Edna O'Brien: New Critical Perspectives*, ed. K. Laing, S. Mooney and M. O'Connor (Dublin, 2006) and *Wild Colonial Girl: Essays on Edna O'Brien*, ed. Lisa Colletta and Maureen O'Connor (2006).

John Banville's short stories are usually neglected in favour of his novels; exceptions include Kersti Tarien, 'Trying to Catch Long Lankin by His Arms: the Evolution of John Banville's *Long Lankin*', *Irish University Review* 31 (2), 2001, 386–403, Joseph McMinn, *John Banville: A Critical Study* (Dublin, 1991) and Rüdiger Imhof, *John Banville: A Critical Introduction* (Dublin, 1997). For material on Brian Friel's short stories, see John Cronin, ' "Donging the Tower": the Past Did Have Meaning: the Short Stories of Brian Friel', in *The Achievement of Brian Friel*, ed. Alan J. Peacock (Gerrards Cross, 1993), pp. 1–13, Richard Pine, *The Diviner: the Art of Brian Friel* (Dublin, 1999), pp. 77–93 and *A Companion to Brian Friel*, ed. Richard Harp and Robert Evans (West Cornwall, CT, 2002), pp. 255–331. John Keyes has a useful introduction to his edition of Robert Harbinson's *Selected Stories* (Belfast, 1996).

1980S TO THE PRESENT

If one excludes McGahern and Trevor, critical opinion has been slow to engage with the contemporary Irish short story, particularly with women's short stories. For a brief recent survey, see George O'Brien, 'Contemporary Prose in English: 1940–2000', in *The Cambridge History of Irish Literature: Volume II: 1890–2000*, ed. Margaret Kelleher and Philip O'Leary (Cambridge, 2006), pp. 452–65. Michael Storey, *Representing the Troubles in Irish Short Fiction* (Washington, DC, 2004), contains a wide range of Northern Irish short stories, both contemporary and from the earlier part of the twentieth century. See also Michael Parker's introduction to his anthology, *The Hurt World: Short Stories of the Troubles* (Belfast, 1995) and Patrick Grant, *Literature, Rhetoric and Violence in Northern Ireland, 1968–98* (Basingstoke and New York, 2001). For individual authors, the following are particularly useful: Catherine Mari, 'Tell-Tale Ellipsis in Colum McCann's *Everything in this Country Must*', *Journal of the Short Story in English* 40 (2003), 47–56, Henri-Dominique Paratte, 'Patrick Boyle's Tragic Humanity', in *The Irish Short Story*, ed. Rafroidi and Brown, pp. 275–87 and Anne Fogarty's introduction to Éilís Ní Dhuibhne, *Midwife to the Fairies: New and Selected Stories* (Dublin, 2003). Jacqueline Fulmer explores Ní Dhuibhne's use of folklore in *Folk Women and Indirection in Morrison, Ní Dhuibhne, Hurston, and Lavin* (Burlington, VT, 2007). John McCourt and Anne Fogarty discuss Colm Tóibín's *Mothers and Sons* in *Reading Colm Tóibín*, ed. Paul Delaney (Dublin, 2008). *Women Write Back: Irish and Catalan Short Stories in Colonial Context* (Dublin, 2003) by Irene Boada-Montague, contains useful discussions of Irish women's stories against a background of feminist and nationalist theory.

Index

Lightning Source UK Ltd.
Milton Keynes UK
UKOW031457310812

198305UK00005I

9 780521 349574